# Sir William C. Macdonald
## A Biography

WILLIAM FONG

Published for The Macdonald-Stewart Foundation by

McGill-Queen's University Press
Montreal & Kingston · London · Ithaca

Legal deposit fourth quarter 2007
Bibliothèque nationale du Québec

Printed in Canada on acid-free paper

McGill-Queen's University Press acknowledges the support of the Canada Council
for the Arts for our publishing program. We also acknowledge the financial support
of the Government of Canada through the Book Publishing Industry
Development Program (BPIDP) for our publishing activities.

LIBRARY AND ARCHIVES CANADA CATALOGUING IN PUBLICATION

Fong, William Jesse, 1948–
Sir William C. Macdonald / William Fong.

Published on the centenary of Macdonald College, Ste Anne de Bellevue.
Includes bibliographical references and index.
ISBN 978-0-7735-3304-2

1. Macdonald, William C. (William Christopher), 1831–1917.   2. Tobacco
industry – Canada – History.   3. McGill University – Endowments – History.
4. Education, Higher – Canada – Endowments – History.   5. Education – Canada –
Endowments – History.   6. Businessmen – Québec (Province – Montréal – Biography.
7. Philanthropists – Canada – Biography.   8. Businessmen – Canada – Biography.
9. Montréal (Québec) – Biography.   1. Macdonald-Stewart Foundation   11. Title.

HD9130.5.F65 2007    338.7´6797092    C2007-903273-7

Frontispiece: oil painting by Wyatt Eaton, 1893,
presented to Macdonald College by Walter M. Stewart

Set in 11/14 Adobe Caslon Pro with Voluta Script
Book design & typesetting by Garet Markvoort, zijn digital

# CONTENTS

# ILLUSTRATIONS

Abbreviations used in captions: ANQ: Archives Nationales du Québec; MSF: Macdonald-Stewart Foundation; MUA: McGill University Archives; Notman: Notman Photographic Archives, McCord Museum, Montreal

To mark the centennial celebrations of the founding of Macdonald College in 1907, we felt it was a fitting tribute to publish the first fully comprehensive story of its principal benefactor, Sir William C. Macdonald, a man who had a passion for the advancement of education.

We are very grateful to the many people and institutions that have made this project possible. A special thanks to the author, Dr William Fong, who, over many months, has patiently and meticulously gathered information on the life of Sir William. We are indebted to Elizabeth F. Hale, our librarian emeritus who, over thirty years, grew to know our holdings in depth; and I also express my deep gratitude to the chancellor of McGill University, Dr Richard Pound, for his fascinating introduction.

In the history of education in Canada, Sir William C. Macdonald stands as a pioneering figure who has made a unique contribution to the youth of our country, the heirs of his generosity and of his dreams.

Liliane M. Stewart

# PREFACE AND ACKNOWLEDGMENTS

Queen Victoria is said to have described Sir William Macdonald as the greatest benefactor to education in the British Empire. Whether or not she in fact did say this, this judgment is probably accurate. Now, almost a century after Macdonald's death in 1917, interest in Imperial history tends to be confined to specialists. Moreover, Victorian benefactors can seem eclipsed by their much richer successors. Nevertheless, because most of Macdonald's benefactions continue to flourish, his name is still far from forgotten. It remains commemorated in Canada, through buildings and institutions, university chairs, the Macdonald-Stewart Foundation, and the tobacco company that he founded. Beyond Canada, people around the world, educated thanks to his endowments in subjects ranging from agronomy to physics to zoology, attest through their careers to the vitality of his legacy.

Yet, for all the thousands that have earned diplomas and made reputations rooted in Macdonald's foresight and gifts, few know much about him, including historians. His name may be remembered, but his reasons for giving most of his fortune to education are largely a mystery. The year 2006–07 marks the hundredth anniversary of the founding of Macdonald College, near Montreal, the institution on which he lavished much of his time and money. The Macdonald-Stewart Foundation invited me in 2005 to try to cast light on at least some of this mystery, to introduce the man behind the benefactions. The Foundation asked me to make a short and simple presentation, unencumbered by heavy scholarly apparatus and yet offering evidence and conclusions to provoke reflection.

As no biography has been published of Macdonald, except for a chapter in a history of Macdonald College, this is a pioneering work. It is bound to contain errors of fact and interpretation; but by putting Macdonald into some context, I hope to at least provoke fresh interest in his era as well as in him. My endnotes acknowledge what I owe to the writers of unpublished material on Macdonald, as well as to authors of a variety of published works on his context, all of whom suggest what future researchers may want to consider in exploring him more deeply.

I first want to thank Mrs Liliane M. Stewart for entrusting me with this task and for writing a foreword, and Bruce Bolton, the executive director of the Macdonald-Stewart Foundation, for his encouragement and help throughout. I am grateful to my old friend Bruce McNiven, who introduced me to the Foundation. Elizabeth F. Hale, the librarian emeritus, guided me through the archives of the Foundation, on which she has been working for many years. These archives contain copies of almost a thousand of Macdonald's letters, both personal and business, from 1886 to 1911, as well as much other material on his life and his tobacco company. Also at the Foundation, Angeline Dazé, Guy Ducharme, and Lucille Riley provided me with other assistance. The staffs of the archives of McGill University, the McCord Museum, the University of Guelph, the University of Prince Edward Island, the provinces of Prince Edward Island and Quebec, the University of British Columbia, and Imperial Tobacco Limited were tireless in lending me their time and effort, as were the staffs of McGill-Queen's University Press and Macdonald College. Judith Turnbull, my editor, worked very hard to meet tight deadlines. Various people, anonymous and other, read drafts and offered remarkably insightful comments. G. Edward MacDonald and Catherine Hennessey in Charlottetown oriented me amid the complexities of Island history. Peter McNally, Robert Michel, Gordon Burr, and Jarrett Rudy at McGill, Nora Hague at the Notman Photographic Archives, and Catharine Currier Francis (a granddaughter of J.W. Robertson) answered many questions. Julia Gersovitz helped with a photograph of Sir Andrew Taylor, and Gary Carroll read through the letterbooks of H.J. Cundall. Frank Buckley provided me with crucial American evidence. To them and to the many others not here named whom I encountered in my research, I also offer my thanks.

The Macdonald-Stewart Foundation, JTI-Macdonald Corp., and the St Andrew's Society of Montreal have all supported the publication of this work, but this interpretation of the life of Macdonald remains mine.

I dedicate this book to the memory of my parents, who introduced me to the McGill campus when I was less than a year old.

A NOTE ON THE SOURCES

This book is written for a broad audience, and it is not thoroughly and closely argued in its treatment of all the issues that it raises. The endnotes may seem excessive to some readers and inadequate to others. Basically, I have tried to identify the primary and secondary authorities that a researcher would find useful in following up information here presented, but not always down to the level of individual documents. Much of the archival material on which this story is based, such as the Robertson Papers at the University of British Columbia, has yet to be thoroughly explored by historians.

If there is much to learn more about, there is also much source material that is now probably irretrievably lost. Some of the manuscripts cited by earlier biographers of Macdonald – in the published J.F. Snell and the unpublished Edgar Andrew Collard and Maurry Epstein – are now untraceable, and citations from them cannot be verified. The Macdonald-Stewart Foundation commissioned the Collard work, but the only copy of it is in the archives of the Foundation. Epstein's work can be seen in his MA thesis, and a copy of it can be found in the library of the Faculty of Education at McGill. Of these three early biographers, only Snell had known Macdonald personally. His research was punctilious, if limited in scope, and he is the source used for largely anecdotal recollections of Macdonald's contemporaries. His notes for his history of Macdonald College survive in the McGill University Archives and are invaluable. Collard and Epstein accepted Snell as accurate though not infallible, and so do I. If there are details in this book that seem to call for a reference but are not supported by one, they probably derive ultimately from Snell, who had no need to provide footnotes for the oral history, generally based on more than hearsay, with which he was familiar. Especially because Collard and Epstein are unpublished, I have drawn heavily on their work, I trust with adequate acknowledgment of it. They both worked very hard and they smoothed my path.

INTRODUCTION

## Richard W. Pound, Chancellor, McGill University

This is the story of a remarkable man.

I remember the first time I saw a photograph of Sir William Macdonald. It was at Macdonald College, many years ago, before I knew much about him other than that, presumably because of his benefaction, some venerable buildings on the downtown McGill campus and the land and college in Ste Anne de Bellevue bore his name. I knew also that Macdonald College was where anyone who wanted to teach in Quebec had to go for certification. Looking back, I realize that this connection of his name with education (and the delivery of it) was perhaps a fitting recognition of the link between Sir William and education in its broadest sense.

Before me was one of the splendid Notman photographs, in which Notman had focused, as only a photographic genius can, on Macdonald's eyes: clear, penetrating, steady, compelling. I said to myself even then that this was a man with a thousand-mile stare, that these were the eyes of a man who obviously lived and achieved in the present but who was also looking far into the future, anticipating new directions for society, mentally clearing fields and ploughing grounds that were as yet undiscovered. That impression has stayed with me ever since.*

As remarkable as the man himself are the manner in which he achieved prominence and success in business and his extraordinary commitment to the education of generations who would follow him, many of whom would have little or no idea of the extent of his impact on their personal development. He was one of those willing to plant trees in whose shade he would never sit. Macdonald was an unusual combination of uncompromising and highly focused drive on the one hand and diffidence on the other. From a difficult beginning, he perse-

---

* The photograph is reproduced on page 240.

vered to become perhaps the wealthiest man in Canada. Despite his wealth, he lived simply, without frills, without pretension, without the trappings of the rich. Because of his wealth, he was able to support activities that interested him and that he believed would benefit the country.

He was especially concerned with a younger generation that was making its way in an increasingly complicated society in which knowledge and education had never been more important. His commitment to educational and country-building causes led him to support them, especially at McGill, on a scale that was (not ignoring the splendid generosity of his friend Lord Strathcona) unprecedented in Canada and perhaps in North America. Only Andrew Carnegie in the United States could be considered a benefactor of similar magnitude. The two met once, at McGill University in 1906, when an honorary degree was conferred on Carnegie, who cheerfully observed to Macdonald that what they had achieved was "not bad for two Scots!" Not bad, indeed.

Macdonald's future could not have been predicted from his beginnings. The family, arriving from Scotland, had settled in Prince Edward Island and had shown no particular promise. Macdonald became estranged from his father (a universally detested landlord) and, caught up in the tensions of a mixed-religion family, was minimally educated and sent into business as a punishment for refusing to comply with his father's academic plans for him. His early work experience as a clerk in Boston gave no hints of any latent brilliance, but such labour was the way one learned business in those times and he developed an appreciation of the measurable and the tangible that was to feed an interest in construction, architecture, tools, machinery, and technology. Boston, a far cry from the rural environment of Prince Edward Island, exposed him to a bigger world, one where there was public and private support for education and a deep commitment to progress. Within a few years he began to apply his developing business acumen and venture into activities of his own, having identified trading, transportation, and, eventually, tobacco as businesses with the potential to grow.

The business that would launch him into prominence was begun in Montreal in 1859. Tobacco, whose use Macdonald himself eschewed and forbade in his presence, proved to be the principal foundation for his wealth. The tobacco business was rife with competition (some fair and some not), politics, risk, discriminatory tariffs, uncertainty of supply (especially during the U.S. Civil War), and economic fluctuations. Macdonald moved carefully and steadily through this jungle, becoming the leading producer of tobacco in Canada and developing a distribution system that ensured the loyalty of his customers and provided secure supplies of the raw materials needed to mix and produce the plug and chewing tobacco then in high demand. He survived a fire that destroyed his

Montreal plant, promptly building a new and better-organized one. He was frugal, reserved, and observant of everything about the business. He paid his bills immediately and insisted on cash or certified cheques from his customers, thus avoiding receivables, payables, or bad debts. By 1868 Macdonald's sole proprietorship was the largest in Canada.

Despite his increasing wealth, he played very little part in the social, political, or cultural life of the community. He never married, was increasingly distant from almost all of his relations, and remained virtually unknown outside a small Montreal circle. In 1870 he began to make gifts to McGill. Having always admired Boston, he wanted McGill to be modelled along the lines of the Massachusetts Institute of Technology and by 1883, when he became a governor of the university, had begun a concerted series of gifts, leading to construction in 1892 of his first building on campus, now known as the Macdonald Engineering Building. A friend of Principal William Dawson, he was fascinated by natural history and its teaching, which led to an increasing choice of McGill as the chief, but by no means only, object of his support.

His generosity extended across a broad range of academia. An example, by no means his largest gift, is his $150,000 donation in 1890 to re-establish the Faculty of Law. In 2007 dollars, this would be the equivalent of $4.75 million. The scale of his support for McGill is almost impossible to grasp, especially given the size of the university at that time. The new Engineering and Physics Buildings were settled with $333,000 in 1892, the equivalent of $10.2 million at the time of writing. It was typical of Macdonald's personality that, at the ceremony to inaugurate the buildings, the chancellor, Sir Donald Smith (later Lord Strathcona), spoke but Macdonald declined any such public platform and was content to silently hand the keys to the governor general for the symbolic opening of the facility. The education McGill provided in engineering and physics made it famous in the sciences throughout the world. Macdonald also admired Dawson's successor, William Peterson, and easily accommodated the new emphasis on the humanities that he brought to McGill.

What separated Macdonald from most people was his ability to see beyond the present and to anticipate what was to come, dealing with the urgent needs of the present as well as providing for the future, taking the calculated risks necessary to implement his ideas. The result was that his investments in education and elsewhere have continued to provide benefits long after the people first involved have passed from the scene and the original ideas have evolved with the expansion of knowledge. The challenges of providing a practical education, to which Macdonald was committed in a variety of ways, would lead eventually to the establishment of Macdonald College in Ste Anne de Bellevue in 1907, based on a donation and endowment totalling, in today's dollars, some $130 million, with, in addition to operating and other support given during his lifetime, a further equivalent of $18.5 million as a bequest in his will. One of the prime objectives of the College was to improve education, particularly rural education, including the training of teachers, and to enhance scientific development in the agricultural disciplines.

While maintaining his focus on practical education and development, Macdonald was also supporting the work of a young physicist, Ernest Rutherford, whose talent he recognized and whose work he did everything possible to foster. Macdonald paid Rutherford an annual stipend that was twice as much as he lived on himself. The proof of his confidence was that Rutherford's work, done at McGill in facilities built by Macdonald and with equipment Macdonald had paid for, was recognized with a Nobel Prize the year after he left McGill. This initiative had recognized a future that was far removed from, but no less important than, the practical good Macdonald could see accomplished all around him as a result of his generosity. Rutherford's work, which Macdonald did not purport to understand, was in a field that might not ever produce anything useful or practical. As it turned out, however, Macdonald was financing the beginning of the atomic age.

Macdonald's most singular feature was that, having become rich, rather than stopping at the accumulation of wealth, he used – he would have said invested – that wealth to produce benefits for the community at large. These benefits have outlasted both him and generations of the original beneficiaries. Upon the death of his friend Lord Strathcona in 1914, Macdonald was prevailed upon to become the fourth chancellor of McGill University. Unfortunately, he was almost immediately stricken with an illness and spent most of his remaining days at home in declining health. His home, in the Prince of Wales Terrace on Sherbrooke Street, was adjacent to McGill, so he could at least watch the transformation in learning that he had made possible though his generosity.

It is as one of his successors as chancellor that I have been invited to contribute these few words of introduction to this work. It is a humbling experience to stand in the shadow of such a giant and an honour to participate in a small way in the recognition afforded Sir William Christopher Macdonald on the occasion of the centenary of his endowment of the College that bears his name and thrives on his values.

Montreal, May 2007

Sir William C. Macdonald

*Chapter One*

## WILL YE NO COME BACK AGAIN?
## MACDONALD'S ANCESTRY AND EARLY INFLUENCES,
## TO 1848

Will ye no come back again?
Better l'ed ye cannot be,
Will ye no come back again?
*Caroline Oliphant, Lady Nairne (1766–1845)*

William Christopher McDonald* was born on 10 February 1831, almost undoubtedly on his father's farm about fifteen miles north of Charlottetown, the capital of what was then the British colony of Prince Edward Island. From there and with little formal education, he would make his mark as a pioneer of the Canadian tobacco industry by the age of twenty-seven and then, over the next sixty years, be considered the most successful manufacturer in the business. At the age of fifty, he was perhaps the richest man in Canada. Over his last three decades, his wealth emboldened him to finance an astonishing variety of initiatives in education, his imaginativeness in this quest perhaps unequalled by that of any other individual. His projects ranged from the improvement of teaching in rural schools to the most advanced atomic research.

Macdonald's story is of more than antiquarian interest. Although he never married or had children, his work has helped to define the lives of many. For over a century now, thousands of people he was never to meet have benefited from his endowments, his scholarships, and his vision, all of which continue to serve – much more usefully than any statue – as his monument. Most of them have undertaken careers as teachers, agronomists, lawyers, physicists, engineers, and

---

* He would change the spelling of his surname to "Macdonald" in 1898. This is the spelling that is used in this book, as it is how history remembers him.

chemists, and from Canada they have spread the fruits of his investment in them all over the world. They are his heirs if not his descendants.

Macdonald died in 1917, and as very little has been published about him anywhere, very few can say much about him now. Even during his life he was a mystery to most of those who encountered him. His manner was by turns painfully shy, studiously courteous, startlingly abrupt, even truculent, and gently self-mocking. Although one of the richest men of his generation in his country, he was renowned among the few who knew him well for his personal modesty, his frugality, and his simplicity of taste. Few of his friends and acquaintances knew about his origins, as he usually refused to discuss them. It is almost as though he had been ashamed of his roots. This is remarkable, as his lineage was as illustrious as any in his ancestral Scotland, a country that has long laid much store by family history in determining character and personality.

Canadians today, almost a century after Macdonald's death, are likely to disagree with Macdonald's contemporaries about the degree to which an individual is shaped by his or her ancestors or even by immediate family members. Macdonald himself would have been the first to have reservations about drawing broad conclusions from genes and breeding. His own life, as we shall see, revealed him to be fundamentally different, in temperament and achievement, both from previous generations of Macdonalds and from his own. Nevertheless, some of Macdonald's more illustrious ancestors were for him a source of quiet pride, and he was no doubt shaped by his early years, which he passed in a deeply divided and troubled home. Although he was not crippled by his childhood, he seems to have found the weaknesses of his relatives, especially of his father and brothers, perplexing as well as embarrassing and distressing. Few of his contemporaries of Scots origin could have been less snobbish or romantic or sentimental than he, probably because he found no reason to be so.

Resolving the mystery of Macdonald's personality cannot be accomplished through a bare description of his success. It involves the peeling away of scar tissue, as he was born within a tradition of at least a thousand years of clannish conflict, devotion, sacrifice, and faith. Over centuries, pride among his ancestors had survived the gradual erosion of their feudal power. Their habits of entitlement and authority survived their migration to North America. Consciousness of their legacy – especially in his Macdonald grandfather, his father, and his eldest brother – bred a reputation for hotheadedness and for standing on dignity and inherited privilege that Macdonald would studiously avoid to the end of his life. Their noble and martial family legacy had degenerated into a bitter obstinacy, and it was a hindrance rather than a help to them. In his generation only Macdonald himself would attach any lustre to this legacy, but he attained success through his maintenance of a sturdy independence of it. Macdonald came to realize late in life that with him would die any hope of a revival of his family's fortunes and distinction, but he turned his regret and childlessness into the realization of a selfless vision wider than any aspirations his ancestors may have had.

## THE MEDIEVAL LEGACY

The Clan Donald, also known as the MacDonalds, the McDonalds, or the Macdonalds – the spellings used by, respectively, William's grandfather, his father, and himself – is largely Gaelic in origin, with an admixture of Viking blood. It has several branches that evolved over centuries, William's being the Clan Ranald.[1] The word *clan* means simply *children*, signifying a tribe but also, as here, a tribe within a tribe. The Clan Ranald was long based on the west coast of Scotland and in the Hebrides, the islands off this coast. This remote area – conservative and rural – was a redoubt of Catholicism for centuries after the Scottish Reformation of the sixteenth century. The chieftains of the Clan Ranald were called the Clanranalds, and they claimed descent from two ancient kings of Ireland, Coilla Uais and Conn of the Hundred Battles, dating back to the second century of the Christian era. The Macdonalds generally exercised a practical sovereignty over the Hebrides and the northeast of Ireland for much of the Middle Ages.[2]

Within the Clan Ranald, William was also a descendant of the Macdonalds of Glenaladale, so named after their family seat. Some of the Clan Ranald claimed to be even more royal than other Macdonalds, as they traced their descent from Robert I, King of Scots (1274–1329, reigning from 1306) – better known as Robert the Bruce, one of the greatest warriors in Scottish history – and from the royal house of Stewart that followed him. By his first wife, Robert had a daughter, Marjorie, who married Walter Stewart, sixth hereditary High Steward of Scotland. By his second wife, he had a son, who succeeded him as King David II (1324–79). Robert the Bruce's grandson through Marjorie succeeded David as King Robert II (1316–90). Robert II was known, after the hereditary office of his father, Walter Stewart, as "the Steward." He was therefore the founder of the Stewart or the Stuart dynasty, which, with the union of the crowns of Scotland and England in 1603, became the ruling house of Great Britain.[3]

The Macdonald family tree actually predates Robert the Bruce by over a century before his accession, and in that century there is another Stewart connection. It starts with Somerled, King of the Isles, who was killed at the Battle of Renfrew in 1164. One Donald eventually succeeded to the kingship of the Isles in 1207. He married a daughter of Walter Stewart (the third, not to be confused with his namesake the sixth, High Steward of Scotland). All the descendants of Donald, King of the Isles, and of his Stewart wife became the Macdonalds (however spelt), the name meaning sons of Donald.

The Glenaladale arms, in a window at Macdonald College,
as borne by Captain John Macdonald (MSF)

This brings us back to the origins of the Clan Ranald Macdonalds. After the reigns of two further kings of the Isles in descent from Donald, the family went into decline and their kingly title fell into disuse. John MacDonald of Islay (1336–86) assumed the more modest title of Lord of the Isles, held by the descendants to 1493.[4] Despite disclaiming the kingship of the Isles, John still controlled much of Scotland and was the greatest landowner in the British Isles after the kings of England and Scotland. His first wife, Amy MacRuairi, was a distant cousin descended from Somerled, and their son Ranald became the first chief of the new Clan Ranald. His second wife, Princess Margaret Stewart, was a great-granddaughter of Robert the Bruce. This second marriage produced no children and thus, contrary to a widespread misunderstanding, there was no genuine descent of the Clan Ranald from Robert the Bruce. No female Macdonald married into the families of Robert I and II either. But the landowning power of the Clan Ranald had predated both reigns, and through their own kingship and later the lordship of the Isles, they enjoyed a position of comparable power to that of the kings of Scotland, in fact if not in dignity.

It took the Clan Ranald almost two centuries from its earliest beginnings to spawn yet a further branch. The seventh Clanranald, called Ian Og, was the most warlike of all its chiefs. His success in the mid-sixteenth century led to his taking up residence in a new house, and he styled himself as the first Glenaladale after its name. The descendants of Ian Og and his brother Allan, who became the eighth Clanranald, proliferated, eventually dividing into the Glenaladale, Bornish, Uist, and Lee lines of Macdonalds. Two and a half centuries after Ian Og's death, the younger son of the fifth Glenaladale, called Angus MacDonald, acquired another family seat, Borrodale, after which he named a further line.

It is with this final division of the Clan Ranald that we see the shape of the family as it was known by William's grandfather, the eighth Glenaladale. This was John MacDonald, and it was he who arranged for the migration in 1772 of members of various branches of the Clan Ranald Macdonalds, especially those of Borrodale and Glenaladale, to the Island of St John (renamed Prince Edward Island in 1799). His action had been influenced by one of the most cataclysmic events in eighteenth-century Scotland.

## THE JACOBITE REBELLION, 1745–1746

Prince Charles Stuart (or Stewart), known as Bonnie Prince Charlie, was the grandson of James II, the last reigning Catholic king of England and Scotland, who had been deposed and had fled into exile in 1688. Prince Charles claimed the throne for his father, the Old Pretender (called James III), a throne lost but not renounced by James II. And when, in the person of Bonnie Prince Charlie disguised as a priest, the Stuarts attempted a return to Scotland in 1745, the Glenaladale Macdonalds entered briefly into an alliance with their traditional enemies, the Camerons, and with certain branches of their own Clan Ranald. They and their allies, the Jacobites, rose in rebellion against those they saw as Hanoverian and Protestant usurpers of what was properly the throne of the Stuarts.

In 1745 the ardently Jacobite Major Alexander MacDonald of the Clanranald Regiment, the seventh Glenaladale and the great-grandfather of William Macdonald, was among the first to welcome the prince from his exile in France. Prince Charles spent his first night in Scotland at Glenaladale, and it was later in the same year that, at Alexander's other house at Glenfinnan, the two men raised the prince's standard in revolt. Bishop Hugh MacDonald, vicar apostolic of the pope in the Highlands, blessed the standard, reaffirming the link between Catholicism and the restoration of the Stuarts. This gathering of the Jacobite clans in rebellion remains one of the most stirring scenes in the Scottish imagination. Their exhilaration was short-lived, however, as their rebellion was over within a few months with the defeat of the Jacobites at the Battle of Culloden in 1746.

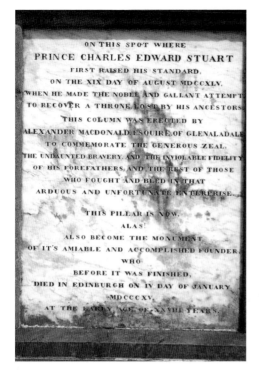

The Glenfinnan Monument commemorating the rising of 1745, erected by
Alexander MacDonald of Glenaladale on Loch Shiel in 1815 (by kind permission
of the National Trust for Scotland)

During Prince Charles's flight from the victorious English and their Scots
allies, Alexander continued to serve as his right-hand man. He hid the prince
in a cave on the estate of his nephew Angus MacDonald of Borrodale, for four
months until it was safe for the prince to return to France. Spurning a £30,000
reward offered by the English to anyone who would betray the prince, Alexander
remained a Jacobite to the end and died in 1761, renowned for his honesty and
faithfulness. For his pains, he had lost much of his property, as did his kinsman,
the Clanranald, but he had indelibly established a family tradition of loyalty that
amounted in some eyes to stubbornness.

### THE MACDONALDS AFTER CULLODEN

After Culloden, the clan system was abolished, and the wearing of Scottish dress
was forbidden. It seemed that the traditional culture of the Highlanders was
doomed and with it Catholicism in what had for centuries been its Highland for-

tress against Calvinism. Catholicism laboured under penal laws and was largely invisible to most Scots, its churches indistinguishable from barns and houses. It would not be until 1793 that public Catholic worship was again permitted. Only with the passage of the Catholic Relief Act in that year did the remaining Catholic lairds, including the Macdonalds, swear allegiance to the House of Hanover and definitively abandon the cause of the Stuart claim to the throne.

As Alexander the seventh Glenaladale was dying in 1761, he summoned home his son John (1742–1810), then a student at the Benedictine college of St James, in Ratisbon near Regensburg. John's education was typical, as the offspring of leading Jacobite families were sent abroad to be educated because they were excluded from attending universities or holding public office in Great Britain until the proclamation of Catholic Emancipation in 1829. Especially in comparison with their typically illiterate tenants, the leading Jacobites were often remarkably sophisticated. Said to be fluent in seven languages, John, only nineteen when he succeeded his father as the Glenaladale, was well educated and a born leader.[5] He was not shy about his talents and would later describe himself as king, priest, and doctor to the settlers he was to lead out of Scotland.[6]

On attaining his majority in 1763, this John MacDonald, William's grandfather, became the senior tacksman of the Clanranald, his cousin, acting as his factor or estate agent. A tacksman served as an intermediary between the chief and his tenants; the position was hereditary. John was also named tanist, or second-in-command, to the Clanranald. He worked in Arisaig and Moidart in Inverness-shire on the Scottish mainland. By the 1760s, many Scottish landowners were beginning to modernize their estates as their English counterparts were doing. A form of capitalism was developing, and money rents were replacing rents in kind. In a Scotland of increasing enterprise and wealth, landowners were abandoning their traditional self-sufficient way of life in favour of producing goods for the marketplace. The upheaval caused by this change, together with the appetite for money it was creating, shredded the traditional habits and allegiances that the previous landowners had developed over centuries. The Clanranald, who was among the reforming landlords, raised his rents and also made a handsome income out of kelping, the gathering of seaweed then used in the manufacture of soap. John MacDonald objected to becoming a businessman, preferring the role of the traditional laird. In the years before his move to the Island of St John in 1773, he could see only the increasing dissolution of everything he held dear.

Unlike their cousin the Clanranald, John and his brother Donald seemed ill-equipped to adjust to the Scotland that was being transformed by the ideas of the Scots moralist and economist Adam Smith. Apparently, they were in any case suffering financially from the failure of the Ayr Bank in 1772.[7] Their difficulty was not a question of their lack of intelligence or education, but was perhaps due to the essentially pre-capitalist and even feudal disposition of the Jacobites. This hypothesis seems confirmed by John's later difficulties entering business in the New World, followed by the failure of all the rest of his family to do likewise, until William and his brother Augustine.

In 1769 Colin MacDonald of Boisdale, the heir of the popular Alexander MacDonald ("Big Sandy") of Boisdale, became the owner of much of the island of South Uist and the tenant of the Clanranald, who was his cousin and the "feud chieftain" of the rest of the island, while of course John MacDonald was still the Clanranald's tacksman and tanist. Colin had abandoned both Jacobitism and the Catholic religion, and had also married a Presbyterian, a heathen Calvinist in the eyes of such men as John.[8] After quarrelling with the parish priest, Colin set out to convert all his Catholic tenants to the Presbyterianism to which he himself had converted. With an infamous yellow stick, he tried to drive his tenants into the Presbyterian chapel he had built. His brutal oppression of his tenants led Bishop George Hay, vicar apostolic of the Lowland District, to conclude that Highland Catholics could find safety only through emigration. Bishop Challoner of the London District in England raised £500 for this purpose, and John MacDonald, who saw little future for the traditions of the lairds after Culloden, undertook to raise the balance necessary.[9] His mind turned to the Island of St John.

## THE DISLOCATION OF THE GLENALADALE MACDONALDS
## TO NORTH AMERICA, 1772–1793

Even before their official surrender to the British through the Treaty of Paris in 1763, the French had abandoned their Île Saint-Jean after the fall of the neighbouring fortress of Louisbourg to the British in 1758. By 1772 the Island was home to a few scattered communities of Acadians, French-speaking and Catholic, who remained in hiding after the expulsion of the greater part of their number, and only a few Protestants. The Acadians were one reason why Scottish Catholics fleeing Scotland mistakenly imagined the Island of St John to be suitable for specifically Catholic settlement, while the intention of the Home or British government was exactly the opposite.

In a single day in 1767, the British divided their new possession into sixty-seven lots of about 20,000 acres each. They auctioned these off largely to speculators in Great Britain, who were intended to pay quitrent to the Crown. Quitrent was a fee payable in place of feudal services, and it was to serve as the seed money needed to develop the infrastructure of the colony for about ten years, after which time the Island was to be presumed self-sufficient. On the Island, quitrent amounted to two to six shillings per acre, varying from lot to lot according to the quality of the land in each lot. The new landlords were expected not only to pay quitrent but also to settle the land, so that their lots would produce revenues both to replace the quitrent and to support the institutions of local government.[10]

In 1770 Sir James Montgomery, the lord advocate of Scotland and one of the major new landowners, sent a first boatload of settlers, from Perthshire, to Lot 34, which he had earlier bought at the first auction of land on the Island. In 1770–71 Lieutenant-Colonel Robert Stewart sent two batches, from Argyll, to Lot 13. In 1770 Montgomery sold Lot 36 to John MacDonald for £600; MacDonald also bought Lot 35, and thus a further 20,000 acres, at about the same time.

John's emigration was to be voluntary and motivated by conscience, like previous Protestant emigrations to Massachusetts and Pennsylvania.[11] He organized the resettlement of his fellow Catholics with the aid of and at the request of his church. In 1772 the lairds' systematic clearance of the inhabitants of the Highlands had not yet begun. It was only in 1780 that the Scottish landlords began to raise sheep, a practice that led to the clearances and to the further and larger emigrations that followed, particularly from 1815 onwards. John probably seldom, if ever, returned to the Highlands. For him, they must have represented little but desolation and loss.

In the 1770s, however, an era still dominated by mercantilist ideas, there was strong official opposition in Scotland to emigration, even by Catholics and the enterprising Highland lairds themselves, including the Clanranald and Colin of Boisdale, even though the population of the Highlands was still growing significantly at the time. The emigration that John was planning was therefore in defiance of his Protestant relation Colin, who wanted to retain his recalcitrant tenants as workers. Moreover, with ideas about the need for labour at home prevailing in England as well, the original British scheme of 1767 for settling the Island of St John had changed radically. Protestants from the American colonies to the south and from other countries – not from the British Isles – were now encouraged to populate the Island in place of the exiled and troublesome Catholic Acadians.

Roman Catholics were considered undesirable by definition, and they were prohibited from holding public office on the Island for almost sixty years, even though the Island was accorded responsible government as early as 1769. This exclusion extended of course to such Catholic leaders as John. He never held a seat in the local House of Assembly, established as early as 1773, from which he could have made the voice of his community heard. It was only after Catholics were permitted to hold office, first in England in 1829 and then on the Island, that in 1830 William's father, Donald, a fervent Catholic, was able to become a member of the House of Assembly.

John's community consisted of two groups totalling 210 people: 100 from the island of South Uist and 110 from Arisaig and Moidart. The first group was largely financed by the Catholic Church and John himself. The second was relatively self-sufficient, even genteel, and seems to have consisted largely of John's relatives, who paid their own way. John began the undertaking by sending his brother Donald out to explore the Island, first in 1770 and then in the following year with a dozen pioneers, the purpose being to build log cabins. Sometime before leaving for the Island himself, John had married Isabella Gordon of Wardhouse, Aberdeenshire. She died in childbirth, and their child shortly thereafter, and he made his brother Donald his heir.

In 1772 John organized the transport of the bulk of his migrants to North America. He chartered a boat from Greenock, the *Alexander*, and included in the party his cousin Father James MacDonald (who died in 1785) as chaplain and Roderick MacDonald (died 1799), another cousin, as physician. Father James's brother Donald came with them; he would become known as the head of the Tracadie Macdonalds, very confusingly as John the Glenaladale's separate estate was also located in Tracadie.

John himself followed on another ship in 1773, arriving after picking up provisions in Boston for his settlers. Unlike most of his fellow landowners, who never moved there, John arrived on the Island of St John with the intention of establishing permanent residence on it, having effectively given up his ancestral lands. He had mortgaged his estates at Glenaladale and Glenfinnan to his cousin Alexander MacDonald of Borrodale, raising enough from this loan to help finance the journey of about half of his emigrants. In return, he expected the emigrants to remain his tenants on the Island and to support him in other ways as they had in Scotland. He himself would pay quitrent or cash in place of the theoretical feudal services that he owed to the Crown. There being no property in Scotland for him to return to, he carved out about 500 acres of Lot 36 for his own use, building a large house facing Tracadie Bay, which he called New Glenaladale.[12] The rest of his two lots, about 39,500 acres in total, he reserved for tenants. Further clusters of immigrants arrived from John's part of the Highlands in 1790–91, but by this time they were among several groups that planned to settle not only on the Island but also in mainland Nova Scotia and Cape Breton.[13]

Of all his family members, only his sister Clementina, who was married, would never leave Scotland. His brother Father Augustine Austin, stayed in Moidart for thirty years and then immigrated in about 1802. It is possible that another brother, Father Hugh, came to the island but died shortly after his arrival. Apart from the siblings already named, the siblings of John who emigrated to the island included Margaret, who would marry Major Ian Mor MacDonald of West River, and Nelly (1750–1803, also known as Helen or Nellie), who in 1791 would marry Captain Ronald MacDonald of Grand Tracadie.

Of the other MacDonald relatives on the *Alexander*, one cousin Donald would establish himself at Allisary and another cousin Donald would live at Bornish, both on the Island but outside John's lots. In 1770, independently of John, his cousin Captain Allan MacDonald had bought half of Lot 25, and in 1775 his relatives would establish there, in Princes County, the Rhetland (or Rhutland) MacDonald line. Captain Allan was also cousin to John Macdonald of Morar, and in the next generation the properties of the two families merged.[14] Similarly, Macdonald settlements cropped up at Three Rivers and elsewhere on the Island.

Although the Macdonalds were prominent among the passengers aboard the *Alexander*, a number of other families were represented – MacEachern, MacKenzie, MacIntosh, MacMillan, MacKinnon, MacPhee, MacCormack, MacRory, Campbell, Beaton, Gillis, and Bain. The boat brought all these settlers to the Island of St John, up the Hillsborough River, from Charlottetown to near Scotchfort, southeast of Tracadie Bay on the north shore, in Queens County. Scotchfort was northeast of Frenchfort, the burnt-out Acadian centre, and Tracadie Cross was between the two. Father James MacDonald built the first Catholic church in Scotchfort, made from logs.

Confounding John's expectations of their loyalty and gratitude, most of the *Alexander*'s passengers, once landed, soon came to consider themselves essentially free to settle not only on John's lot but on adjoining lots or beyond, where there were no resident landlords or rent collectors. In contrast to the still largely feudal country, populated by tenants, that the 210 immigrants had left behind, the Island seemed eminently suitable for squatters and pioneers. This fact condemned in their eyes the very system of tenancies as old-fashioned and irrelevant to the future of relative freedom that they wanted to carve out for themselves. They almost immediately rebelled against the harshness of life in their new land, even though John had secured them supplies from Boston and Quebec City. Many spread out of Lot 36 to other parts of the Island, to Cape Breton Island, north of Nova Scotia, and even farther afield.

As the American colonies to the south were approaching revolt, John was having trouble earning a living from his land. With few tenants, he had little income for quitrent. In 1775 he and his brother Donald joined His Majesty's Royal Highland Emigrant Regiment, later known as the 84th Regiment of Foot.[15] Lieutenant-Colonel Allan MacLean had raised the first battalion, and Major John Small the second.[16] For this second battalion, Captain John raised thirty-three recruits on the Island and in Newfoundland and was appointed commandant at Halifax, where he remained for the duration of the American Revolution – six years – apart from a period in Annapolis. He seems to have acquitted himself honourably in military service and was thereafter generally known as Captain John. Donald, however, died fighting the French in about 1780, leaving John without an heir.

While absent from the Island, Captain John was still unable to pay his quit-rent. His cousin Nelly was in charge of Lot 36 and its ninety head of cattle, but his few remaining tenants had nowhere to sell their goods and they were unable to contribute to the payment of his quitrent. Walter Patterson (also spelt as Paterson), the governor of the Island since 1773, was trying, for his own profit, to confiscate the lands of proprietors in arrears of quitrent. In 1781 the Island receiver of quitrents informed John that he would have to pay all his quitrent in arrears in hard cash within six months or face the sale of Lot 36. This lot was not in fact auctioned off, but his Lot 35 was.

In the mistaken belief that he had lost both of his lots, John went to London in 1781–83 to petition with other proprietors for the restoration of whatever lots had been auctioned for failure to pay quitrents. The petitioners argued that the war had made these payments impossible and that they had been given insufficient notice of the auctions. They obtained a favourable ruling from Lord North in 1783, which Patterson ignored. As a consequence, MacDonald, from 1785 onward, campaigned for Patterson's removal as governor. In 1789 he attended Patterson's hearing, to account for his actions, before the Privy Council in London. But the property seized for sale in 1781 still could not be recovered. In 1790 MacDonald returned from England and offered to represent his fellow injured proprietors in a suit against the now ex-governor Patterson and his associates. It was only after Patterson had landed in debtors' prison in 1792 that Captain John was able to repurchase Lot 35.[17]

On a visit to Scotland in 1792, John met and married Margaret Moran McDonald of Ghernish (died 1836), by whom he had five children. The first, Flora Anna Maria (born in 1794), was educated at the Ursuline Convent in Quebec and later married and had children. The second, William (born in about 1797), is said to have become a priest. It is probable that the subject of this biography was named after him, as there seem to be no Williams among our subject's mother's brothers. A third child, Lieutenant-Colonel Roderick (circa 1800–1857), belonged to the 30th Castle Tioram Regiment of Highlanders, named after the ancient eyrie of the Glenaladales.[18] A fourth child became a priest and was known as Father John (1808–1874). William was to know him well, in addition to John's remaining child, William's own father, Donald (1795–1854).

In Tracadie, considerable acreage on both sides of the Hillsborough River belonged to John MacDonald's family. John dispensed the traditional hospitality of a chieftain, and his house, often full of visitors, was compared to a public house. All his instincts remained deeply paternalistic and feudal. Nevertheless, he overcame his Jacobite legitimism and accepted the Protestant Hanoverian George III as his king. He was also remarkably tolerant religiously and was one of the first subscribers to the building of a Protestant church in Charlottetown.

Silhouette of Captain John MacDonald
(*The Island Magazine* 29 [Spring/Summer 1991], 35)

There were aspects of life on the Island, however, that Captain John could not tolerate. He quarrelled with the second governor, Edmund Fanning (1739–1818), when the governor, like his predecessor Patterson, apparently tried to press for escheat (the reversion to the Crown of the property of landowners in arrears of quitrent payments) in order to benefit personally from the anticipated forced land sales.[19] In 1796 a pamphlet written by a Loyalist refugee from South Carolina, Lieutenant-Colonel Joseph Robinson, had called for the introduction of Crown escheat courts to take back unimproved lots from inactive proprietors. Captain John believed that Fanning and his Stewart allies, led by Chief Justice Peter Stewart, were actually behind this move. Becoming "increasingly loud and shrill," he urged Attorney General Joseph Aplin to prosecute Robinson for libel.

In 1797 the speaker of the House of Assembly, "Hellfire Jack" Stewart, stung by Captain John's criticism of the Stewarts, took on the captain in a fight. Stewart was armed with a regimental broadsword and Captain John with a Highland dirk. Both survived. Fanning refused to receive, much less transmit to the duke of Kent at Halifax as the captain had requested, Captain John's complaints about escheating revolutionaries on the Island, whom the captain had compared to revolutionaries in France. The House summoned Captain John to explain his accusations, but when he refused to appear before it, it condemned him for being of "turbulent and reckless and factious character and disposition." The House also condemned his "baneful and pernicious endeavours" and "highly reprehensible and refractory conduct and behaviour," as well as his "wanton and wicked" disposition and "shameless scurrility, misrepresentation and falsehood."

Despite John's efforts, the House of Assembly proceeded to adopt a series of resolutions in response to various petitions for an escheat court. Probably under the influence of Jack Stewart, it sorted the lots into four categories, ranging from those totally unsettled to those settled in accordance with the provisions of their original grants. It placed Captain John's Lots 35 and 36 in this last category, that of properly settled land. The House was generous in this categorization, as John had not complied with the official stipulation that his settlers be non-British Protestants. Rather than insisting that the captain's lands be surrendered to an escheat court for non-payment of quitrent, the House called for the settlement of those lands of non-resident proprietors that were not yet settled, leaving the payment of his arrears an open question.

These resolutions of the House were significant in demonstrating that the House now recognized that the language of quitrents and escheat was no longer adequate in addressing the practical problems faced by the landowners since the first days of the settlement program, more than twenty-five years before. The House still condemned John's almost hysterical comparison of Fanning and his associates to the revolutionaries then terrorizing France, and it left him liable to paying quitrent, but the resolutions it had passed pointed to a future less encumbered by historical and legal technicalities.

In 1801–02 Captain John was in London, again defending the non-performing or defaulting proprietors from the threat of escheat. The Home Government did eventually rule in favour of these proprietors, but curiously it did so under the influence of Hellfire Jack Stewart. The tide had actually begun to turn in Captain John's favour with the House resolutions of 1797. He was on the way to rehabilitation, slowly consolidating his own reputation as a devoted resident landowner, unlike many of the others whom he was defending.

John's finances continued to deteriorate, however. The fifth earl of Selkirk had lent him money in the 1790s to carry on, but John could not discharge his debts. The quitrents he owed continued to cripple him, and by 1805 he was planning to sell his land. By 1806, however, the House of Assembly was praising him as an exemplary landlord and petitioning the Crown for him to be relieved of the obligation to pay quitrent, but the Crown did not comply. John thus remained under the threat of the forced sale of his property to pay arrears. His creditor, Selkirk, had brought out his own settlers to the Island, in 1803, and in 1809 he invited John to lead a new colonization expedition to the Red River, in what is

The gravestone of Captain John MacDonald and of his daughter
Flora in Prince Edward Island (MSF)

now Manitoba and where there were presumably no quitrents, but by then the captain was exhausted. The matter of his property unresolved, he died towards the end of 1810 or in early 1811.

Captain John MacDonald's life of continuous struggle would haunt his descendants, from his son Donald to his grandsons, first John Archibald and then William, the last owner of most of his grandfather's lands before they were finally expropriated in 1873–76. While it is no easy task to determine precisely what the captain's legacy was and how it may have shaped William, one aspect of his influence, already suggested, may have lain in his sheer inability to adjust to the modern world, to a capitalist society that was disinclined to deference and dependency. He had tried to escape this world by leaving Scotland, only to find it making inroads on the Island of St John. For centuries, his family had been proud to resist many of the prevailing trends in Scotland. Few families could have been more Scottish culturally but also less Presbyterian or less inclined to engage in business. With their memories of their stubbornly intimate links to the Old Religion, the Old Pretender, and the Auld Alliance (between Scotland and France), the Macdonalds were supremely unlikely to be counted among those Scots credited with shaping the modern world. But was Captain John truly as inflexible and hopeless at business as his unfortunate financial affairs might suggest?

It has been claimed in an early unpublished biography of Sir William Macdonald, that Captain John studied the specific characteristics of crop growing in North America. He set up his own farm as a model for his tenants, hoping to turn them – formerly shepherds and cowherds in Scotland, for the most part – into educated agriculturists. He was also an early advocate of conservation, preventing erosion of his land, for example, by refusing to allow either the spruce trees to be felled or the sand-hill grass to be cut along the north shore of the Hillsborough.[20] According to a more recent account, however, Captain John preferred to raise cattle rather than clear, plough, and cultivate the land for crops because he was afraid that his settlers would fail to plough and manure properly. He banked the salt marshes along the north shore in order to drain them and thus protect the farmsteads for the storage of hay, which was to be a cash crop as well as food for his cattle. He intended to maintain his tenants in their old agricultural practices, having them raise only enough grain and vegetables for food, while he himself concentrated on livestock production with the help of their labour.[21] Even the earlier account cites a letter from Captain John in 1806 claiming that he had to support "with straw and hay this winter 120 heads of near breeding-stock, 16 large bullocks, 16 horses and 100 sheep." It therefore seems fair to conclude that his farm was largely devoted to livestock, that he had taken up something quite unlike anything he had done in Scotland, and that he was far from being simply an unrepentantly feudal rent collector. He was trying to be self-sufficient.[22]

Furthermore, over the years Captain John quite correctly defined the reasons why the landholding system was absurd. The conditions stipulated in the original grants were, in his words, "useless, intricate, nonsensical, even hurtful or impracticable." He understood that the escheators were simply trying to profit from this unfairness, but he was unwilling to abandon all that he had sacrificed for his property. He preferred instead to condemn the many cases of conflict of interest on the Island, where the same people were "Prosecutors, Judges and Inquest or Jury," and all were hostile to proprietors. Moreover, he observed that the official class could not be trusted "on points of Intention, probity and truth," presumably referring to Patterson and Fanning.[23]

The captain habitually exhibited suspicion of, if not hostility towards, authority. Unfortunately, by persisting in associating himself with even the non-performing non-resident proprietors, he also ensured the continuing hostility of Islanders, especially tenants, towards his own family. The result was that the Macdonalds were to remain isolated and increasingly mistrustful. Over three generations, their farming probably brought little profit, compelling them to squeeze what they could out of their tenants. Captain John's legacy was thus of land that did not pay. Almost a century later, this was the only sensible conclusion that his clear-headed businessman grandson, William, could draw from it.

## WILLIAM'S PARENTS AND HIS BIRTH, 1819–1831

Donald McDonald, William's father, shared the inheritance of Captain John's land with his brother Father John MacDonald and his sister Flora Anna Maria, who married Alex MacDonnell (or MacDonald) of Glengarry. In 1819, in a sharp break with family tradition and Catholic practice, Donald married a Protestant, Anna Matilda (1797–1877), a daughter of Ralph Brecken. At a time when it was still generally accepted by Catholics that Protestants went to hell, and vice versa, theirs was a marriage apparently entered into out of desperation. Donald had previously applied in vain for dispensation to marry a first cousin, the sister of his cousin John Small Macdonald, a Catholic. In the almost incestuous world of Catholic Macdonalds that he knew, there were no other suitable Catholic women who were unrelated to him and of comparable social rank. Donald made rank his primary criterion in his continuing search.

What Anna Matilda lacked for Donald in religious affiliation she compensated for in political connections. Her brother Ralph was speaker of the House of Assembly in 1812–13. Her brother John was elected to the House in 1829 and served as a member of the Legislative Council (essentially the preserve of landowners), sitting with Donald in 1839–52. Among her sisters, one married Thomas H. Haviland, whose career included such posts as those of president of the Legislative Council, assistant justice of the Supreme Court, colonial treasurer and secretary, and mayor of Charlottetown. Another sister married James Peake, a member of the House of Assembly and later a president of the Legislative Council. A third sister married Dr James Mackieson, a surgeon general. From these, there followed a new generation of politicians, contemporaries of William and his cousins. Thomas H. Haviland's son Heath was thrice a colonial secretary, a father of Confederation, a Dominion senator, and finally, in 1879–84, lieutenant-governor of Prince Edward Island. John Brecken's son Frederick de St Croix twice served as attorney general and was later William's legal adviser on the expropriation of the tenanted lands inherited from Captain John.

The Honourable Donald McDonald (Archives of
Prince Edward Island, accession no. 3466, item no. HF75.113.1)

Anna Matilda's maternal grandfather, Joseph Robinson, had fled South Carolina as a Loyalist. After establishing himself on the Island, he became speaker
of the House of Assembly as well as assistant justice of the Supreme Court and
a member of the Executive Council. Robinson's daughter Rebecca, Anna Matilda's aunt, married Robert Hodgson, another speaker of the Assembly. He was
the father of Anna Matilda's cousin Sir Robert Hodgson (1798–1880), who served
as attorney general (1829–51), president of the Legislative Council (1840–53), chief
justice (1852–74), lieutenant-governor (1874–79), and thrice as administrator of
the government. What compounded the peculiarity of the marriage of William's
parents was the fact that both his mother's grandfather Robinson and her uncle
Hodgson had been among Captain John's bitterest enemies under Governor

Fanning. The union of the Breckens with the Macdonalds in 1819 thus marked the acceptance by the Protestant establishment of the latter, an acceptance made easier now that Captain John had been dead for about two decades and Catholics had been free to hold public office for about the same length of time.

Marriages in 1819 were, in any case, seldom love matches. They were alliances of property and interests. In 1808 Captain John had divided all his land on Lots 36 and 35 into seven estates, one for his wife, one to be sold for the payment of his debts, and one for each of his five children. His trustees were to be one William McDonald, an Edinburgh advocate, and his cousin Alexander MacDonald of Borrodale. Through his and Anna Matilda's marriage settlement, dated 22 January 1819, Donald McDonald assigned the St Martin's Estate on Lot 35 to trustees until the wedding. If, in the course of the marriage, Donald died first, Anna Matilda was to receive the rents from Lot 35 for life or an annuity of £200 not subject to the control of any subsequent husband. This annuity would be in addition to her dower, or right of support as a widow, on Donald's property. If Donald survived Anna Matilda, the estate on Lot 35 would remain his.[24] Although there was nothing unusual about this arrangement, it confirms that the marriage was probably a strategic alliance for both parties. It certainly did no harm to Donald, who was elected to the House of Assembly in 1830, sitting there for twenty-three years before his elevation to the Legislative Council, in which he served as president until his death in 1854. He was also elected as sheriff of Charlottetown for a year, in 1836. It seemed that his children were well positioned for lives of ease if not success.

This prospect was an illusion. William's parentage conveyed to him at best a contradictory inheritance, both Catholic and Protestant, revolutionary and counter-revolutionary. It was a legacy full of pride but inherently precarious because it was rooted in the dispossession of his father's family in post-Culloden Scotland and of some of his mother's in revolutionary America. Captain John had lost all the family property in Scotland, and now his grandson Donald was facing calls for the expropriation of most of the family land on the Island.

The Honourable Donald and Anna Matilda McDonald produced three sons, John Archibald (1825–1903), Augustine Ralph (1827–1900?), and William Christopher (1831–1917). They also had four daughters, Matilda Alice and Anna Rebecca, who became Ursuline nuns; Margaret, who married and lived on the Island; and Helen Jane, who converted to Protestantism and never married.[25] Of these seven children, only John Archibald married and had children.

No vestige seems to remain of the house in which William was born, and there is now little indication of the graves in Prince Edward Island where his ancestors and siblings were buried. It appears likely that William was born and grew up in Arisaig Cottage, a house that his aunt Nelly had had erected during the American Revolution, near the site of New Glenaladale, the original house built by Captain John, which had probably disappeared by William's time. Arisaig Cottage was burned down, most probably by arsonists, in 1850.[26]

## WILLIAM'S ISLAND EDUCATION AND THE FAMILY TRADITION

Many in William's family were not only well educated but also unusually interested in education and philanthropy. His uncle Roderick McDonald, a lieutenant-colonel, became paymaster of the 30th Castle Tioram Regiment in order "to devote all his pecuniary resources in endeavouring to procure school-masters and books" for the Highland youth of the Maritime colonies. It was the work of Roderick and Sir Samuel Cunard for the Highland Society of London that established, at their own expense, ten of the earliest schools in the Maritimes, serving 10,000 children. He had organized five branches of the Highland Society to care for Scottish exiles, both Protestant and Catholic. William's father was the society's first president on the Island, while Roderick was its chief in Nova Scotia.[27]

As described above, William's grandfather, John MacDonald, had attended the Benedictine college at Ratisbon in Germany. His father, Donald, and his two brothers, John Archibald and Augustine, had been educated at the Jesuit college of Stonyhurst in England. It was Donald's wish that William should also go to Stonyhurst and, as such Jesuit schools promised, there be shaped for life. This was not to be. William studied first at home with his uncle, Father John, who had received a good education in Paris and Rome and had taught at the Grand Seminary in Quebec City. He also attended a school run by a Mrs Hubbard. This was his only experience of a rural school, but its probable inadequacies likely marked him enough to make rural education one of his chief interests in later life. Then, for a few months in 1844, William attended the Central Academy in Charlottetown, the predecessor of Prince of Wales College, as it was to become in 1861. It is not known why William did not stay at the academy, but it was after his time there, in about 1845, that Donald was planning to enrol him at Stonyhurst. The boy absolutely refused to go, and so Donald determined that he would instead have his son gain a practical education in business.

In sending William into business, Donald intended to punish him. After all, this was an occupation that no other close relative had likely ever engaged in. According to his early biographers, Snell and Collard, William was ejected from Donald's house and sent to work as an apprentice, delivering parcels for his cousin Daniel Brennan, a merchant in Charlottetown. William's pay is unknown, but it included £15 per annum for clothes and laundry. William, it seems, once found himself short-changed and so took the amount he considered his due from the till. He was discovered and dismissed.

This story makes William out as the black sheep of his family, and his refusal to attend a Catholic school suggests that he was hostile to the religion of his father. In themselves, the long-standing and still-unresolved issues of discontented tenants and unpaid quitrent were not enough to make a future on the Island unattractive to William. But the friction over land management and religious issues was enough to make this future impossible for him, much as similar factors had prompted Captain John to quit Scotland. Not long after his dismissal from his first cousin's employ, in 1848, William left the Island and made his way to Boston, rejecting the home, hearth, and religion of his family. He was, however, not the first Macdonald to find himself at odds with the church.

## THE PROBLEMS OF THE MACDONALDS WITH THE CATHOLIC CHURCH AND THE ST ANDREW'S PROJECT

Chronologically and socially, the Macdonalds were the first Scottish Catholic family on the Island. Religion was inextricably linked to the family's settlement. As already noted, Captain John's cousin Father James was the first priest in their community, and he was followed by Captain John's brother Father Augustine Austin in 1802–07. In the following generation, Donald's brother Father John became a prominent landlord as a co-heir of Captain John's estate. In 1830 he had brought out 106 mainly Irish Roman Catholics to the family property at Fort Augustus in Tracadie. Even after 1845, when he returned to England for good, he demonstrated that property ownership was not incompatible with priestly status. It is possible that William himself had been intended by Donald for the priesthood as well as for landownership, as it was traditional for each generation to produce at least one priest and neither of William's older brothers had shown any interest in a priestly vocation. His namesake uncle had been a priest, and William's was the first in probably many generations that did not produce one.

Nevertheless, the family had difficulties with the Catholic Church, beginning as far back as 1771–72, when Captain John became suspicious that the church's subsidy of his poorer emigrants might lead to troublesome tenants. Moreover, with the arrival of other Scottish Catholic settlers – not sponsored by John – in 1790, all from the Clanranald's or other Catholic estates, John found that he was no longer the undisputed leader of the Scots Catholics on the Island. And, as described above, his own tenants had been melting away to other lots, diminishing his rental income to such an extent that he was never free of serious financial problems. In effect, he not only had lost his position as the undisputed leading

Catholic layman with the power to determine the course of the Catholic community as a whole, but had also become incapable of providing for the needs of his family and his tenants.

In addition, Captain John's controversial position on the nature and development of a seminary at St Andrew's near his own estate led to an uneasy relationship with the church, one that would affect his descendants, including William.[28] The problem began in 1794, when John agreed to help raise the £250 needed to purchase a 200-acre farm at St Andrew's, on Lot 37, to serve as the site of a seminary. He is said to have envisioned a distinctly Catholic community in which the Scots Catholics of the Island would be bound with the largely Irish Catholics of Halifax.

In 1805, when John was in England, Bishop Denaut, of the diocese of Quebec of which the Island was a part, decided to attach a large church to the intended seminary at St Andrew's. On his return to the Island in 1806, John protested that spending a projected £2,000 on the church would leave little money for chapels elsewhere. He proposed £500 or £600 for the church and about half this sum for missionary chapels. Father John C. MacMillan, an early historian of the Catholic Church on the Island, concluded that Captain John was trapped in a conflict of interest in opposing the new church, as he actually wanted a church to be built nearer his house for the use of his brother, the infirm Father Augustine Austin.

It is true that Captain John protested that St Andrew's was too distant for all but six families among his tenants, and that the problem was compounded by the bishop's having forbidden the saying of Mass in private houses, but it appears that John did not want a large church near his house, where there were few to serve in any case. He wanted a "snugg" chapel, such as had been common among Catholic recusants in Scotland and Ireland. There seems to be no reason why John could not have had both the church at St Andrew's and the chapel that he was proposing or why the two would have been inappropriate for the population they could serve. But the bishop seems to have turned John's proposal for financing against him.

As the church at St Andrew's was to be on Lot 37, to the east of his own Lot 36, Captain John called for an assessment to be made from Catholics "at large" on the Island, not simply from his own tenants, to pay for it. One historian concludes that the St Andrew's assessment committee "could do nothing except express disgust with MacDonald's arrogance" and that "this attitude was subsequently handed down orally to succeeding generations." His position may have made sound financial sense, but his "ferocity in this instance worked to confirm the ambiguous attitude towards him that still persists among the descendants of his settlers."[29] The quarrel was perhaps more between John and the bishop of Quebec, with Father Bernard MacEachern, the vicar general, and the assessment committee of St Andrew's caught in the middle and obliged in the end to defer to the bishop.

In his last years, John felt financially strapped. After Governor Patterson had sold Lot 35 at auction to General Alexander Maitland in 1781 because of John's failure to pay arrears of quitrent, John was able to buy it back in 1792, but only at the exorbitant price of £1,200. This amount he had to borrow from his rich cousin Alexander of Borrodale. Alexander had already foreclosed on John's Scottish estates, mortgaged to him in 1770, but in 1792 Alexander became once again a creditor of the captain. The new debt was in addition to the quitrent still owed by John to the government. Even by William's birth in 1831, his father Donald and his uncle Father John had still not discharged the Borrodale mortgage on Lot 35. In Captain John's last years, other land of his, probably Lot 36, was also mortgaged to the earl of Selkirk for over £600, which was what the captain had paid for it in 1770. Although he had a few tenants left, there was almost no rental income from them, and his family was forced to live off the sale of hay and cattle.

Their problem appears to have derived from the captain's failure to enter into long-term written leases with his tenants, both before and after his absence in the American War of Independence. Even after his return and while a resident landlord, he was losing or evicting tenants. In 1795 he had had seventy tenant families, but in 1798 he had only forty-six. One possible reason for his refusal to enter into long-term leases was the threat of an escheat court, which was already depressing land values because it threatened to break up the lots into smaller units after they had been forfeited by their landowners for non-payment of quitrent. Moreover, long-term leases would necessitate the essentially permanent "location" of long-term tenants, as well as the provision of fences for them, which might serve as the basis for the smaller units forcibly purchased through escheat. Fundraising for St Andrew's went on after John's death, but it has been speculated that Islanders contributed little because of the reluctance of the widow of Captain John to grant long-term leases to her tenants, who in consequence felt no security sufficient to want so to invest in the community.

In any case, St Andrew's College and Church did open, and over the thirteen years of the existence of the seminary, 1831–44, it was closely tied to William's family, with many of his relatives, both close and distant, serving it in various capacities.[30] Brennan, the relative to whom William was to be apprenticed in 1845 or so, had applied for its incorporation and served as its treasurer. Donald McDonald was secretary. The remaining lay trustees were Donald's first cousin, on his father's side, John Small Macdonald, who was also Brennan's brother-in-law and whose sister Donald himself had courted, and Angus Macdonald of Brudenell, who was a first cousin of John Small Macdonald on the latter's moth-

Father John MacDonald
(John C . Macmillan, *History of the Early Catholic Church on Prince Edward Island*
[Quebec: L'Evenement Press, 1906], between pages 42 and 43)

er's side and related to Donald McDonald more distantly. Of the three clerical
members of the board, one was also related to Donald, being from the Borrodale
settlement at Allisary; this was Father Bernard Donald Macdonald (1797–1859),
who was to become bishop of Charlottetown in 1837.

The St Andrew's project turned out to be less than inspiring. The first two rec-
tors of the college, the Irishmen Fathers Edmund Walsh and Charles McDonald
(apparently no relation of William's), left under a cloud. Father James Brady
was the next to serve as rector, and St Andrew's deteriorated further under his
leadership. His successor in 1843, Father Pius MacPhee, seems to have been even
more lax as an administrator, and the college closed within a year of his arrival.

The tenant issue was tied to the fate of the college, in its last year, in the person
of Father John, William's uncle. He had joined the trustees after the death of
Bishop MacEachern in 1835, but friction with his tenants at Fort Augustus,
which he had colonized five years before, resulted in his transfer from Tracadie
to St Margaret's in Kings County. Although he held no property in that area, he

was suspected of aiding in the enforcement of rents even there, and he billeted soldiers sent there to enforce rent collection. In 1843 Bishop Macdonald asked him to resign from St Margaret's, but Father John refused, only to find himself forced out four months later by dissident parishioners and obliged to leave for England two years later, never to return.

In 1843 Donald, doubtless irked by the treatment of his brother Father John, began to find fault with Bishop Macdonald's interference in college affairs. Donald and Father John attacked Father James MacIntyre, the professor of philosophy at St Andrew's, accusing him of having undermined Father John at St Margaret's and conspiring for his recall. Donald described both MacIntyre and Brady, whom MacIntyre was replacing in missionary work in Tracadie, as levellers and escheators. In October 1844 Donald McDonald and Father John MacDonald, and someone named Angus Macdonald, resigned as trustees of St Andrew's, which had already ceased its functions.

Thus, five years before William's departure from the Island, his father and uncle were carrying on a feud with the Catholic Church begun by his grandfather almost forty years earlier. William's break with Catholicism was a decision separate from this feud, but probably contemporaneous with the closure of St Andrew's.

## WILLIAM'S REJECTION OF CATHOLICISM AND GENERAL PERSPECTIVE ON RELIGION

William probably attended St Andrew's Church, although it closed in 1844 when he was only thirteen. Alternatively, he may have gone to the Church of St John the Evangelist in what became Tracadie Cross. Whatever interest he might have had in religion barely lasted beyond his childhood. In later years William confessed to Professor Percy Nobbs of McGill University that he had broken with Catholicism because of "some traumatic experience, apparently during his service as a choirboy or acolyte." Nobbs recorded that Macdonald's face had "reddened with shame and anger" as he was speaking, as the incident had made a "deep and horrible" impression on him.[31] We do not know the nature of the experience or exactly how it affected William's thinking, but by his own admission, it led to his abandonment of his faith, and he is said to have developed "a passionate aversion to the ritual and tenets of the church."[32]

With the closure of St Andrew's, there was no local school to which William could be sent, and this would explain his attendance at the Central Academy in the autumn of 1844. St Andrew's troubled existence may also have led to his refusal to attend the very Catholic Stonyhurst. William's ultimate loss of faith contributed to his leaving the Island for good in 1848. Catholicism was part of his

tortured legacy of Jacobitism, anti-American loyalism, feudal obligations, and
rebellious tenants, a legacy that made no real sense to William, full of vigour at
the age of seventeen.

William was always wary about discussing religion, seeing it as a private
matter with no place in the public sphere. When asked about his religious views,
he is reported to have replied that he "could not conceive how so sacred a matter
should interest anyone but himself."[33] But it would be rash to say that he became
an atheist or even an agnostic. And as he occasionally attended church with
his mother and his Protestant sister in the 1870s – and reportedly attended a
revival meeting featuring Dwight Moody, a fiery evangelical preacher as late
as the 1890s – he was probably not anti-Christian. Like many of his time, he
was afflicted with doubt but also curiosity about religion, finding it increasingly
incomprehensible as time passed.

In 1900 he told one correspondent that he had contributed to causes related
to religion up to about 1875. Towards the very end of his life, however, William
explicitly disclaimed an interest in religious controversy of any kind. Still, he
passed happy hours with two Macdonald relations who were Jesuits, and he is
said to have been able to recite prayers in Latin.[34] His surviving correspondence
reveals that there was always a core of sweetness and gentleness in him, something deeply forgiving and hopeful, but in marked contrast to his grandfather
and his father, both firm believers, he had a total lack of interest in dogma. He
was always very courteous with clergymen of all denominations, but he firmly
refused a request for aid from Bishop's College in Lennoxville when approached
by its principal, an Anglican priest. By about the time his mother died, in 1877,
he had developed a very different sort of faith, one in scientific progress.

## MACDONALD'S MATRILINEAL INFLUENCES AND
## HIS SIBLINGS' CHOICES OF RELIGION

Perhaps we can conclude from this look at William's Macdonald antecedents, his
youth, and his religious orientation that he was not a typical Macdonald at all.
In looking for influences, genealogists might do better to look at his matrilineal
line. William was much closer to his mother than to his father, and his correspondence contains many letters to his Protestant cousins on his Brecken side
and almost none to his Macdonald cousins. Moreover, unlike the Macdonalds,
the Breckens were generally prosperous businessmen and professionals.

It is not clear whether William's mother, Anna Matilda, ever converted to
Catholicism as a result of her marriage. If she did, she later reverted to her native
Protestantism, probably by the early 1850s. William's sister Helen abandoned
Catholicism at the same time, a decision Donald described to John Archibald as

worse for him "than an Assasin's [*sic*] Knife or Bullet," adding that it would "drive me to perfect madness."[35] Macdonald had already left the church, although he would never follow his mother and sister to Protestantism. By the time William was in his teens, and possibly before, he was living in a family divided emotionally as well as religiously. Anna Matilda and Helen moved out of Donald's house in about 1851. In early 1852 William wrote to his brother John Archibald about their father: "I trust he will have no interference with the family in the future."[36] William, having himself left the family home in 1848, naturally sided with his mother and his sister, and within the decade he would invite them to live with him in Montreal. William's two sisters in the Ursuline convent, however, would never leave Catholicism, and his two brothers, John Archibald and Augustine, likely remained Catholic. Augustine seems to have been writing a book on the lives of saints towards the end of his life as he descended into utter madness. But long before this descent, Augustine was William's business partner, often brilliant and successful, and it is to this happier period that we now turn.

*Chapter Two*

## MACDONALD'S EARLY CAREER IN NORTH AMERICA: FROM BOOKKEEPER TO TOBACCO MANUFACTURER, 1848–1861

Chì duine acrach fad uaithe.
[A hungry person can see a good distance.]
*Gaelic maxim*[1]

You must exert yourself and push on, letting nothing stop you … If you must loose [*sic*] all, stop not to grieve, it is unbecoming in a man as well as useless – but stop only to plan, continue and devise means to meet your ends. Let your aim next to Heaven be your Superiority, let Onward and Upward be your motto – never be second when it is within your power to be first. In the words of a Roman general, "If you are sleeping, awake; if you are running, fly." Read Franklin's life – see how he rose from a poor printer's boy – a tallow chandler's son to be second only to the immortal Washington – how he persevered in his studies as well as his business – losing no time late or early – not only being industrious but endeavouring to appear so.

William C. McDonald

I shan't stop until that name is GOLD wherever it may go.
*William to his brother John Archibald McDonald, 6 January 1852*[2]

In the first five or so years following his departure from Prince Edward Island, William Macdonald developed habits and interests that would stay with him for the rest of his life. He left the Atlantic colonies probably in August 1848, as this is the date on his receipt for £3 for passage from Charlottetown to Quebec City on the schooner *Swift*.[3] It seems to have taken William some time to find a new home. From 1848 to 1854 he worked, it is said, in Nova Scotia, Newfoundland, Quebec City, Boston, New York, and Montreal. This period included a year in the produce business in St John's, an endeavour that failed.[4] More importantly, it

The Geo. H. Gray Building, Boston (Boston Athenaeum A B64B6 Sh.g.#1)

included the years he spent as a bookkeeper in Boston, from 1849 to 1852. These years proved to be the most formative for his future, giving him practical business experience and acquainting him with a much broader culture than he had so far encountered – a culture unknown to his father and his siblings, apart from Augustine, who had gone to Boston before him. Boston educated him as Stonyhurst could never have done.

In mid-1849 William secured employment in the counting house, or bookkeeping department, of George H. Gray, a wholesale hardware merchant in Boston harbour. Gray worked with his partners, Isaac W. Gray and I.W. Danforth, in their store on Broad Street opposite Arch Wharf. The sign on the building described Geo. H. Gray & Co. as commission merchants as well as exporters and importers, dealing in hardware, anvils, vices, and steel. Sharing the building was W. & S. Butcher's Files, Edge Tools, & Steel.

Having to account for metal objects did more than ground William's mind and keep it from turning to the fanciful or abstract thoughts typical of someone his age; it also fostered in him an intense preoccupation with the measurable and the tangible and a lifelong interest in construction and architecture. In Boston he gained knowledge of tools and machinery, which he would later apply in equipping his factory in Montreal with the most up-to-date technology in all of Canada and in providing the city with some of the best educational workshops and laboratories in the world.

Employment as a junior bookkeeper in a counting house entailed rubbing shoulders with exporters and commission agents, and it proved to be an ideal background for an aspiring merchant. Bookkeepers gained an ever-broadening and deeply detailed picture of the operations of the business. Ideally, they noted and recorded every cent earned and spent and every bit of raw material or product used or produced by the firm. Their job permitted little creativity or fudging.

These were the days before businesses were subject to government regulations, when it was rare even to encounter investors unknown to the principals. Bookkeepers did not gather figures for audited financial statements for external eyes as they would later, but did so for the owners alone. The hard numbers of bookkeeping were tangible and verifiable to the owners of George H. Gray, and they generated an unsentimental and even a harsh view of reality. When he was later an owner himself, William, having had such training, would always resent having to be accountable to or to rely on others. He disliked outside interference and remained deeply proud of his self-sufficiency and frugality.

At least initially, life in Boston must have been desperately difficult for William. He wrote to his father threatening to run off to the gold rush in California if Donald would not send him £20.[5] His derisory salary did not pay "half his board," forcing him to seek ways of supplementing his income. Before long, however, he was earning more than a living wage and making enough outside Gray's to save and even invest. He probably did supplemental work as an agent in 1850–51, purchasing farm equipment in Boston for someone in Prince Edward Island, perhaps his brother John Archibald or another relative. Very late in his life, he remarked, "I started working at $1.00 a day and from that day to the present I have always banked or invested half of what I earned."[6]

While working in Boston, William maintained his ties with family, nearly all of whom were still on the Island. By now, Donald (his father) and John Archibald recognized that they had to make money through other means than rents alone, as it seemed almost impossible to collect from their rebellious tenants. William warned John Archibald not to do business with Donald, however, as their father had "no credit at home or any place" and was "regarded everywhere contemptuously."[7] The torching of Donald's property on 21 July 1850 (described in note 26 in chapter 1), probably by irate tenants, and the attempt on his life on 8 August of the same year were ample evidence of his unpopularity.[8] On hearing that Donald had recovered from his gunshot wounds, William assured John Archibald, "He'll live forty years longer if he keeps a revolver in his pocket."[9] William was not exaggerating the dangers to his father if the contemporary account of the English traveller Isabella Lucy Bird, who toured the Island in 1854, is to be believed:

Conspiracies were formed against him [Donald], his cows and carts were destroyed, and night after night the country was lighted by the flames of his barns and mills. At length he gave loaded muskets to some of his farm-boys, telling them to shoot any one they saw upon his premises after dusk. The same evening he went into his orchard, and was standing with his watch in his hand waiting to set it by the evening gun, when the boys fired, and he fell severely wounded. When he recovered from this, he was riding out one evening, when he was shot through the hat and hip by men on each side of the road, and fell weltering in his blood. So detested was he, that several persons passed by without rendering him any assistance. At length one of his own tenantry, coming by, took him into Charlotte Town in his own cart, but was obliged shortly afterwards to leave the island, to escape from the vengeance which would have overtaken the succourer of a tyrant. Tracadie [Donald] was shot at four or six different times.[10]

William proposed that he himself enter into business with John Archibald. John Archibald was planning to open a general store in Charlottetown, and the brothers agreed that John Archibald should work as William's salaried agent rather than as his full partner, selling West Indian goods and "Yankee notions" on William's behalf. This salary arrangement was to be secret, and the store was to be operated in the name of John Archibald alone because of "prejudice" against William in town after his troubled apprenticeship there with Daniel Brennan. Although only twenty years of age, William warned John Archibald that he would not be content to limit himself to selling £1,000 worth of goods. He advised his older brother on bookkeeping and on how to deal with customs, and he also recommended that his older brother be courteous to customers and avoid politics.[11]

William arranged for a shipment to Charlottetown of liquors (rum, gin, brandy, and wine), molasses, raisins, whiting, currants, scales, and stoves at the end of 1851. Although the ship, the *Responsible*, was wrecked, its cargo was salvaged, arriving in Charlottetown three months late. Ignoring William's entreaties, John Archibald did not bother to collect what had been salvaged, with the result that William lost all his investment in the cargo. William, infuriated, described John Archibald's conduct as "almost unpardonable, to say the least of it, [and] unwarrantable."[12] The incident hardened William, much as his dispute with his cousin Brennan in Charlottetown had about four years before.

Complicating the matter was Augustine's possible involvement in the affair, reported on, but later retracted, in the Boston press. According to the report, a Charlottetown firm of wholesalers, Elliott & Greig, had won a court award against Augustine for a debt that he had owed the firm for some years, and it was now seeking to recover its judgment debt from the salvage of the *Responsible*. If there was any truth to the report, Augustine must have held some legal interest in the cargo – that is, he too must have invested in the venture. John Archibald assumed that Augustine did owe the debt, but William believed that Augustine's dispute with Elliot & Greig amounted to no more than a "knee scrape." This scrape may have been what prompted Augustine to leave the Island for Boston sometime in the late 1840s, probably 1847. There is speculation that Augustine's entanglement in the affair lay behind John Archibald's refusal to retrieve the salvage. William accused Elliot & Greig of deliberately trying to ruin his business because they feared competition from John Archibald and himself.[13]

Augustine had registered as a student at Harvard Law School in 1848, and in William's judgment, he would have made an excellent mercantile or patent lawyer. However, he left the school the following year, apparently for health reasons, though whether mental or physical it is unclear. Harvard Law School was at low ebb at the time, having reduced its teaching staff to one professor and two part-time lecturers.[14] Some time in the period 1848–51 Augustine worked for about a year as an articled clerk at the law firm of Rufus Choate (1799–1859).

Choate was among the foremost Massachusetts, if not American, advocates of his day, along with his mentor Daniel Webster. He had become a specialist in patent law, and in 1850 Harvard Law School tried to induce him to join its teaching staff, but he declined. He likewise declined a seat on the supreme courts of both Massachusetts and the United States in order to keep working in his lucrative private practice.[15] Choate stood for the views of nearly all the rich merchants of Boston, whom William undoubtedly was studying closely, both while living there and after he had left the city. With their wealth in combination with their austerity and their public spirit, these merchants resembled what William himself was to become. Their lives offered William a compelling vision of a civic, educated society, as well as of the obligations of businessmen in both its creation and its maintenance.

William was at the very impressionable age of twenty in 1851, and Boston, the first place he spent considerable time after leaving the Island, had a lasting influence on him. What in the long term William learned from Boston, we can just glimpse in his correspondence, which essentially survives only from the 1880s onwards, when he was taking the Massachusetts Institute of Technology (MIT) as his model for expanding McGill University. His ideas for his educational projects in this later period were also inspired by places other than Boston – elsewhere in the United States and in England, Scotland, and Germany – but it was only in Boston that he had lived and worked. His observations and impressions of the city as early as 1850–51 therefore deserve our attention. His admitted adulation of George Washington and Bostonian Benjamin Franklin – both rebels in the eyes of his grandfather Captain John and his great-grandfather Robinson – suggests how far he had already escaped the Island intellectually.

## BOSTON AS THE ATHENS OF AMERICA[16]

In 1851 Boston, with a population of over 100,000, was enjoying a golden age of economic influence and prosperity. It was still the city of merchants, traders, and exporters, dependent on sailing vessels, that it had been in the eighteenth century, but it was now also a city of textile manufacturers, who operated huge mills just outside town. With its thriving businesses, the Boston area was a magnet for the ambitious and the simply unemployed from Nova Scotia, New Brunswick, Newfoundland, and Prince Edward Island. Far more than Halifax, the largest town in the British Atlantic colonies, Boston was both a cultural and an economic capital.

The personally frugal and yet culturally innovative plutocracy of Boston was well established by the 1850s.[17] Its members were more modest in dress and deportment than they were in their self-regard. Called "Brahmins" by their contemporary chronicler Dr Oliver Wendell Holmes, after the priestly caste of Hindus that set moral standards, they stood for humanitarianism and for what they saw as the march of the mind. They were noted as well for their Yankee shrewdness and New England exclusivity.[18] Under Mayor Josiah Quincy, their foetid colonial town had become a modern, sanitary city. Their ideal of Boston was republican but not revolutionary, hostile to excess and luxury but standing for integrity, statesmanship, and devotion to the public good.

Although often perceived by others as haughty aristocrats, the Boston Brahmins of the 1850s were hardly more than a generation away from the builders of the factories that were the main source of their prosperity. Members of the Cabot family and others had set up the first cotton manufactory in Beverly, Massachusetts, in 1787, and at roughly the same time Moses Brown of Rhode Island induced an Englishman to reveal the secrets of the Arkwright machinery used in the English cotton industry.[19] The introduction of power (as opposed to hand) looms, the use of incorporation to attract outside capital, and improved managerial planning had all led to great fortunes for such Massachusetts families as the Lowells and the Appletons by the 1830s. Following them, still-newer families such as the Lawrences used their stores as local outlets for their own manufactured goods, becoming merchants as well as manufacturers. Employing the newest technology and hundreds of hands, these entrepreneurs were as important to the industrialization of America early in William's life as Pittsburgh, under his friend Andrew Carnegie, would be in his later life.

The Boston Brahmins were conservative with their money. They were oriented to the future, investing in railways and financial institutions, just as William himself would soon be doing. They were also Whigs, or thinking conservatives, and leaders in setting new standards for public education and social responsibility, building on the reverence for education preached by their predecessors as leaders of the community, the Puritans, who had founded Harvard University. The Brahmins studied the classics of ancient Greece and Rome and admired the Athenian spirit of inquiry and love of invention. Just as Edinburgh, with its flourishing academies, economists, and moralists, had seen itself as a new Athens for the eighteenth century, Boston, with its fresh cultural ideas, technological innovations, and increasing prosperity, fancied itself as a still-newer Athens for the nineteenth.

The Brahmins hoped that their own "city on a hill," through its superior cultural institutions and virtue, would provide a model for America. They were far more practical than the ancients they admired – less speculative philosophers and poets than seekers of knowledge to improve their health, their homes, their farms, and their businesses. Many were indeed what no ancients could have been: scientists. Their preferred subjects were botany, mineralogy, geology, and chemistry, all branches of "applied" as opposed to "pure" science. Even their philosophers, such as Ralph Waldo Emerson and David Thoreau, were preoccupied with living according to nature and with fulfilling themselves, rather than with pure abstractions.

The most striking difference between William's Prince Edward Island and Boston was probably religious. The Irish were migrating to Boston in great numbers after the potato famine in 1847, and so this city, once occupied almost exclusively by Puritans, was becoming increasingly Catholic. Massachusetts had been very anti-Catholic since the landing of the Pilgrims in 1620, as seen most strikingly in the burning down by a Protestant mob of the Ursuline convent in Boston as late as 1834. The Boston that William knew at mid-century remained overwhelmingly Protestant, but it was well past the anti-Catholicism and mob bigotry displayed in the riot of 1834. Even before the 1830s, a highly rationalistic, tolerant, and indeed liberal Unitarianism had largely displaced, among the rich and the educated, the Calvinistic Puritanism associated with the Congregational Church, from which the Unitarians had formally split in 1825. William's sojourn in Boston fell exactly in the middle of what is generally considered the golden age of Unitarianism, 1835–65. And although he may not have known it, Unitarianism had already spread to substantial merchants in Montreal, some of whom he would soon befriend and work with closely.

Although derived from ancient Christian controversies about the nature of God, Unitarianism was peculiarly suited to the expansiveness of the New World. It rejected the deterministic view of salvation of the Calvinist Puritans, which saw the fate of souls as determined by birth. It rejected also what it saw as the unduly complex concept of the Trinity, or the three persons of God of both Catholics and Protestants. The Unitarians saw divine and moral perfection everywhere, and they were firmly oriented towards the salvation of all humanity in this world rather than in the next. They injected a radical openness into the life of Boston generally, proclaiming both complete religious tolerance and the goodness of all mankind, with reason and conscience as the only grounds of religious truth. Under Unitarian influence, Boston developed tolerance even for Catholics, who reciprocated with an openness far removed from their defensive posture on Prince Edward Island.

In particular, the Catholic bishop John Bernard Fitzpatrick (1812–1866) was quietly an ally of such Whigs as Choate and the textile magnates Amos and Abbott Lawrence and Nathan Appleton. He joined businessmen, chemists, geologists, astronomers, and lawyers in weekly meetings to discuss the physical sciences, manufacturing, commerce, and social reform, thus demonstrating his belief that there was a wider society from which Catholics could not afford to be excluded. In contrast to many of his fellow bishops, Fitzpatrick did not believe in the creation of a Catholic parochial-school system. He insisted that Catholic children should be educated with Protestants in the emerging common-school system of the city. Fitzpatrick's stand was bold for its time and in stark contrast to the deepening divisions between Catholics and Protestants over the issue elsewhere, including in William's own nominally non-sectarian Central Academy in Charlottetown.[20]

Whatever William learned in Boston must have distanced him from his roots. When he returned to Charlottetown for his first visit, about eight years after he had left, he was astonished that it now seemed "more like an Indian village than the important Town I supposed it to be when I left it as a lad."[21] To the end of his life, William continued to feel that Canada had much to learn from America. Yet, while he acknowledged the superior wealth and quality of American educational institutions, he was never intimidated by them. They threw out a challenge to Canadians that he took personally.

One such institution was Girard College in Philadelphia, which in 1848, a year before William's arrival in Boston, opened to educate male orphans. It had an endowment of over $6 million, the bulk of an estate left in 1831 by Stephen Girard (1750–1831), a one-time French sailor who became a Philadelphia banker, merchant, West Indies trader, financier, and philanthropist. His wife died in a lunatic asylum, and he quarrelled with his brother John, although he assumed the care of John's daughters after they had been orphaned. A lapsed Catholic, Girard had supported causes of various denominations and had led a life of extreme frugality and simplicity. His great passion had been work, and he was remembered for declaring, "If I knew I should die tomorrow, I should plant a tree today." There were many uncanny parallels between Girard's life and what was unfolding as William's. William is said to have recognized this. If not truly a model, Girard was certainly William's inspiration for what was to come. Towards the very end of William's life, he lent the principal of McGill University, Sir William Peterson, a copy of a handbook to Girard College in which there were the words, carefully marked, of Bishop Lightfoot of the Church of England that summed up what may have been William's new view of catholicity even in Boston: "The holy season extends all the year round, the temple confined only by the limits of the habitable world, a priesthood co-extensive with the human race." Peterson concluded "Those words he must have taken as a confession of his faith."[22]

Rufus Choate also had much to teach William about public education, though less positively, as his views, like those of the Brahmins generally, were already becoming old-fashioned. Although eventually a congressman and then a senator, Choate found politics generally dispiriting. He was, however, engrossed in how to shape public education for citizenship. While in Washington, he joined the National Institution for the Promotion of Science (founded in 1840), which in its almost universal scope of interest resembled an eighteenth-century philosophical society. It only superficially resembled the Boston Athenaeum, founded as a private library in 1807, where as a young man Choate had educated himself in the classics of Greece and Rome. The Boston Athenaeum was the hushed preserve of doctors and lawyers and scholars, modelled on the Liverpool Lyceum, founded in 1797, which was concerned chiefly with art and literature.[23]

Much more ambitious than the Boston Athenaeum, the National Institution for the Promotion of Science was attempting to attract the interest of all of America in all branches of science – astronomy, geography, natural philosophy, natural history, geology, mineralogy, chemistry, agriculture, American history, and antiquities, as well as literature and the fine arts. It collected specimens of geology and mineralogy and other objects of natural history, and its first head was no less than the sitting U.S. secretary of war, which suggested that its activities were becoming integrated into a strategy for national development. With its emphasis on present-day, rather than past, inventions, the institution was at the forefront in promoting science as the way to meet the practical needs of a new, robust country.[24]

The United States at this time was grappling with two competing cultural visions, the Whig and the Jacksonian, to define the soul and the mission of the republic. This conflict had come to a head in 1844–45 but it was to take almost a decade more to resolve. The issue centred on what to do with an unsolicited legacy to the country of over $500,000 from John Smithson "for the increase and diffusion of knowledge among men." Choate, the self-educated classicist who was regarded by the ascendant Jacksonian Democrats as almost insufferably elitist, sat on a Senate committee to decide on how to use the money. He proposed "a grand and noble public library," like the Boston Athenaeum, with lectures by eminent scientific and literary figures. Senator Benjamin Tappan wanted a big institution consisting of a natural-history museum, a technical school, and a station for agricultural experiments, as well as a library concerned with "the ordinary business of life." Outside Congress, some were pressing for schools for the blind, or for women, or for practical science, the last resembling the French École Polytechnique.

There seemed to be an emerging consensus that the bequest should be used for the advancement of science, but there was no consensus on what constituted science. By 1854, Senator Tappan had won and Choate had lost. The new Smithsonian Institution incorporated the National Institution for the Promotion of Science, and it became the powerhouse of a national effort to make knowledge both useful and popular. This national commitment to a broadening of access to scientific and technical knowledge was simultaneously beginning in England. But it would take almost four more decades for Macdonald to help to finance the beginnings of a comparable commitment in Canada.

### SELF-IMPROVEMENT AND PHILANTHROPY IN NEW ENGLAND

Rufus Choate described the American spirit as "free, busy, and aspiring," a sort of civic humanism.[25] By mid-century the movement for popular education as part of civil humanism was assuming a national dimension, and it was continuing to flourish locally and not least in New England. The Mercantile Library Association, founded in 1846, for example, maintained libraries not only in Boston but also in Cincinnati, New York, St Louis, and elsewhere. These were social and educational centres as well as lending libraries, and they offered lectures, conversaziones, and even courses. They catered not so much to manual workers as to clerks, shopkeepers, ministers, doctors, and small manufacturers. As such, they were not for the masses, but neither were they for the privileged. They diffused inspiring, practical, and timely insight and information to the ambitious.

William joined the Mercantile Library Association of Boston in 1850–51, thus beginning his own career of over sixty-five years of intellectual self-improvement. It was from here that he probably borrowed the many books he mentioned to John Archibald.[26] He may have heard lecturers such as Choate, Emerson, and Longfellow. American thinkers such as these were among the many lecturers at the Mercantile Library up to 1877, when it became a branch of the Boston Public Library, itself founded in 1848 as the first large municipal free library in America, in sharp contrast to the exclusive Boston Athenaeum.

The American Mercantile Libraries were thoroughly nineteenth century in inspiration, just as the Athenaeum had been thoroughly eighteenth century.

Mercantile Library Association Building, Boston
(Boston Athenaeum, A B64B6 L.m.1856)

They resembled the Mechanics' Institutes that were spreading almost exclusively within the British Empire. George Birkbeck (1776–1841), professor of natural philosophy at the Anderson's Institute in Glasgow, had established the first Mechanics' Institute in 1820, in Edinburgh, with classes, a library, and apparatus for scientific experiments. Imitators broadened their membership to include clerical as well as manual workers. In 1828 Montreal, with the aid of such businessmen as John Molson and the politician Louis-Joseph Papineau, established its own Mechanics' Institution (renamed the Mechanics' Institute in 1840) as the first free lending library in British North America. By 1841 there were 300 Mechanics' Institutes in Great Britain alone.

A general and widespread public thirst for literature, the arts, and the sciences prompted other initiatives. In the 1820s Josiah Holbrook organized community groups in Massachusetts called "lyceums," for "mutual education," and by 1839 the American Institute of Instruction and the American Lyceum Association could boast a thousand local societies in New England. In addition to its own lyceum, Boston had its Useful Knowledge Society, Natural History Society, Mechanics' Apprentice Association, and Lowell Institute.[27] The Lowell Institute provided free lectures for citizens on moral, intellectual, and physical instruction,

Nᵒ 7339          Boston, *July 24* 1850

*Received of Mr. Wm C McDonald*

*Two Dollars, being his first annual assessment, as member*

*of the* **Mercantile Library Association.**

*C B Patten*

*For the Treasurer.*

Macdonald's membership card for the Mercantile Library Association, 1850 (MSF)

attracting eight to ten thousand to a lecture by, say, Jacob Bigelow, a Harvard botanist, on technology, a word that he popularized. "Technology," was rapidly entering the popular vocabulary as referring to "practical" as opposed to "pure" science. The Massachusetts Institute of Technology would soon emerge as a rival to both the Lowell Institute and Harvard. All these were privately funded institutions requiring the imagination and support of individuals.

One such individual, born not far from Boston, and known to nearly everyone in the 1850s, was George Peabody (1795–1869), often described as the father of philanthropy. Peabody was a lifelong bachelor with no inherited advantages, and he refused to support religious or political causes, instead emphasizing education for all. Peabody personally underwrote the American participation in the Great Exhibition in London of 1851. He then began to give to his native America, with $1.717 million going to three Peabody institutes, essentially libraries and foundations for adult education, in 1852–57, with other public libraries to follow.

These various popularizing institutions saw education as rooted not so much in literary tradition as in the practical. They catered not to hereditary elites but to hardworking individuals. They taught not religious dogma but self-knowledge through experiment. William, through the Mercantile Library Association, seems to have absorbed their message thoroughly. The motto attached to the Glenaladale arms had been "My hope is constant in Thee," whereas William's, as is clear from his letter to John Archibald in 1852, was already "Onward and Upward."

A self-made scholar and lawyer, Choate was not blind to the future as belonging to self-made individuals. At the dedication of the Peabody Institute in Peabody's hometown of Danvers in 1854, aging but with an eye to the future, he continued to attack popular education that was purely utilitarian, but he did not despair. He admitted that labour was the lot of everyone, but he saw this fact as no reason "why we should not aspire to the love and attainment of learning, and to the bettering of the mind." "Have you not a conscious nature," he demanded, "other than that which tills the earth, drives the plane, squares the stone, creates the fabric of art?" This was, he concluded, a "nature intellectual, spiritual, moral, capacious of science, capacious of truth beyond the sphere of sense, with large discourse of reason."[28] Here he was reasserting the humanism of Boston against mere technical training. He was reasserting even a highly technical education as the basis of good citizenship, another lesson that William seems to have absorbed thoroughly.

Most of Boston's major institutions expanded in the period leading up to the American Civil War and continued to grow after it. An important development for the future Sir William Macdonald would take place in the Mercantile Building in Boston proper, the home of the Mercantile Library Association. It was here that the Massachusetts Institute of Technology, with the Boston Natural History Society, would be established in 1861.[29] For the moment, it is enough to say that Boston was William's first exposure to a world of ideas, of public and private funding for educational institutions, and of deep commitment to progress. In the over half-century that remained to him, he would never lose interest in Boston, and by the 1880s he would find it more inspiring than ever.

## MACDONALD IN NEW YORK, 1852

By the end of 1851, William was looking for employment in New York. Geo. H. Gray & Co. recommended him to Long & Davenport of Platt Street in New York for his "industry, integrity, and [as] capable of filling any situation for which he might represent himself qualified,"[30] but it is not clear whether Long & Davenport hired him, whether he worked for them on commission, or whether he worked for them at all. He was in New York in February 1852,[31] and later in the year he replied to an advertisement in the *Journal of Commerce* for an assistant bookkeeper, mentioning only that he had worked for two and a half years in Boston.[32]

Although William spent only approximately a year in New York at this time, it is likely that he nevertheless maintained strong links with the city. In fact, he and Augustine spent considerable time there during the Civil War. New York was already the commercial capital and the principal port of the United States, and even to the increasingly restive Southern states, it was more important than any Southern city. The South, though, was also integral to the prosperity of New York. When William was in New York in 1851–52, a railway boom was taking place under the shadow of growing fears of civil war. There was little admiration for or even tolerance of slavery in New York, but if abolition meant civil war, most New Yorkers probably preferred the status quo.

## TRADE ROUTES AND THE RAILWAY BOOM, 1851–1853

In 1850 Augustine left Boston for Montreal, and in 1852 or 1853 Macdonald followed him there from New York. Precisely why they went to Montreal is not clear, but it may have been simply that Augustine had found a business opportunity. They no doubt could have stayed in America – and indeed Augustine would return to spend most of his life there – but the Loyalist traditions of Captain John and of their mother's family may have inclined them to prefer life under the British flag. Augustine, despite decades of residence in the United States, never gave up his status as a British subject, and Macdonald in later life was determined to make Montreal a worthy rival of Boston, at least academically.

In any case, in the 1850s it was not unusual for even native New Englanders to move to Montreal to work. New Englanders had been setting up businesses in the city even before the American Revolution, bringing with them American experience and an American spirit of enterprise. They saw in Montreal and the St Lawrence River an economy that rivalled that of the eastern seaboard of the United States. In *The Empire of the St. Lawrence*, Donald Creighton describes the rise and the fall of this economy, which was based on the export of such staples as fur and wheat from the vast area northwest of Montreal and largely bypassed Boston and New York. The American immigrants to Montreal joined in the creation of this empire, but many retained a distinctive American identity. Although they readily acquired both French- and English-speaking local business and marriage partners, they favoured two churches, the American Presbyterian and the Unitarian, and they maintained lively familial and intellectual links with the United States.

As Creighton describes it, the commercial empire of the St Lawrence had collapsed by 1849 as a result of England's adoption of free trade. Through the repeal of the Corn Laws in 1846, Great Britain had abolished colonial preferences, and traders were immediately forced to seek new markets. The United States responded by passing the Drawback Act, which cancelled the duties on imports from foreign countries that were re-exported to Canada. This aided the traders, especially those in Toronto, who chafed against the high freight rates on the St Lawrence. Imports of refined sugar through Montreal, for example, fell by about 50 per cent in that year. In 1849 the repeal of the Navigation Acts "completed the destruction of the old mercantile system of the empire" and "the commercial empire of the St. Lawrence was bankrupt."[33]

While Canada continued to trade with England and while Montreal was certainly not excluded from the east-west trade of British North America, Montrealers now looked to the south for their prosperity as they had not done before.
So great was the anger of several Montreal merchants that they came to promote
union with the United States, forming the short-lived Annexation Movement of
1849. Despite the failure of this movement, the Montreal that Augustine moved
to in 1850, and William two or three years later, was already busily reorienting
itself to new commercial and transport links with the United States. In developing water power and in adding railways to the canal system that linked it to the
Great Lakes, the city was transforming itself into a centre of industry as well as
of commerce and was on the verge of unprecedented expansion. William and
Augustine could hardly have failed to notice the opportunities for growth Montreal now offered.

At that time, however, nobody could predict precisely how the new transport
links with the United States might evolve, and thus even business partners in
Montreal were investing in rival ventures. In about 1851, two years before his
arrival in Montreal and presumably on the advice of Augustine, who was already
there, William himself invested in the earliest railway to extend from Montreal
into the United States, the Champlain and St Lawrence, the initial stage of
which had been completed in 1832.[34] By 1851 the Champlain and St Lawrence
was running from St Lambert, just south of Montreal, to Rouses' Point in Vermont. As this line was an adjunct of a railway network in northern New England
that pushed up from Boston, Boston was said to be entertaining hopes of making
Montreal a virtual fiefdom.[35] One American contractor in that year held more
than one-quarter of the shares of this railway.

Prominent among the directors of the Champlain and St Lawrence in
1851 were the iron wholesaler William Workman (1807–1878), the hardware
wholesaler Benjamin Brewster, and Sir George Simpson (1786–1860), governor
of the Hudson's Bay Company. Workman was of Irish origin but had been
born in Montreal; Brewster was an American operating in the Ottawa Valley;
and Simpson was a Scotsman who headed one of the richest British trading
companies. Workman and Brewster were also prominent in the Montreal City
Bank, much favoured by American investors, in which Macdonald was also
invested.

It is unlikely that Macdonald bought shares in the Champlain and St Lawrence
before 1850, but by 1851 he was doubling his holdings in the railway, just as
Workman, Simpson, the brewer John Molson (1787–1860), and several others
were.[36] (We do not know the size of his initial holding or where he obtained his
capital.) The railway was the only outlet from Montreal to the Atlantic, more
specifically to the American markets of the eastern seaboard, and was Montreal's

only winter outlet to England. Its revenues grew by 25 per cent in 1851 and by a further 30 per cent in 1852.

In 1853 the rival St Lawrence and Atlantic Railway (begun in 1844) briefly entered into active competition with the Champlain and St Lawrence. This line extended from Longueuil, on the south shore of the St Lawrence opposite Montreal, to Portland, Maine, and it also extended from Montreal to Plattsburgh, New York. Its attraction to Montreal investors was that Portland, unlike Boston, was unlikely ever to rival Montreal, even though it was closer to Britain than was either Boston or New York. When work began on the St Lawrence and Atlantic in 1844, its leading promoters in Montreal included two Americans, John Frothingham, business partner of William Workman, who was still backing the Champlain and St Lawrence, from Maine and Harrison Stephens (1801–1881) from Vermont.

The St Lawrence and Atlantic grew slowly, mainly in 1846 and 1851. Many of its early promoters disappeared, but new investors transferred their allegiance to it from the Champlain and St Lawrence, despite the profitability of the latter. By the time of its recapitalization in 1851, notable among its new investors were the grocer and speculator in steamboats John Torrance (1786–1870); Peter McGill, president of the Bank of Montreal in 1834–60; McGill's father-in-law, Joseph Shuter; and the hardware and drygoods merchant and politician George Moffatt (1787–1865). William Workman counted himself among them shortly afterwards. These men had been maintaining close ties with Americans, apparently afraid of a serious eclipse of Montreal's business influence if a rail link to Boston or New York were left unchallenged.

Such men as the drug manufacturer William Lyman (1794–1857), of Massachusetts descent; Charles Grant, seigneur and fifth baron of Longueuil and future landlord of Macdonald's; and A.T. Galt (1817–1893), a son-in-law of John Torrance, were also among the influential backers of the St Lawrence and Atlantic in 1851–53. They said expressly that the American drawback legislation of 1846, which permitted exports from Canada to pass through the United States in bond, might accentuate the advantages held by Boston and New York and endanger Montreal. With the St Lawrence and Atlantic complementing canals on the St Lawrence, they argued, Montreal would be able to attract a quarter of the American wheat shipped from the Great Lakes to the Atlantic.[37]

Finally, the very success of the Champlain and St Lawrence in 1851–53 seems to have increased trade between Montreal and the United States. Even so, the St Lawrence and Atlantic proved to be a failure compared with the Champlain and St Lawrence, chiefly because Portland never became a major centre for export and import, much less for banking, insurance, and shipping, which Boston and New York clearly were. The railway merged in 1853 with the newly incorporated

Grand Trunk Railway, which had a better chance of securing the traditional Montreal markets in the West. The Grand Trunk had been set up to provide a railway between Montreal and Kingston, its three chief shareholders being Galt, Luther Holton, and D.L. MacPherson, with the financing guaranteed by the government of the Province of Canada in 1851. By the time of Macdonald's arrival in Montreal, the government's relationships with businessmen, particularly investors, were becoming increasingly complicated.[38]

In 1852 a third competitor, the Montreal and New York Railway, began to challenge the Champlain and St Lawrence. This railway had started out in 1848 as an extension from Caughnawaga (now Kahnawake, on the south shore of the St Lawrence) of the Montreal and Lachine Railway, begun in 1846 to connect Montreal with the Ottawa Valley and points to the west. The promoters of the Montreal and New York included John Torrance and others associated with the Montreal and Lachine Railway. The Montreal and New York was intended to join the Northern or Ogdensburg Railroad in New York State and ultimately provide a link with New York City. Its terminus was to be Plattsburgh, on Lake Champlain, and the Champlain and St Lawrence correctly saw it as a direct threat. A price war broke out between the two railways in 1853, and the Champlain and St Lawrence was victorious. In 1855 it absorbed the Montreal and New York under the name of the Champlain and New York Railway. By 1872 all three of the railways that had been competing so vigorously in 1853 had been merged into the Grand Trunk.

Macdonald is said to have been a shareholder in the Champlain and New York and a director of both the St Lawrence and Atlantic and the Montreal and New York Railways, all apparently between 1852 and 1853.[39] This is extraordinary for at least two reasons. First, it means that he had the capital, even if not a large amount, to invest in the railways within three years of leaving Prince Edward Island. More importantly, he may have been unique in investing in the three simultaneously. As we have seen, Torrance, McGill, Shuter, Moffatt, and Workman switched their allegiance from the Champlain to the St Lawrence before or shortly after 1851, and Torrance probably did not join the Montreal and New York until he had left the Champlain. But Macdonald was betting on all three, which suggests that from the start of his career in Montreal he was obsessed with the transport links of the city with the United States, however they might develop. He was probably indifferent to which of his three investments paid off, as at least one of the railways was bound to prevail.

Such a link was to prove crucial to his future success, not least because his fellow directors and shareholders included some of the most powerful businessmen in the city. Men such as Molson, Workman, and Frothingham were much like the Lowells, the Cabots, and others he had admired in Boston. Indeed, some, such as Frothingham, were actually from New England. He felt a natural intellectual affinity with them, but perhaps more importantly, the railway links that in the end prevailed would ensure him supplies from the United States.

We have already cited Macdonald's recollection, in later life, that probably from his time in Boston his habit was to invest half of whatever money he made. Unfortunately, no portfolio of his has survived, and it is impossible to trace exactly how he succeeded as an investor. In view of the fluctuations in tobacco prices, it is possible that he made even more money from his investments than from his tobacco, with which he was primarily associated. Late in life, he would give shares instead of cash to the institutions that he favoured, especially McGill University. Most of these shares were in railways, including local ones such as the tramways in Ottawa and Montreal. It seems likely that a large part of his fortune grew out of the vast expansion of rail transport in Canada throughout his lifetime, beginning with the investments just described.

## MACDONALD AS A COMMISSION AGENT AND IN PARTNERSHIP WITH AUGUSTINE, 1852–1859

In 1871, in rather vague testimony before a mixed British-American commission on claims arising out of the American Civil War, including his own, Augustine recalled that in "about the year 1850, he engaged in the business of manufacturing tobacco" in Montreal "in partnership with others until the year 1862," except for 1853 "or thereabouts" and "also a short period in 1857."[40] While all of this is possible, his partner in 1851–52 could not have been William, who was then in the United States. According to their own mother's testimony before the same commission, Augustine went to the United States in 1848, stayed there "until 1851 or 1852," and then went into business in Montreal. She visited him in Montreal "in 1855 and 1863" and found him residing there, after which he was in the United States.[41]

It seems reasonable to accept that Augustine had a more accurate memory of his movements than his mother did and that he had indeed left Boston for Montreal in 1850, to be followed by William in 1852 or 1853. If William's understanding of Augustine's wholesale business in Charlottetown was accurate, it is likely that Augustine had already spent considerable time in Montreal, buying goods for resale and possibly dabbling in tobacco manufacture, before going to Harvard in 1848. At any rate, in the early 1850s Augustine's experience in tobacco manufacture could not have been extensive, principally because he had no money for a tobacco factory of his own and, in any case, mechanization in tobacco manufacture would not be introduced in any significant way for another twenty years or so.[42] It was possible, however, to manufacture tobacco on a small scale. In cigar-making, for example, machinery was not as important as labour. All that was needed was a small hand knife for cutting the wrapper, a board for rolling the cigar, and a tuck-cutter for measuring and finishing the cigar. Plug-making, as we shall see, was only slightly more complicated.

In April 1853 Macdonald (as we shall now call the adult William) and Augustine decided to go into business together, and they registered their partnership as "McDonald, Brother & Co." in Montreal on 18 May. Augustine seems to have been the senior partner, and their stated business was as "importers of Oil," although by 1855 they were also dealing in paint and glass.[43] On 21 January 1854, the brothers registered new articles of partnership, by which Macdonald was to furnish all the necessary capital. The partners were now also in the business of selling various goods as commission agents. Augustine was to receive £200 per annum in quarterly instalments and 5 per cent of all net profits, the remainder of which was to go to Macdonald.[44]

A commission agency was the standard way for young men to start in business, as it required little capital but much energy. As commission agents, the brothers could have sold anything. As noted, they advertised themselves as specialist oil merchants. What kinds of oil they sold we do not know. In that era, they could have sold any of a vast variety of animal or vegetable oils or petroleum products: menhaden, cod, and whale oils (marine animals); neat's foot, horse, lard (pig), tallow, and elaine oils (terrestrial animals); linseed, Chinese wood, poppyseed, and sunflower oils (drying vegetable oils); corn, cottonseed, sesame-seed, and castor oils (semi-drying vegetable oils); almond, peanut, olive, rosin, turpentine, palm, and coconut oils (non-drying vegetable oils); and naphthas, gasolenes (so spelt), kerosenes, and lubricants (petroleum products). They may also have sold waste fats.[45] If one sort of oil was the most likely, it was that of the sperm whale, a major product from Boston. They also sold tobacco, probably manufactured in the United States.

Augustine later suggested that his partnership with William had not been easy. He testified in 1871 that when he arrived in Montreal in 1851, he had not been worth more than £2,000 – a sum he had received from Donald. He had first engaged in the commission business, selling tobacco among other things, with a Robert Underwood and then "with my brother a year or two." As he recalled, "[W]e dissolved, I think, and he went on alone; did not do much for some time; perhaps [in 1853, apparently] I assisted him."[46]

It is not clear why the brothers began to sell tobacco, but it is probable that Augustine had developed links with tobacco suppliers in 1851–52. Boston and New York were headquarters for both cotton and tobacco factors, who sold crops from the South to manufacturers in the northern states and beyond. If the brothers were buying sperm whale oil in Boston, it would have been quite natural for them to buy tobacco there as well. Moreover, the tobacco trade between Glasgow and America had flourished from the mid- to late seventeenth century, establish-

**Admit**

Into the Lobby of the Legislative Council, on Thurs-
day the 10th day of February, 1853.

DONALD M'DONALD,

*President.*

To the Doorkeeper.

Admittance ticket to the Legislative Council of
Prince Edward Island, 1853 (MSF)

ing a tradition of Scots in the tobacco business.[47] Many Scots came to the United States to manufacture tobacco, especially near Petersburg in Virginia.[48]

What sort of tobacco products did Macdonald sell in the years 1854–55? He may have sold cigars from the Connecticut Valley, but it is more likely that he sold plug tobacco for chewing that he bought on consignment from Boston, a city that had for long sent ships to the West Indies to buy tobacco leaf and molasses, among other products. By the 1850s snuff had come to be considered European and effete, but chewing tobacco was seen as quintessentially North American. In combination with hardtack, fat pork, and molasses, tobacco was one of the staples of Canadian life.

Among Macdonald's papers is an admittance ticket, dated 1853, to the lobby of the Legislative Council of Prince Edward Island, signed by his father, Donald McDonald.[49] Donald had been a member of the council since 1839, and as a leading if unpopular landowner, he had just assumed its presidency in 1853. In July 1854 he surprised his sons by calling at their office on St Peter Street in Montreal. It was on this visit that Macdonald must have received the admittance ticket from his father, as at that time he had not returned to the Island since leaving it in 1848. Donald arrived with their sister Margaret, whom he was about to enrol as a student at the Ursuline convent in Quebec City. To his delight he was able to report of William, "At the sight of me, he called out 'My God,' and jumped to us both, embracing each with perfect greed and delight."[50] Donald found that his two sons were clearing revenues of £40,000 a year and were hoping to clear savings of £20,000 after five years.[51] The reunion led to a reconciliation between Donald and William and even to the idea that Donald would move to Montreal to live with his youngest son, as he found the situation on the Island too hostile for his comfort. Donald expressed this as his intention – at "whatever rate" he might sell his land on the Island.[52] But Donald died within days of the reconciliation. After travelling to Quebec City to enrol Margaret at the convent and visit two other daughters already there, he succumbed to cholera in the epidemic then raging in the city.

He died intestate, and it is unclear how his land devolved to his family, principally to his three sons, William, Augustine, and John Archibald. Anna Matilda presumably retained the St Martin's estate on Lot 35, given to her in her prenuptial settlement, and their uncle Father John likely retained his own lands of some standing, although he had been living in England since 1845. In sworn testimony to the mixed Anglo-American committee on claims arising out of the American Civil War, in 1872, Augustine claimed that he had sold to William the approximately 4,000 acres of the Glenaladale estate that Donald had left to him. Whether Augustine ever formally passed title to William, or indeed how Augustine himself had obtained title to this land, is unclear. The proceeds from this sale he "invested in a commercial business."[53] In view of the tenants' hatred of the family, it is unlikely that the brothers' inheritance was particularly profitable.

The four years following Donald's death, from 1854 to 1858, were prosperous ones for the Province of Canada and also it seems for Macdonald. In 1856 there was a shift in the relationship of the two brothers in Montreal, for on 13 February they registered an agreement by which Augustine was to be merely Macdonald's "clerk." It recited that as of the previous 1 January Augustine "shall and will faithfully and diligently serve the said William C. Macdonald, his secrets keep, shall do no damage to his said employer or see it done by others without giving instant information thereof." Augustine was in "all things" to "demean himself as a good and faithful clerk ought and is bound to do." For this service, Macdonald was to pay him £250 for a year, exclusive of all travelling expenses.[54] This reference to expenses suggests that Augustine was to be a buyer, possibly of tobacco leaf, in the United States.

Macdonald's purchase on 5 January 1858 of a barque, or boat, presumably for importing, suggests that he was intending to remain as a commission agent indefinitely and to export from Montreal to places in the Great Lakes. At a distress sale, he paid £430 in Halifax currency for the "Barque St. George, her tackle, and apparel." However, the years of prosperity were about to end. The British economy had begun to slump early in the previous year, and this economic depression had spread to New York in September 1857 with the failure of the Ohio Life Insurance and Trust Company. English and Scottish banks then failed, and in November Great Britain suspended the operation of its Bank Act. It took some time for the depression to grip Montreal, and even then the city would be less affected than many parts of British North America, reporting only 15 failures out of 909 businesses.[55] In 1857 Canadian imports fell from their level of the previous year, and in 1858 they fell again. In March 1858 a creditor named William D.B. James, a forwarding agent and trader, sued Macdonald over a dishonoured bill of exchange. The barque must have been worth much more than £430, for to pay off his debt Macdonald accepted £1,000 for it from James.[56]

## THE ROLE OF TARIFFS IN MACDONALD'S EMERGENCE AS A TOBACCO MANUFACTURER, 1854–1862

In 1854 the ratification of the Reciprocity Treaty between Britain's North American colonies and the United States guaranteed the free exchange of raw materials such as tobacco leaf and sugar cane on the continent. In addition to benefiting existing manufacturers, the treaty encouraged new ones. John Redpath, who opened his sugar refinery in Montreal in 1854, was one new manufacturer to benefit from reciprocity, and William Macdonald was another, embarking on his career as a Montreal-based manufacturer of tobacco products in the following year, 1855. As we have seen, in 1853–54 he had sold imported tobacco from the United States, probably fully manufactured. Because he was then simply an agent, his profit on each sale would have been small compared with that of the manufacturer.

Because American manufacturers had not yet attained the commanding position to enter Canada that they would enjoy twenty years later and colonial manufacturers were few, local monopolies were very possible. For Macdonald, it must have seemed the ideal time to import American leaf directly, process it with sugar and other ingredients, and sell it within British North America.[57] He made a start, but in the mid-1850s he probably lacked sufficient capital to set up the large factory he envisioned as necessary for manufacture.

The tariff situation changed again in 1858, when the Tariff Act of the Province of Canada was passed to protect Canadian industry. The effect of protective legislation was the inverse of that of the Reciprocity Treaty still in effect. While reciprocity meant that raw materials, such as tobacco leaf, were admitted duty-free from the United States, the Tariff Act levied a duty on imported finished goods, such as manufactured tobacco. It was the combined effect of reciprocity and protective legislation that probably encouraged Macdonald to open his factory. Not only was the unprocessed leaf that was to be his chief factor of production admitted free of duty, but what he had been selling, namely tobacco manufactured in the United States, was now to be subject to import duty, which made it more expensive to his customers and uncompetitive with his own manufactured product.

Isaac Buchanan (1810–1883), a Hamilton merchant from Glasgow with operations near Montreal, had been a staunch supporter of the passage of the Tariff
Act. He had organized meetings of businessmen in Toronto and Montreal to call
for protection and had followed these up with petitions. While the introduction
of protection was not really in Buchanan's own interest as a wholesale grocer, he
had won a seat in the Legislative Assembly in 1857 and saw it as his public duty
to encourage the development of Canadian industry.[58]

As it turned out, while the 1858 tariff encouraged entrepreneurs such as Macdonald and Redpath to manufacture, it failed to increase government revenues.[59]
Consequently, A.T. Galt, the inspector general, introduced a new act in 1859,
one that imposed a tariff on revenue rather than on imports. In effect, this excise
tariff was a sales tax. Although Macdonald was obliged to pay this tariff on his
manufactured goods, or to pass it on to his distributors, the 1859 act proved to be
more beneficial to the economy generally than the 1858 act. By 1862 Galt was able
to report an increase in government revenue over expenditure. Moreover, the
value of all imports had increased by 67.1 per cent between 1858 and 1862. Reciprocity imports accounted for most of this rise, those from the United States,
including tobacco leaf, increasing by 160 per cent.

Galt's Tariff Act of 1859 also placed *ad valorem* rates instead of specific duties on
non-reciprocity goods. Although these rates did not affect Macdonald's imported
leaf, they made non-reciprocity imported goods from countries other than the
United States more competitive with American goods. They therefore favoured
the merchants of Montreal by encouraging the import of goods from Europe via
the St Lawrence and over the troubled Grand Trunk. Reciprocity goods from the
United States still tended to enter Canada West through the Great Lakes. With
these new *ad valorem* provisions, non-reciprocity imports from outside the United
States increased by 75.1 per cent in 1858–62, while American imports increased
by only 6.7 per cent.[60] Protection of local manufacture, together with the revival
of the St Lawrence as a trade route, enabled Canada and Montreal in particular
to recover quickly from the depression of 1858. The renewed general prosperity
favoured Macdonald as he set about developing a network of wholesalers for
his manufactured tobacco out of the distribution channels that he had used as a
commission agent.

## McDONALD BROS. & CO., MANUFACTURERS OF TOBACCO, 1859–1861

Augustine was to recall in 1871 that "in 1857, or just after, I began alone in the
tobacco business."[61] In any case, on 1 March 1859 Augustine entered into partnership with his brother William and Alexander Ross of Charlottetown. They formed

# TOBACCO WORKS
## 20 Water Street.

Messrs. FORESTER, MOIR & CO.,
17 St. HELEN STREET,
Are Agents for the sale in Canada, of all our Tobaccos.

We manufacture the following WELL KNOWN and FAVOURITE BRANDS:

| Brand | Size | Brand | Size |
|---|---|---|---|
| Lion, | 5's & 10's. | Henrico, | 12's. |
| Crown, | 5's & 10's. | Britannia, | 4's. |
| Union, | 10's. | Royal Arms, | 4's. |
| Diamond, | 12's. | Victoria, | 4's. |
| Anderson, | 12's. | Forget-me-not, | 4's. |
| Huberton, | 12's. | &c. &c. | |

## A large assortment of Leaf Tobacco constantly in Stock.

Shippers and other large buyers can purchase from us with unusual advantage, our Tobaccos being made to keep in any climate.

CAUTION.

As several manufacturers have imitated our "CROWN" and "DIAMOND" brands, our card an Trade Mark, as above, will be hereafter stencilled upon every Box, for protection to the Trade as buyers, and to ourselves as manufacturers.

McDonald Bros. advertisement (*Mackay's Montreal Directory 1864–65,*
between pages 288 and 289, Rare Books and Special Collections, McGill University)

McDonald Brothers & Co., Tobacco Manufacturers of Montreal,[62] and established a factory at 163 (or 20, in an earlier numbering) Water Street (later known as Commissioners Street and still later as De la Commune Street). Near the port, the building was well situated to receive hogsheads of tobacco leaf and other supplies. In area it was 135 by 35 feet, but the business expanded rapidly to the corner of Wellington and McGill Streets. The head office was at 232 St Paul Street, and there seem to have been annexes at 14 George Street and 1 Grey Nun Street.

Ross supplemented the capital of the brothers, who four years before had been earning revenues of £40,000 a year, according to their father. If they had succeeded in their plan to save by now £20,000, they would have been reasonably prosperous, even apart from their legacies from Donald's estate. They now had the capital to invest in the new business of tobacco manufacture. Their involvement with commissioned sales in Montreal had by 1859 given them almost six years to solidify their links with tobacco factors, or agents between retailers and wholesalers, in New York City and elsewhere. This experience was in addition to their possible involvement in the tobacco trade in Boston and New York in 1848–52. Without doubt, Macdonald had become a fairly experienced businessman by this time. He may not have been leading an ostentatious way of life – he preferred to board at the Ottawa Hotel in Montreal than buy a house, for example – but by 1859 he was a director of both the City Bank and the Montreal and Champlain Railroad. And now he was positioned to become a tobacco manufacturer.

### TOBACCO MANUFACTURE AND THE CONDITIONS FOR SUCCESS

Had McDonald Brothers & Co. wanted to make cigars, they would not have needed any machinery, since – as noted – cigars were essentially made by hand. However, the plan was to make plug tobacco, and so the new Macdonald plant would need the equipment necessary for the manufacturing process – a machine to pulverize the leaf into flakes or shreds after the midrib was removed; vats of "sauces" and "flavours" (sugar, licorice, and alcohol) in which the workers dipped the pulverized leaf; wringers to squeeze the surplus liquid out of the flakes; equipment to cut, press, and shape the tobacco into cakes; and cases or boxes into which these cakes were pressed and packed.[63] This was the basic process that Macdonald would employ for his entire career in the manufacture of plug tobacco. It will be described in greater detail in chapter 3. The changes that took place in his plant over the next sixty years or so were changes of scale and were driven by mechanization rather than by radical changes in his product line. To the extent that he was manufacturing chewing tobacco, his primary product was essentially a nicotine-laced candy, as it was very sweet. His secondary product, pipe tobacco, was largely made of the dregs of his chewing tobacco.

Ottawa Hotel, St James Street, 1879 (ANQ, Cote 1Q 1888)

Manufacturing was just one aspect of the business. Successful marketing was another. Because of the simplicity of its ingredients and its growing popularity owing to its addictive properties, processed tobacco lent itself to large profits. Macdonald was doubtless aware that the consumption of tobacco had been growing. In the United Kingdom, consumption per head was 11.71 ounces in 1821; 16.87 in 1851; 22.60 in 1881; and 31.20 in 1905; in Canada, 32.24 ounces per head in 1905 and 46.37 in fiscal year 1907/8.[64] Nevertheless, success was not guaranteed. Macdonald was dealing with a business where there were few barriers to entry and therefore a potential glut of product on the market. His main task was to differentiate his product from that of his competitors and to buy up or otherwise neutralize his competition when at all possible. To maintain his differentiation, he also had to ensure a fair degree of uniformity in the flavours identified with his brand. This meant purchasing the same quality of leaf, as much as possible, year after year. It also meant advertising his product and paying special attention to his reputation.

Above all, however, Macdonald needed to be technologically up to date. As the mechanization of manufacture advanced, the advantages of economies of scale became more apparent, especially in the manufacture of plug tobacco compared to that of cigars. In the period 1860–70 the average capital investment in an American cigar factory was $3,000. In contrast, the average tobacco factory required $15,000 in 1860 and $25,000 in 1870. In 1880 the figure was $40,000, and in 1890, $75,000. These increasing capital requirements led to a concentration of the tobacco factories in the United States (and to a lesser extent in Canada), from 626 establishments in 1860 to 433 in 1905. And while in 1860 the average number of employees per establishment was thirty, with an average annual output of $35,000, by 1905 the corresponding figures were fifty-five and $270,000, proving the worth of ongoing mechanization.[65]

New firms in direct competition with Macdonald continued to enter the market, more and more of them as time went by. Thus, Macdonald's task from 1859 involved more than creating a mass taste for his products; he also had to fight off his competitors. He was able to do this by buying them up or otherwise neutralizing them, but he also had to protect his sources of supply and his distribution network. Early on he had cultivated not only links with tobacco growers and their agents, including factors in the northern states, but also links with wholesale grocers in various parts of the gradually uniting British North America. These grocers were the backbone or perhaps the spinal cord of his distribution, as he never sold directly to retailers. As tobacco is habit-forming and as his American-origin tobacco was probably the first tobacco that many of his countrymen had ever tasted, his distribution channels lasted him for the rest of his life. Augustine, however, was later unable to recall what their profits had been from 1857 to 1861: "I know that it was not profitable; *i.e.*, it was a threadbare business."[66]

*Chapter Three*

# MACDONALD THE TOBACCO KING, 1861–1917

'S a Chanada a nall d'ainig,

Aite b'fhearr dhomh dùbailt.

[Then I came over to Canada, A place twice as good for me.]

*Gaelic maxim*[1]

What led him to manufacture tobacco nobody has ever explained. He would have made as much money had he decided to make sugar, cotton or lumber. But tobacco was a Canadian institution. Lumber camps were as much in need of tobacco as a modern army. Hard tack, fat pork, and molasses needed plug tobacco to complete the luxury of living. The tobacco made by Macdonald was one of the first Canadian-made to go to the outpost places; smoked and chewed in lumber camps, mining camps, Eskimo igloos, prospectors' tents, and Indian tepees; in half-breed shacks and factory yards; on trains and steamships and trails; in the outermost marches of the Arctic where the hip-pocket and its plug are a constant joy; on the soft blowing Pacific where the weed from Montreal is as common as canned salmon; on the cod-banks of the Atlantic where the fisherman's pipe is the joy of living; and even in down-town clubs of Canadian cities you will find men who, scorning the fine-cut and the patent package, discreetly haul out from the hip-pocket a plug of Macdonald tobacco and proceed to demonstrate the joy that comes from the art of getting ready to smoke.

*Augustus Bridle, Sons of Canada (1916)*[2]

## TOBACCO: CHARACTERISTICS AND A BRIEF HISTORY

Tobacco is native to the Americas and is now grown all over the world.[3] A very delicate plant, its successful growth requires unusual amounts of time and effort. Aboriginal peoples have used tobacco in rituals, in friendship ceremonies, and as medicine. Columbus was the first European to encounter it when he arrived in what is now El Salvador in 1492. In North America, tobacco is cultivated as far north as Quebec and Ontario and as far south as North Carolina. When smoked or chewed, it varies considerably in flavour, depending on where it was grown, what kind of weather prevailed in the year that it took to produce a crop, and the skill of those cultivating, packing, transporting, and processing it.

Virginia tobacco, the most famous American tobacco, takes its name from the state of Virginia but also grows in North Carolina; together the two states form the Virginia District of tobacco growing. The first Virginia tobacco (*Nicotiana rustica*), exported from Chesapeake Bay to England in 1610, was extremely bitter. The colonists in Virginia quickly switched to so-called Spanish tobacco (*Nicotiana tobacum*), named for its origins in Spain and in the Spanish West Indies, Venezuela, and Trinidad. They planted this new variety on their own farms, and from there it spread to Maryland. By the early eighteenth century, the colonists were exporting annually 20 million pounds of tobacco; by mid-century, they were shipping 70 million pounds; and in 1775, the eve of the American Revolution, they were shipping 100 million pounds. Through most of that century, tobacco was the most important staple exported from the British colonies in America and then from the United States. By the time Macdonald began selling imported American-made tobacco, he was benefiting from the almost 250 years that American tobacco – particularly Virginian – had been building its reputation.

In British North America, particularly in what is now roughly the province of Quebec, farmers long raised tobacco on their own land, much of it for their own consumption, probably following the practice of the Aboriginals. Late in Macdonald's career, this local tobacco was to prove the most formidable long-term threat to his success. Duties on imported American leaf, imposed by politicians to protect both the growers and manufacturers of local tobacco, effectively made his products more expensive than local ones. There was no widespread enthusiasm for Canadian tobacco, although people did acquire a taste for it. Many found it extremely harsh on the tongue, and it has never been accepted internationally. And even among those who used it, Canadian tobacco did not seem as desirable for chewing as for smoking.

From the manufacturer's point of view, chewing tobacco – whatever the source of its leaf – was the ideal product. With its nicotine, sugar, and other additives, it was essentially addictive, which ensured repeat purchases, and it was at times extremely fashionable, which led to a proliferation of new product lines defined by flavour, packaging, and target markets. There were in Macdonald's time also many sellers and makers of cigars, the best of whom used only Cuban rather than American leaf, but they catered largely to the rich or at least to the urban. After the end of the American Civil War in 1865, a public appetite grew for cigarettes, and within thirty years cigarettes were becoming more popular than chewing tobacco or cigars. But since they were at least as habit-forming as other ways of consuming tobacco, they offered a new opportunity to tobacco manufacturers. Macdonald, though, while catering to a growing need for tobacco generally, focused on tobacco for chewing and pipe-smoking, so that new competitors did not necessarily take business away from him.

## MACDONALD'S PRACTICE OF AND ATTITUDE TOWARDS HIS TOBACCO BUSINESS

The writing of business history is typically dogged by the meagreness of evidence left behind. This is especially true of Macdonald Tobacco. Macdonald did not believe in wasting paper, and he never used letterhead stationery, seeing no need for it. He was the sole proprietor from 1863 until the end of his life, and so was under no obligation to disclose information to anyone except the revenue authorities. His company had no board of directors to report to and no taxes to pay apart from duty on imported leaf and other goods. Macdonald never employed more than a handful of trusted associates at one time, generally about three. He did his business on a cash basis, and he apparently kept no ledgers. He hated the press and he kept no scrapbooks of press clippings. He almost never wrote or kept letters containing significant information. Furthermore, very few of the scant records that he did keep survive. Augustine, in his testimony before a Civil War claims commission, admitted that he had burnt all of the company's records, up to the year 1864 or so.[4] There do exist minuscule scraps of papers containing production and sales figures for various years, as well as other shreds of evidence. While these data are far from comprehensive, chronologically and otherwise, they do give us an idea of how Macdonald did business and why his business took up so much of his energy.

Remarkably, Macdonald often declared that he was ashamed of his career. He did not approve of tobacco; he described the chewing of it as a filthy and disgusting habit and even forbade its consumption in his presence. He saw the use of tobacco as reflecting moral weakness, much as he saw the consumption of alcohol. In discussing his philanthropy, he once said, "I am not proud of my business, and that feeling, perhaps, has been the reason of my donations."[5]

Disdainful as Macdonald may have been about manufacturing tobacco, he was unusually successful at it. The years 1859–68 saw the consolidation of his fortune, and significantly, these years encompassed the American Civil War (1861–65). Macdonald's first plant was established in 1859, three years before the outbreak of war; by the war's end, it had more work than it could handle. While the war did not prompt Macdonald to start his "threadbare" business, from 1861 onwards it certainly enabled it to thrive.

William C. Macdonald, 1863 (Notman 1-8843)

## MACDONALD'S TOBACCO BUSINESS DURING
## THE AMERICAN CIVIL WAR, 1861–1865

The event that marked the start of hostilities – the rebel attack on Fort Sumter in April 1861 – was a surprise to nearly everyone. Even so, tensions between the Southern cotton and tobacco states and the northern manufacturing states, over issues related to slavery, had been building since the 1850s, when Macdonald was still in Boston. In December 1860, South Carolina, Mississippi, Florida, Alabama, Georgia, Louisiana, and Texas had seceded from the Union. Then, delegates from these states, with the exception of Texas, met in February 1861 to establish the Confederate States of America. The cotton, but none of the tobacco, states were included in the Confederacy, giving Macdonald time to anticipate the leaf shortages that would come when the tobacco states followed. It was only after Lincoln had mobilized troops in response to Sumter in April that the six tobacco states split their allegiances, half of them leaving the Union – Virginia, North Carolina, and Tennessee. The rest stayed, although a part of Kentucky was from time to time under the control of Confederate forces.

In the antebellum or pre-1861 South, there had been tobacco factories in Richmond, Petersburg, Lynchburg, and Danville in Virginia, and also in North Carolina, Kentucky, Tennessee, and Missouri.[6] In 1860, 90 per cent of manufactured tobacco came from the slave states, and 56 per cent of that proportion from slave-owning Virginia. Richmond had fifty-odd factories employing 3,400 hands and producing goods valued at $5 million.[7] It was from Virginia, through New York factors, that Macdonald had probably bought the tobacco plugs and twists that he first sold in 1855–58, and also his tobacco leaf in 1858–61.

The rebellious tobacco states produced much less tobacco during the war than before, as they needed their fields for raising food, and from 1862 onwards, it was official Confederate policy to discourage tobacco growing. Once the Northern blockade extended to New Orleans in 1863, of the old tobacco towns in what was now the Confederacy, only Danville, Virginia, prospered, chiefly because of its rail link to Richmond. Richmond was both the capital of the Confederacy and a port from which ships could run the blockade to break through to the British colonies in the Atlantic and the West Indies.

Initially, with the outbreak of war, Maryland, Kentucky, and Missouri, loyal to the Union, could continue to supply tobacco leaf to their traditional customers outside the Confederacy, and the delay before the three Confederate tobacco states – Virginia, North Carolina, and Tennessee – were blockaded allowed these states to do the same for a brief time. Even after the Confederacy had been blockaded, the border between North and South remained somewhat porous, like the border between the North and British North America. The British Empire was

Tobacco plants, probably growing in Kentucky early in the twentieth century (MSF)

officially neutral in the conflict, and thus Macdonald and Augustine were not deemed enemies by either side and they could do business with both. As they could not predict the course of the conflict any better than anyone else, their task was to secure supplies when and where they could.

On the Northern side, Kentucky replaced Virginia as the chief tobacco-producing state. The disruption of the South as the centre of tobacco manufacture and as the main source of raw leaf encouraged tobacco manufacture even considerably north of Kentucky, in New York City and Montreal. Macdonald now bought his tobacco from Louisville, Kentucky, and as he had been manufacturing tobacco since 1859, he bought leaf rather than manufactured plug. With the dislocations provoked by battle, Macdonald was probably as worried about the security of his supply as he was about how to profit from the war. Tobacco leaf could not be stored indefinitely, and the quality as well as the quantity of the harvest of each year was crucial for profits.

To Macdonald's contemporaries, the significance of the coincidence between the consolidation of his business and the war was a mystery. They knew that he had not been doing well up to the outbreak of war. As his tobacco leaf had prob-

Tobacco for purchase in Danville, Virginia, probably early in
the twentieth century (MSF)

ably come overwhelmingly from the Virginia District, some may have seen his
most pressing problem as being how to overcome or evade the blockade imposed
to stop the flow of goods from the rebellious South to the North. There was even
speculation that during the conflict he engaged in blockade running.

To expand his manufactured-tobacco business during the war, Macdonald needed a much surer source of supply than such expediencies as blockade
running. He was actually unusually well placed to profit from the war. He had
been dealing in tobacco in Montreal since about seven years before its start, and
through his work in Boston and New York, he had become intimately familiar
with American business practice. Almost as soon as war broke out, Augustine
rushed to New York to buy manufactured tobacco, and only a few months later,
by the end of 1861, he was worth $100,000, having realized as much as a 600
per cent profit on what he had bought.[8] In the same year, he bought tobacco in
Mobile, Alabama; and in 1862–63, he bought tobacco "in the west, which was
then within United States lines," all over Missouri, Tennessee, and Kentucky,
"doing business bordering $2,000,000 a year." His purchase in west Tennessee,

Augustine McDonald, 1867 (Notman 1-28762.1)

of $200,000, was "with paper payable after the war closed."[9] Augustine recalled that his grandfather, presumably Captain John, had bought £100,000 in British Exchequer bills for £48 on the hundred. Perhaps eager to imitate his forebear, he speculated wildly on currency as well as on tobacco and cotton prices, but he was careful to "neutralize" much of the profit he secured in British pounds, leaving his pound notes with friends from New York City to St Louis, Missouri.

We do not know how much of the tobacco Augustine bought reached Montreal, but it was likely a fair amount. From testimony during Augustine's litigation after the war, we can glean hints. C.C. Mengel, a tobacco and commission agent in Brooklyn, had first met Augustine in St Louis in 1859 when Mengel was working for the tobacco firm of Brown & Whiting in Boston. From 1859 to 1864 his purchases for Augustine amounted to $400,000 a year. We cannot assume

David Stewart, Montreal, 1863 (Notman I-9725.I)

that all of this tobacco went to the factory in Montreal, however, since Mengel also seems to have been involved in the resale of tobacco, on rising markets, on behalf of Augustine. "I know," Mengel would recall in 1871, that "I sold for him at great advance, sixteen or eighteen cents, when it costs six or seven." He had never sold "at a loss" for him, and he did not know Augustine's customers in Montreal or how much Macdonald Tobacco was making in profit.[10]

And there is further evidence of Augustine's helping Macdonald to procure tobacco during the war. John Bryan, a New York banker and broker in both cotton and tobacco, had met Augustine in 1858, three years before the outbreak of the Civil War. As a banker, Bryan was doing $20 million in business; as a broker, $6 to $10 million. He apparently sold consignments of tobacco to Augustine after the conflict began and to Macdonald himself in 1863–64, his proceeds in his dealings with Macdonald Tobacco being from $40,000 to $60,000.[11] A tobacco commission merchant from Louisville, Alexander Harthill, spent two days in Montreal in 1863 and found Macdonald's works to be "the largest factory on the continent, working ten or eleven hundred hands," with about one and a half million pounds of manufactured tobacco in stock worth $400,000, and leaf worth $30,000 to $50,000. He reported that he sold Macdonald $100,000 in raw leaf.[12] Harthill's figure for "hands," like all other figures given for the number of employees, must be qualified, as Macdonald's labour was largely seasonal and even in season many if not most of the workers were part-time and were in any case divided into two shifts.

Augustine was doing so well by 1863 that he started to speculate increasingly in cotton, that other great crop of the South. He moved to Louisville in Kentucky and in that same year withdrew from his partnership in Macdonald's tobacco business. Macdonald had been very fortunate to find David Stewart to replace Augustine as clerk in 1857. Such was Macdonald's confidence in Stewart that he gave him power of attorney in 1866.[13] Stewart remained his right-hand man until both men were stricken with illness in 1914.

By the end of the American Civil War, largely thanks to Augustine's efforts early in the conflict to establish secure supply routes for tobacco from outside the Confederacy, Macdonald had a secure and flourishing business in Montreal. Contrary to rumour, these supply routes probably did not involve running the Unionist blockade of Confederate ports. Also contrary to rumour, his success did not come from a contract under which he, as a neutral, supplied Union troops with tobacco imported from the Confederacy, processed in Montreal, and then exported manufactured tobacco to the North.

Instead, Augustine had ensured Macdonald's security of supply from the North at a time when Macdonald had no strong competitors in Montreal. Northern tobacco did go to Montreal, where Macdonald processed it, but it did not go from there to either side during the war. It went to customers in British North America, who felt as much in need of tobacco as the warring Americans. Macdonald was also expanding the links with wholesalers in British North America that would be an integral part of his business as long as he lived. All of this put him in a good position at the end of the war, and it would be about thirty years before he was to face effective competition.

## MACDONALD'S LEAF AND TOBACCO PRODUCTS

Macdonald's leaf was nearly always American, and with the exception of one year, about 1860, he refused to countenance any other. He processed his American leaf only for chewing tobacco or pipe-smoking. Both products may be called "plugs," but plugs more often refer to highly compacted chewing tobacco alone, as tobacco for pipes is shredded leaf. Macdonald Tobacco did not manufacture cigarettes until 1922, after Macdonald's death, and it never manufactured snuff or cigars.

Macdonald's chewing tobacco was more popular than his pipe tobacco. There was already a market for chewing tobacco when he began to make it, and it was a simpler and safer habit for most working people than clenching a pipe between the teeth. Chewing tobacco was comforting, like betel nut in Asia or other mild narcotics chewed in Africa and the Americas. One of his brands was actually called "Solace." Chewing tobacco encouraged sociability, and along with Macdonald's pipe tobacco, it found a loyal market among the miners, lumbermen, and railway builders who were transforming British North America in the mid-nineteenth century in both the countryside and the towns. Brown lines of expectorated tobacco followed trails through the wilderness, and in winter they were especially visible on the snow-covered streets leading to factories. The use of chewing tobacco spread to all classes, including professionals and politicians, and cuspidors could be seen throughout Canada well into the twentieth century, including on the floor of the House of Commons in Ottawa.

### A New Kentucky Leaf

Macdonald's chewing and pipe tobaccos were relatively affordable for the masses, although because they were known as Virginian, they were still perceived as being of high quality. While he often faced robust competition, he was probably the first manufacturer in Canada to use only American leaf, and certainly the most enduring. He was also probably the Canadian manufacturer with the best-established links to American sources. This consistency of supply meant that he was able to develop recognition of his brand early and thus secure consumers loyal to his product.

The American Civil War intervened before Macdonald had fully developed this brand loyalty. Virginia, as we have seen, was blockaded as a Confederate state, and so Macdonald had to look elsewhere for leaf as attractive as the Virginia leaf he had been selling. Kentucky, which was not blockaded, also grew the so-called Virginia leaf. Its accessibility to Macdonald during the war, already described, was not the only advantage Kentucky offered him.

Kentucky was exporting a new kind of tobacco that was particularly suited to the chewing tobacco Macdonald was selling. This was bright, or yellow, tobacco, discovered in Kentucky in 1853–55 in one of the oddest developments in the history of agriculture. Farmers found that the traditional dark, or black, tobacco that they were growing had lost colour as a result of inadequate watering. Not wanting to lose their crop, they cured it in the normal manner, and to their surprise they found that it yielded a much sweeter product than had been possible before.

Bright tobacco swiftly spread to other states, and it became a new product in the hands of manufacturers. It did not supplant the traditional dark or burley tobacco, but it created a new market for a very distinct tobacco. And during the war it had the advantage of growing not in the traditional Virginia District but on land to the west, outside the Confederacy. Other new strains of tobacco followed. The so-called Kentucky white burley was discovered in Ohio in 1864, giving manufacturers such as Macdonald the opportunity to add new flavours to their product line.[14]

The blockade between North and South affected trade both ways. It not only cut off the supply of Virginia tobacco to the North and by extension to Canada, but also prevented the export of tobacco leaf from Kentucky to the South. The expanding railways of Kentucky could export only to the North during the war, as the state bordered the Confederacy to the south. Thus, both the attractiveness of the new, sweeter tobacco and the exclusive redirection of the trade route from Kentucky northwards during the war ensured success to any Canadian tobacco manufacturer that had established the necessary supply links to Kentucky. And this, as we have seen, the Macdonald brothers had certainly done.

### Bright and Dark Tobacco after the War

At the end of the war, in April 1865, looters stole a supply of bright tobacco held by John Ruffin Green of Durham Station (later Durham) in North Carolina. These looters spread a taste for Green's product like a virus, so that bright tobacco, granulated, became highly sought after all over the country. Green adopted the Durham Bull as his trademark, and his factory became one of the largest in the world, expanding from about a dozen workers in 1869 to about 900 in 1884.

It seems that the popularity of the new tobacco drew Macdonald back to the United States, if only temporarily. The city directory for Louisville shows that Macdonald was living in the city in 1867 and Augustine as well. Augustine is listed as a resident of Louisville until 1875 and as working for "Macdonald & Co." In his later testimony, he said that he had been "manufacturing" tobacco there, and it does appear that his enterprise was separate from his brother's business. But as the two were both living in Louisville in 1867, it is not unlikely that from 1867 to 1874 Augustine bought tobacco leaf in Louisville for Macdonald's works in Montreal.

Such was the global popularity of bright tobacco after the war that it came to be cultivated extensively in the Virginia District as well as in Kentucky and elsewhere, and thus Virginia tobacco could now be either dark or bright. By 1884

Macdonald was buying his dark tobacco from Kentucky and Missouri, and his bright from Virginia, a probable reversal from his prewar – and certainly his wartime – patterns of purchase. He was now buying three times as much dark as bright, however, which is why he was dealing so much with Danville in Virginia, as well as with Louisville in Kentucky. The dark purchases formed the bulk of his chewing tobacco, with only his wrappers coming from the bright, giving the plug its unique lemon-coloured appearance and a distinctive sweetness to complement the licorice-impregnated and even sweeter dark.

### Cavendish Tobacco

Sir Thomas Cavendish, an Elizabethan admiral, had discovered in the 1590s that the bitter Virginia tobacco tasted better when mixed with sugar, and he lent his name to attempts to improve the flavour of the leaf. The process involved flavouring and then pressing the tobacco leaves in layers, cutting or shredding them, and then applying heat from fire or steam. The tobacco was then allowed to ferment slowly over several days or several weeks. The Cavendish tobacco that finally emerged varied in colour and taste, depending on the blend of leaves used and the flavourings added.

There was much speculation about what went into each product. People spoke of molasses, cayenne pepper, copperas, opium, strychnine, and Indian hemp. Despite popular conception that it was an essential ingredient, molasses was out of the question, as it would cause the tobacco to ferment too quickly. Macdonald used Demerara sugar and possibly maple sugar instead. Opium, at $15 a pound at the end of the nineteenth century, was also out of the question. But rum, brandy, and port may have been used in the more expensive brands, and licorice was probably used in all of them.[15] Macdonald and his direct competitors added value to the leaf they imported by performing all the manufacture themselves. Macdonald called himself a manufacturer of Cavendish tobacco.[16]

## MACDONALD'S MANUFACTURING PROCESS

The factories of the American South were indeed the obvious and perhaps the only possible models for Macdonald's plant. Following his early biographer Collard, who interviewed long-time employees of Macdonald Tobacco, we can trace how Macdonald's tobacco manufacture took place in the various rooms of whatever plant he was using. Apart from the leaf room, which was presumably for storage and stemming, there were rooms for flavouring, lump-making or twisting, filling, wrapping, and prizing. The tobacco leaf arrived at the factory in half-ton cakes. These cakes had already been tightly pressed on the plantations and then broken in two three places at inspection warehouses in the United States.[17]

After moistening the leaves, the stemmers ripped from each leaf the coarse and harsh-flavoured mid-vein (the stem). The leaves would then be dried again, some to be used as filler and some put aside for use as unflavoured wrappers.

Next, dippers soaked the stemmed tobacco for filler in a black, syrupy compound of licorice and sugar that had been cooked in massive iron kettles. The filler leaves were then aired, and a final bouquet was prepared. This consisted of a fragrant concoction of rum, sweet oil, and spices that was sprinkled on the leaves, the flavours varying from product to product. The leaves were then either fashioned into "twists" or hammered into neat, rectangular plugs. A senior worker, called the adjustor, weighed the precise amount of filler to go into each plug; this was determined by the excise tax to be levied. He used trimming knives and scales to ensure the correct weight.

The wrappers then wrapped each plug in a choice, unflavoured leaf that had been set aside while the tobacco for filler was being cooked and flavoured. They used a tucker or sharpened screw to puncture the wrapper, and then they inserted the end of the wrapping leaf into the hole to seal it. There was a rigorous inspection and counting of plugs, and defective products were placed on an "honour table" for remaking. Macdonald himself knew how to deal with even extreme defects. On one visit to the works, he was shown some plugs green with mould. He sat a woman down at a table and had her wipe the mould off with a rag soaked in gin, and after a month the plugs were found to be in excellent condition.[18]

The wrapped plugs then went to the pressroom, where prizers or screw-men placed them in multi-divided wooden "shapes" or pattern-boxes, swinging giant wing-screw presses to force them into the desired shape and firmness. This process was repeated several times until the edges of the plugs were perfectly aligned so that the pieces could fit into the boxes to be packed.

Macdonald's pipe tobacco consisted of parings from plug tobacco, both dark and bright, mixed with various flavours. Scrap and stems often found themselves shredded with these parings in cutters, resulting in distinctive pipe tobaccos – sold in tins – for a variety of customers.

## THE EFFECT OF TARIFFS ON TOBACCO MANUFACTURE, 1863–1868

If his operations were very American in inspiration, Macdonald faced throughout his career a problem that was distinctly Canadian. In 1863 Macdonald became the sole proprietor of his business, and he would remain so for the rest of his life.[19] He probably bought out his brother Augustine, who, as noted above, returned to the United States in that year, and Alexander Ross, his two main partners since 1860. Other partners from 1860 – Donald Campbell of Halifax,

Walter R. Edwards of Boston, and Benjamin F. Atwood of Philadelphia – seem to have withdrawn before 1863.

Then, a year later, in 1864, he found himself facing a severe challenge in the form of an unexpected excise tax of 10 cents per pound levied on the sale of locally manufactured products made from foreign leaf, except for snuff and cigars.[20] The tax, which was one of the measures of the Inland Revenue Act of that year, made the imported American-manufactured tobacco much more attractive, but Macdonald had already stopped selling it. To remain competitive, he now had to reduce the price of his own Canadian-manufactured goods by 9 cents a pound, from 28 cents to 19, and then again to 16. The question of protection was to remain a nagging one for Macdonald throughout his career.[21] He himself had used Canadian leaf in tobacco manufacture for about a year, in 1860 or so, but his customers had found the result unsatisfactory. Now this excise tax provoked the greatest price drop he had yet suffered, and it alerted him to the ever-present threat from Canadian leaf.

Isaac Buchanan, who as we saw in the last chapter had been behind tariff reform ten years earlier, lobbied John A. Macdonald, then prime minister of the United Province of Canada, for relief for the tobacco manufacturers from the excise tax of 1864. He reported that eight tobacco factories in Hamilton alone were going bankrupt. His appeal failed, and he resigned his position as president of the council in the government of Sir Etienne-Pascal Taché and John A. Macdonald.[22]

By 1866 the duty on imported, largely American, tobacco was 15 cents per pound. In 1867 the Canadian manufacturers petitioned the government for an additional *ad valorem* duty of 25 per cent on imported manufactured tobacco (that is, on the estimated market value of the goods), but they received from the new Dominion only a 5 per cent *ad valorem* duty as supplementary protection.

In consequence, Macdonald felt, the Canadian market was under threat from damaged manufactured tobaccos, both bright and dark, which were worthless in the United States but could be sold very cheaply north of the American border. The American manufacturers had been inducing Canadians, presumably merchants, to accept the damaged tobacco by paying the freight charges for parcels of it up to the border, and in so doing, they were also defrauding the U.S. Internal Revenue Department of tax on parcels of sound and saleable tobaccos.

Then, in December 1867, an excise tax, replacing the 10 cents for every pound imposed three years earlier, was levied on all tobacco sold in Canada, so that it was now 5 to 15 cents a pound, again except for cigars and snuff. These taxes, both the duty on American imports and the excise on sales in Canada, seem to have had little adverse effect on Macdonald. It is unclear whether Canadian-manufactured tobacco was taxed at the lower end of the range, say at 5 cents a pound, while American-manufactured tobacco was taxed at the higher end, say at 15 cents a pound. But if, as seems not unlikely, this was the case, then Macdonald actually benefited from the 1867 excise tax, as he did from the duty on American manufactured imports.

Trial balances survive for his business from January 1867 and January 1868. Two entries are notable and show growth. From one January to the next, the capital account increased from $137,066 to $208,787 and the inventory increased from $58,685 to $104,690. The balance for January 1868 suggests that Macdonald was incurring some increasing, if minor, debt,[23] but it can still be said that by 1868, three years after the end of the American Civil War, Macdonald was the owner of the largest tobacco firm in Canada.

Nevertheless, the 1864 excise tax imposed on tobacco products sold locally continued to inflict pain on Canadian manufacturers generally. On 31 January 1868 a protest meeting of wholesale and retail dealers and licensed manufacturers of tobacco was held in Montreal, with A. Dubord in the chair.[24] The resolutions emerging from this meeting described the Inland Revenue Act of 1864 as having been "subject to the most glaring frauds and impositions on the revenue of the country" committed by unlicensed manufacturers of tobacco, cigars, and snuff. These businesses had paid no excise taxes, and in addition, the official returns of trade and navigation in June 1867 incorrectly indicated that Montreal, Quebec City, and St Francis were the only places in Lower Canada where tobacco manufacture occurred. In fact, "it is notorious that Tobacco is cut and manufactured in nearly every small town and country place in the Eastern Townships."

Those attending the meeting called for the levying of duty on both leaf and manufactured tobacco. They also noted that it had proved impossible to enforce and collect duty on leaf owing to "exportations [re-exportations] and the necessity of drawback duty." To cure this, they called for a bonded system with nominal duty on importations and production, "leaving it optional with the importer to manufacture his Tobacco in bond or duty paid." Twenty-four men signed a petition for relief, but Macdonald was not among them, possibly because his business was not directly affected by manufacturers that were using the still relatively unpopular Canadian leaf. In the following year, 1868, Canadian manufacturers would only use 169,206 pounds of Canadian leaf as against 5,130,270 pounds of American leaf.[25]

Macdonald's own position became clear on 30 March 1868, when he wrote to W.P. Howland, the minister of inland revenue in Ottawa.[26] Although not suffering like manufacturers of Canadian leaf that were being undercut by evaders of the excise tax, Macdonald did not hesitate to associate himself with them in calling for protection against the importation of American-manufactured leaf, which directly competed with his product. This protection he defined as an

McDonald Bros. & Co.'s Tobacco Works, Water Street, 1865 (MSF)

import duty on foreign-manufactured tobacco that exceeded the excise on home-manufactured tobacco by 10 cents per pound and 10 per cent *ad valorem.*

Macdonald complained that, in the previous six years in Montreal alone, "six factories have ceased to exist, one half of the proprietors being possessed of ample capital to continue if they had found it sufficiently profitable." Although in the end he failed to win from Howland the protection that he was lobbying for, he was actually still prospering, possibly because so much of his competition had disappeared. As he admitted to Howland in his appeal for protection, he had paid the government $180,000 in excise between January 1867 and January 1868, and he expected to pay a further $200,000 by the following January.

## MACDONALD'S FIRST PLANT, 1858–1865

Since about 1858, Macdonald's business had occupied premises at 163 Water Street, later expanding to a building at Wellington and McGill Streets and to 1 Grey Nun and 14 Duke (formerly George) Streets. The building on Water Street had been a stone granary dating back to the French regime. Macdonald's

Tobacco sorting room at the Macdonald works, 1941 (MSF)

landlord was Charles Grant, the baron de Longueuil. By about 1865 Macdonald was employing about a thousand men, women, and children, off and on, in two work shifts, from seven on Monday morning until eleven on Saturday evening. His workers could produce between 120 and 150 boxes of tobacco a day. The Montreal *Gazette* reported in late 1865 that Macdonald's production exceeded the daily demand in Canada. Perhaps complying with the laws of supply and demand, Macdonald reduced his price from 27½ cents a pound to 20 cents and then to 16 cents.

## PLANT EXPANSION, 1866–1874

Despite its enormously thick stone walls, the plant on Water Street was almost completely destroyed by fire in November 1865. Immediately after the fire, Macdonald rebuilt the plant, reopening it on New Year's Day, 1866 – not a small feat. Moreover, he now consolidated his scattered operations within the rebuilt structure. In addition to its basement, the new factory occupied five storeys, two of them new, and with its new machinery and utensils the business was valued

# THE DUPLEX

## AUTOMATIC TOBACCO PRESS.

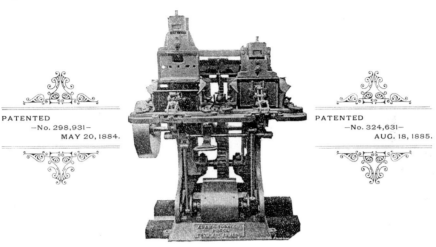

PATENTED
—No. 298,931—
MAY 20, 1884.

PATENTED
—No. 324,631—
AUG. 18, 1885.

Tobacco press patented by Adams Tobacco Press Co., Quincy, Illinois (MSF)

at about $40,000. The fifth storey was used for drying and flavouring. The fourth contained leaf and sorting rooms and was fitted with boilers to dissolve the one-half to three-quarters of a ton of licorice used daily. The third and second storeys housed the rolling-rooms, used in making plugs out of rolls. Each room contained a hundred work tables, and each table could accommodate up to five workers, so that each room could accommodate up to 500 workers at one time, apart from overseers and attendants.

The first storey housed the pressroom, with its nine hydraulic presses for the shapers and finishers, as well as steam-driven pumps. There were twenty-five heavy iron compress boxes or finishers, each of which had its retainer, and a hundred iron screw presses. One of the hydraulic presses could deal with a hogshead of leaf at a time and also press stems. A connected shed housed a bonded warehouse and equipment. In the cellar were two large sweating-rooms capable of holding 500 boxes at a time. A steam-driven hoisting apparatus, with a safety platform to carry material from the cellar, could move at more than fifty feet per minute and carry 4,000 pounds. In a ten-hour day, the plant could easily

Table 1: Selected Data on Assets and Liabilities, March 1866 to January 1867, Taken from Every Second Month and Rounded to the Nearest Dollar

| ASSET | 3/66 | 5/66 | 7/66 | 9/66 | 11/66 | 1/67 |
|-------|------|------|------|------|-------|------|
| 1  Leaf | 7,647 | 15,582 | 22,910 | 21,479 | 23,595 | 20,927 |
| 2  Improvement | 57 | 2,922 | 3,466 | 3,472 | 3,472 | 3,472 |
| 3  Machinery | 8,741 | 11,588 | 14,535 | 14,880 | 14,880 | 15,394 |
| 4  Licorice | 4,814 | 8,556 | 9,197 | 9,917 | 9,917 | 8,596 |
| 5  Flavour | 368 | 2,405 | 4,296 | 4,681 | 4,681 | 4,681 |
| 6  Wages | 85 | 3,114 | 7,513 | 8,951 | 106 | 1,341 |
| 7  Drayage | 4 | 66 | 100 | 100 | 106 | 118 |
| 8  A.R. McD | 2 | 476 | 776 | 796 | 946 | 1,054* |
| 9  Cash | 3,240 | 1,626 | 2,204 | 3,227 | 5,254 | unknown |
| 10  Freight | n/a | 587 | 621 | 615 | 648 | 648 |
| 11  Box | n/a | 840 | 2,014 | 2,345 | 2.351 | 2,308 |
| 12  Nail | n/a | 17 | 75 | 75 | 115 | 115 |
| 13  W.C. McD | n/a | n/a | 284 | 578 | 918 | 918 |
| 14  Tax | n/a | n/a | 2,276 | 2,276 | 3,174 | 10,668 |

* This entry appears to refer to leaf bought by Augustine, the purchase price of which was still owed to him personally.

manufacture up to 150 boxes of tobacco, each weighing from 105 to 110 pounds.[27] For Montreal at this time, this was industrialization on a grand scale, ensuring Macdonald's dominance as a tobacco manufacturer by virtue of his investment in plant and machinery, apart from his skills as a businessman.

Macdonald's production capacity was not greater than it had been in the three buildings he had occupied between 1863 and 1865, but his operations were now consolidated and could be rationalized. Lists of assets and liabilities for his business survive from March 1866 to January 1867 (see Table 1). The assets in this period vary considerably in value, particularly the raw materials used in production, reflecting the seasonality of the business.

In about 1870 Macdonald moved his head offices, as opposed to his "works," from Water Street to Notre-Dame Street, where he was to stay until 1910. The offices occupied the second floor of a modest stone structure of three storeys, a former house. Macdonald and David Stewart each occupied a former bedroom, and there was a "general office" for the bookkeeper, William John Greer, and an office boy. Macdonald's office, about twelve by twelve feet, retained its original bedroom wallpaper, faded and cracked, with the full imprint of a dirty hand upon it.

One journalist described the offices as "a bit of a counting house from the pages of Dickens'." They contained "plain and substantial furniture," which some described as more suitable for a kitchen, and had "an air of quietness." The floors were covered with oilcloth "of a quiet pattern," but this seems to have been a late luxury, for in the early days the offices had wide painted boards as flooring.[28] In his later years there, Macdonald would resist using a telephone and even a typewriter and filing cabinet, although he eventually installed telegraphic and telephone communication, but only in his factory. When Bell Telephone asked him to become a customer, he replied, "You'd like well to let the public have me by the ear any time they wished, wouldn't you? Well, they'll not!"[29] He hated noise and would tolerate only the sound of a ticking clock. He used no letterhead stationery, as noted earlier, and he sometimes wrote letters on brown wrapping paper. He had no secretary, and he did not welcome casual visitors, for whom there was a hard wooden bench just outside the office.

Macdonald seldom visited the shop floor of the factory, leaving that end of the business, from 1870 to 1889, to his superintendent Sam Wells, from Dumfriesshire, and, under Wells, to overseers or foremen, three for men and one for women. The male overseers wore black bowler hats, and all the overseers exercised direct control over the workers, even having the power to fine them. The working language was French, although some of the foremen could not speak it and had to use sign language. All foreign workers were called Polish, whatever their real origin.

By 1871 Macdonald is said to have acquired $250,000 in capital and to be employing 550 workers who produced more than $500,000 in goods annually.[30] This number of workers seems to be only half of those that he had been reported as employing in 1863, but it probably related to only one of two shifts, as his production was growing rather than falling.

## MACDONALD'S NEW WORKS, 1874

In 1874 Macdonald moved his entire plant, but not his head offices, outside the city, to the village of Hochelaga where it met the eastern boundary of the Montreal ward of Ste Marie. Ste Marie had been a centre of industry in the city since 1782 and was the location of Montreal's first brewery, which was later taken over by the Molson family. By the 1870s various manufacturers were working to establish Hochelaga as an industrial suburb, particularly the Rolland brothers, manufacturers of fine papers, and the Hudon brothers, manufacturers of textiles. The promoters of Hochelaga had laid down streets, provided public services, and offered bonuses and subsidies to manufacturers and railways. The Canadian Pacific Railway (CPR) locomotive yards and two branches of the

Macdonald Tobacco Works, Ontario Street, in the nineteenth century (MSF)

Hudons' Hochelaga Cotton Mill were located south of St Catherine Street, then becoming the principal commercial thoroughfare of Montreal. The new plants of Canadian Rubber, Dominion Oilcloth, and, after 1885, Empire Tobacco were also built there.

The new Macdonald plant occupied a city block bounded by Ontario, Iberville, Dufresne, and Larivière Streets. Before the plant was built, this had been farmland, unlike the more established industrial district to the south. Like its Water Street predecessor, the new factory had five floors, including a basement, but it covered almost five and a half acres, permitting Macdonald to double both his machinery and his workforce. He built it of the strongest possible materials, including Montreal limestone and granite pillars from Aberdeen that he bought cheaply as unneeded ballast from Scottish ships.

He ensured that his rolling and pressrooms were filled with air and light and that the building was as fireproof as he could make it, with fire escapes for use when necessary. The unusually large skylights and windows reduced the need for gas lighting, which he made his workers pay for in any case. The building was constructed of red brick, with trimmings in yellow brick around its doors and

Alexander Cowper Hutchison, architect of the new
Macdonald Tobacco Works, about 1910 (Notman 11-180836)

windows. A massive central tower incorporated the main entrance, a gigantic clock with four dials, and a flagpole set atop its 140 feet. Inside the tower a staircase eight feet in width was to serve as a fire-escape route. The roof was made of tin to protect against sparks and embers in the wind. Macdonald even bought up all the buildings adjacent to the four sides of the plant so that it could stand alone. As the site was not far from the port and just west of the CPR line, the plant could readily ship in its raw products in bulk and then ship them out processed for distribution.

Macdonald continued to work out of his downtown office on Notre-Dame Street, again delegating the management of the workers to his superintendent. Although he doubtless kept a sharp eye on every aspect of the plant's operations, he now concentrated on ensuring his supply of raw materials and on expanding his customer base. Macdonald paid close attention to the layout of his new factory, as he was installing big, new machinery to be operated mainly by women and children. Mechanization and rationalization, together with the physical separation of ownership and upper management from the workforce, made for a relatively very modern plant.

## LABOUR, SUPPLIES, AND STOCK, 1874–1889

Apart from raw materials, the most important factor of production was the cost of labour. An interesting question is how Macdonald may have adapted American methods to his own operations, especially as both the growing and the manufacture of tobacco had been so associated with slavery. President Lincoln did not proclaim the emancipation of the slaves until 1863. Even before the war, however, the slaves in the tobacco factories had been paid for their labour. It was very expensive to buy a slave, and so from about 1840 to 1861, especially in Richmond and Petersburg, tobacco manufacturers routinely hired slaves from their owners as the demands of manufacture increased. By the 1850s half of the slaves in the larger tobacco-manufacturing towns were hired annually. Good workers could receive fortnightly bonuses, and at Christmas they might even change employers as they pleased.

Repulsive as the idea of slavery was to most in British North America, the reality was that slave workers in the American tobacco factories were to some extent free agents and willing hands, their slavery being essentially their legal status. They often worked side by side with freed slaves, and no distinction was made between them.[31] In consequence, from the point of view of labour, tobacco manufacture was not all that different after the war from the way it had been before the war, even in the former Confederacy, and in itself slavery did not make American procedures unsuitable as a model for Macdonald in Montreal.

For the most part, Macdonald hired hundreds of semi-skilled women and children, probably not long off the farm. The planners of Hochelaga had mapped out and subdivided working-class lots, and workers flocked to the suburb to be near the new mills, there being no electrified public transit in Montreal until the 1890s. Generations of the same families worked for his company, and the works were a centre of community life. Fathers, mothers, children, cousins, aunts, and uncles worked side by side. Unlike nearly all his competitors, Macdonald stayed in business for decades, forty-nine years by the time of his death. Also unlike them, he also paid what he had promised, and so there was for his workers some reassurance in working for him.

Nevertheless, daily life was precarious for most of Macdonald's workers. Employment was seasonal, and the wages for women could be half those of men, although sometimes they were actually higher. Every morning casual job-seekers would gather at the entrance of his works in the hope of being hired for the day, and one result of Macdonald's move to Hochelaga was an almost constant supply

Table 2: Figures for the Week Ending 1 June 1876

| | |
|---|---|
| Fillers (69 benches) | 51,152 lbs x $1.75 per 100 lbs= $895 |
| Mechanics and watchmen (28) | $207.29 |
| Carpenters (39) | $317.65 |
| Total weight of work per week | 87,214 lbs* |
| Average weight of work per day | 14,563 lbs |
| Increased weight of work per day | 1,853 lbs |

* The discrepancy between the total weight of work for that week and the weight of work produced by the fillers may perhaps be accounted for by the fact that there remained work in process (before filling) at the end of the week.

of cheap labour. His superintendent, first Sam Wells and then Howard Stewart (a son of David Stewart), chose these workers. There was no job security for anyone, no union, and no way of airing grievances. Macdonald did not hesitate to cut his workforce if business was slow, generally keeping his bench-owners in order of seniority.

Work at Macdonald's was seasonal chiefly because tobacco was harvested at roughly the same time each year. Table 2 conveys a sense of the factory as a whole, at the stage of production when fillers were required. Furthermore, winter made year-round shipment to or from Montreal impossible. At the end of October 1887, however, several employees sent a pitiful request for payment of the same wages "during the next winter season as they are now getting," as they were doing "as much work in winter as in summer" and in winter their expenses were greater. This letter appears to have been from the skeleton force in the plant during the winter, as actual production would have closed down or been at least considerably less at this time.[32]

The workforce was administratively divided between those who maintained the plant and shipped from it, on the one hand, and those who did the actual tobacco manufacturing, on the other. In the first category, we find that in 12–25 November 1875 only thirteen mechanics, four labourers, and four watchmen were employed. By the first week of April 1876, when production had presumably resumed, Macdonald was employing at least sixteen mechanics, two watchmen, seven labourers, and thirty-five carpenters, with the records suggesting another twenty-seven workers, possibly part-time. In the third week of the same April, there suddenly appeared twenty-seven scrubbers. In the week ending 1 June of that year, sixty-nine "benches" of fillers, twenty-eight mechanics and watchmen, and thirty-nine carpenters were employed. In 11–17 August 1876, there were sixty-four workers in the pressroom, and a week later there were twenty-two storemen. From the distribution of workers in this period, from April to August, we can correlate the labour, both bench and other, used at the various stages of production "in season." The weekly wages also varied with who was doing what. A mechanic made between $6.00 and $10.00; a labourer between $6.00 and $7.00; a watchman between $7.00 and $8.17; a scrubber between $2.17 and $4.00; a presser between $43.00 and $65.00; and a storeman between $35.00 and $60.00.

There was one strike in the 1880s. When informed one day that his machinery was at a standstill, Macdonald went to his works and asked why the workers had laid down their tools. When told that his wages were insufficient, he ordered the door padlocked, which it remained for several weeks. Eventually a delegation of workers went to his office and gave him a list of those who were willing to work for his wages. He returned to his works and unlocked the padlock with his own hands, warning that he would never open again if they struck again, which they did not.

Macdonald was a stern employer, but by the standards of the day he was also a fairly humane one. In his testimony before the Royal Commission on the Relations of Labor and Capital appointed in 1886,[33] he explained that he employed between ten and eleven hundred hands, about 500 males and 550 females.[34] He could not say how many of the males were boys, but he denied knowingly employing boys below the age of twelve, although some lied about their age. His superintendent admitted to inadvertently employing girls under the age of fourteen, which was against the law.

Macdonald's workers began at seven in the morning and left at six in the evening, stopping only for an hour to eat. The meal was typically taken at the workbenches, and hot water for tea came in a big pail. There were spittoons for workers who chewed tobacco themselves. In the shipping department, and only rarely, they might work until nine or ten in the evening, preparing the goods for delivery.

Each year, overseers imposed fines of $150 to $300 on workers, for infractions of various rules, and these fines were donated to the Montreal General Hospital. The fines were only a tiny fraction of the wages that he paid out, and they were imposed essentially for raucous behaviour, damage to equipment, or carelessness. Names appeared on a blackboard with the pertinent misdemeanours and fines, and they were erased when the fines were paid. This was the limit of Macdonald's discipline, in contrast to say that of J.M. Fortier, a prominent manufacturer of cigars, who admitted to beating apprentices with a ruler or his hands or even a mould.[35]

Macdonald testified further that he paid out more than $200,000 annually to his workers. He paid them in little numbered tin boxes so as to avoid the expense of envelopes. Once a week, the paymaster and two assistants would bring the boxes out on a big tray and pour coins out into outstretched, tightly cupped palms. The wages of boys, twelve to eighteen, varied from $1.50 to $5.50 a week, and those of men from $6 to $8.50, but this was the average over the year and Macdonald actually reduced wages in the fall. To those, like his petitioners in October 1887, who pleaded that their winter expenses were greater than their summer expenses, Macdonald was not sympathetic. "When they have good wages they should save for the short period" was his counsel. There were actually more workers in winter than in summer, although the work was lighter, and "we have got to thin them out." Women and girls made from $2.50 to $3.75 a week, if they worked "by day." Those who worked "by the piece" could make between $5 and $15.

Macdonald set his wages according to supply and demand. When asked whether he worked "for charity," he replied "I do not sir. I am in business for the purpose of business," for making money. When challenged on why he was charging higher prices for his tobacco than in the previous spring (apparently that of 1886) and yet paying lower salaries than then, he replied that some of his raw material now cost 50 per cent more than then, and that he was selling it for below its cost, even apart from charging nothing for the labour, such was the current "condition of the trade."

Macdonald confessed that he had been "very desirous" of permitting his employees to share in his profits apart from the wages they were making. But he could not see "how it is going to be brought about with any degree of safety to the capitalist." He gave bonuses on occasion – "I have no partners in the business, so that I may be generous sometimes – when I can afford it."

One of Macdonald's great achievements was to subcontract the work of manufacture to bench-owners, although to what extent he adopted this method from American or other models is unclear. The benches resembled picnic tables, and each occupied about six square feet. The bench-owners would in turn hire workmates, called in Macdonald's testimony to the royal commission "stumpers, stringers and coverers," to form teams, and about half of all of Macdonald's workers were in the bench system. It was the wages of the bench-owners, or subcontractors, that Macdonald reduced in the fall. The bench-owners then reduced the wages of their own workmates. If the bench-owners did not pay their workmates at all, Macdonald, himself or through his superintendent would intervene, threatening to dismiss the non-paying bench-owners.

Macdonald sold raw leaf to the bench-owners, and they established, by contract, what he would pay them for the finished product. He was not responsible for productivity or spoilage, for rates of production, or for hiring and firing the workmates of bench-owners. In the 1880s his approximately 180 bench-owners each employed three or four colleagues or helpers, and he typically met them only occasionally. The bench-owners competed with one another and even sold finished product from one bench to another when the market price was rising, thus also making profits from one another. In a recession, bench-owners might form partnerships and reduce the number of their helpers. Macdonald's works became a virtual laboratory of capitalist enterprise and were completely consistent with his own desire to be as independent as possible, of his own workers as well as of his competitors and his customers.[36]

## MACDONALD'S PRODUCTS AND THE MAINTENANCE OF HIS BRAND

Very early in his business, in about 1864–65, Macdonald found that his products were spawning imitators. Like American tobacco manufacturers, he realized that it was very important to preserve his trademark and name, as brand loyalty was essential to his success. He appointed Forester, Moir and Company as his exclusive agents in Montreal and broadcast their appointment in full-page ads.[37] It was probably at about this time that he began to insert little tin hearts into his plugs, and his product became known throughout the country as the tobacco "with a heart."

The inspiration for his tin heart may have been the Scottish heart brooches that were very common at the time, inspired by the heart brooches made by silversmith Robert Cruikshank (who had come to Montreal in 1773) and exchanged with Native people for skins.[38] As late as 1876, when he discovered that competitors were using the names of his Penners and Defiance brands, Macdonald issued a warning to consumers: "Retail Grocers and Tobacconists are warned to be on their guard against purchasing a very low grade of Tobacco having tin stamps upon the plugs, and falsely represented as being of my manufacture. All my best Tobaccos have a tin stamp on every plug, with my name and address on each stamp. Those who prefer my make of Tobacco can only be certain they are getting it by seeing my name on the stamp."[39] This stamp was his registered trademark.

Macdonald's products varied over time, increasing but sometimes also decreasing in number. In 1869 he advertised British Consols made from fancy bright tobacco; Britannia from bright; Royal Arms from mahogany; and Navy, Victoria, Diamond, and Prince of Wales from dark sweet chewing. By 1872 he had significantly added to the variety of his packaging and product line. Fancy bright still yielded British Consols, but ordinary bright could also be medium bright, for example. In 1875–76 his products included Navy 3s and 6s, Solace (Britannia, Royal Arms, and Extra), Victoria 4s and 8s, Little Favorite 12s, Diamond 12s, Prince of Wales 12s, Navy (Nelson, Short and Long), British

*Above* : The Macdonald
heart (MSF)

*Right*: Macdonald
Tobacco trademark (MSF)

Consols, and Twin Gold Bars, among others. The numbers (e.g., "3s") referred to how many plugs there were in each package. His trade names had become very patriotically British. In 1878, in contrast to the American Uncle Sam, Daniel Webster, and Diadem of Old Virginia brands, he offered British Consols, Queens, Viceregals, Chancellors, Britannia, Royal Arms, Nelson Navy, Crown, and Prince of Wales products. He did not restrict himself to British names, however, as he also offered Napoleon tobacco and products with such evocative names as Laurel, Brier, Ingots, Honeysuckle, Brunette, and Lovely.

Macdonald continued to develop new products, and by 1885 he was making more bright than dark tobacco. Evidence suggests that he tended to carry a sizable inventory and certainly did not engage in what would be later called "just in time" production. Table 3 offers a glimpse into the size of his production and its costs.

Macdonald Tobacco tin, Prince of Wales Chewing Tobacco
(McCord Museum M2002.69.1798)

Macdonald Tobacco tin, Pilot Pipe Tobacco (MSF)

Table 3: Data for the Week Ending 1 June 1876 and the Week Ending 5 November 1885, Showing the Difference between Product Lines and the Trend to Dark Tobacco

PRODUCTS GENERATED AND THEIR COSTS OF PRODUCTION
IN THE WEEK ENDING 1 JUNE 1876

|  | WEIGHT | COSTS |
|---|---|---|
| Favorites | 11,299 lbs | $197 |
| Solace No. 1 | 6,441 lbs | $160 |
| Short Bright Eights | 5,775 lbs | $129 |
| Gold Bars | 4,209 lbs | $126 |
| Consols | 2,047 lbs | $61 |
| Recovered work | 1,908 lbs | $13 |
| Scrap | 6,281 lbs | $106 |

AVERAGE PRODUCTION, APPARENTLY IN THOUSANDS OF POUNDS,
IN THE WEEK ENDING 5 NOVEMBER 1885

| Dark tobacco | | Bright tobacco | |
|---|---|---|---|
| Prince of Wales | 3.76 | Honeysuckle | 15.02 |
| Favorites | 6.49 | Napoleon | 12.01 |
| Favorites Double | 10.27 | Solace no. 2 | 7.72 |
| Crown | 6.21 | Solace Double | 13.91 |
| Dark Navy 4s | 11.12 | Pilot 8s | 8.74 |
| Dark Navy 12s | 9.05 | Brier 6s | 14.56 |
| Dark Twist | 2.33 | Laurel 3s | 11.18 |
| Dark scrap | 4.70 | Recovered work | 6.94 |
| Total dark average | 5.44 | Total bright average | 11.60 |

## MACDONALD'S SUPPLY AND DISTRIBUTION CHANNELS

The manufacture of tobacco was only one stage in the journey from the cultivation of the leaf to its consumption. Typically, the tobacco went from the farmer to the factor or agent; from the factor or agent to the manufacturer; from the manufacturer to the jobber or wholesale grocer; from the jobber or wholesale grocer to the retailer; and from the retailer – finally – to the consumer. Until 1858 Macdonald sold only imported manufactured tobacco and only as a commission agent, which was like a jobber, and he bought his stock from American factors. He subsequently sold his own manufactured tobacco, made from imported raw-leaf tobacco, to jobbers or wholesalers.

Table 4: Order Book for the Week Ending 7 June 1876

1   L. Chaput Fils & Co., City,* 40 cads* Argyle Solace
2   Harvey Stuart & Co., Hamilton, 50 cads Solace
3   Wm. Ramsay & Co., Toronto, 25 Solace, 25 Edwards Solace, 25 Bright Navy 3s, 50 Solace
    3 (all cads)
4   J. Rattray & Co., City, 11 boxes Prince of Wales 50 cads Mahogany Napoleon
5   Lord Magor & Mum, City, 20 boxes Defiance 10s, for export
6   Richard Dunbar, Toronto, 100 cads Solace no. 2, 10 boxes Prince of Wales no. 2
7   Geo. Watt & Sons, Brantford, 25 boxes Prince of Wales no. 1
8   J. Rattray & Co., City, 50 cads Solace 2, 22 cads Sunnyside Solace
9   R. Blackburn, New Edinburgh via Prescott, 25 cads L. Favorite, 25 cads Solace no. 2, 10
    cads Solace
10  Jardine & Co., St. John, NB, order of 22 May cancelled
11  Edw. Adams & Co., London, 28 cads Nelson Navy 6s
12  Hossack Woods & Co., Quebec, Richelieu Line, 20 boxes Harpers 10s
13  Vaughan Clarke & Co., St. Stephen, NB, GTR, 25 boxes Crown 12s
14  Sinclair, Jack & Co., City, 25 boxes Prince of Wales no. 1
15  Robertson & Lightbound, City, 25 boxes Prince of Wales no. 1

*(continued on next page)*

When Macdonald began his business in Montreal, it is likely that he sold to any buyer he could find. According to one story, in the mid-1850s he used to go from shop to shop with a basket of the manufactured tobacco he was importing. When his factory opened in 1858, he probably did not face much direct competition initially. In the mid-1860s, using Forester, Moir as his exclusive agents in Montreal, he developed a network of wholesalers to distribute his products, almost exclusively in eastern Canada. Those outside Montreal he probably found through commission agents.

By March 1869 he had ninety-one distributors, including thirty in Montreal, six in Quebec City, ten in Halifax, nine in Saint John, New Brunswick, and the rest in Ontario. By 1874 he had distributors in Newfoundland and Labrador and sales in the United States and the British Isles, although sales outside eastern Canada were to remain a minor part of his total sales.[40] He resolutely refused to sell directly to retailers, except for very large ones, and he maintained this stand even while refusing to enter into a price-fixing scheme with his own wholesalers. Table 4 conveys the nature of his trade over one week. The few retailers that he did serve, and only in his later years, had to buy 1,000 pounds of tobacco a week, and settlement was by either cash or sight draft, payable within ten days. He did not generally trust cheques, and he took them only if they had been marked as accepted or certified by their issuing bank.

16 A. Yum & Co., Kingston, 15 boxes Prince of Wales no. 1, 10 boxes Johnson 10s

17 Edw. Adams & Co., London, 25 boxes Prince of Wales no. 1, 50 boxes Prince of Wales no. 2

18 Lord Magor & Mum 50 boxes Peimers (?) 100s, 58 boxes Defiance 100s, 58 boxes Defiance 2 ½ 100s

19 A. Shannon & Co., City, 50 cads A S and 600 Solace

20 Brown, Routh & Co., Hamilton, 20 boxes Prince of Wales no. 2, 50 cads L. Favorite

21 E. Morrison & Co., Halifax, 25 boxes Crown 12s, no. 1 and 25 boxes Crown 12s, no. 2

22 Logan, Lindsay & Co., St. John, N B, 45 boxes Crown 12s, no. 2, 25 half boxes Mahogany Navy, 10 half boxes Rich Dark, 30 cads Mahogany Napoleon

23 A. Cusson, City, 50 cads Nelson Navy

24 Perkins Inco & Co., Toronto, 25 boxes Prince of Wales no. 2

25 Jno. Ross & Co., Quebec, boat, 25 boxes Prince of Wales no. 2

26 J. Rattray & Co., City, 25 boxes Prince of Wales no. 2

27 Robertson & Lightbound, City, 25 cads Chancellors 3s (Fancy Navy)

28 Nerlich & Co., Toronto, 25 cads L. Favorite, no. 1, 30 cads Solace no. 2

30 Hossack Woods & Co., Quebec, boat, 28 cads, Solace no. 2, 28 cads Solace

31 A. Beattie & Co., St. Marys, 30 cads L. Favorite no. 1, 15 cads Nelson Navy,

32 F. McHardy & Co., Toronto, 25 cads Solace no. 1, 50 cads Solace no. 2, 25 cads Twin Gold Bar, 25 cads Nelson Navy no. 2, 25 cads Queens 3s

33 Geo. Robertson & Son, Kingston 20 cads L. Favorite no. 1, 10 cads Nelson Navy, 10 cads Mahogany Napoleon, 6 cads British Consols no. 1

34 Kingan & Kinloch, City, 25 cads Solace no. 2, 10 cads Twin Gold Bar

35 Jas. McCussie & Co., Guelph, 25 boxes Prince of Wales no. 1

36 J. Rattray & Co., City, 25 cads Nelson Navy, 25 cads Twin Gold Bar, 25 cads Solace no. 1, 25 cads Pall Mall Solace

37. Lawson Harrington & Co., Halifax, 58 boxes Crown 12s.

---

\* "Cads" are caddies and "City" is Montreal. Caddies and boxes varied in weight from manufacturer to manufacturer. In the case of Macdonald Tobacco, a caddy was about 20 pounds and a box ranged from 100 to 110 pounds.

Note: Of the thirty-seven entries above, one was for a cancelled order, four were from J. Rattray & Co., and two were from Lord Magor & Mum. There were therefore thirty different wholesalers that placed orders with Macdonald in that week.

As almost the first in the field, Macdonald was free to find his agents and to develop a market for his product. He was buying his raw leaf from New York factors and then from agents in the South, but he tried to keep the distribution of his manufactured product simple.[41] As Canadians increased their tobacco consumption, intermediaries emerged to serve them, notably wholesale grocers and commercial travellers. Macdonald liked neither of these groups, and the two groups did not like each other, but his chief concern was with his competition. Keeping things simple gave him an advantage. Macdonald insisted that his wholesalers pay him in cash or by certified cheque, as he paid all his own suppliers immediately, in cash. Consequently, he had no accounts receivable, no accounts payable, and no bad debts – an enviable position to be in.

## MACDONALD'S COMPETITION, 1874–1885

Through the years, Macdonald faced competition. By the end of his career, he was said to have fought off about twenty competitors altogether. Testifying to the McTavish Royal Commission on the Tobacco Trade in 1902, he professed not to remember many of them, but he recalled McMullen & Adams (later Adams Tobacco); Porcheron; Paegels & Ferguson; and Moore – all of Montreal – as well as Scales of Toronto; Globe of Windsor; and Mayflower (Smith) of Halifax. Beyond these, there were tobacco firms in Quebec that Macdonald did not mention, although to the extent that they made cigarettes or cigars, they were not in direct competition with him. Those that used Canadian leaf were also not direct competitors. There had been even less Canadian leaf used by Canadian manufacturers in 1873 than in 1868 – only 201,782 pounds as opposed to 7,767,437 pounds of American leaf.[42] Macdonald denied ever having tried to buy out his competitors, although he admitted buying machinery from failed businesses to prevent it falling into the hands of new competitors.

Macdonald had competitors from the time he opened his business in 1859. The family firm of Tuckett Tobacco of Hamilton had started up two years earlier, but its market seems to have been largely in Canada West, which became Ontario in 1867. Thus, although it endured well into the twentieth century, it was not a direct competitor of Macdonald's except in Canada West. In about 1870, when it was known as Tuckett and Billings, this company began manufacturing T & B Myrtle Navy plug tobacco, a product that was highly thought of even overseas, made as it was from the American leaf of high quality that Macdonald favoured. But Macdonald shipped very little to overseas markets, and so even this product did not compete with his, and in any case it sold for 88 cents a pound (in 1916), about four times what Macdonald was charging.[43]

Distribution was not easy, especially in the winter to far-flung places, and consequently tobacco manufacturers sprang up in Halifax, Quebec City, and elsewhere. But to compete seriously with Macdonald, these businesses had to manufacture products very similar to his, namely tobacco for chewing and for pipe-smoking. As we have seen, cigarettes were almost unknown, even in the United States, until about 1870, and they did not become popular in Canada until the 1890s. Cigars were popular, and Quebec boasted many cigar makers, but Macdonald's products required a much larger investment in plant. Until 1874 he seems to have been essentially unchallenged within his own territory centred in Montreal.

In the 1870s and 1880s Adams Tobacco (formerly McMullen & Adams) of Montreal made the most serious attempt – to that point – to unseat Macdonald Tobacco as the leader in chewing and pipe tobacco. It obtained its charter in January 1874, its directors including Sir Hugh Allan, John H.R. Molson, and William Angus, as well as James L. Adams and Edgar McMullen. In December of that year, it cheekily invited Macdonald to a ball to celebrate its start in business. The principal directors were rich and well known to Macdonald, and they presumably thought that they could emulate his success by selling the same products from the same city but expanding farther afield. Adams doubled the size of its plant in its first year and invested heavily in the newest machinery. It advertised "Virginia Home Spun" tobacco, a plug that – through a spinning process – became more pliant than other plugs.

Adams appeared at an awkward time for Macdonald. The duty on imported leaf, such as Macdonald was buying, rose from none in 1868, when it had to be bonded on importation, to 20 cents a pound in 1874, although it would fall to 12 cents in 1883.[44] Macdonald was now, however, in such a dominant position that he probably felt confident enough to shift the risk of import duties onto his customers, essentially wholesalers. They had to collect his manufactured product at his bonded warehouse and pay the import duty and excise tax on it there before taking collection; Macdonald refused to deliver to them, although he would arrange transport out of Montreal. Even in the face of competition from Adams, Macdonald managed to sell more tobacco to the rest of Canada in July 1874 than all his Montreal competitors combined, 170,414 pounds compared with 83,387 pounds. In the previous month, June, he had shipped only 79,116 pounds out of Montreal, while his Montreal competitors had shipped 98,013.[45]

Macdonald seems to have remained, though with some difficulty, supreme in his product lines in, for example, the first quarter of 1876, ending on 31 March (see Tables 5, 6, and 7).[46] He was still buying more foreign leaf than his closest competitor, Adams, although he manufactured less Cavendish tobacco in this quarter. Yet, while Macdonald was buying more than Adams in the first quarter of 1876, on an annualized basis he was manufacturing less than he had been in 1873. Adams by contrast was producing both more than Macdonald in 1876 and more than the company itself had produced in 1873.

Although well capitalized, however, Adams did not survive much beyond 1885, officially winding up its business on 5 February 1886 on the petition of the Merchants' Bank of Canada. The reasons for Adams's demise are unclear, but Macdonald appears to have undercut its prices throughout its existence. See Table 8 for comparative prices of the two companies' major products. The backers

Table 5: Comparative Costs in $, First Quarter 1876

| MANUFACTURER | FOREIGN LEAF | LICORICE | SUGAR | GUM | TOTAL |
|---|---|---|---|---|---|
| Macdonald | 622,556 | 99,760 | 340,116 | 2,200 | 758,632 |
| P&F | 73,715 | 1,942 | – | 175 | 75,832 |
| Adams | 596,593 | 57,683 | 19,190 | – | 673,466 |
| Smith | 41,350 | 14,043 | 12,568 | – | 67,961 |

(P&F = Paegels & Ferguson of Montreal; Adams = Adams of Montreal; Smith = Smith of Halifax)

Table 6: Comparative Values in $ of Cavendish Tobacco Manufactured, Tariff Paid on the Raw Leaf Used in Its Manufacture, Excise Paid on Its Sale (Ex Factory), and Amounts Warehoused, in the First Quarter of 1876

| MANUFACTURER | CAVENDISH | DUTY PAID[*] | DUTY EX FACTORY | WAREHOUSED |
|---|---|---|---|---|
| Macdonald | 374,949 | 27,556 | 5,511.20 | 347,393 |
| P&F | 43,259 | 16,568 | 3,313.60 | 26,691 |
| Adams | 393,189 | 75,168 | 15,033.70 | 318,020 |
| Smith | 61,233 | 19,779 | 3,955.80 | 41,454 |

[*] "Duty" refers to both the "tariff" imposed on imports (or exports), and the "excise" imposed on sales within the country, and in this table the first duty refers to the tariff paid on raw leaf by the manufacturers, and the second duty refers to the excise paid by them on delivery of manufactured goods from their factories.

Note: The extreme discrepancy between the total duties paid by these companies may be due to clerical error.

Table 7: Comparative Performance during Economic Depression: Cavendish Production Figures in $ for 1873 and 1876

| MANUFACTURER | 1873 | 1876 ANNUALIZED | DIFFERENCE |
|---|---|---|---|
| Macdonald | 2,425,181 | 1,499,796 | -925,385 |
| McMullen Adams | 1,245,424 | 1,572,756 | +327,332 |
| Smith | 372,997 | 244,932 | -128,065 |
| Total production | 4,043,602 | 3,317,484 | -726,188 |

Source: MSF/WCM, folder 028.

Note: McMullen Adams was the predecessor to Adams Tobacco, and P&F figures are unavailable for 1873, possibly because it was no longer in business.

Table 8: Comparative Prices between Major Macdonald and Adams Products, 1874–85 (defined on 2 July 1877; cents per pound; all figures approximate)

A. BLACK CHEWING TOBACCOS

| Adams price list dated: | Sept. 7/74 | Aug. 26/76 | Mar. 2/85 |
|---|---|---|---|
| Challenge | 24 | 18 | 16.5 |
| Sensation | 23 | 17 | – |
| Princess Louise | 22 | 17 | – |
| Sailors' Solace | 24 | 19 | – |
| Sailors' Solace Extra | 25 | 20 | – |
| Navy, quarter pounds and sixes | 24 | 19 | – |
| Black Hawk | – | – | 9.5 |
| Adams averages | 23.6 | 18.3 | 13 |

| Macdonald price lists dated: | Mar. 21/74 | Jan. 22/76 | Mar. 2/85 |
|---|---|---|---|
| Nelson or Prince of Wales Navy | 20 | 17.5 to 19.5 | 19.5 |
| Navy | 20.5 | 17.5 to 19.5 | – |
| Victoria | 20.5 | – | – |
| Little Favorite | 20.5 | 17.5 to 19.5 | – |
| Prince of Wales | 17 to 21 | 14 to 19 | 17.5 |
| Macdonald averages | 19.9 | 17.5 | 18.5 |

*(continued on next page)*

of Adams Tobacco bore Macdonald no grudge for his success. Indeed Andrew Allan, the brother of Sir Hugh, acknowledged his victory by inviting him to join the board of the Merchants' Bank, an offer Macdonald declined.

Macdonald did not have long to gloat. In May 1886 he bid $40,000 for Adams's equipment, plant, and charter in order to forestall competition, but he lost to the Empire Tobacco Company of Granby.[47] This failure, as he confessed to L.N.P. Landrum, his agent in Louisville, caused him worry. By February 1888, however, he recorded that his competition had not "accomplished anything worth speaking of."[48] Empire used Canadian as well as American leaf, so at least part of its business was not in direct competition with Macdonald's all-American-leaf products. Furthermore, as the demand for tobacco was growing, Empire was able to find new markets.

An increase in the tariff against raw American leaf – justified by the need to protect the Canadian tobacco farmer – could have in itself tipped the balance against Macdonald. In 1884 La Compagnie de Tabac de Joliette began manufacturing Canadian leaf exclusively for smoking tobacco, and in the following year D. Ritchie and the American Cigarette Company did the same in Montreal.

B. BRIGHT SMOKING-TOBACCOS

| Adams price list dated: | Sept. 7/74 | Aug. 26/76 | Mar. 2/85 |
|---|---|---|---|
| Rough 'n Ready | 37 | 32 (50 lbs) | 40 (25 lbs) |
| Crown Jewel Navy | – | 32 (7 lbs) | 32 (10 lbs) |
| British Navy | – | 27 (18 lbs) | – |
| Solaces | 23 to 45 | 21 to 28 (18 lbs) | 18 to 24 (20 lbs) |
| Adams averages | 35 | 28 | 28.5 |
| | | | |
| Macdonald price lists dated: | Mar. 21/74 | Jan. 22/76 | Mar. 2/85 |
| British Consols | 36 to 44 | 32 to 38 | 35 |
| Various brights | 23 to 28 | 21 to 32 | 22 to 30 |
| Solaces | 20 to 25 | 19 to 22.5 | 15.5 to 28 |
| Macdonald averages | 29.3 | 27.4 | 26.1 |

*Source:* MSF/WCM, folder 040.

Notes:

Macdonald's prices were lower than those of Adams in 1874, 1876, and 1885 except for black tobacco in 1885. Although these figures are based on incomplete data and rough averages, the conclusion is consistent except for 1885, when Macdonald was charging only half a cent more per pound for black chewing tobaccos.

The data here are from price lists in the Macdonald papers and have been coordinated as closely as possible. Apart from the facts that only two lists coincide in date, the products listed are only approximately the same, and only rough average prices are calculated. Adams manufactured other products for which Macdonald had no equivalent, and only approximately comparable products are listed here.

Samuel Davis, a Montreal cigar manufacturer, bought but did not amalgamate with Ritchie in 1888. Aside from manufacturers of both Canadian and American pipe and chewing tobacco, there were long-established Montreal firms (Landau & Cormack, for example) that specialized in cigarettes made from Turkish and Egyptian blends. Louis Grothé and Samuel Davis made their cigars in Montreal, but such was the diversity and extent of the consumer demand for tobacco that these manufacturers were hardly competitors to Macdonald at all.[49]

Notwithstanding his success, Macdonald could never sleep easily in the face of competition. Within a decade an even more formidable challenger than Adams would emerge in the form of the American Tobacco Company. Nor was this the only kind of challenge he had to face. A fire at his plant in June 1895 resulted in the deaths of four of his employees. While he was relieved to find only the roof of his main building and one floor destroyed, he must have seen the litigation that followed as unwanted publicity, preoccupied as he had been since 1858 with preventing fire in his works. Altogether he lost $100,000 in property, including 1,000 pounds of manufactured tobacco damaged by water, but he was back in business within a few weeks.[50]

There were various public inquiries to respond to as well, notably into relations between labour and capital and into exclusive contracts in the tobacco trade. In 1885 Macdonald's own exclusive distributors, the wholesale grocers, began to pressure him to join in a scheme to fix or at least to maintain prices in the face of price-cutting by retailers.

## THE WHOLESALE GROCERS' PRICE-FIXING PLAN, 1883–1910

Macdonald liked to attribute his success to his continued exclusive use of wholesalers to distribute his products, in contrast to Adams and then Empire, which both used commercial travellers.[51] Nevertheless, after 1885 one of his most serious annoyances came from his partners in distribution, the wholesalers.

In 1902 Macdonald testified to the Royal Commission on the Tobacco Trade that he had always used wholesale grocers exclusively in the distribution of his products, except to the extent that some of them were also retailers.[52] He also admitted that some retailers "buy from me," although he did not "sell" to them. Here he was referring to tobacconists "who job a good deal and do retail some times." He had never dealt directly with commercial travellers or, until late in his career, with those who were exclusively retailers. He had never "entertained the idea" of any "exclusive contract system." He found that distributing through retailers "would be costly and excessively troublesome."

Wholesalers depended on a slice of the profits to survive, but in the mid-1880s they were finding themselves undercut by commercial travellers, who did not hesitate to offer the retailers (their customers) "loss leaders," products they sold at a loss to induce retailers to buy other goods they had on offer. So thin was the wholesalers' margin that they also undercut one another. To combat this practice, a large majority of wholesalers banded together to fix a common wholesale price for a given product, hoping at least to squeeze out those undercutting it among their own number. They still faced competition from the individual travellers, but they hoped that with their unified front that threat could be contained. As we have seen, one of Macdonald's chief advantages was that he had been able to establish links with wholesalers before any other significant tobacco manufacturer. He had created customer loyalty through the early distribution of his product, and thus the wholesalers were now much more dependent on him than he on them. He calculated the prices that he would charge the wholesalers on the basis of his study of the comparative production figures, from month to month, that appear to have been published in a guide called the *Blue Book*.

Macdonald's unwavering belief in real competition, together with his resolute independence, is evident in his refusal to help these wholesalers, even though his trade depended on them. He firmly believed that he was responsible only for his own profits, just as his bench-owners and wholesalers were responsible only for theirs. That his wholesalers were facing reduced margins was not his responsibility, nor was it even within his control. Because Macdonald's products were so popular, the wholesalers had no choice but to stock them, giving Macdonald little reason to help them with their price-fixing, even if he wanted to. Manufacturers of other products, from sugar to starch, felt that they could not afford to resist the wholesalers. Macdonald's unique resistance, as well as his ultimate triumph, suggests how strong his market position must have been.

The Montreal Wholesale Grocers' Association began in 1883 as a local branch of the Dominion Wholesale Grocers' Association, based in Toronto, which had been established in the previous year and included some of Macdonald's biggest customers, such as Hudon Hébert and Lightbound, Ralston & Co.[53] The Dominion Wholesale Grocers' Association sought to fix the terms and discounts on invoices in order to eliminate price-cutting by commercial travellers. It also hoped to set the maximum prices at which retailers might sell their goods and thus to eliminate price-cutting by wholesalers not among their members. The vast majority of the wholesalers in eastern Canada probably joined the association (renamed the Dominion Wholesale Grocers' Guild in 1884),[54] as did 95 per cent of the grocers in Montreal and all the manufacturers of tobacco, except for Macdonald, in eastern Canada.

For two years, the wholesalers struggled to convince Macdonald to conform. But by June 1886 even the secretary of the Dominion Wholesale Grocers' Guild admitted that although price-fixing was working "like a charm in the West," Macdonald had stymied it in Quebec. The secretary did not think that a proposal made by the Montreal branch – to sell only Macdonald's tobacco or to boycott his tobacco to coerce him to conform, a tactic that had worked in Hamilton a few years before – was "practicable."[55]

What the wholesalers wanted from the manufacturers was their commitment to sell to neither undercutting wholesalers nor commercial travellers directly. Macdonald was willing to refuse to sell to commercial travellers, as this had always been his policy, but he was not willing to refuse to do business with undercutting wholesalers. The wholesalers feared that if Macdonald sold directly to even a few undercutting wholesalers, their price-maintenance system would be threatened. All the other manufacturers, even Tuckett in Ontario, reached agreements with the wholesalers, but with Macdonald – the biggest manufacturer in the country – refusing to comply (he could always sell his popular product directly to retailers if the wholesalers chose to boycott him), the wholesalers could not but feel insecure.

They pleaded their case with him early in November 1885, and in a "characteristic" letter, he refused "to take part in such combination," news that they greeted with general "disapprobation." As they confessed a few weeks later, "We still have fresh in our memories the unsuccessful issue of the *Tobacco Memorial* from which we had hoped so much, and our affection will not warm toward Mr. W.C. McDonald, whose notable indifference to our concern has left us still in the mire and full of discontent as to our profits on Tobacco."[56]

By as early as May 1886, the Montreal Wholesale Grocers' Association was beginning to lose members. Ransom Forbes, most probably a founding member, withdrew because the renegade wholesaler J.A. Mathewson was offering Forbes's customers more liberal terms, in credit and discounts, and hoisting the association on its own petard by citing its inflated and discriminatory pricing. Later in that year, major wholesalers in Kingston and Deseronto withdrew from the Dominion association, particularly from the price-fixing agreement with respect to tobacco. In the following year Macdonald was still holding to his position, doggedly refusing to apply pressure on a Montreal wholesaler named Leroux, who seems to have been selling at a cent or two below the price fixed by the association.

Beginning towards the end of 1887, however, Macdonald relented for about a year and applied pressure, on behalf of the Dominion association, on the recalcitrant wholesalers Rathbun of Deseronto and Fortier of Sherbrooke, as well as on two other firms. Nevertheless, by refusing for the most part to cooperate with the wholesalers in their price-fixing from 1885 to 1897, and again from 1898 to 1902, Macdonald ensured that a good part of the tobacco trade was beyond the reach of the scheme for sixteen years. To the extent that the tobacco agreement that the Montreal association had with other wholesalers and manufacturers tended to fall apart, it was inferior to the agreement that the association reached with all the sugar refiners between 1887 and 1892, when sugar made up 40 per cent of their sales. The association reached similar agreements over wooden ware, molasses, rice, and starch in 1890–91.

In the tobacco trade, no one but Macdonald and a few fearless and rebellious retailers and wholesalers, notably Mathewson, defied the Montreal association. A select committee of the House of Commons on the restraint of trade convened in 1888, but neither it nor anti-combines legislation in 1889 could prevent the Dominion Wholesale Grocers' Guild from enforcing the agreements reached in 1887–92 on other products. George Lightbound, of Lightbound, Ralston, testified in 1888 against the agreement between the sugar refiners and the guild. But then it was revealed that he had been a founding member of the Montreal association and was aggrieved only because he did not want to be bound by guild restrictions west of Montreal, although he was quite willing to accept them in other directions.[57]

Macdonald had neither time nor need for such hypocrisy. His dominant position in the market allowed him to ignore his wholesale critics, but his refusal to join or even to support tacitly a monopoly or oligopoly confirmed more generally his deep-seated belief in open and fair competition among manufacturers as well as wholesalers. In this he was almost but not quite unique. J.A. Mathewson in Montreal and Joseph Flavelle in Toronto were two others.

Buttressing him, however, was the retailers' organized opposition to the wholesalers. In an 1890 meeting between the Toronto Wholesale Grocers' Guild and the Retail Grocers' Association, the retailers took issue with the wholesalers for not discriminating between large and small buyers in their price-fixing, and argued that large wholesale buyers of tobacco in particular should receive better terms.[58] The two groups managed to reach an accommodation at this meeting, but the agreement fell apart in 1892 when James Lumbers, a wholesaler in Toronto, induced other wholesalers to leave the guild, thus breaking its stranglehold, and convinced the sugar refiners to abandon their agreement with the guild as well.[59] The guild continued to apply strong-arm tactics against its remaining members, but it was too weak to threaten Macdonald, who in 1894 publicly declared to all his wholesale distributors that they might sell to retailers at whatever price they desired.

### MACDONALD'S CONCERNS WITH SECURITY OF SUPPLY, 1885–1895

In addition to securing the distribution of his product through established, if sometimes exasperated, wholesalers, Macdonald took steps to stabilize his supplies of American leaf that his agents bought in bulk from tobacco agents in the South. By the 1880s if not before, he had consolidated the storage of his raw leaf in warehouses in the United States. Augustine, as noted earlier, may have bought leaf for Macdonald in Louisville beginning in 1865, but he stopped these purchases in about 1875, when he moved to New York. It is unclear who bought for Macdonald afterwards, but at some stage his agent became L.P.N. Landrum of Louisville. Surviving data suggest that about 6 per cent of the American leaf arrived in Montreal via Halifax. The rest must have come directly by rail.

Macdonald divided his raw leaf into Western Production and Virginia Production. The Western tobacco probably came from Louisville, where Chiles & Campbell & Company and then Landrum seem to have been his agents. The Virginia tobacco came from Danville and Lynchburg. Table 9 sums up the costs of each kind of leaf as well as the amounts bought over specific periods in 1876 and 1877.

Table 9: The Cost of Leaf and the Value of Stock in 1886, after the End of Competition from Adams

FOR NOVEMBER 1886

*A. Western production (black leaf) from Kentucky and Missouri*

| ITEM BOUGHT | POUNDS | AVERAGE COST ($) | TOTAL BOUGHT ($) |
|---|---|---|---|
| Raw leaf | 384,940 | 5.75 | 22,146.01 |

| PRODUCT MADE | POUNDS | AVERAGE COST ($) | TOTAL VALUE ($) |
|---|---|---|---|
| Pilot | 24,021 | 6.01 | 1,443.63 |
| Solace | 60,024 | 5.92 | 3,550.96 |
| Twist | 9,903 | 5.39 | 534.16 |
| Prince of Wales | 220,849 | 5.63 | 12,432.70 |
| Napoleon | 41,811 | 6.53 | 2,731.47 |
| Honey Suckle | 14,186 | 8.50 | 1,209.71 |
| Scrap | 5,005 | 4.86 | 243.38 |

*B. Virginia production (bright leaf)*

| ITEM BOUGHT | POUNDS | AVERAGE COST ($) | TOTAL BOUGHT ($) |
|---|---|---|---|
| Raw leaf | 140,044 | 13.53 | 18,950.09 |

| PRODUCT MADE | POUNDS | AVERAGE COST ($) | TOTAL VALUE ($) |
|---|---|---|---|
| Consols etc. | 247 | 51.65 | 127.60 |
| Brier etc. | 7,119 | 39.84 | 2,836.11 |
| Pilot | 12,508 | 28.25 | 3,534.35 |
| Fillers | 12,436 | 11.46 | 1,426.16 |

FROM 1 JANUARY TO 30 NOVEMBER 1886

*A. Western production (black leaf)*

| ITEM BOUGHT | POUNDS | AVERAGE COST ($) | TOTAL BOUGHT ($) |
|---|---|---|---|
| Raw leaf | 4,125,041 | 5.88 | 242,478.31 |

| PRODUCT MADE | POUNDS | AVERAGE COST ($) | TOTAL VALUE ($) |
|---|---|---|---|
| Pilot | 316,083 | 6.11 | 19,309.10 |
| Solace | 770,468 | 5.97 | 45,997.87 |
| Twist | 116,528 | 5.86 | 6,829.23 |
| Prince of Wales | 2,433,860 | 5.64 | 137,318.65 |
| Napoleon | 300,308 | 6.82 | 20,492.36 |
| Honey Suckle | 137,588 | 8.63 | 11,869.72 |
| Scrap | 14,859 | 4.45 | 661.38 |

*(continued on next page)*

*B. Virginia production (bright leaf)*

| ITEM BOUGHT | POUNDS | AVERAGE COST ($) | TOTAL BOUGHT ($) |
|---|---|---|---|
| Raw leaf | 1,440,563 | 14.11 | 203,232.63 |

| PRODUCT MADE | POUNDS | AVERAGE COST ($) | TOTAL VALUE ($) |
|---|---|---|---|
| Consols, etc. | 3,610 | 58.03 | 2,094.99 |
| Brier, etc. | 78,405 | 40.12 | 31,458.58 |
| Pilot | 129,660 | 26.35 | 34,116.65 |
| Fillers | 164,919 | 13.49 | 22,246.91 |

*The following figures appear in Macdonald's stock book as of 1 December 1886:*

| ITEM | POUNDS | AVERAGE COST ($) | TOTAL VALUE ($) |
|---|---|---|---|
| Black leaf | 2,214,246 | 5.91 | 130,755.75 |
| Honey Suckle | 128,030 | 9.00 | 11,524.77 |
| Med. Bt. Wrap* | 11,090 | 36.59 | 4,058.25 |
| Short Bt. Wrap | 9,318 | 24.80 | 2,310.75 |
| Gold Bar Fills | 175,804 | 14.00 | 24,616.34 |
| Nutmeg no. 1 | 472,072 | 11.21 | 52,938.71 |
| Nutmeg no. 2 | 511,748 | 8.80 | 45,043.28 |
| Scrap | 5,170 | 4.75 | 245.57 |
| Damaged (in Danville) | 270 | | |

*Source:* MSF/WCM, folder 028, item 1.

* "Bt." seems to mean "Bright."

Note: This table shows how raw leaf was converted into different products and whether the product was made of Western black leaf or Virginia bright leaf. The amounts, from Macdonald's cost book as of 31 December 1886, show how much he spent on each kind of leaf, first for the the month of November and then for the eleven months from 1 January to 30 November 1886. The average costs listed refer to the dollars expended on each hundred pounds of tobacco, more or less. The average cost of each product varied from the average cost of the raw leaf bought presumably because each product was made from a blend of different kinds of raw leaf, and these blends are not broken down in these data.

After manufacture, Macdonald's products were stored in warehouses in Hamilton and Toronto as well as in Montreal. His Ontario markets were so important that it was cheaper to maintain separate warehouses in that province than to try to satisfy individual orders by shipping directly from Montreal. Records for the years 1886 to 1888 suggest a significant upward trend in the pounds of tobacco products stored in Ontario: in Toronto, from 274,170 in 1886 to 560,159 in 1888; and in Hamilton, from 37,328 in 1886 to 180,649 in 1888.

## AMERICAN TOBACCO, IMPERIAL TOBACCO, AND THE TOBACCO TRUST, 1895–1911

It was the American tobacco trust, operating in Canada as the American Tobacco Company, that would take Macdonald on head to head. The company had already gained a stranglehold over almost all aspects of the industry in the United States, including the manufacturers of chewing and pipe tobacco. The consolidation movement had begun with J.B. Duke of Durham, North Carolina, who seized the opportunity offered by a new development in tobacco use since the Civil War – Americans' growing taste for cigarettes.

By 1885 the United States was producing more than a billion cigarettes a year, and four years later Americans were consuming 2.1 billion, 940 million of which were manufactured by Duke. In the same year, Duke, together with his four remaining competitors in cigarette manufacture, formed the American Tobacco Company to control virtually all cigarette manufacture in the country. Duke obtained exclusive rights to the Bonsack cigarette machine, the most advanced available. He devised "consignment agreements," to eliminate price-cutting. These agreements bound both wholesalers and retailers not to sell at prices below the price fixed by the new monopoly, and jobbers were reduced to a profit margin of 10 per cent. By 1890 his combination of dealers and manufacturers of cigarettes was known as the "tobacco trust."

In 1891 Duke took over a manufacturer of chewing tobacco in Louisville, two similar firms in Baltimore, and even a cheroot firm in Richmond, making it clear that he intended to control the entire tobacco industry. He recognized chewing tobacco as important, for as late as 1897 twice as much of it was being consumed in the United States as smoking tobacco, 182 million versus 91 million pounds.[60] Major manufacturers of chewing tobacco had organized themselves into a price-fixing organization as early as 1884, but they did not have a monopoly. Using his profits from cigarettes, he had his own chewing-tobacco factories lower their price of a pound of plug from 50 cents to as little as 20 cents, and then he bought out his chief rivals among the plug manufacturers, merging them into a company called Continental Tobacco. By 1899 American and Continental together formed an enlarged tobacco trust that went on to take a controlling interest in still more companies without obliterating their identities.[61]

Meanwhile, in Canada in 1895, the American Tobacco Company of the United States bought Ritchie and the American Cigarette Company of Montreal. The separate American Tobacco Company of Canada Ltd was incorporated to run the U.S. company's Canadian holdings. It bought 80 per cent of Empire Tobacco in 1899 and B. Houde of Quebec City in 1903. To the extent that it continued to use American leaf, American Tobacco, and thus the American tobacco trust, was a director competitor of Macdonald's in 1899.

In that same year, in addition to the growing threat from the trust, Macdonald was facing renewed pressure from his own wholesalers to support price-fixing. Although the Dominion Wholesale Grocers' Guild had largely stopped fixing retail prices between 1892 and 1898, there was a resurgence of the practice in 1899 that even survived prosecution under the anti-combines provisions of the Criminal Code in 1906–10. Tuckett Tobacco had submitted to the guild's demand for cooperation in 1885, and Empire Tobacco complied in 1887. It seems that American Tobacco, on buying control of Empire in 1899, was also willing, at least initially, to adhere to the same tobacco agreement. Canadians were developing an appetite for cigarettes, which American specialized in manufacturing and which Macdonald did not.

Macdonald had foreseen a growing challenge when he noticed his profits falling in 1896, and he could see "no prospects for improvement." As he told Landrum, "Whether war, in either near or distant future, will be brought on by Trust Companies I am not able to judge, but it is wisest to be *prepared* for all *emergencies*."[62] Macdonald appeared vulnerable to being eventually boycotted by the wholesalers in the guild if they decided that they could afford to drop his products in favour of those manufactured by American. Not surprisingly perhaps, his position towards the guild suddenly changed in 1901. He agreed with Maritime merchants not to sell, directly or indirectly, any of his tobacco at less than an advance, on his invoice gross price, of 4 cents a pound for thirty days and 5¼ cents a pound for three months.[63]

By 1905 Macdonald's jobbers, or wholesalers, were in difficulty. They were selling his thirteen products at 5 cents above their duty-paid FOB (free on board) cost at Montreal, which meant that they were responsible for all carriage, freight, and insurance charges from his bonded warehouse in Montreal after they had paid the excise tax or duty on what they were buying from him. In 1906, however, the Montreal wholesalers realized that Empire was cutting wholesalers out of new, as opposed to established, accounts by establishing direct contracts of sale with retailers. Empire had bought peace with the guild by adhering to its agreement with established wholesalers, but this new development was not welcomed by the guild, as it threatened its power in the long term.

Between 1895 and 1901 American Tobacco established exclusive contracts with retailers of the products, chiefly cigarettes, that it was making from Canadian tobacco. It seemed only a matter of time before the trust established similar contracts for whatever products it made from imported leaf. Such was the power of the trust that it probably could have eventually squeezed Macdonald out of the market or taken him over. Macdonald admitted to the 1902 Royal Commission on the Tobacco Trade that it would have been almost "prohibitive" to begin selling manufactured tobacco had such contracts existed when he started his business. In 1902 Macdonald still considered Tuckett his most formidable competitor, but he puckishly described both Tuckett and American Tobacco as his "good friends" and "confreres."

The purpose of the 1902 commission was to inquire into the "alleged exclusive contract system adopted by the American Tobacco Company of Canada, Limited, and The Empire Tobacco Company, Limited," in 1895 and 1901 respectively, so as to create a monopoly in the sale of cigarettes, affecting both the manufacturers and the growers of tobacco.[64] The commission noted that Canadian manufacturers had used 690,141 pounds of Canadian leaf in 1897, 1,949,429 in 1898, and 3,041,687 in 1901, in addition to 1,244,411 pounds of "combination" leaf, Canadian mixed with American, also in 1901.

As Macdonald did not use Canadian leaf or make cigarettes or enter into exclusive contracts, he was not the direct subject of the inquiry. He did, however, testify, and the barrister O.E. Fleming, who described him as "the father of the tobacco industry of Canada" and its "largest tobacco manufacturer," questioned him sharply on what was widely perceived as Macdonald's own monopoly. Macdonald was almost playful in responding:

Q.   I understand that you never suffered from competition to any extent?
A.   I do not know what you call suffering.
Q.   But any competition that you have had to meet has not prevented you from carry-
     ing on a very successful business in tobacco?
A.   Oh, well, you see my head is bald.[65]

Macdonald could not deny that he dominated the market in his line of products, but he took the occasion to attack exclusive contracts, "greedy" monopolies and the "exorbitant" prices they asked of the consumer, and the tariffs that favoured Canadian leaf, declaring that "competition is the life of business."

Because of his early capture of the Canadian market for smoking and chewing tobacco made from American leaf, even as late as 1902 Macdonald saw other manufacturers who used American leaf as no more an immediate threat than cigarette manufacturers. He had doubtless recognized the intrusion into Canada of the American tobacco trust as a long-term threat, which is why he caved into the guild in 1901, and now the trust threatened to expand its intrusion. In 1908 the new Imperial Tobacco Company of Canada took over American Tobacco of Canada, including Empire and B. Houde, but Imperial remained an instrument of the American trust. By incorporating the American leaf part of the old Empire Tobacco, Imperial was to that extent, as American Tobacco had been, a direct competitor of Macdonald's. Backed by the trust, it seemed that Imperial might conceivably undercut Macdonald's prices just as Duke had undercut those of his plug competitors in 1891–99.

There was, however, a growing resistance against trusts generally, as they threatened the livelihoods of far more people than Macdonald had done as a rich manufacturer. The tobacco trust threatened Canadian farmers, for example, as it was in a position to dictate the price it would pay them for their Canadian tobacco. Parliament was still toying with legislation against such trust practices as exclusive contracts when, in 1911, the Supreme Court of the United States broke up the tobacco trust on the ground that it was in violation of the Sherman Anti-Trust Law. With the collapse of the trust, its operations in Canada and Great Britain lost much of their extraordinary financial power, although they continued to flourish. Their threat to Macdonald's enterprise, though, was greatly diminished.

### THE PERENNIAL PROBLEM OF TARIFFS

As we have seen, the pre-Confederation excise of 10 cents on locally manufactured products using imported tobacco leaf had risen to 15 cents by 1868. By 1880 it was 20 cents a pound, which it remained at least until 1885, except for 1883 when it was 12 cents. By contrast, in an effort to encourage tobacco growing in Ontario and Quebec, the federal government imposed an excise tax on domestic leaf of 8 cents in 1882, 2 cents in 1883, and 5 cents in 1885. In 1902 Macdonald objected to the fact that Canadian leaf was protected to the extent of 34 cents a pound, which he saw as a tax on the Canadian consumer to pay for an inferior product, in particular a product inferior to his.

It was clearly government policy to favour domestically produced leaf, and this was precisely what led to the expansion of the Canadian cigarette industry and the exclusive contracts that the royal commission of 1902 would examine. In 1888, however, cigarettes fell into a separate category for excise and were taxed at 60 cents per thousand; in 1890 the tax rose to $1.50 per thousand. This development reduced the advantage of Canadian tobacco to the cigarette manufacturers. Had the previous excise rates applied to cigarettes, the tax would have been the equivalent of 25 cents per thousand in 1867 and about 50 cents per thousand in 1885.

It was constantly a battle for Macdonald and other manufacturers to deal with tariff changes, which were determined largely by the lobbying efforts of groups both within and beyond a given industry. Under the National Policy of Sir John A. Macdonald in 1890, the duty on raw sugar was removed and that on refined sugar reduced, all to encourage the burgeoning Canadian sugar-refining

Table 10: Pounds of Tobacco Leaf, Manufactured in Montreal, for Selected Months, Showing How Much Was Subject to the New Tax of 1909

| DATE | FOREIGN (lbs) | CANADIAN (lbs) | COMBINATION (lbs) |
|------|--------------|----------------|-------------------|
| March 1907 | 394,848 | 41,472 | 24,162 |
| March 1908 | 490,820 | 42,211 | 35,506 |
| April 1909 | 204,720* | n/a | 529 |
| April 1910 | 826,480 | n/a | n/a |

Source: Canadian Cigar and Tobacco Journal, 1908 and 1910.

* This was the figure for the new duty; 108 lbs in 1909 was subject to the old duty.

industry. The loss to the government of 15 per cent of total tariff revenue was offset by a rise in both tariff and excise duties on tobacco (and liquor).

Similarly, in an effort to win support from Canadian tobacco farmers, Sir Wilfrid Laurier raised the tax on Canadian-manufactured imported raw leaf in 1909, and this had a direct effect on Macdonald's price structure. Table 10 shows that although Montreal manufacturers used monthly almost twice as much imported leaf in 1910 as in 1907–08, the 1909 tax briefly reduced their use of it to less than half. By 1909 there was no tax at all on manufactured Canadian leaf. On the assumption that his proportion of Canadian purchases of imported raw leaf remained constant through 1908–10, it is clear that Macdonald's tariff costs almost quadrupled, while those of manufacturers using Canadian leaf disappeared. The strong protection of Canadian tobacco farmers was to continue, forcing Macdonald Tobacco to use only Canadian leaf in due course, but only after the death of Macdonald. On this note, and on the eve of the breakup of the American tobacco trust, we can conclude that for over fifty years he was the consummate survivor in the business. His business life was never easy, but its success struck awe in others.

## MACDONALD AS A BUSINESS LEGEND

Macdonald began to lessen his involvement in his tobacco business in the 1890s. David Stewart and his son Walter gradually took over, although David would predecease Macdonald by a few months. David's sons Walter and Howard would ultimately inherit the firm. By the turn of the century Macdonald was probably concerning himself only with leaf purchases.

In 1902 an article in the Canadian Cigar and Tobacco Journal attempted to sum up the careers of Macdonald and his arch-rival Mortimer B. Davis (later of Imperial Tobacco), describing the two men as "The Tobacco Kings of Canada."[66]

Of Macdonald's company and Davis's, it emphasized in italics: "*Both industries represent a one-man power. Both men are autocrats.*" Although Macdonald studiously ignored this journal, its editors had always held him in awe. Macdonald had "for half a century virtually ruled the tobacco trade in Canada." As a "strong, self-centred Scotchman," he combined "all the caution and stubborn persistence of his race." The article concluded: "Reserved in manner, deferential in speech, and small of stature, he has, nevertheless, an iron will, and a singleness of purpose that has kept in his hands for many years the practical control of the plug tobacco market, in which he has fixed both price and profit."

In May 1910 the same journal noted that Macdonald had finally, after forty years, moved his office from Notre-Dame Street to "a more modern building" on St James Street, the Guardian Building. The battered furniture moved with him. Under his feet was nothing so luxurious as linoleum but bare floorboards again, painted in terracotta by a worker from his factory. Now, when he came to the office at noon, the article suggested, he could take an elevator to the seventh floor rather than walk up a flight of stairs.[67] Here Macdonald was underestimated. He would climb the stairs to his new office almost every day, and before that climb he would walk from his home on Sherbrooke Street, down Beaver Hall Hill, a distance of perhaps two miles. But then, in 1914, some sort of disability left him partially paralysed, and thereafter he spent most of his time at home, still, however, the sole owner of one of the largest businesses in Canada and the longest-surviving tobacco manufacturer in the country.

*Chapter Four*

# THE ISLAND LEGACY, DOMESTIC LIFE, AND THE END OF CAPTAIN JOHN'S DREAM, 1864–1906

At your age I had been maintaining myself for nearly seven years. I had intended that the amount of the bequest [$500 from his sister Helen] should remain intact and be handed to you when you started out for yourself, and not for a moment [was I] looking forward to the disappointment and regret, over your negligent habits, experienced on the receipt of such a wretched specimen of attempted account-keeping as your book disclosed.

*Macdonald to his nephew Fred, the last Glenaladale, 17 April 1890*[1]

Nothing would induce me, voluntarily, to risk the recurrence of the distress I underwent from Sunday Dec. 11/92 to Jan. 3/93. Confidence is a plant of slow growth in an experienced bosom, and my confidence received such a cruel shock on 11th Dec. last, that I have not yet recovered from it, and I fear I never can, as respect those received.

"O what a tangled web we weave,

When first we practise to deceive."

*Macdonald to his niece Anna, 21 August 1893, after she had left his home on 3 January 1893*

I have acquired a knowledge of my family history, not otherwise obtainable than from this box of old papers. Much of the matter is entirely new to me, and it is very very interesting. What an amount of labor my grandfather went through, and little money came out of the property even ninety years later.

*Macdonald to Judge Alley, 13 June 1893*

Macdonald never married or sired children, and over the years he became increasingly estranged from many of his relations. He generally shunned society, had no interest in politics and little in the arts, and was virtually unknown except to a very small circle in a city where most people habitually spoke French, which he himself could not understand. To many, he must have seemed a solitary figure with few family concerns. It is true that for much of his life Macdonald was no more of a family man than any confirmed bachelor, but if we take Prince Edward Island into account, he had almost too much family – distant perhaps, but still very demanding.

### THE FATE OF THE PRINCE EDWARD ISLAND LEGACY

In the first chapter, we saw how Macdonald turned his back on his native Prince Edward Island in 1848, at about the age of seventeen, never to return there to live. But the final loosening of his PEI family ties would take much longer – indeed almost the rest of his eighty-six years. After Macdonald's departure in 1848, his family's situation rapidly deteriorated. As we have seen, Donald lost his house to arson and was almost assassinated in 1850 and then succumbed to cholera in 1854.

In 1864–67, a decade or so after Donald's death, the Tenant League of Prince Edward Island began to agitate against landowners such as the Macdonalds. Modelling itself on similar resistance movements in Ireland, the league organized a tenant boycott of both rents and arrears of rent. In March 1865 James Curtis, a deputy sheriff, served writs on defaulting tenants in Fort Augustus and on the Monaghan Settlement on Lot 36. Father John, whose land this was, had been absent in England for twenty years, but he was still insisting on his rents or on the eviction of defaulters. Curtis went in search of James Callaghan, a tavern keeper and known leader of the Tenant League. When he found himself faced with men armed with sticks, a gun, and a pitchfork, he beat a hasty retreat.[2]

There followed two fires on the Glenaladale estate in the next two months. The first, at John Archibald's residence on 14 April, was never officially attributed to arsonists. In fact, a story in the press suggested that John Archibald had set it himself in order to collect an insurance payout that was twice the real value of the house. The second fire, on 27 May, consumed an uninsured barn and a stable worth £150.[3] This second fire seems to have been set by a tenant in arrears of rent who was under extreme pressure from John Archibald to pay. Chief Justice Robert Hodgson tied this fire to the serving of writs, and George Dundas, the lieutenant-governor, connected it to the league. Despite a £500 reward for information leading to the conviction of the person or persons responsible for this second fire, no one came forward to give information.

Edward Whelan, the editor of the Charlottetown *Examiner*, condemned the league but did not accuse it of arson. He reserved his choicest words for John Archibald's tenants, "the poorest of their kind in the Colony": "Their rents are high, their leases shamefully short, and their arrears of rent have risen to such an amount as to render liquidation impossible. Of personal property, stock and farm implements, they have little or none; and improvements about their farms are almost imperceptible. They never had any heart to make improvements – how could they on a forty year's [sic] lease … It was a cruel thing to entice unfortunate people to settle on any property on such conditions. Poverty, squalor and discontent, might surely be expected to be their companions through life."[4] Nevertheless, Whelan agreed that anarchy must not be permitted to prevail. Troops in aid of the civil power arrived in October and swept through the Island over ten days in November 1865, stopping first at Lots 35 and 36 to serve writs. They met only passive resistance. Robert Haythorne, who lived on Lot 34, reported hearing of wholesale distraints by John Archibald, with the seizures of crops, horses, and cattle.[5]

Despite the collapse of the league and the prosecution of some of its members in the courts, the landlords were beginning to buckle under the pressure. In 1866 the Cunards sold their estate, the largest on the Island, to the government. Major families with political connections – James Pope, T. Heath Haviland, Jr, and the Palmers, among others – followed suit.[6] By 1871 there were no defenders of the leasehold system in the Legislature. Two years later, when the Island entered into the Canadian confederation, an act, never implemented, was passed for the compulsory purchase of all still-leased lands, but later in the same year more draconian legislation was passed for the same purpose, the Land Purchase Act of 1873.

In 1875, three years after Augustine had testified before the British-American Mixed Commission, the Land Purchase Commission of Prince Edward Island was still confused about how much, if any, of the land originally bought by Captain John belonged to William Macdonald as opposed to John Archibald. The mandate of the Land Purchase Commission was to expropriate all the remaining leased land on the Island from the proprietors, in accordance with the new Land Purchase Act of 1875. This act had been passed under the strong influence of Louis Davies, head of the provincial Liberals, who had viewed its predecessor, the Land Purchase Act of 1873, as too favourable to the proprietors. The 1875 act empowered the commission to set the price for the leased land, and following expropriation the tenants were to buy this same land with the aid of loans from the government. Davies would serve as the chief prosecutor under the act in his capacity as counsel for the tenantry at the commission hearings in 1875–76.[7]

Macdonald was incensed by this assault on what he saw as the property rights of his family, and he even considered contesting the legality of the 1875 legislation. H.J. Cundall, his agent on the Island, found both Macdonald and his sister Helen "very angry" about it, and also with "Hn and Bn." These latter were probably their cousins (through their Brecken mother) Edward Jarvis Hodgson, a lawyer, and Frederick de St Croix Brecken, the attorney general, neither of whom had been successful in opposing Davies. Such was popular feeling against the Macdonalds and other landlords that the commission found no impediment to proceeding immediately to hearings on the valuation of leased lands.[8]

Hodgson served as counsel for the landlords before the commission. He explained, presumably with regard to the division of property after Donald's death in 1854, that "John Archibald received a conveyance of the shares of William and A[u]gustine. He thus had four fifths of the whole estate; so the matter stood for some time, and afterwards [in 1869] William became possessed of [his sister] Margaret's share, and afterwards – in 1873 – he [Macdonald] became possessed of John Archibald's four sixths. He [Macdonald] thus represents at present five sixths of the property – one sixth being still owned by [Macdonald's sister] Helen."

Macdonald was thus charged with winding up a considerable legacy, emotional as well as physical, as since the death of his father in 1854 he had effectively been the last financial resort for all his family. He was – in theory but not in fact – to be the beneficiary of any compensation by the Land Purchase Commission, but the fact that he received significantly less than his claim solidified his resentment of Prince Edward Island over the following thirty years. Only in 1906 would he relent and build a consolidated school and an extension to Prince of Wales College there, as will be described. He did not need money, and it was not the paltry compensation that antagonized him so much as his family's humiliation in the face of the hatred expressed towards it, especially towards John Archibald, at the hearings. He also resented the vindictiveness of the Liberal leader Davies.

Macdonald's resentment was likely compounded by his opposition to expropriation on principle, seeing it as subversive of property rights. When, over a decade after the hearings, his relation Robert F. DeBlois (probably a son of Macdonald's cousin, Mrs George W. DeBlois, and a brother of George D. DeBlois, later lieutenant-governor) invited him to buy stock in the Charlottetown Gas Company, Macdonald replied dryly: "My experience does not incline me to look favourably upon Prince Edward Island as a desirable place in which to invest with the hope of securing satisfactory returns."[10]

As we saw in chapter 1, since first coming to the Island in 1773 the Macdonalds had been far from absentee landowners. In contrast to the owners who resided in Great Britain, whose inefficient agents would collect rents for them if they were lucky, the Macdonalds were all too present in the lives of their tenants. As one historian has put it, the Macdonalds of Tracadie were tenacious landlords, "notorious for their short leases, high rents, and ruthlessness in the use of distraint and eviction; freehold was highly uncommon on the two townships [Lots 35 and 36], accounting for only 3.6 per cent of the occupiers of land listed in the 1861 census."[11] As John Archibald himself admitted to the commission in 1875, "Where they [tenants] did not pay I either sued or distrained ... I would take a pound of money even where it would have to come from a pound of flesh."[12]

John Archibald admitted that few leases had survived from his father's time because, ever since Captain John, the family had always wanted flexibility in using their land. One effect of John Archibald's policy of entering into only short leases was that his tenants felt insecure and were thus reluctant to make improvements. This in turn led to the tenants' being described as the poorest on the Island and as rendered incapable of meeting their rent by their own landlord. A further effect was that over time the unimproved land was denuded of wood, was subject to erosion, and progressively became worth less to the family itself.

Throughout the fifty-two years that John Archibald had left to live after failing to claim the salvage from the boatload of goods that Macdonald had shipped to him in 1851, he was never to be trusted by Macdonald for his business ability. He was likely not alone in this low opinion. John Archibald was questioned sharply by the Land Commission inquiry of 1860 about everything from whether Father John had repaid money that he had obtained from the Glasgow settlers whom he had brought over thirty years before, to whether Donald had ever prevented his tenants from cutting timber on the land, to whether his present tenants were not the most miserable on the Island. A Mr Ryan testified that he had taken over a lease on the Tracadie estate from one Campbell, who had fallen into arrears of rent owed to John Archibald. Ryan had paid these arrears but was now about to see his short lease end and to be forced to leave with no compensation for his improvements on the land. John Archibald said that he would renew Ryan's lease if Macdonald consented, which was curious, as Macdonald likely had no interest in the land until 1873. There was also the suggestion that John Archibald was stealing the timber of his tenants. The commissioners effectively told John Archibald that he was lying when he testified that he had concluded a lease stipulating that the cutting of wood was reserved to him, when in fact it was not.[13]

Fifteen years later, in 1875–76, the deliberations of the Land Purchase Commission over what value to place on the Tracadie estate as the basis for compensation served to dredge up other alleged iniquities of John Archibald, causing the lawyer Hodgson to lament, "This estate is made the scape-goat for all the sins of proprietors, real or imaginary."[14] There was even speculation about whether Macdonald might have been engaged in some sharp practices with his brother. Macdonald's agent McLean vigorously asserted that the Land Purchase Act, insofar as it required payments made to the owner over the previous six years to be credited to the tenants, did not apply to Macdonald. The justification was that Macdonald had been owner for only three years, since 1873, and thus any payments made by tenants to John Archibald before then could not now be credited to the tenants and thus reduce the amount of compensation due to Macdonald.

John Archibald, however, confessed that he could not remember what Macdonald had paid for his land in 1873, as, although there was a deed, the true consideration for the property was the debts of John Archibald, then "over head and ears in debts," that Macdonald had been paying off and was continuing to pay off. Hodgson – here in his capacity as an agent for the land formerly owned by Macdonald's sister Margaret – confirmed that Macdonald was still paying off John Archibald's debts, including a recent judgment against him for £700, although the debts Macdonald had already paid extended back over twenty years and amounted to thousands of dollars. The question was now whether Macdonald had ever truly divested himself of the property that he himself had possibly inherited from Donald in 1854, by selling it to John Archibald before purportedly buying it "back," in addition to buying John Archibald's other share inherited directly from Donald, in 1873.[15]

Davies refused Hodgson's proposal to capitalize Macdonald's net rental receipts as an alternative basis for valuation because, Davies claimed, Macdonald had actually withheld his leases from examination by the commission. Davies described John Archibald's own valuation of £4 to £8 an acre as coming from "a diseased imagination" and John Archibald's record as a landlord as "diabolical," as "so black and damning that it has never had a parallel in this country," and as destructive of life "mentally and physically."[17]

Hodgson, concluding for Macdonald and distancing him from John Archibald, invoked the Magna Carta on the rights of the subject to hold property. Macdonald himself had been, he reminded the commission, charged with nothing at all and yet felt "like a man with the grasp of the hangman at his throat," and thus was determined to "contest every step in these proceedings." Hodgson declared that Macdonald's leases were ready for examination and would show a valuation of 2 shillings per acre if capitalized. He reviewed how Island statutes had "all been turned like the guns of a battery upon the rights of proprietors" ever since Captain John.

In the end, the commission awarded $34,000 for John Archibald's land, $3,700 for Helen's, and $7,592 for Anna Matilda's dower, for a total of $45,292 on 22,847 acres, or about $2 an acre. This was all that was left from Captain John's 40,000 acres, apart from whatever land remained to the family for their own use. In its award the commission did not mention William Macdonald, and why it did not is unclear.[18] We are left to wonder whether it recognized the purported transfer of land from John Archibald to Macdonald. At any rate, with this award the conflict of three generations of Macdonalds with the government came to an end. Despite further litigation by the family in which they challenged the legitimacy of the commission, a battle that dragged on through 1878, they found themselves beaten. Their land under lease, as opposed to what John Archibald still owned for his own use, was finally conveyed to the government in 1878, 105 years after Captain John's settlers had landed at Scotchfort.

Also in the end, it was not really the monetary compensation that mattered to Macdonald. It was the apparent unfairness, even injustice, of life that had again manifested itself in the final unravelling of the family legacy. While there was no shame attached to his tenuous links to the Tracadie estate, he could feel no pride in the way the land had been run by three generations of his family. The commission's lawyer Davies had portrayed them, one of the founding families of Prince Edward Island, as one of its greatest scourges. Speaking of their tenants and of John Archibald's refusal to compensate them for their improvements when they were evicted, Davies had exclaimed:

That these poor wretches, who went upon the bogs, and swamps and sand hills of the Tracadie Estate, and sank themselves morally and physically, should now have their little improvements taken from them seems to me too monstrous a thing to conceive of … This estate has been next thing to bathed in blood. For years and years these poor people have struggled, not with the adversities of nature only – with the poverty of the soil, and the distance from markets, – but have struggled against a grasping, avaricious landlord [John Archibald], who exacted not merely his pound of flesh, but where he could by any means on earth do so, took two pounds.[19]

At the time of Davies's vociferous campaign against the Macdonalds, he was becoming as distinguished an Islander as Macdonald himself, and he would do much to define the place of the family in the history of the Island. He became premier of Prince Edward Island in 1877, even before the family gave up their resistance, but only served until 1879. In 1896 he was knighted and named Dominion minister of marine and fisheries, and five years later he became a justice of the Supreme Court of Canada. He ended his career as chief justice of Canada, serving from 1918 to 1924. Thus, Davies outlived both Macdonald and John Archibald and was occupying high political and judicial office as Macdonald's own reputation was at its apogee.

The new Glenaladale farm was owned and lavishly supported by Macdonald after 1878, but it was disastrously run by John Archibald and two of his sons. It limped on until 1906, when it was finally sold outside the family. Captain John's dream of replicating a feudal estate in the New World was at last over.

St Lawrence Hall, St James Street, about 1894, when it was the Canadian Pacific Express Building (ANQ, MAS 6-136-d, no. 11)

## MACDONALD ESTABLISHES HIS OWN HOME IN MONTREAL

For his first fifteen years in Montreal, ever since he arrived at age twenty-two in 1853, Macdonald had lived alone in hotels, apart from possible short periods with his brother Augustine. He had stayed at the Ottawa Hotel before the Civil War, and then in the war years had taken up residence at St Lawrence Hall, a luxurious hotel at the corner of St James and St François Xavier Streets next to the head office of the Bank of Montreal.[20] However, having his factory renovated in 1866 seems to have stimulated Macdonald to contemplate changing both his residence and his way of life.

In 1868 Macdonald visited his mother, Anna Matilda, and his sister Helen on the Island and invited them to come to Montreal to live with him. This they agreed to do, in the following year. For them and himself he rented, and in 1896

Anna Matilda McDonald, 1870 (Notman 1-48896.1)

bought, no. 3 Prince of Wales Terrace at 891 Sherbrooke Street, between Peel and McTavish Streets, just around the corner from McGill University. Newly built in 1859–60 by Sir George Simpson, governor of the Hudson's Bay Company, the Terrace had been named in honour of the Prince of Wales's visit to Montreal. Macdonald's was one in a row of identical houses notably modern in their gas lighting and running water, which he held out as an attraction to his mother and sister, others being its proximity to Protestant churches, three or four servants, horses, carriages, and sleighs.[21] Anna Matilda and Helen attended the Anglican Church of St James the Apostle on St Catherine Street, while he attended no church, except possibly on occasion to accompany them.

The austerity of the Terrace recalled the eighteenth-century squares of Edinburgh, and until its demolition in 1971 it stood out in "its classical grandeur, its well-balanced appearance, its sober taste, inside as well as outside."[22] A visitor

Helen Jane McDonald, 1863 (Notman 1-8831.1)

was to recollect Macdonald's library on the ground floor of his very plain house. Its shelves, tables, chairs, and sofa were overflowing with magazines and reports, with few bound volumes. "Here, standing at a lectern, he read for hours on end in his untiring quest for information."[23] Macdonald refused to buy paintings for his new home, which contributed to its rather stark appearance. As late as 1899, he declared that for years he had "resisted the importunities of my friends to buy *Oil paintings* and I have none in my house except portraits of my late sister and myself, and have the same desire to avoid a beginning, in that direction, that a temperate man would have, to avoid the first glass of spirits."[24]

Exterior view of Prince of Wales Terrace, probably in the 1960s (MSF)

Over the years, Macdonald retreated to the top floor, where he read most of the time, leaving the lower floors to his servants, essentially a chambermaid, a kitchen maid, a cook, and a driver. Even at the end of his life, his bedroom was furnished with merely an old iron bed, a chest of drawers, and two chairs.[25] As he seldom or never entertained, he had no butler. The location enabled him to participate in the life of the university, and he became very close to Principals William Dawson and then William Peterson and their families, friendships he would keep to the end of his life.

Macdonald, Anna Matilda, and Helen, in the nine years they all lived together, seldom, if ever, saw Macdonald's brothers or the two sisters who were nuns. Anna Matilda died in Montreal in 1878, and Helen, frequently in poor health, continued to live with him until her death eleven years later in 1889. Their home had probably always been a very quiet one; with Helen's death, it became even quieter. Macdonald would not remain alone, however: his niece

Interior view of Prince of Wales Terrace (MSF)

Anna, a daughter of John Archibald's, came to live with him in 1890. He had paid for her schooling in England, at Falconberg House in Cheltenham and had been favourably impressed with the accuracy of the accounts that she kept there. Anna managed his household until her marriage in 1893 to a distant cousin, Alain Chartier de Lotbinière Macdonald, of which Macdonald very much disapproved.

## HIS BROTHER AUGUSTINE'S BUSINESS VENTURES
### AND IGNOMINIOUS END

In the last chapter, we saw Augustine, the brother to whom Macdonald had long been closest, as a manufacturer of tobacco in Louisville in his own right, up to 1875, and as a buyer of leaf for Macdonald as well. Augustine's career as a purchaser of and a speculator in cotton during the Civil War is much more colourful than any aspect of William's career.[26] It began in July 1863 when President Abraham Lincoln himself commissioned Augustine, as a subject of Great Britain, which was neutral during the war, to negotiate a secret deal with the Confederate commander of the Trans-Mississippi Department to buy cotton from Southern cotton factors and to hold it without threat of destruction by either warring side. Lincoln's object was to continue supplying Northern cotton mills, especially those in Massachusetts, using a route through the relatively peaceful Southern states west of the Mississippi. He lacked the gold necessary to pay for the cotton being shipped by the Confederacy to Liverpool in defiance of his blockade of the South.

Augustine's task was both dangerous and challenging. Lincoln told naval and military authorities to protect him, and the assistant adjutant general of the United States authorized him to carry one gun and one revolver. His assignment, authorized by the U.S. Treasury, was to buy between 6,000 and 10,000 bales of cotton, each weighing about 450 pounds. Building on tobacco connections established before the war, in May and June 1864 Augustine established an agency in Memphis. Through two agents, he bought 600 bales of cotton in Arkansas and Louisiana, which he stored in those states, some in sheds under gin houses on Bayou Bartholomew, others in a log house and a sawmill, all near swamps, with a view to shipping them north. By this time, southeastern Arkansas and northern Louisiana, west of the Mississippi where these stores were located, were protected from Confederate troops by the Northern occupation of the river. Then, in about July of that year, the U.S. Congress changed the regulations that had allowed neutrals to buy Southern cotton. It vested the right to purchase cotton solely with the United States and compelled the disclosure of the identities of all sellers of cotton, previously secret. This made it impossible for Augustine to export the 600 bales, as doing so would have endangered his suppliers, who might be suspected of being in possession of stolen money.

In a single day, Augustine is said, probably wrongly, to have had $40 million in cotton transferred to him in trust. He definitely bought $2 million in cotton on his own account. In early February 1865, a Unionist Colonel Osband (sometimes described as General Osborne) systematically put to the torch Augustine's Arkansas and Louisiana warehouses and shelters for cotton, and Augustine lost all his stock. Osband, who laid waste to other property in the South, apologized to an American for burning his cotton as well. But he was very proud that he had destroyed "that damned Englishman's, McDonald's, cotton, and had literally ruined him." He declared that "such damned scoundrels had no business in this country, and that if he had his way, would hang them all."[27]

Augustine's loss of $2 million led to his bankruptcy and to his appeal for compensation before the British-American Mixed Commission of 1871 (alluded to earlier) on claims arising out of losses during the Civil War. He retained a Memphis lawyer, Moyers, to present his claim, and Moyers retained the Washington firm of Harvey & Dole to act for Augustine in Washington. This they did, for a contingency fee based on whatever might be awarded. Augustine later claimed not to have approved of this fee, and when he was awarded $200,000, he refused to pay the fees of Harvey & Dole. In June 1878 this Washington firm successfully won a judgment for $50,000 from Augustine. Augustine left or perhaps fled Washington without satisfying the judgment and was then adjudged in contempt of court. He was discovered in Brooklyn the following February, and Hovey & Dole sued him in New York for the wrongful taking and detention of property, namely the $50,000 awarded to it. Upon Augustine's refusal to answer to the charge against him, he was imprisoned in Ludlow Jail in New York City.

The rector of Grace Chapel found him there six years later, in 1885, and a former judge, William H. Arnoux, applied for a fresh trial. This time Augustine refused to appear, even after the new trial was granted. James C. McEachen, with Arnoux and James H. Laird, appeared as his counsel, apparently without fees, and General Charles E. Hovey, General H.P. Titus, and Thomas H. Wheeler represented Hovey & Dole. Wheeler noted that Augustine, while living in Cincinnati in 1869, had filed for bankruptcy with stated debts of $250,000. Hovey & Dole's only concern was what Augustine had done with his $200,000 award. The answer seems to have been that he had lost it all on Wall Street.

Augustine's counsel claimed that Augustine had not even known of the judgment for $50,000 against him when he left Washington, and in any case his imprisonment of six years was out of proportion to the offence of contempt. Augustine told a newspaper reporter that he could have taken a poor debtor's oath and walked out of prison, but "[t]hat would have been a confession on my part."

It is not clear why or how Augustine was released from jail after his trial in 1885, although it is probable that he did take the poor debtor's oath. Collard suggests that he blamed his brother William for his suffering and "tormented" him thereafter, chiefly by publishing his memoirs in 1893.[28] Unfortunately, the corrupt municipal officials of Tammany Hall that he criticized in these memoirs seem to have bought up most of the copies, and there is not one even in the Library of Congress. In any case, it is clear from an extant letter from Macdonald to Augustine that, at least in 1889 and for over a decade more, he lived in Bridgeport, Connecticut. To Montrealers who remembered Augustine, it seemed that Macdonald had little to do with his brother from 1878 onwards. Some, it is said, commented on Macdonald's callousness, and it seems that a purse was collected in Montreal to aid in Augustine's defence. Most of Macdonald's letters from before 1886 have disappeared, and thus it is hard to know how much he may have helped Augustine. His letters from then on reveal that he may have paid for all of Augustine's rent and meals in Bridgeport and for much else. All that can be

H.J. Cundall, portrait by Robert Harris
(Confederation Centre, Charlottetown, CAG H-309)

safely said is that this former business partner of Macdonald's had proved himself permanently insolvent, though not half so much trouble as John Archibald.

### HENRY JOHN CUNDALL AND JOHN ARCHIBALD

Macdonald met his lifelong friend, Henry John Cundall (1833–1916), in 1844,
when they were both pupils at the Central Academy. Cundall's grandfather,
Robert Cundall, had come, through marriage, to own half of Lot 20, and his
father, William Cundall, held a mortgage on the Macdonald property at Tracadie. Henry Cundall himself became a successful land surveyor, notably for
the P.E.I. Railway and, as a land agent, collected rent on several estates. It was
natural that after his father's death in 1876 Henry should follow him in caring for
the Tracadie estate, on which he probably inherited the mortgage.

After the exhausting litigation over the Land Purchase Act of 1873, in 1878
Henry assumed responsibility for transferring all the leased property of the Macdonalds to the government and for managing the money that former proprietors
now received in exchange for their estates.[29] Cundall was thus transformed from

a land agent into a trustee. His father had himself received money through the sale of Cundall land under the act, and so through inheritance Henry became a man of some means. Famed for his punctuality, his scrupulousness, his honesty, and his discretion, he was perfect as Macdonald's agent – specifically as the person to look out for John Archibald. Cundall's vast surviving correspondence and diaries, especially from 1882 to 1893, suggest that Macdonald was his principal trust client.

By his wife Mary Ellen Weeks, whom he had married in 1866, John Archibald had twelve children, nine surviving infancy. It is not clear whether Mrs McDonald, as Macdonald always addressed her, was Protestant, but as we shall see in chapter 6, Macdonald paid for the education of at least some of John Archibald's children in distinctly non-Catholic schools. Although a number of John Archibald's children were to cause Macdonald much distress, they made up the whole of the next generation of the Glenaladale Macdonalds and for this reason were important to him. Macdonald and his spinster sister Helen were extremely devoted as surrogate parents to several of them who lived off the Island, in Montreal, the United States, England, and Scotland. As John Archibald was often severely ill with digestive problems and incapable of managing money, Macdonald arranged for Cundall to look after most of his affairs, and at least by the 1880s John Archibald was receiving, through Cundall, $1,000 a year from his youngest brother.

In 1883, in a last effort to restore a vestige of the Macdonald presence on Lot or Township 36 on the Island, Macdonald offered to build John Archibald and his family a big new house. In all, he spent about $50,000 on the house and a huge barn. Cundall and James Hodgson supervised the erection of all the buildings and the draining of the swamp near them. Macdonald had three stoves installed in the house, along with sofas and rugs. The farm received from him harnesses, barrels, horses, and cattle. Designed by Andrew Hutchison, one of Macdonald's Montreal architects, "New Glenaladale," as the house was predictably named, was on the land that remained to the family after 1878, still legally belonging to Macdonald himself to keep it out of the hands of John Archibald's creditors. Macdonald and Helen visited it in 1884 and on several occasions in later years, and he paid for all the upkeep of the property, the feeding of John Archibald's huge family, as well as the education of most of his children. He paid for his sister-in-law, Mrs McDonald, to come to Montreal for surgery and for the eminent doctor F.J. Shepherd to perform the surgery on her. But she was as much a spendthrift as her husband and children, and although she eventually left John Archibald, still fully expected – and received – an allowance from Macdonald.

Macdonald's fireproofing of the house and emphasis on animal husbandry in the estate foreshadowed his building of Macdonald College in Ste Anne de Bellevue about twenty-five years later. John Archibald and his family, however,

New Glenaladale, built by William Macdonald for John Archibald McDonald (MSF)

were incapable of making the farm a going concern. In 1878 Cundall had bought Arisaig for John Archibald, property that had been part of the leased lands surrendered to the government and had previously belonged to his uncle Roderick, but only a few years later, when John Archibald was contemplating selling it, he could not recall whether it was really his.[30]

For Macdonald, New Glenaladale now seemed to be a distinctly shaky inheritance, despite his continued investment in it. Although he remained the legal owner for years before transferring it to John Archibald in about 1898, it was essentially a write-off. Cundall was to oversee the final residue of this acquisition, John Archibald's farm. Within less than thirty years, by 1906, even it was lost to John Archibald's family.

Long before this time, Macdonald had given up on his family heritage. He had his own home in Montreal, and he did not return to the Island in the new century. He had changed, the Island had changed, and even Scotland had changed. But with the final and complete abandonment of the family lands in Prince Edward Island, the ghost of Captain John was exorcised. And already a new Macdonald legacy was largely in place, one far more productive than even Captain John could have dreamt.

William C. Macdonald, 1870 (Notman I-45493)

*Chapter Five*

# THE EVOLUTION OF PRACTICAL EDUCATION
## AT McGILL, CIRCA 1850–1880

The analysis of new mineral species, while they directly regard a scientific result, must always have an economic bearing. You cannot tell whether a new substance is to be profitably available or not until you have ascertained its properties ... Thus economics lead to science, and science to economics ... I am not a naturalist. I do not describe fossils, but use them. They are geological friends who direct me in the way to what is valuable ... Some tell of coal; they are cosmopolites; while some give local intelligence of gypsum, or salt, or building-stone, and so on ... My whole connection with geology is of a practical character. I am by profession a miner and a metallurgist.

*William Logan, in testimony to the Select Committee on the Geological Survey of the*
*Parliament of the Province of Canada, October 1854*[1]

Macdonald's arrival in Montreal in 1853 coincided with a major reorientation of the local economy. Many of its old certainties, such as an overwhelming dependence on the staples trade with Europe, were gone. New routes were opening west and south from the city, and Montrealers were tasting prosperity through industrialization. There were changes in the intellectual and religious lives of Montrealers as well, reflected in the preoccupations of scientists, particularly geologists, and in new ideas about higher education. These economic and social upheavals would touch Macdonald personally. Over the last half of the nineteenth century, they would coincide with a reconsolidation of his personal life with his growing commitment to McGill University. In various ways, there emerged a convergence between the interests of the university, on the one side, and those of the industrializing society and Macdonald's thriving investments in it, on the other.

GEOLOGY: INTELLECTUAL TREMORS AND
DIGGING FOR TRUTH

Although it has suffered no major earthquake for hundreds of years, Montreal
lies in a geologically less stable zone than most cities in North America. In the
nineteenth century it was home to two eminent geologists, Sir William Logan
and Sir William Dawson. These men were acutely aware not only of the sea and
the lava from which the old volcano of Mount Royal, on which the city is built
and after which it is named, had emerged, but also of the plants and animals that
had once flourished on the mountain and that were now extinct or superseded,
and above all of the effects of ice floes on the St Lawrence. There was great
curiosity in Macdonald's time generally about the age of the earth and about
whether outcrops of rock were the result of erosion or the product of other geological forces. Geologists were discovering the past everywhere, but they were
pursuing questions that dated back only a century.

In the eighteenth century, the Scottish lawyer, medical doctor, and father
of modern geology, James Hutton (1726–1797), had found at Cairngorm in the
Scottish Highlands molten granite penetrating foliated metamorphic schists,
which themselves showed layers of different minerals split into thin irregular
plates. After finding other instances of layered and penetrated rock, he concluded
that these formations indicated several cycles of deposit and erosion, a discovery
so startling that his friend John Playfair found his mind giddy as it looked
through the deposits far into "the abyss of time."[2]

Hutton provided educated minds with verifiable evidence that the present
was a guide to the past, that the geological processes still underway were
replicating processes of the past that had taken place long before. Hutton's
"uniformitarianism" stood in sharp contrast to more traditional and scriptural
theories (such as that of the Great Flood) of why rocks look as they do. For
Hutton, these rocks were obviously not uniform, but the processes that had
created them had been, in the sense that they had recurred without any apparent
external, including divine, intervention to disrupt their recurrence. He saw the
earth and the life on it as marked by deep, even immeasurable, time, as opposed
to being marked by a biblical type of catastrophe. He opened the door to theories
of the natural variation of species, if not of their evolution.

Even granite, symbolic of the solidity of Scotland, was far from permanent.
Moreover, contrary to received opinion, granite was a young rock, as Hutton
revealed to the duke of Atholl in 1785 while investigating a great swathe of it
stretching from Aberdeen across the Grampians. And rocks had long been
convertible to structures for human use. The Scots, for example, had been
excavating granite as early as 1741. Knowledge of geology, then, was not only
interesting, but also potentially useful and profitable.

One Montreal businessman – the building contractor and much later sugar refiner John Redpath (1796–1869) – made his fortune through stone. Born in Berwickshire, where Hutton had explored shale, and later a stonemason in Aberdeen, Redpath knew well the granite studied by Hutton. Equipped with practical training in geology and having settled in Montreal, Redpath provided the stone for Notre-Dame Church and the Lachine Canal. With the fortune that he had made through these ventures in granite, he invested in mining and smelting, coal, slate, and copper companies. What had appeared to many as adamantine rock was for Redpath a source of immense wealth. Geology was of use to more than masons and builders; it was the intellectual basis of the Canadian mining industry. Any geologist was bound to be not only an explorer but also an entrepreneur alert to the profits hidden underground.

### AN INTELLECTUAL REVOLUTION IN SCOTLAND

Through the eighteenth century, at least from the Battle of Culloden onwards, Scotland enjoyed a period of rebirth, becoming a centre of bold new ideas in the realms of philosophy, religion, economics, and science and an inspiration for boldly thoughtful people everywhere. Its capital, Edinburgh, became known as a centre of intellectual activity. Previously better known for its venomous theological disputations and tribal feuds, Scotland now became renowned throughout Europe and America as the home of such towering thinkers as David Hume and Adam Smith. While historians may differ on the dates and content of the Scottish Enlightenment, they would agree that it was led by a tight group of brilliant people, probably numbering no more than a dozen. James Hutton, the geologist who exposed the abyss of time through rocks, could count himself among them, and his friends formed the bulk of its leadership. The Enlightenment shaped education all over the British Empire, from Canada to New Zealand, as well as in the United States and beyond. It was this Scotland that Captain John had left.

The more intellectual content of Scottish Enlightenment thought covered a wide field, from painting to economics, and it raised fearlessly searching questions to which there still remain no definitive answers or rebuttals.[3] The work of Smith, for example, resounds more loudly now than ever before, at least politically. But the radical scepticism of Hume has always been the hardest to refute or supersede, for he hurled a challenge to future generations to prove the very plausibility of knowledge itself, in particular of all experience and intellectual claims, and more especially of revealed religion, with its propositions from scripture. It was to the practical extension to Canadian higher education of the mixed legacy of Hume, Hutton, and other Enlightenment figures that Macdonald would – largely unconsciously – devote the bulk of his fortune.

What Hume's scepticism and Hutton's geology most exhibited in common was a preoccupation with the experience of the individual as investigator and as the judge of truth. Hume's *Natural History of Religion*, for example, addressed the social and psychological factors that induced people to believe in religion. As a modern professor of logic and rhetoric at Glasgow has summed him up, Hume concluded that "[t]he near-universality of belief in a deity points to near-universal features in human nature, while at the same time carrying no implication whatever for the truth, or otherwise, of what is believed."[4]

Hutton always invoked observation as the authority for any statement, even for conclusions that he could not definitively demonstrate through direct experiment, such as his view that the earth was an engine of heat. In his *Abstract of a Dissertation Concerning the System of the Earth, Its Duration, and Stability,* Hutton did not "deny that the world had a beginning in time, but he [did] deny that anything we see indicates such a beginning."[5] In the practice of geology, scientific investigation grounded the more extravagant Humean expressions of scepticism in terms comprehensible to those seeking practical results and even profits. Geology did not assuage doubts about religion, but it did not unequivocally encourage them either. It formed a common ground for a diversity of temperaments and beliefs, an intellectual basis for a new kind of higher education in the second half of the nineteenth century.

## THE CHANGING NATURE OF THE UNIVERSITY

Although there have been academies and other institutions of higher education in different cultures since ancient times, Canadian universities such as McGill emerged from a European tradition going back to the Middle Ages. The medieval university by definition strove to teach the "universe of knowledge," and Catholic theology was central to its view of this universe.[6] With the Protestant Reformation, this theology fragmented and with it fragmented the idea of what was universal. The role of theology in the universe of knowledge no longer rested on a general consensus among Christians. Non-Catholic universities, although they might architecturally hark back to medieval Oxford and Cambridge, were heirs to this fragmentation and to the denominational conflicts among the Protestants themselves.

By the mid-nineteenth century in the British Isles, theology was largely a marginal subject for many university students or not a subject for them at all. In 1852 the prominent convert from Protestantism to Catholicism, John Henry Cardinal Newman, doubted the future of theology as a serious subject even in Catholic universities. At the opening of a Catholic university in Ireland, he felt obliged to defend its courses in theology as being as basic to the modern curriculum as the sciences.[7]

McGill College, 1869 (Notman VIEW-7071.0)

In Quebec City, Laval University was run by priests who did not abandon the central role of theology in their curriculum. Theological orthodoxy was also a necessary requirement for entry into early Protestant Canadian institutions, such as King's College in Nova Scotia and King's College in Toronto, both Anglican. An exception was Dalhousie College in Halifax. The founder, Lord Dalhousie, was a Presbyterian, and he did not favour any religious tests for students or staff.[8]

In Montreal, the English-speaking Protestant population had rejected an exclusively Anglican university very early. The original charter of McGill University in 1821, as well as its revised charter of 1853, stipulated that it was not to be a denominational institution, and so McGill was open to Jews and Catholics, and potentially to people of other religions or of none, as students. There was nothing anti-Protestant or anti-Christian in a non-denominational university – if it taught theology, it taught it as a kind of truth but not *the* truth. But it was officially without any distinct affiliation with one church or another. On the periphery of McGill stood colleges for the training of Anglican, Congregational, Methodist, and Presbyterian ministers, and their students often took the arts course at McGill to supplement their theological studies; but the university itself remained studiously neutral in religious disputes. Shorn of an official commitment to even Protestant theology, the universe of knowledge to be covered at McGill was fundamentally different from that at Laval. Still, the idea of universal knowledge was not dead even at McGill. Having persisted through the Renaissance and the Enlightenment, it survived in the curriculum as natural philosophy and history.

## NATURAL PHILOSOPHY AND HISTORY

Long before Christian theology, Aristotle had asked where knowledge came from, and "natural" philosophers following him tried to derive general conclusions from the observation of phenomena.[9] Medieval scholasticism emphasized Aristotle's deductive approach and did not encourage any verification of such observations. It tried to fit them into *a priori* assumptions derived from "revealed" truths of Christianity in scripture, as defined by theology.

Practical experimentation to test the truth of ideas of natural philosophy was not articulated until the sixteenth and seventeenth centuries. Sir Francis Bacon proposed induction and research instead of deduction from limited observation. Sir Robert Boyle insisted on the publication of detailed experimental results, including those of failed experiments, and on the replication of experiments to validate observational claims. It was only after Boyle that science, which had previously meant merely knowledge, became differentiated from natural philosophy in its emphasis on experimental verification. Its practice became firmly inductive and detached from religious presuppositions. From Boyle onwards, civility characterized scientific discussion as it had never characterized theological disputes. Observation and verification became the supreme authority rather than scripture. This and other developments of the seventeenth century led to the creation of the "philosophical societies" of the eighteenth and early nineteenth centuries, such as the Boston Athenaeum.[10] Almost until the end of the nineteenth century, McGill University was buying "philosophical apparatus" for use in its laboratories. This term was a throwback to the old natural philosophy. But observation through experiment takes time and patience, and from natural philosophy emerged natural history.

If natural philosophy emphasized deduction, natural history consisted of recording of what was observable in nature. Early in the Christian era, Pliny offered a mathematical and physical description of the world: he dealt with geography, ethnography, anthropology, human physiology, zoology, botany (including agriculture), horticulture, pharmacology, and mineralogy. The incorporation of time into natural philosophy led to the idea of natural history. Pliny transformed the experience of nature over time into an academic inquiry and discipline in itself. Although he was more analytical than observational, he was essentially accumulating "facts." During the Renaissance there developed a passion for collecting and categorizing specimens of minerals, vegetables, and animals. Then Linnaeus in the eighteenth century boldly tried to organize species into taxonomic groups. The domains of natural history more generally, from minerals to animals, formed a "great chain of being," on a linear scale of increasing perfection. Collections of "natural history" included not merely what could be seen every day but also vestiges of the distant past, such as dinosaur bones, rocks, and minerals.[11]

Although the practice of collecting specimens of natural history originated in amateur enthusiasms and although it still generates specialist hobbies, such as the study of birds, butterflies, or wild flowers, it has always been the foundation of great institutions. The Smithsonian National Museum of Natural History, now the Smithsonian Institution in Washington, and the Redpath Museum in Montreal are early examples. Geologists were the first collectors for natural science museums, which to this day tend to be filled with rocks, fossils, and minerals. But botanists, taxidermists, ethnographers, and even astronomers were pioneers in exploring natural history as well.

Initially, natural history was not divided into what became known as the pure and the applied (or practical) sciences. The growth of the university in the nineteenth century is largely the story of the emergence of this division, as well as of the increasing specialization of the sciences into different disciplines, new departments, and even new faculties.[12]

### EARLY GEOLOGY IN CANADA[13]

At the beginning of this chapter, we saw how James Hutton proposed that processes of heating and erosion in rocks were recurrent and had been so indefinitely and might continue so indefinitely. In 1798, very shortly after Hutton's death, William Logan was born in Montreal of a Scots family.[14] Logan went to Edinburgh to study and then found employment, first at a counting house in London and then as a bookkeeper at a copper-smelting works in Wales. In Wales he became interested in the copper itself and in the coalfields around him, and his mapmaking skills were such that he joined the staff of the local geological survey. Returning to Canada in 1840, Logan studied the geology of the Eastern Townships and Maine. In the following year, he met Sir Charles Lyell, the most eminent of English geologists, and also John William Dawson (always known as William), a young local geologist from Nova Scotia who had been studying in Edinburgh.

Born in Pictou in 1820, Dawson was the grandson of a Scots farmer and the son of a businessman.[15] In 1833 he entered Pictou Academy, where he developed a passion for collecting shells, fossils, insects, and rare birds. His headmaster, Thomas McCulloch, introduced him to electricity, magnetism, motion, pneumatics, hydrostatics, and elementary physics, as well as the classics and mathematics. Outside school, Dawson met Richard Brown, an eminent geologist and the engineering manager of the Sydney coalmines. These mines were being developed by the General Mining Association of London, which until 1858 would hold a monopoly over the exploitation of natural resources in Nova Scotia. Brown had discovered coal seams at South Joggins, near the Bay of Fundy, and Dawson proceeded to explore them in greater depth. Dawson also set up a chemistry laboratory at home and learned taxidermy from his headmaster's son, who helped him collect birds, butterflies, and moths.

From studying Lyell's writings, Dawson learned that facts discoverable in the earth's crust and changes now observable could be linked through an identification of causes and an identification of effects. He saw this as Lyell's "greatest contribution to the growth of modern geology," but he did not explicitly link Lyell's conclusion to Hutton's uniformitarianism, possibly because Lyell believed in a creative intelligence that did not find a place in Hutton's theory.

In the meantime, in 1834, Dawson's father had set up the Pictou Literary and Scientific Society. It resembled the Halifax Mechanics' Institute founded three years before. In 1836, when he was only sixteen, the younger Dawson delivered a lecture to the Pictou group on the structure and the history of the earth. His father's printing business brought him to Boston, where Dawson became acquainted with the Natural History Society there, with its valuable collections of fossils.

Dawson wanted to be a preacher and had become proficient in Hebrew, but his parents sent him to Edinburgh University in 1840, where he studied physical geography, minerals and rocks, and palaeobotany (the study of the geological distribution of plant fossils). His principal teacher there, Robert Jameson, articulated the Neptunist or catastrophic-flood theory of rock variation as opposed to Hutton's uniformitarianism. Jameson firmly believed in the unity of natural history. Dawson was obliged to return to Nova Scotia within a year. This return was providential, as by chance he met both Logan and Lyell. Like Brown, his two new friends were looking for coal.

Of all the researchers into natural history, geologists were initially the best funded, as their work could lead to mining prospects. There was no bar to their also becoming palaeontologists, but they were perhaps the first to engage in practical, or applied, science. The applied sciences included various kinds of engineering, and mining engineers were thought of as "professionals" rather than as mere miners or indeed mere researchers. Around the time that Logan, Dawson, and Lyell were becoming acquainted, the new United Province of Canada decided to

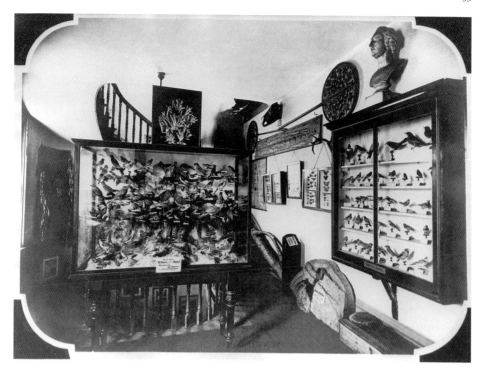

Natural History Society Museum, about 1900 (Notman MP-0000.113.1)

establish a geological survey to discover what in its rocks might be economically exploited. The York Literary and Philosophical Society of Toronto, the Natural History Society of Montreal, and the Literary and Historical Society of Quebec, all made up of amateur collectors, supported this pioneering effort, which entailed making a comprehensive inventory of mineral resources. In 1842 Logan became the first director of the Canadian Geological Survey. He opened an office in Montreal and established a collection of geological specimens.

In 1854 the government appointed a select committee on the future of the Canadian Geological Survey. When asked how his work led to practical economic results, Logan replied that much geology "is devoted to tracing out the distribution of the various formations that come from beneath one another and spread over the surface of a country, the mode of representing them being by colours on a map." This was a "classification of the surface into parts," delimiting "where to look for known materials." Effectively, Logan was explaining how Hutton's early insights had led to a possible key to Canadian prosperity.[16] In the following year, he organized a Canadian collection at the Paris Industrial

Exhibition, and for this and his work at the London Great Exhibition of 1851, he received a knighthood. Logan declared that he was not himself a naturalist, in the sense of a fossil specialist, but he saw "fossils as an indispensable means of research" into economic minerals and their proper description as necessary for the entry of minerals into "the educational systems of the country."[17]

Meanwhile, Dawson resumed his education at Edinburgh in 1846. Two years later, in 1848, he conducted a geological survey of Cape Breton and carried out assays and evaluations of coal and iron deposits for the government. He lectured at the Pictou Academy in the same year, and in 1850 he taught an extension course in natural history (botany, zoology, mineralogy, and geology) at Dalhousie College. Dawson became superintendent of education with a view to introducing agricultural courses in the higher schools and to establishing a Normal School. For over three years, he travelled from county to county, convening meetings of school commissioners, examining schools, collecting statistics, lecturing on education, introducing agricultural studies and uniform textbooks, and "carrying on a geological reconnaissance." He established a Normal School at Truro and set up mixed school commissions for both Catholics and Protestants, so as to avoid separate confessional systems except in the larger towns.

In 1853 Dawson published his great work, *Acadian Geology*, and in the following year, his reputation as an educator soaring, he worked with a commission under Egerton Ryerson, superintendent of education for Canada West, to reorganize King's College, Fredericton, later the University of New Brunswick. Sir Charles Lyell invited him to apply for the chair of natural history at Edinburgh, until recently held by Dawson's mentor Jameson. Dawson's application, made in 1855, failed, probably because of prejudice against him as a colonial, but almost simultaneously Judge Charles Dewey Day, president of the board of governors at McGill, invited him to apply to be principal of McGill.

### McGILL REBORN UNDER DAWSON

When Dawson arrived in Montreal in October, he found McGill physically in shambles:

Materially, it was represented by two blocks of unfinished and partly ruinous buildings, standing amid a wilderness of excavators' and masons' rubbish, overgrown with weeds and bushes. The grounds were unfenced, pastured at will, by herds of cattle, which not only cropped the grass, but browsed on the shrubs, leaving unhurt only one great elm ... The only access from the town was by a circuitous and ungraded cart track, almost impassable at night. The buildings had been abandoned by the new Board [... and my residence] was destitute of every requisite of civilised life.[18]

Sir William Dawson, 1882 (Notman II-63320)

There were only three faculties – Medicine (ten professors and one demonstrator), Law (two professors and two lecturers), and Arts (four professors and one lecturer, most part-time). Quite naturally, the university was largely perceived as being little more than a medical school. Dawson found the board of governors, however, "a body of able and earnest men."

Despite his own deeply held religious beliefs, Dawson fully accepted that McGill must remain without religious affiliation. His experience at Dalhousie College had provided him with a model of a non-denominational institution. By contrast, the Disruption of 1843 among Scottish Presbyterians and the Oxford Movement of 1833–45 had demonstrated how theological disputes could disrupt the most established universities.[19] As McGill had already evolved into an institution to serve the non-Catholic community generally, though no particular denomination within it, there was no point in its teaching controversial dogmas such as might divide non-Catholics. The university might accommodate, say, Christian apologetics in its philosophy courses, or perhaps even in its geology courses if Dawson himself was teaching, but effectively the emerging McGill avoided theological controversy.

In sharp contrast to, say, the motto of Oxford, "Dominus illuminatio mea" (The Lord my light), even before Dawson McGill had adopted the motto "Grandescunt aucta labore" (All is accomplished through work). There was nothing anti-religious about this motto, and Dawson remained firmly and almost ostentatiously religious all his life, but there was nothing religious about it either. It signified at least a change of emphasis, however, rather than a repudiation of religion by the university. In the twentieth century, it typically appeared under the McGill crest, which featured an open book proclaiming, "In domino confido" (In the Lord I trust), the motto of James McGill.

Dawson knew that the university could not rely on endowments from religious institutions in the way that ancient European universities had, and to rescue McGill from virtual insolvency, he sought private funding from as wide a range of donors as possible. Dawson went to Toronto, then the capital of the Province of Canada, by canoe and in the snow to seek government aid, but even his patron Sir Edmund Head and George-Étienne Cartier, the prime minister, could do little to help McGill. He then appealed to the citizens of Montreal, and here he was more successful. John H.R. Molson gave $40,000 to endow a chair in English, and other supporters of the university together gave $35,000 more.

In his inaugural address as principal in 1855, Dawson made it clear that McGill had been marked by "too great an emphasis on the old type of learning," by which he meant the study of the classics. He was afraid that graduates might "go forth from our college with an antique panoply more fitted for the cases of a museum than to appear in the walks of actual life." He rejected the Oxford model in favour of "practical results" suitable for Canada.[20] This was probably exactly what many potential donors – a large segment of them without a degree or any sort of university background – wanted to hear. It was what Macdonald certainly heard, for when Dawson retired in 1893, Macdonald reminded him of this address and the vision it had defined. He praised Dawson for fulfilling so much of his vision over the course of his thirty-eight years as principal, and expressed gratitude for having been able to aid Dawson in this effort: "I am in hopes that we both may live to see the institution of the broad and model university you conceived of and sketched in your inaugural address of 1855, and that we may rejoice in the great amount of good it will do for *all time* for the people of this Dominion."[21]

Inspired though Macdonald may have been in 1855 if he was present to hear Dawson deliver his inaugural address, fifteen years would pass before he would begin to give to the university and about thirteen years further before he would launch upon a concentrated series of much greater donations. In the meantime, Dawson and McGill faced formidable challenges in keeping afloat. A building "in town," that is, to the south of the abandoned campus, was housing both the Faculty of Arts (including the Department of Natural History and Mathematics, created two years before) and the High School of Montreal. In 1856 this building burned to the ground, taking with it the faculty's few books, Dawson's collections of specimens, and scientific apparatus.

A year later, in 1857, Logan and Dawson invited the American Association for the Advancement of Science to meet in Montreal. This was the first effort to bring together scientists from all over the continent, and it demonstrated their hope that McGill would teach subjects closer to their own interests. For Logan and Dawson, geology was only one of several disciplines of natural history that deserved to be pursued. But in the same year Logan's Geological Survey found its annual budget halved to £2,500 ($10,000).

In 1860, when McGill's arts students at last exceeded fifty, their faculty was able to occupy a building site up to then abandoned. The Arts Building, containing classrooms, a library, a museum, a room for chemistry and assaying, as well as residences for the families of Dawson and university secretary William Baynes, was completed with the generous aid of William Molson. It would take until 1880 for McGill to receive a major gift from the Redpaths; this would be the Redpath Museum, given by Peter Redpath, a son of John Redpath. It would take until 1893 for McGill to receive a comparable building from Macdonald, in the form of the new Technical Building, later known as the Macdonald Engineering and Physics Buildings.

In the quarter century between Dawson's arrival and the opening of the Redpath Museum, McGill benefited from the generosity of other supporters. The largest were from the Molson brewing family, which was in its third generation of wealth, and from families that had begun wholesale businesses earlier in the century and were now in their second generation of wealth. Examples of these latter are the Frothingham and Workman families, which were partners in wholesaling hardware, and the Greenshields family, which managed the major dry goods business in the city.

In Montreal as in Boston, there was considerable public interest in popular education outside the university. One of Dawson's chief interests was the Natural History Society of Montreal, which he served as president for nearly the entire period from 1855 to 1895. This was his forum for introducing the public to scientific work that interested him, one that he shared with others who also gave lectures to the society's members. The nineteenth century witnessed many gentlemanly enthusiasts of natural history. William Esson, a minister at the St Gabriel's Street Presbyterian Church in Montreal, founded the Natural History Society in 1827 and the Mechanics' Institution a year later.[22] Other clergymen who joined the Natural History Society in its first year were James Somerville, another minister at St Gabriel's; Alexander Mathieson, the minister at St Andrew's Presbyterian Church; and John Bethune, Anglican rector of Montreal and principal of McGill from 1835 to 1846. Among the major collectors of specimens was Dr Andrew Fernando Holmes, who taught medicine at McGill and was another stalwart of the society, serving as its president before Dawson. Macdonald himself did not join the society until 1874, and then he found himself in the company of McGill governor Donald A. Smith, later Lord Strathcona, whom he was to succeed as chancellor of the university forty years later.

Another favourite educational cause of both amateur scientists and business-men was libraries. Mercantile Association Library of Montreal opened in 1843, with G.H. Frothingham as one of its incorporators, and four years later it bought the books of a predecessor, the Montreal Library, founded in 1796. Like its counterpart in Boston, the Mercantile Association Library in Montreal for some years shared a building with the local Natural History Society, as well as with the Mechanics' Institute, re-established as an "Institute" rather than "Institution" in 1845 by John Redpath after having been shut down with the Rebellion of 1837. In 1866 the library relocated to a new building, which it shared with the Art Association of Montreal, later known as the Montreal Museum of Fine Arts. Peter Redpath became president of the library in the following year.

The library tried to attract senior clerks, who earned £25 or more a year; junior clerks, who earned less; and merchants. It offered lectures; classrooms for the study of literature, the arts and sciences, and commerce; and a museum of natu-ral history and curiosities. It did not succeed, however, in attracting many clerks, and its lecture program and other ventures, apart from its collection of books, seem to have failed almost from the start. At its height in 1853, when Macdonald may have joined it, its membership included only 49 of the 400 clerks in Mon-treal but 505 merchants.[23]

If the great universities of England and even of Scotland were not Dawson's model, Owens College in Manchester, founded in 1851 by a local textile mer-chant, was.[24] John Owens, a Nonconformist, or dissenter from the Established Church of England, and a bachelor, had left almost £90,000 to establish the college, stipulating that it must be non-sectarian, like University College in London. The college had a shaky start, going into a sharp decline and closing its doors as a result of the economic depression in England in the mid-1850s.

George H. Frothingham, 1862 (Notman I-2770.1)

But as industrial England matured, there grew a demand for professionals with degrees, diplomas, and similar qualifications. These Owens College decided to offer. Its new charter in 1858 provided for a bachelor of science degree that required knowledge of mathematics, chemistry, biology, physics, logic, and ethics.[25] Oxford was not to confer a similar degree until 1895. Supported by two Unitarian friends, Owens College reopened in 1870, and in the 1880s it joined colleges in Leeds and Liverpool to become part of a new Victoria University. One governor of McGill from 1864 to 1894, Peter Redpath, was probably unusually well informed on Owens. He had gone to Manchester in about 1837 to study business and ten years later married Grace Wood, the daughter of a prominent businessman there. Both Peter and Grace Redpath were to be among the most generous benefactors to McGill.[26]

Peter Redpath, 1892 (Notman 11-99021)

Most of the members of the Natural History Society, the Mercantile Library Association, the Mechanics' Institute, and similar organizations in Montreal from the 1850s onwards were similar to the backers of Owens College. Nearly all of them were businessmen, some of them were Unitarians, and most of them saw the need for McGill to expand its professional teaching beyond its faculties of medicine and law. In Owens College, a vision for a future McGill not only existed but was being implemented.

For McGill to implement this vision, however, it had first to sort out the teaching of science, both pure and applied, as it had already evolved at the university. Although chemistry was taught in the Faculty of Medicine, it was also taught in the Faculty of Arts, as were all the other disciplines that might be considered scientific, including mathematics, geology, and natural history. The pressing question for Dawson from the start was how such emerging classes of professionals as engineers could be accommodated at the university.

Before it became an academic subject, engineering had been a profession, which it was to remain. It had evolved from a long tradition of trades and crafts and was a natural outgrowth of geology and mining. A dictionary definition of an engine, the etymological basis of the word "engineer," is a mechanical contrivance consisting of several parts working together, especially as a source of power. In the nineteenth century, engineering was seen as an applied science, and the first engineers were probably the makers of armaments – "engines of war" – in the Middle Ages, the antecedents of the corps of Royal Engineers of today. The steam engine was one of the drivers of the Industrial Revolution, and its inventors were by definition engineers, as were its operators. It was not necessary, or even possible, for these engineers to have engineering degrees, but industrialization generated a momentum of its own. The railways of the late eighteenth and early nineteenth centuries demanded industrial processes, particularly for making the steel for tracks and bridges.

Mining engineers were essential to the process, but civil engineers – those who designed roads, bridges, canals, and gasworks and thus shaped the way steel was used – were also required. Macdonald became familiar with their work in 1859, when he hired John McDougall (circa 1825–1892) of the Caledonian Iron Works to help rebuild his factory on Water Street. His new works on Ontario Street, which he built in the 1870s, were an even more spectacular example of engineering, which he frequently filled with new kinds of machinery. Engineers became solvers of technical problems, branching out from mining engineering into the specialties of mechanical, electrical, and chemical engineering, and, more recently, human and social engineering.

In Canada, civil engineers became widely known through the extensive canal building that went on between 1824 and 1848, designed to circumvent Niagara Falls and the rapids of the St Lawrence.[27] As described in chapter 2, the 1850s saw a railway boom with the building of four lines between Canada and the United States, in all of which Macdonald was an investor.

Then there was the Victoria Bridge, designed by the engineer Thomas Keefer (with Robert Stephenson, son of the great British railway engineer George Stephenson) and opened by the Prince of Wales in 1860. A mile and a quarter long, this was the longest tubular bridge in the world. It linked the eastern and western divisions of the Grand Trunk, the longest railway in the world, and it connected the Island of Montreal to the south shore of the St Lawrence, eliminating the need to cross the river on horse-boats or, in winter, by sleigh.

Another railway boom followed Confederation in 1867, and by 1888 Canada could claim more railway miles per capita than any other country. The railways led to a demand for rolling-stock, and rolling-mills, foundries, and car and motor works arose – and with them the need for mechanical engineers. As the nineteenth century progressed, large cities increasingly needed the services of municipal engineers, who designed safe water and gas supplies, sewers, and lighted streets.

Dawson had no professional designation as an engineer, but few others had either, even those who practised engineering.[28] On becoming principal in 1855, Dawson inaugurated a series of popular lectures on applied science, in the Faculty of Arts, and in 1856 he instituted the first diploma program in civil engineering in British North America. This latter was shut down in 1860 owing to lack of interest, but there was a sudden reversal in public opinion in the same year with the opening of the Victoria Bridge. Both Keefer and Stephenson had used William Logan's study of ice floes in their design of the bridge, and its completion made the benefits of civil engineering obvious to everyone.

These perceived practical benefits of applied science did not translate, however, into adequate funding for a school of engineering. It was not overwhelmingly clear that a university education, as opposed to work experience, was an absolute prerequisite for an aspiring engineer. Similar doubts had persisted about the worth to the economy of the Canadian Geological Survey. In 1863, for example, Logan had published his enormous book *The Geology of Canada* and found it immediately criticized for its emphasis on fossils rather than on exploitable minerals.

Nevertheless, by 1871, as a result of fundraising for an engineering school begun in the previous year, Dawson had obtained pledges amounting to $1,800 a year from the English-speaking community. He was perhaps emboldened by his success to apply to the Quebec minister of public instruction, P.J.O. Chauveau, who was also the premier and a friend of his, for annual grants of $3,000 for a new school of engineering and of $2,500 for a school of mines.

Chauveau wished to be seen as even-handed by the French-speaking community and first offered the Montreal branch of Laval University $3,000 a year to maintain a school of applied science. In contrast to its appeal for a grant about twenty years later, Laval refused this grant in 1873 on the ground that provincial funding was a threat to its independence as a religious institution. Two years later, the Catholic School Commission of Montreal agreed to accept $3,000 a year for a school of applied science at the Catholic École des Hautes Études Commerciales.

It is unclear when – or even whether – and for how long McGill received the annual grants that Dawson applied for in 1871. It is clear, however, that from the earliest days of the Department of Applied Science (predecessor of the Faculty of Engineering), private funding was essential and difficult. In 1871 J.H.R. Molson,

William C. Macdonald, portrait by Robert Harris (McCord Museum M-970.65)

Peter Redpath, and G.H. Frothingham pledged $400 a year for five years to pay Bernard J. Harrington, lecturer in practical science. In that same year, George Frederick Armstrong was serving as the first professor of civil engineering. A school of civil and mining engineering seems to have opened in 1874, replacing the school of mining and metallurgy run by Logan from 1868 to 1871. A chair in mining engineering followed, and in 1876 Henry Bovey succeeded Armstrong in the chair of civil engineering. Bovey was one of the few formally qualified engineers in Canada, in the company of such men as Sir Casimir Gzowski, and had not merely graduated from Cambridge but also worked on the Merseyside Docks in Lancashire.

Then, in 1879–81, the Geological Survey moved from Montreal to Ottawa, and with the consequent loss of an emphasis on geology at McGill, it was obvious that engineering at McGill must continue to include much more than geology and mining. Much was in place for an expansion of engineering and the sciences at McGill, including popular interest, a precedent in Owens College, the leadership of Dawson, and the location of the university in an increasingly prosperous and industrial city. What was most obviously lacking, however, was firm funding. The province was politically unable to finance first-rate facilities for engineering and science at McGill unless it did the same for Laval or purely technical French-speaking institutions. Provincial revenues in any case were probably insufficient for even one such bold venture.

What McGill needed was a benefactor of industrial background, very familiar with engineering and scientific processes, and with experience in building up a big project from nothing or at least very little. As we shall see in chapter 6, such a benefactor did not emerge until 1889, and then in the person of Thomas Workman, president of Molsons Bank, whose fortune had come out of the largest hardware business in North America, Frothingham & Workman. Unfortunately, he was by then dead, and his desire to build a new "Technical Building" took the form of a bequest. Unfortunately also, his legacy almost immediately proved inadequate to equip his building. It was a stroke of extremely good fortune that another industrialist, both very much alive and with much deeper pockets, was now ready to expand Workman's vision beyond what even Dawson could imagine. This was William Macdonald.

*Chapter Six*

## MACDONALD'S EARLY PHILANTHROPY:
## THE FRASER INSTITUTE, McGILL UNIVERSITY, AND
## HIS SEARCH FOR FAMILY, CIRCA 1870–1892

I look on the engineering profession as one of the most important professions, if not the most important profession, of this or any other country, and I have a keen appreciation of the great benefits it has conferred, on the human family the world over. "May its progress never cease, and its knowledge with the years increase."

> *Macdonald to C.H. McLeod, Secretary of the Canadian Society of Civil Engineers,*
> *on accepting honorary membership in the society, 11 January 1896*[1]

### THE FRASER INSTITUTE

In 1870 Hugh Fraser, a bachelor merchant resident of St Lawrence Hall, as Macdonald had until recently been, died.[2] In his will, after specific bequests, he left the Honourable John Abbott and Judge Frederick Torrance the residue of his estate for the purpose of establishing a free lending library, museum, and art gallery. Fraser's brother John, who had been left nothing, immediately contested the will. His litigation ultimately went to the Privy Council in London, which in 1874 ruled the will valid. Abbott and Torrance had in any case incorporated the Fraser Institute in the year of Fraser's death, with Thomas Workman, Peter Redpath, and Alexander Molson joining them as governors. On hearing the ruling of the Privy Council, they began to plan a building for the institute, but they were impeded by John Fraser, who up until 1883 carried on other bitter litigation, challenging the very legality of the institute as well as the validity of his brother's will. For a further fifteen years, he would conduct other kinds of futile harassment.

In the meantime, William Dawson proposed that the Natural History Society should merge with the Fraser Institute. Other support for the institute came

The Fraser Institute, Dorchester Street
(ANQ, cote: MAS-2-65-c, No de séquence O273210)

forward. The Mercantile Library Association and the Institut Canadien (an anti-clerical society) offered to give their books to the Fraser. It has been said that Dawson first met Macdonald at a meeting of the Fraser Institute.[3] In any case, Macdonald, the brewer John H.R. Molson, Duncan McIntyre and R.B. Angus of the Canadian Pacific Railway, and Hugh McLennan of the Harbour Board set up a fund to pay for a building for the institute. With the exception of McIntyre, these men were all present or future governors of McGill. In 1885 Principal Dawson was at last able to join Macdonald and other friends of McGill – Sir Donald A. Smith of the Hudson's Bay Company; Matthew Hamilton Gault, MP, of the Sun Life Assurance Company; and the textile manufacturer David Morrice, among others – at the opening of the Fraser Institute. Macdonald served from the start on its executive committee, not retiring until 1894.

The Fraser Institute hardly compared in distinction to the great libraries in Edinburgh or Boston, but it signalled a firm commitment by leading Montreal businessmen to the diffusion of popular education – and at a time when they were likewise committing themselves to McGill. The saga of its birth, from 1870 to 1885, also coincided with Dawson's concerted efforts, firstly, to put McGill on a sounder financial footing, and secondly, to develop within it the sort of technical institution that he was watching develop elsewhere, such as at Owens College in Manchester. Owens College, as we saw in chapter 5, was founded by businessmen for businessmen, primarily to confer the new bachelor of science degree and to prepare students for such professions as that of engineering. Essential to both his goals was the support of the local business community. The Fraser was the most obvious stepping stone to and link with McGill for businessmen like Macdonald, who had rarely, if ever, set foot in a university. Dawson's proposal to merge the Natural History Society with the Fraser Institute did not take place, but they did share facilities with the Mercantile Library Association, much as the Natural History Society and the Mercantile Library Association in Boston had shared facilities in Macdonald's time there.

## McGill University

Dawson, Logan, and many others associated with McGill had been educated at Edinburgh, while in Montreal they came into contact with developments in Boston. To some extent, then, the McGill they were trying to create was heir to both of these cities. The influence of Edinburgh was very clear in the McGill medical school in particular. And, traceable to Boston, Unitarianism, which was not so much a religion as a radical openness to new ideas, exercised a comparable influence on the board of governors. By the 1870s many of the Montreal merchants who supported the university were Unitarians with New England, if not Bostonian, antecedents.

The first Montreal Unitarian congregation was established in 1844 and erected its church, the Church of the Messiah, in 1846. Here it was to flourish well into the twentieth century. Among the founders of the Messiah were William Workman, twice mayor of Montreal and partner in the largest hardware wholesaler in North America, Frothingham & Workman, with his brother Thomas; John Young, trader, contractor, and chairman of the Harbour Commission; Sir Francis Hincks, banker and prime minister; Harrison Stephens, a merchant from Vermont and sometime partner of Young's; and Benjamin Holmes, cashier of the Bank of Montreal, politician, and another partner of Young's.

Further generations of Unitarians perpetuated their extremely liberal influence on public life, such as the lawyer George Washington Stephens I (son-in-law of Harrison), followed by his own son of the same name, a politician and merchant. Other prominent citizens who joined the church were Sir William Van Horne of the CPR and John H.R. Molson, head of Molson's Brewery and

Thomas Workman, 1869 (Notman 1-36832)

of Molsons Bank, and his wife, Louisa Frothingham. The Unitarianism of the
Workmans, the Frothinghams, and at least one Molson ensured that Macdonald should be not alone in wanting to ensure the non-sectarian character of the
McGill. Along with such Presbyterians as Peter Redpath and Donald Smith,
these Unitarians would be his models as benefactors.[4]

Up until 1890 Macdonald seems to have been unsure about quite what to do for
McGill, apart from responding to general fundraising appeals. He is said to have
given the university $1,750 for biological equipment in 1867, but there seems to be
no record of this in the minutes of the governors.[5] His first documented connection to the university is his endowment of scholarships in 1870. His endowment
of $1,250 annually, until 1881 and therefore amounting to $15,000, was part of the
total of $54,000 collected in what was the university's first fundraising campaign

Mr and Mrs John H.R. Molson (Notman II-124740.0)

since 1856. The Macdonald scholarships (held for one year) and exhibitions (held for two years) were not confined to students of any particular subject, but were open to all students, then only male, through competition.[6]

In 1871 Macdonald gave $5,000 to the general endowment of the university and a great number of books and butterflies. These included the T.D. King Shakespeare collection of 214 volumes (with Donald Smith), the Ribbeck collection of classical literature of about 4,000 volumes, and the Bowles collection of lepidoptera (with J.H. Burland), as well as his own collection of the same. But he did not contribute to a campaign to raise funds for the Department of Applied Science within the Faculty of Arts, an area that would be his chief interest in later years. Many others did, though, led by Daniel Torrance with $5,000; George Moffatt, C.J. Brydges, and Robert J. Rechie with $1,000 each; and James Ferrier, Peter

Graduates in applied science, 1873. Pictured: C.J. McLeod, D.A. Stewart, R.J. Brodie, H.K. Wickstte, G.T. Kennedy, and J.F. Torrance (Notman 1-84433.0.3)

Redpath, J.H.R. Molson, G.H. Frothingham, and T.J. Claxton, among others, with much lesser amounts. In 1870 the expenses of the department – totalling $4,570 – were covered by a small grant from the provincial Superior Education Fund, student fees, and income from an endowment of $8,000, together with $1,500 in annual subscriptions, some expiring, from friends.[7]

The governors' memorandum to potential subscribers, seeking a total of $2,000 to $5,000, had begun as follows: "The University has long regarded the promotion of practical scientific culture, with the view of fitting the young men of this country for prosecuting the higher industrial arts and professions, as one of its leading functions. To this end it has established its Department of Applied Science in which students may receive an adequate preparatory training for the professions of civil engineering, mechanical engineering, mining engineering, assaying and chemistry."[8]

The memorandum explained that the staff of the department consisted of H.T. Bovey, MA, CE, fellow of Queen's College, Cambridge, and professor of

Geological Club in Pointe Claire, with Sir William Dawson, 1890
(Notman MP-0000.87)

civil engineering and applied mechanics; Gilbert P. Girdwood, MD, professor
of practical chemistry; Bernard J. Harrington, BA, PhD, professor of assaying
and mining and lecturer in chemistry; C.H. McLeod, lecturer in surveying and
drawing; J.W. Dawson, lecturer in geology and palaeontology; and Alexander
Johnson, LLD, lecturer in mathematics and natural philosophy. In addition,
there were lecturers in mathematics, English, German, and French. There were
no hard divisions between the department and the Faculty of Arts, of which it
was a part.

It was not until 1878, seven years later, that McGill decided to establish a Faculty of Applied Science separate from the Faculty of Arts. It approved a bachelor
of applied science degree for graduates in civil engineering later in that year,
with Dawson himself as professor of civil engineering and applied mechanics
and dean. He was also to hold the new Logan Chair in Geology in addition
to remaining as principal. Dawson launched a new campaign for funds for the
new faculty at the end of the year, but again Macdonald did not contribute. The
contributors were much the same as those to the previous campaign, with annual

subscriptions for five years of fairly small amounts – Peter Redpath and J.H.R. Molson for $400 per year each; and Hugh McLennan, A.F. Gault, James Ferrier, and T.J. Claxton for $100 each. Miss May L. Frothingham gave $400 a year for three years, and there were other smaller amounts.[9]

Just why Macdonald did not contribute to the 1878 fundraising campaign remains unclear. Perhaps he was not yet interested in the applied sciences, but it is also possible that he did not know Dawson or anyone else at McGill very well in this period. He had, however, moved to Prince of Wales Terrace in 1868, not far from Dawson, who was living in the east wing of the Arts Building, and he was even closer to mathematics lecturer and vice-principal Alexander Johnson, who lived in no. 5 of the Terrace, almost next to Macdonald's no. 3. The most significant event in Macdonald's life in 1878 was almost undoubtedly the death of his mother, and he was also much preoccupied with the final surrender of the tenanted lands of the family in Prince Edward Island. While Macdonald probably began associating with the Dawsons before his mother died, it was certainly after this event that he had much more time to develop this association.

### PERSONAL RELATIONS BETWEEN MACDONALD AND THE DAWSONS

William Dawson and his wife (née Margaret Ann Young Mercer) were extremely sociable. They invited students to visit them informally and also extended formal invitations to musical recitals, lectures, and scientific displays at their home. Macdonald probably attended some of these, as over time he had become increasingly fond of music and greatly enjoyed talking to students and their teachers.

In 1875 Dawson established a summer cottage at Little Métis, a resort on the lower St Lawrence near Pleistocene and Palaeozoic deposits. He spent happy summers with his family there, writing scientific papers and books and collecting fossils. At least from the 1880s and possibly before, Macdonald visited Little Métis on several occasions and very probably stayed with the Dawsons. There developed unusual bonds of warmth and candour between him and the Dawson family, both at Little Métis and in Montreal. Much later, for example, when in 1892 the principal asked Macdonald what to do about his shy son, William Bell, Macdonald advised that the boy should stay in business, as he would make a poor professor.[10]

Macdonald was especially close to another Dawson son, the troubled Rankine, whose education he supported, and to Anna, Dawson's daughter. He could be very stern with Rankine. In 1891, after being told by Lady Dawson that Rankine seemed to be abandoning his medical studies in favour of a career as a business promoter, Macdonald wrote to him: "If you had been pursuing your profession and needed assistance, I would most willingly have helped you without ever looking for a return, but if you have taken the business of Financing, at which

Sir William and Lady Dawson (Notman 11-118899.0)

you must yet be a novice, and to a large extent in the hands of some one else, of whom I know absolutely nothing, it is not surprising that I should decline even the first small request."[11] Macdonald was gentler with Anna. In 1876 she married Bernard Harrington, another geologist and a lecturer at the university. Macdonald was delighted with the match, and he would later build a chemistry building for the department that Harrington would head. He bought a house for the couple in Métis and visited them there.

Bernard J. Harrington, 1885 (Notman 11-77336)

The time that Macdonald spent with the Dawsons allowed him to become as well acquainted with the administrative problems of the university as any governor. Nobody was better placed than Dawson and Harrington to educate Macdonald on the evolving needs of both research and teaching at McGill. And nobody was better placed to influence his giving in favour of science and engineering.

## DAWSON'S CHRISTIANITY

One factor that may have given Macdonald pause, however, was Dawson's staunchly Christian response to what he saw as the tendency of new theories of science, especially Charles Darwin's on the evolution of species, to undermine the truths of the gospel. Dawson was not only fundamentally hostile to the scepticism of Hume but also determined to reaffirm Christian belief in the new Darwinian era of scepticism. He worked throughout his almost forty years at McGill to create a creationist apologetics consistent with his work as a scientist. He did not base his creationism on a literal interpretation of the biblical account in Genesis – that the world had been created in one week – but all his efforts were aimed at establishing that the biblical account was basically scientifically plausible. Some of his work presumed that translations from the original Hebrew were incorrect, and he took up the study of Hebrew and even took a year of leave to travel through the Middle East.

As he was known as a scientist of the first rank in Great Britain, the United States, and Canada, Dawson became famous as a formidable defender of Christianity, and he was eagerly taken up by American universities, theological colleges, and journals that shared his views. But as a scientist he was also largely isolated, at least in his later years, in his quest to reconcile science with Christianity. He was dogmatic even in comparison to some of his close contemporaries. Logan, for example, had seldom entered a kirk, and even Lyell, Dawson's Christian patron, found his positions too extreme. In 1883, before delivering his lecture as president of the British Association for the Advancement of Science, Dawson was warned not to engage in apologetics, as nobody else there would share his views. His son George Mercer Dawson, moreover, perhaps even a greater geologist than he was, studied under that great scourge of Christianity, T.H. Huxley.

While they held Dawson's administrative abilities, energy, and learning in high esteem, it is unlikely that any of the governors in his time, including Macdonald, shared his religious views. In any case, these views did not intrude upon Dawson's administration or impede his solicitation of aid for the university. Moreover, Dawson was completely open to the development of new disciplines and departments at McGill, whatever their implications for religious faith. Such was his own certitude about the truths of Christianity that he did not fear any lethal threat to them, particularly from science.

With such openness to a specialization of the curriculum, Dawson was able to cultivate the openly unbelieving Macdonald as a friend as well as a benefactor, and he was able to encourage the reorganization of the teaching of natural history. They were both happy to see not only the development of such established branches of natural history as chemistry and botany and mathematics as distinct departments in the university, but also the rise of the new academic discipline of engineering to train professionals. It was a combination of his personal respect for Dawson and his quick understanding of the practical needs at the university that made Macdonald's partnership with Dawson, especially from 1883 to 1893, so easy and effective. This respect and understanding were certainly preconditions of their partnership, but another precondition may have been Macdonald's deteriorating relations with his family.

## MACDONALD'S FAMILY TIES, 1878–1903

A rich man in Macdonald's time could have spent his money on hospitals, schools, charities, his family, and himself. Up to 1893, Macdonald spent little on himself but did contribute generously to these other causes, and certainly to the welfare of his family – his mother and his sister Helen at their home in Prince of Wales Terrace, his brother Augustine, and his brother John Archibald and his wife and children.[12]

Macdonald was loyal to his family, despite rifts that had arisen over religion. Of his immediate family, only he, his mother, and Helen had publicly repudiated Catholicism. The rupture in the family dated back to 1849–54, when Donald McDonald had broken first with William and then with his wife and finally with his daughter Helen. So deeply wounded was he by Helen's apostasy, by his own confession in 1854, it seems the closeness of the three apostates was at least in part rooted in their continued repudiation of him.

The deaths of his mother in 1878 and of Helen in 1889 fundamentally loosened Macdonald's attachment to his roots and left him disconsolate. No letters survive on the death of his mother, though it is known that when the three were together at Prince of Wales Terrace, they formed a very close-knit home. His letters on the death of Helen, which occurred while they were touring Europe together, convey unbearable grief but not despair.

Macdonald's invitation in 1891 to his niece, John Archibald's daughter Anna, to live with him was his last effort to revive a family atmosphere in his house. She has been described mistakenly as his housekeeper, while in fact he had servants and she did not perform the duties of a housekeeper as they would have been understood at the time. Neither was she a chatelaine or a hostess, as he almost never entertained. Anna was a great help to him, however, in looking after her own younger siblings – as Helen had been before her – when they passed through Montreal from time to time. This they would do when Macdonald arranged for their passage between various schools and Prince Edward Island. Anna was in effect a surrogate elder daughter to him, and her siblings were his other surrogate children.

With the expropriation of the leased family land in Prince Edward Island looming, from about 1876 Macdonald undertook to support the chronically ill John Archibald, his wife, and, by the late 1880s, their nine surviving children. These children he clothed and educated and sometimes took on holidays, for roughly a decade beginning in 1888. He wrote to them regularly, arranged for their schooling in Scotland, England, Massachusetts, and Ontario, and paid all their expenses as well as those of their parents. Macdonald was the first to admit that he knew nothing about children, but he arranged their trips between the

Island and their schools and even, with the aid of Helen and then Anna, put them up for extended periods at Prince of Wales Terrace.

These children and their parents would have tried the patience of anyone. As only his many letters to them survive, and not their replies, it is not possible to see their points of view, but of his generosity, his patience, and ultimately his broken heart in relation to them there can be no doubt. He demanded, usually in vain, that they send him accounts of how they had spent the allowances he was sending them, which were in addition to their school fees, which he was also paying.

Of the nine children, Fred, the eldest and therefore the prospective heir to the ghostly Glenaladale chiefdom, disappointed him the most. Fred aspired to take over John Archibald's farm, and with this in mind, Macdonald sent him to the Massachusetts Agricultural College in Amherst in 1888. Fred dropped out after a year, showing little regard even for the special tuition in chemistry paid for by his uncle, and spent a year at Glenaladale before going to New Mexico in search of something new to do. Macdonald offered him a second chance: "If you will heartily second my efforts it will be a great pleasure to me to help you up. But the work has to be done by you, I can only help. You only can masticate, assimilate and digest *your* food – you only can acquire your own knowledge."[13]

Donald, Willie, Roderick, and Johnie (so spelt) were not much better. Macdonald sent Donald and Roderick to Miss Lauder's school in Montreal, and at the suggestion of the Reverend Dr James Barclay, of St Paul's Presbyterian Church in Montreal, he then sent some of them to the Merchiston Castle School in Edinburgh in 1891 and 1892. Barclay had himself been educated there, and he was sending two of his sons to accompany Donald, the first of John Archibald's boys to go, in 1891. Although founded by a brother of the originator of the Disruption in the Church of Scotland, Thomas Chalmers, Merchiston was not a religious foundation. In any case, Macdonald wanted Donald, then fourteen, to study commerce, science, and the pianoforte. Donald did not turn out to be a strong student, but of the four boys he seems to have been the closest to his uncle, receiving his moral support for the longest period. Only Donald seems to have found a career, eventually becoming a tea planter in Assam.

By November of 1891, it was becoming clear that Fred would not succeed in finding his fortune in New Mexico. Macdonald stepped in again and in the spring of 1892 sent him and Willie, who had been similarly unemployed, to study at the Ontario Agricultural College in Guelph.[14] Fred did not last long at the college, for after a few weeks he had decided to return to Prince Edward Island and take over the family farm. Macdonald helped Fred even in this venture, authorizing Cundall to buy, in Macdonald's name, animal stock (worth $6,000) and farm implements for Fred. Nothing, Macdonald warned, was to be owned in the names of either Fred or his parents. He considered them all spendthrifts whose property might be attached for debt at any time. Macdonald warned Fred: "If you disappoint me, I can easily bear the loss, but I doubt if you can." But within two days Fred was demanding extra travelling expenses beyond his personal living expenses.[15]

Willie lasted at Guelph a little longer, but he decided not to return in September 1893 and went back to Glenaladale.[16] Macdonald refused to help him enter the dairy business:

Your knowledge of horses and cattle, their care and treatment; your knowledge of the various kinds of soils, their fertility, resources and requirements, is of the most limited sort imaginable, and not such as to induce me to look for anything but failure from such effort as you could put forth. You imagine that because Fred is having much work done this year that he will necessarily make it successful. Like every body else, he finds it very easy to spend other people's money, but that is very different from making farming pay. That part of the operation has yet to be proven.[17]

By the following spring, Fred was asking his uncle for a loan of $300. Macdonald despaired of his nephew's foresight and warned Willie, too, that his patience was coming to an end. Willie continued, however, to run up unauthorized debts in Macdonald's name: within only eight months in 1893–94, for example, he ordered eight suits of clothes, six pairs of pants, and two pairs of football pants from a tailor, who passed the bill on to the rich uncle.

When, in 1892, Roderick (thirteen) and Johnie (ten) went to Merchiston, Macdonald found that they were mentally feeble. Roderick left the school about four years later but was so "painfully backward" that he could not enter McGill except as a part-time student in drawing, wood-turning, carpentry, smithy, and foundry. Johnie remained longer, and Macdonald asked the headmaster to give him special instruction for his "weak intellect."[18]

Of John Archibald's girls, Macdonald sent Tillie and Maggie to Falconberg School in Cheltenham at about the same time. Tillie seems to have been quite bright, and she passed her Oxford examination. Macdonald wrote enthusiastically to her headmistress, urging her to broaden Tillie's interests. Forestry, he observed, added "much to the pleasures of life and travel" and physics was "a most important part of a liberal education." His enthusiasm did not last long. For some reason, the girls repudiated him for interfering in their lives, just as their sister Anna was about to do.

Anna and Macdonald quarrelled in December 1892, apparently after he learned of her intention to marry the Catholic Alain Chartier de Lotbinière Macdonald.[19] Anna left in the following January, declaring that she would rather live in Timbuctoo than with her uncle. The quarrel left a very deep wound in Macdonald, who confessed months later that he had not recovered from it.[20] Anna's departure was deeply upsetting to him not merely because she was the last member of his family to live with him but also because it meant that he would no longer see his other nieces and nephews in his home, as he had been doing over the previous five years. With Helen's death in 1889, Macdonald had sought distraction first in a tour of American technical schools and then in erecting his first buildings for McGill. Anna's departure less than four years later would lead to even more buildings and indeed to an ever-growing tide of gifts to McGill.

Macdonald wrote to John Archibald's wife in September 1893, condemning the "perverse course" of all her girls and declaring that his "responsibility for the family, either *financially or morally*, is permanently at an end."[21] His disclaimer did not last long, for on the same day he sent Fred $1,000 for twenty more cows and in October he sent Mrs McDonald $500 for household expenses.

Two years later, at the end of 1895, he declined to offer Fred advice on how he might continue on the farm, on the ground that he, Macdonald, was "entirely ignorant of Agriculture," but he noted that Fred was still unable to make enough money even to pay his workers and feed his stock. Fred's venture had totally collapsed, and he went to western Canada in search of other employment. Writing to John Archibald in January 1896, Macdonald refused to take any interest in the recovery of the farm.[22] By now, he had buried his mother and his sister Helen in the Mount Royal Cemetery in Montreal. He had even bought plots there for himself and John Archibald to lie in forever, side by side. Although these were not to be used, they demonstrated his fixed determination to break with the Island even in death. He maintained allowances for John Archibald and his wife, however, only to discover in January 1898 that they had separated. Apparently John Archibald had become enraged when he discovered that his wife and Fred had secretly decided to sell timber rights on the farm. So great was his "uncontrollable temper" that Mrs McDonald feared "personal violence" from him.[23] Macdonald tried to force their reconciliation by refusing to pay them separate allowances, but to no permanent avail.

In the following year, Macdonald reported to John Archibald that Johnie was doing fairly well at Merchiston but still had "not his heart in his work" and seemed "content not to learn very much." "I am grieved," Macdonald continued, "for I feel much as the man did who undertook to make an empty bag stand upright." As for Roderick, Macdonald concluded that he "was able to do two things in a very effective manner, viz. sleeping and smoking, but beyond these he seemed heedless of his future."[24]

Macdonald remained in frequent correspondence with John Archibald in Prince Edward Island until John Archibald's death in 1903, and he occasionally wrote to Augustine in the United States before the latter's death on an unknown date. In this period, he seems to have seen John Archibald only about three times and Augustine possibly never. Macdonald had irretrievably lost respect for John Archibald as early as 1851, although his pity for him increased over the years, perhaps because of his precarious health and difficult family life. Augustine was even feebler, a recluse who between the years 1892 and 1897 could not afford to pay for his room in a boarding house in Connecticut, although he never told Macdonald of his plight. He seems gradually to have gone mad and to have died in an asylum for the mentally ill. Macdonald's last letters concerning Augustine, in 1899–1900, relate to an asylum and to hiring an assistant to keep him clean.[25]

By the turn of the century, then, hardly any of Captain John's legacy was left. As we have seen, in the year of the death of Macdonald's mother, 1878, the leased lands of the Glenaladale estate on Prince Edward Island were finally expropriated. In 1893, as he was reviewing documents from Captain John's life, Macdonald bitterly reflected on how little his family's struggle of almost a century had yielded and what a poor investment Prince Edward Island had been.[26] In 1902 he wrote to his agent H.J. Cundall that "Glenaladale is not now of any more importance to me than a last year's bird's nest. It is quite improbable that I shall ever see it again," and he did not.[27]

## MACDONALD ADOPTS McGILL AS HIS NEW FAMILY, 1881–1892

A man other than Macdonald might have given up on the young and devoted his energies elsewhere. But Macdonald, despite his forbidding exterior, was extremely compassionate towards the young – one would have to say positive in his thinking – for the disappointments of his roughly two decades as a surrogate father simply reinforced his hopes for the formal education of productive young people. He was under no illusion about how easily lives could be wasted, and his experiences with his relations bring the benefactions about to be described into relief. As his friend Susan Cameron, the wife of McGill's bursar Walter Vaughan, would recall of his treatment of others:

He had to be convinced of the latent ability of the candidate [a young student] and the actuality of the need, and to that end he made himself familiar with all the circumstances, became the sympathetic friend of child, parents and teachers, and followed every step in the progress of his protégé. He was not interested in supporting weakness, and had no wish to assume responsibilities which properly belonged to others; but once convinced that he had found a promising field, he poured out his irrigating wealth with a hand as lavish as it was unpretentious.[28]

In 1890, writing to his cousin Margaret Small McDonald about her impecunious brother, Macdonald remarked: "It shews you the faulty state of education which does not provide a training by which every healthy member of the human family might be able, if necessary, to become self-supporting. In this Country, there is no difficulty in every intelligent person procuring the small requirements of good raiment and shelter, in the station of life in which they have been reared, if the proper instruction has been given to them, while young."[29] This proper instruction became his mission, but it was for him not an easy one to define practically and he was to take time in finding his stride.

The deterioration of Macdonald's family relations just described extended over decades. The substitution of McGill as the chief object of his assistance was similarly a gradual process. It required others to serve first as exemplary benefactors, and he initially continued his contributions to the university gingerly. After the fundraising campaign for the Faculty of Applied Science in 1878, Peter Redpath announced that he would build a special museum for McGill to show specimens of geology, palaeontology, zoology, botany, and archaeology, all in honour of the twenty-fifth anniversary of Dawson's principalship.[30] This was the first purpose-built museum in Canada, and it signalled a new era for the sciences at the university.

## FUNDRAISING AT MCGILL AND MACDONALD'S ELECTION AS A GOVERNOR, 1881–1883

Despite the announced Peter Redpath Museum, McGill was far from rich. Its balance sheet for 1880 revealed that there had been government grants of only $2,500 from the province and $1,650 from the Superior Education Fund, with $1,500 from the Dominion government for the McGill University Observatory. The Faculty of Arts yielded only $686 in fees, and the Faculty of Applied Science yielded $1,025. Annual donations to the Faculty of Applied Science amounted to only $2,375.50. There was a deficiency in matching expenses to revenues of $6,500. Archdeacon William Turnbull Leach, the dean of arts, and Abraham de Sola, professor of Hebrew, had their salaries cut; the expenditure for new books for the library was confined to $200, and the gymnasium, which had cost $2,500 a year, was simply abandoned. Prizes in both faculties were suspended, and all annual salaries above $1,000 were reduced by 12.5 per cent.

George Hague, manager of the Merchants' Bank of Canada, proposed a campaign for an endowment of $150,000 for McGill. This marvellously successful effort took place in October and November 1881, Macdonald surpassing all other donors with $25,000 in new scholarships in the Faculty of Arts.[31] Clearly he had pledged his troth. The campaign continued into 1882–83, and other contributions followed over these years. Miss Barbara Scott gave $30,000 for the William Scott Chair in Engineering, Hiram Mills $43,000 for a chair in classics, and the estate of David J. Greenshields $40,000 for a chair in chemistry and mineralogy. The Gale Chair in Law was endowed with $25,000, and the Choil and Campbell endowments of medicine were $50,000 each. Donald Smith's endowment of the Donalda courses for women alone totalled $120,000.[32] Suddenly, the university seemed about to enter a stage of development as yet unimagined. A statement by the governors of McGill of their financial position in 1886 was to reveal a new endowment of $33,500, with annual subscriptions for two to eight years of $3,500 a year. While investments totalled $385,000 in 1881, by 1885 they would reach $721,000, in addition to an increase in special endowments of $190,000.[33]

George Moffatt, one of the early supporters of the Mercantile Library, and C.J. Brydges of the CPR resigned as governors in May 1883, and Macdonald, George Hague, and Hugh McLennan were elected to the board to fill these two vacancies and one other. In March 1884 Macdonald offered to repair the abandoned gymnasium for $256 and sent his architect, Andrew Taylor, to do the job. In June he pledged $500 for five years for a chair in botany and vegetable physiology, which was occupied in the following October by David Pearce Penhallow.

The year 1884 was a decisive one. The British Association for the Advancement of Science met in Montreal, and Macdonald joined J.H.R. Molson on the governors' planning committee to organize a conversazione in connection with the event. He seems to have attended sessions spellbound, including a lecture by the eminent physicist Oliver Lodge. In the meantime, Donald Smith had joined Peter Redpath as a benefactor to the university unprecedented in his generosity. In September 1884 Smith gave McGill $50,000 and was elected chairman of the governors a few weeks later.

In 1885 the dean of medicine, R. Palmer Howard – whose son had married Smith's daughter – proposed expanding the medical buildings at a cost estimated at $21,150. Macdonald had joined the estates committee of the board, which administered the buildings and the real estate of the university, and he and Molson were charged with finding funds for this project. They recommended using part of endowments from Choil and Campbell, but there was some doubt about whether this would be sufficient. Macdonald added $1,000 to the Campbell Memorial Endowment. Financial stringency returned with a drop in interest rates in 1886–87 and the consequent fall in the yield of investments, so that there was a deficit of $2,500 in that year. In 1886 he gave $2,075 for fittings of the Upper Chemical Laboratory, and in the following year he contributed $3,000 for current expenses, followed in 1888 with $3,000 for classrooms for the Faculty of Applied Science.

## MACDONALD AND THE FACULTY OF LAW
### AT McGILL, 1887–1893

At the start of 1887, Macdonald pledged to provide McGill with new chemistry laboratories, but in March of that year his interests suddenly turned to the Faculty of Law. The Bar was proposing the introduction of an examination, which it would administrate, as a prerequisite for joining the legal profession. In the face of this proposal, the Faculty of Law was urging the governors to petition the Legislative Assembly of Quebec to retain as sufficient qualification for entering the legal profession either Protestant matriculation or the degree of bachelor of arts from McGill. The question of whether a McGill degree was sufficient to earn entrance into a profession was a vital one, as the assumption that it was would constitute an attraction to funding and enrolment. If the Bar alone was responsible for qualifying lawyers, at a time when a university degree was not necessary for lawyers in any case, it might effectively remove the need for a law degree from McGill. In the 1870s, for example, the Dominion Lands Act had not accepted the McGill bachelor of applied science degree as the equivalent of a diploma in civil engineering, a fact that lessened, if temporarily, the practical value of the McGill degree. Legislation around these issues could be very hazardous.

In this new case, the Faculty of Law also perceived a more general threat to the guarantees of Protestant education in Quebec under the British North America Act. The province was unsympathetic to the plea from the McGill governors, and it proceeded to pass a Bar Act to make entry into the legal profession dependent on criteria that the Bar itself would set. The university later appealed to the governor general to disallow this act, but its appeal was rejected.[34] Early in 1888, Macdonald and J.H.R. Molson eased the situation somewhat by pledging $3,000 for the renovation of the east wing of the Arts Building, then housing the law faculty.[35] It was not until 1889, however, that the province, after vigorous representations by board members Sir A.T. Galt and Judge Church, both McGill governors, provided McGill with some relief from the exclusive jurisdiction of the Bar to educate lawyers.

The future of the Faculty of Law was complex because it was the professional school of McGill most clearly connected to French Quebec. Because its graduates were expected to function in the Quebec legal system, which was dominated by French-speaking judges and juries and had its own civil code, largely derived from France, the McGill law school was far from a bastion of Anglo-Saxon isolationism. The origins of Macdonald's particular concern for the law faculty are unclear, but in the context of the time he probably saw potentially Catholic interference with the legal system and in particular with the ultimate survival of non-Catholic Quebec. A more general crisis over the funding of Protestant education had begun with an appeal to the province by Laval University for $20,000 a year. The McGill governors likewise petitioned the province, in February 1889, for financial assistance. The university implicitly used such benefactions as Macdonald's as a reason for more, not less, funding from government. McGill requested an amount

equal to that given to Roman Catholic Institutions, inasmuch as such grants to Collegiate Institutions cannot reasonably or justly be apportioned, in the income of the Common School Funds, according to population, because the value of these Institutions is to be tested, *not by any standard of general population, but by their number of students and their appliances for education and by the necessary expenditure for the kind of education which they give, and also because those Institutions are not chargeable in the taxes of one community, but sustained by voluntary endowments, the magnitude of which should be considered in the public ends granted to them.*[36]

At about this time, the board appointed a special committee on the future of the law faculty in particular. The committee included J.S. Hall, QC, MPP; the lawyers Charles J. Fleet and R.D. McGibbon; and the dean of the faculty, N.W. Trenholme. Its report noted that the faculty had "been mainly dependent for its continuance as a branch of the University on the labor and efforts of a few men busily engaged in their profession, whose services have been throughout all these years given without any adequate remuneration or reward other than that of duty discharged."[37] Even with the Gale endowment, the average faculty member received only $300 a year.

As the only English-language law school in Quebec, McGill was threatened by the "French colleges," to which it might have to abandon "the all important field of Jurisprudence and kindred subjects." The loss of the law faculty would mean that McGill would "renounce all participation in the training of the men who must necessarily be our Bar, our Judges and largely our Legislators and Occupants of high offices of Public trust." The committee noted that Laval University in Quebec City had established a branch in Montreal. To put the McGill faculty on a firmer footing, it called for a permanent professor of law and an assistant, costing $1,000 per year; annual scholarships and prizes worth $1,800 per year; a library; and a separate building. The committee noted that Harvard, Columbia, and Michigan universities had full-time law professors, unlike McGill, and estimated that $118,000 needed to be raised for the law faculty, although even $60,000 would be sufficient for the moment. It could make do, temporarily, with the lecture rooms and library at the Fraser Institute.

In April 1890, in response to this report, Macdonald gave $150,000 to re-establish the Faculty of Law. Initially, this amount was mixed with grants for the "Technical and Physics Buildings" and for a chair in experimental physics, but later the full amount was confirmed for the funding of two Macdonald chairs in law. The holder of one was to be in charge of the "management and advancement" of the faculty, and the other was to act as secretary. The governors noted that this was the largest benefaction "hitherto received by this University, and that it merited our most earnest and cordial thanks."[38] They added to the name of the Faculty of Law the words "McDonald Foundation," although this designation has not survived. By 1913 he had given $232,500 to the Faculty of Law.

## MACDONALD AND ENGINEERING AND PHYSICS AT McGILL, 1889–1893

In about 1889 Macdonald was reported to have $260,000 invested in the Bank of Montreal, $150,000 in the Merchants' Bank, $150,000 in the Bank of Commerce, and property worth $56,700, for a total of $616,700. The whole Molson family was said to have property worth $643,000, with a further $200,000 invested in the Bank of Montreal, $60,000 in the Merchants' Bank, $630,150 in Molsons Bank, $30,000 in the Bank of Commerce, and $164,000 in the Savings Bank, for a total of $1,733,150. The Redpath family had $187,500 invested in its refinery, property worth $510,000, and $100,000 in the Bank of Montreal, for a total of $797,500. The Stephens family was worth $800,000, and the Allan family had $590,000 invested in the Merchants' Bank and $40,000 in an assurance company, for a total of $630,000. These figures are at best approximate, and it is not certain whether they include the value of all businesses owned. Nevertheless, they suggest that in 1889 Macdonald, with no immediate family or obvious heirs, was the richest individual in Montreal and in Canada. The closest other individual was Stanley Bagg, who is said to have owned property worth more than $500,000. Whatever the inaccuracies of these figures, they indicate that Macdonald was free to pursue almost any project he desired through both his profits and his investments.[39]

More particularly, Macdonald was in a position to join the ranks of the Frothinghams and the Workmans, the partners in hardware who in 1889 made two handsome endowments to McGill. First, the Reverend Frederick Frothingham, a Unitarian minister, and his sister Mrs J.H.R. Molson gave $40,000 for the principalship in the form of the John Frothingham Principal's Fund. The only condition was their "hope and expectation that the fund shall be administered in the broadest spirit of Protestant freedom. Its purpose is to serve that generous education which knows no limits of sect and creed."[40]

Then the estate of Thomas Workman included $60,000 for the endowment of both a professorship of mechanical engineering and a building for the Department of Mechanical Engineering in the Department (now Faculty) of Applied

H.T. Bovey in his office, Macdonald Engineering Building, 1893 (Notman VIEW-2668)

Science. This $60,000 was also intended to finance the construction of the Work-man Technical Building as well as its machinery and apparatus. The building had to be opened within two years of Workman's death. It stipulated that the Workman executors might present four students a year for free tuition in the department, and also that McGill must remain governed in an non-sectarian, non-denominational manner, and "not by or under the control or direction of any one Religious sect or denomination."[41] With their stipulations of non-sectarian education, both of these endowments must have appealed to Macdonald. Initially, there was no reason for him to supplement or emulate either of them, but when the inadequacy of the Workman endowment became apparent, Macdonald was prompted to give his financial support to engineering.

In the early 1880s, as noted earlier, Barbara Scott gave $30,000 to endow a separate chair in civil engineering. While the Workman gift in 1889 was twice as large as Scott's gift, it was not enough to pay for the mechanical workshops of the Department of Applied Science, partly because the equipment was difficult to budget for and was growing in complexity. Henry Bovey presented a list of the equipment needed for the new Workman Technical Building, as it was initially called, and by November 1889 he had raised funds for this purpose from

Smith's shop, Workman wing, Macdonald Engineering Building, about 1901
(Notman MP-0000.25.286)

J.H. Burland of the British American Bank Note Company ($6,000), Mrs John McDougall (wife of the ironmaster, $4,000), and then much less from many others, and secured pledges from companies to contribute in kind.

But it was far from clear whether the amount was enough for the modern facilities envisaged, and Bovey made a direct appeal to Macdonald, apparently just after his sister Helen Jane's death in December 1889. The board had already authorized Bovey to conduct "a tour of Institutions of a like character [to that of the Workman Technical Building] in the United States, in order to obtain all possible information on their construction, arrangement and conduct."[42] Macdonald agreed to accompany Bovey and architect Andrew Taylor on this mission, which took them to New York City, Brooklyn, Cambridge and Worcester in Massachusetts, New Haven, Newark, Philadelphia, Baltimore, and Ithaca early in 1890.[43]

The journey opened Macdonald's eyes to how far American technical education had advanced. Boston's Massachusetts Institute of Technology seems to have impressed him the most. After decades of great difficulty after its founding in 1861, MIT had established itself as one of the foremost technical institutions anywhere. Its president, General Amasa Walker, was a towering figure, physically and intellectually, a hero of the civil war, a classicist, a scientist, and a renowned pedagogue. Macdonald no doubt saw Walker's school as a worthy model, as is clear in a letter he wrote to him in 1891: "To have such an educational establishment as your Institute of Technology would be a source of great pleasure to us all, and an immense benefit to the whole Dominion; but that is more than we can look for, for a long time to come. We must however keep that aspiration before our minds, and make it a matter of ambition to strive to equal you in perfection, of equipment and instruction, though we cannot hope to, and do *not need* to equal your great Institute in extent."[44]

In September 1890 the governors, continuing to sense that the Workman project might prove more expensive to complete than originally envisaged, petitioned the Quebec government for $10,000 for the Faculty of Applied Science, proposing a new department of electrical engineering. Premier Honoré Mercier flatly refused to help.[45] Macdonald stepped into the breach and agreed to complete Workman's project, initially giving $10,000, including $4,000 to pay for the necessary fuel for the equipment as well as for a professor of mechanical engineering for 1890–92, a machinist, a workshop superintendent, a pattern maker, a blacksmith, a foundry man, a fireman, and an engine driver.[46] Then, deciding against implementing Workman's more limited building plan, Macdonald donated $248,662 for the erection of entirely new engineering and physics buildings, both named after himself, and he also gave $85,000 for their lighting, heating, insurance, and maintenance, as well as for the salaries of a mechanic and a caretaker.

Macdonald found other ways to bolster the Workman endowment of 1889. With $40,000, he endowed a separate chair in electrical engineering, and he permitted Charles Carus-Wilson, a former demonstrator in the mechanical laboratory of the Royal Engineering College, Coopers Hill, to switch to this chair from the Workman Chair in Mechanical Engineering that he had only recently taken up.[47] John F. Nicholson took over the Workman chair.[48] For C.H. McLeod, he set up a chair in surveying and geodesy and also a lectureship in descriptive geometry.[49]

Macdonald's interest in physics dated from his hearing the lecture by Oliver Lodge at the meeting of the British Association for the Advancement of Science in Montreal in 1884. Physics was not covered by the Workman endowment, but in taking over the project, Macdonald took the occasion to incorporate the subject into his expanded plans. He had already approved the appointment, in June 1890, of John Cox, late fellow of Trinity College, Cambridge, warden of Cavendish College, and a lecturer in physics at the university extension school in Cambridge, as the first "William C. McDonald Professor of Experimental Physics in the Faculty of Arts with a seat in the Faculty of Applied Science."[50]

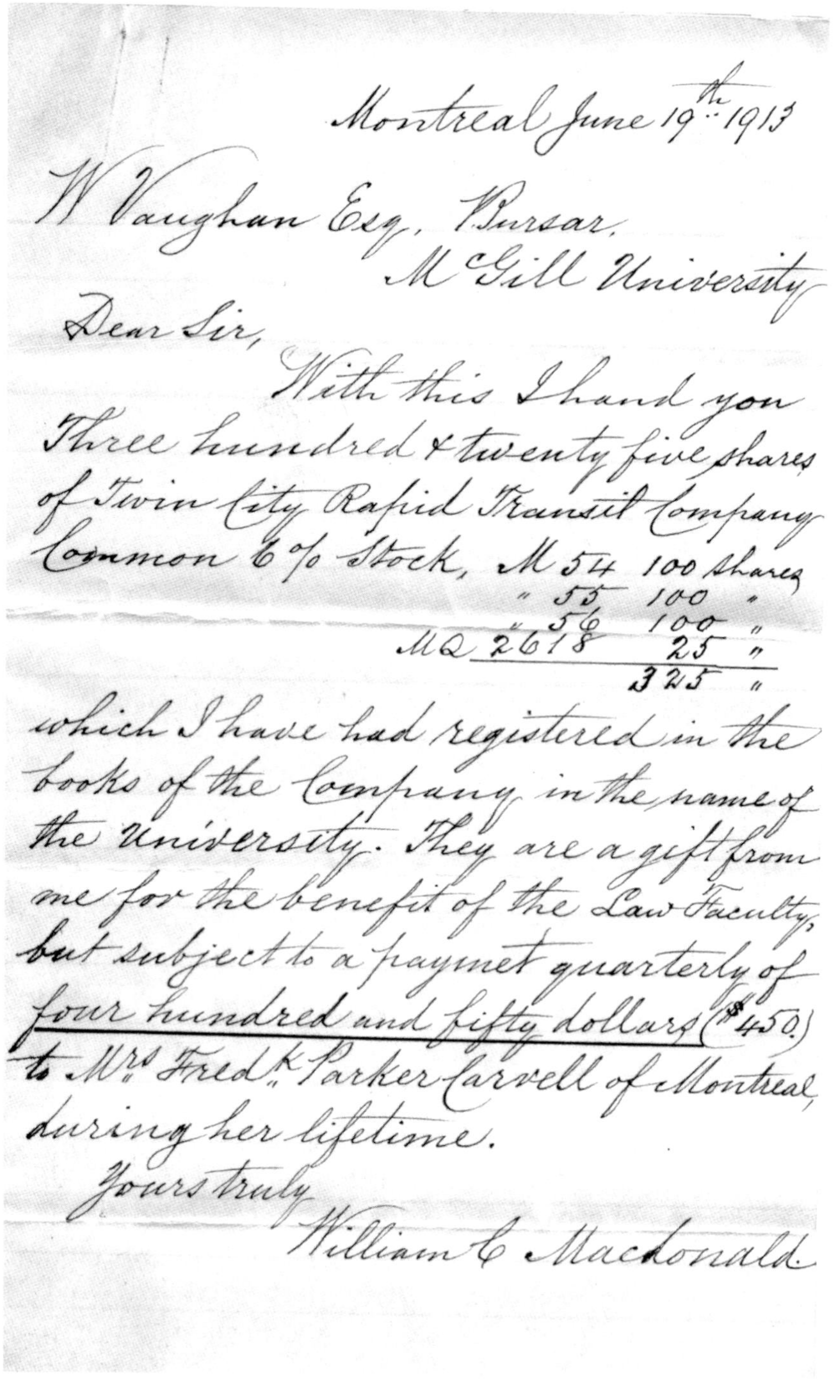

Montreal June 19th 1913

W Vaughan Esq, Bursar,
      McGill University

Dear Sir,

With this I hand you
Three hundred & twenty five shares
of Twin City Rapid Transit Company
Common 6% Stock, M 54    100 shares
                  "  55    100  "
                  "  56    100  "
         MQ 2618          25  "
                         325  "

which I have had registered in the
books of the Company in the name of
the University. They are a gift from
me for the benefit of the Law Faculty,
but subject to a paymet quarterly of
four hundred and fifty dollars ($450.)
to Mrs Fredk Parker Carvell of Montreal,
during her lifetime.
      Yours truly
            William C Macdonald

Example of Macdonald's handwriting in a letter conveying an endowment, 1913
(MUA, RG 4, C 504)

Composite picture for the opening of the Macdonald Engineering Building, 1893
(Notman VIEW-2658)

This was on the same day that Carus-Wilson was appointed the first Workman Professor of Mechanical Engineering in the Department of Applied Science. It was also on the same day that Professor C.H. McLeod reported on a visit he had taken, apparently at Macdonald's expense, to engineering schools all over the United States to gather information on modern surveying and geodetic equipment. McLeod reported that he needed $1,500 in equipment, and Macdonald immediately agreed to pay for it.

The new Macdonald Engineering and Physics Buildings opened in February 1893. Sir Donald Smith, on behalf of the McGill governors, presented an address to Governor General Lord Stanley of Preston. Macdonald shyly and silently gave

Andrew Thomas Taylor,
architect of the Macdonald Engineering and Physics Building
(*Canadian Architect and Builder* 9, no. 2 (1896): 174)

Stanley the keys to the buildings, and Stanley addressed the assembly present and then inspected the apparatus that Macdonald had installed. Although Macdonald refused to speak at the opening ceremony, he was proud to invite President Walker of MIT and Professor George Barker of the University of Pennsylvania to attend the ceremony and to stay with him at Prince of Wales Terrace.[51]

With the opening of his Engineering and Physics Buildings, Macdonald decisively marked McGill University, not merely by anchoring the northeast corner of its campus with an imposing technical complex, but also by ensuring its commitment to being second to none in research and practical training. His buildings complemented Peter Redpath's library and museum but they also outstripped them, and now Macdonald's task was to ensure that they met their great potential. But his vision was also extending way beyond the centre of Montreal.

*Chapter Seven*

# THE MACDONALD-ROBERTSON MOVEMENT AND
# THE FOUNDING OF MACDONALD COLLEGE,
# 1899–1909

When I say that intelligent labor rests upon education I do not mean to say that it rests upon the number of days a man may have gone to school or the number of days or years he may have attended college. What I mean is that it rests on the experiences of life that lead to ability to think, to know, to do and to manage life and things ...

Education itself is a series of experiences leading up to personal intelligence, ability and unselfishness. It is not a remembrance of names, although sometimes memorized knowledge of a second-hand sort has been counted its object. It is a series of experiences from the doing of things, whereby ability is gained to enjoy things and to enjoy life. In every sense education does pay. It is the one thing that enriches the life of individuals and nations ...

Education always stands for some sort of power – power to see, power to know, to understand, to do, and therefore to be.

*James W. Robertson, "Education for the Improvement of Agriculture,"*
*an address in the Assembly Chamber, Halifax, 4 March 1903*

I leave you Sir William's thought of you, and venture to join him in the expression of it, "We like you, we wish you well and ever rejoice when we hear of your happiness and prosperity."

*James W. Robertson, "Education for the Improvement of Rural Conditions,"*
*an address at Charlottetown, 20 July 1907*

I must beg of you to make the article [on consolidated schools] complete without my picture, for I have the greatest possible aversion to being paraded before the public in any way, that can be, properly, avoided.

Professor Robertson is the man upon whom falls the burden of work in this connection. He it is who deserves recognition, not I, who am merely the paymaster.

*Sir William Macdonald, letter to C.B. Allardice,*
*managing editor of the* Weekly Star, *29 January 1903*

In the period encompassing the last three years of Queen Victoria's reign and almost the entire reign of King Edward VII, 1899–1909, William Macdonald had two formidable partners in his efforts in educational reform, the renowned educator James Wilson Robertson (1857–1930) and McGill principal William Peterson (1856–1921). Peterson's role will be described in the following chapter; in this one we shall look at the partnership that resulted in the Macdonald-Robertson movement.* Through Robertson's decade of close work with Macdonald, beginning in 1899, there emerged across Canada a wave of interest in thoroughly practical education, among adults as well as children. Together the two men boldly implemented a fresh vision for the twentieth century only imagined in the eighteenth and still largely untried in the nineteenth. The results of their efforts varied considerably, but among them was Macdonald College, the institution of international reputation that is the most lasting monument to both men.

Born and raised in Dunlop, Scotland, Robertson was a grandson of a Free Church Presbyterian cheese importer. He was also the only surviving son of a farmer and part-time Baptist minister.[1] His grandfather did not approve of his father's becoming a Baptist and eventually disowned him. In 1863, probably to put some distance between themselves and the grandfather, Robertson's family moved from their farm to a small mining and steelmaking town. It was here that his father became an evangelist, working for compulsory education and opposing child labour in the mills. The family returned after a few years to their farm, where Robertson attended school until the age of fourteen. He was then apprenticed to a leather firm in Glasgow, where he learned how to keep accounts. Although he also completed a course at the Cunningham Institute in Glasgow – which included Latin, French, and other subjects necessary for university matriculation – all his university degrees in later years were to be honorary.

In 1875, when Robertson was seventeen, his family moved to Canada, and it was not long before he found employment as the assistant manager of a cheese factory near London, Ontario. Within a year he was hired as the manager of another cheese factory, and by 1881 he had bought his own factory. He was able to manage a cooperative of eight cheese factories, specializing in product for export, the reverse of what his grandfather had done. Ever restless, he raised chickens in his spare hours.

Exporting cheese brought him to Europe, where he studied not only British produce but also the butter of Denmark, the bacon of Ireland, and the eggs and

---

*  In Macdonald's time, their partnership was often referred to simply as the Macdonald movement, but sometimes it was called the Macdonald-Robertson movement. As Macdonald himself admitted that its inspiration and administration were Robertson's, it seems appropriate here to attribute the movement to both men.

poultry of France. These products, like the apples of the United States, were all superior to their Canadian equivalents, and Robertson was determined to raise the standards of more than Canadian cheese. He grasped that the quality of food generally depended on several interrelated factors. Cheese, for example, would depend on the quality of milk from the cow, the milk on the health of the cow, the cow on the quality of the fodder, and the fodder, traditionally hay, on the richness of the soil. Because hay depleted the soil of minerals, he recommended using corn instead. The quality of this corn depended on the quality of the seeds and on their conditions of growth. These conditions became Robertson's chief interest, and he conducted a systematic study of the elements of successful agriculture generally. He returned from his travels with knowledge of improved strains of cattle and swine, of new apparatus for creameries and cheese factories, and of better methods for fattening and shaping chicken for the market. He had studied every stage in the process of preparing food for export, from its planting or raising through to its purchase by the end user.

## THE BUSINESS OF AGRICULTURE AND SCIENCE IN AGRICULTURAL EDUCATION

Robertson's systematic study of agriculture as an integral part of international trade took place in the midst of a long-standing debate about what farmers needed to know in order to be successful. On one side, it was argued that farmers needed only practical advice in order to increase profits and that experimental farms were the ideal place to train them. On the other, it was argued that farmers needed to understand the science of agriculture – they needed to adopt a thoroughly scientific approach rooted in experimental research – and that university laboratories should be built for their training. Although there was widespread agreement that agriculture must be improved, public funding for agricultural schools was limited, uncertain, and subject to political pressures.

Agricultural colleges began to appear in the United States in 1862 as part of the free land grant movement.[2] Despite the establishment of the federal Department of Agriculture and the Ontario Bureau of Agriculture in 1867, agricultural colleges started slowly in Canada, though not for lack of encouragement. Egerton Ryerson, the father of public education in Ontario, saw the need for agriculture in the university curriculum, and the historian Daniel Wilson, later president of the University of Toronto, argued for its inclusion. McGill principal William Dawson, who was especially interested in agriculture, wrote several pamphlets on the subject. The University of Toronto ran an experimental farm in Toronto from 1851 to 1864, but it failed. In Quebec, small agricultural colleges had emerged, notably in Ste Anne de la Pocatière in 1859, but only for French-speaking Catholics.

In 1871 free and compulsory elementary education was established across Ontario, and land for an agricultural school was bought at Mimico Station, southwest of Toronto. This land proved to be clay, hopeless for farming, and so in 1873 the province bought land in Guelph, further south and west. There it established the Ontario School of Agriculture and Experimental Farm, which opened its doors in 1874. With its emphasis on manual labour and practical experience, the school was largely divorced from the more scientific experimentation and liberal arts programs that were taking over the curriculum of the better American agricultural colleges. It was attended by boys of fifteen and older who had been nominated by township councils; these boys would work up to seven or even ten hours a day on farm tasks, leaving little time for study. Thus, as its name suggested, the institution was more an experimental farm than a school.

The first two principals of the Ontario School of Agriculture left their posts ignominiously amid scandal in the first year of the school. The third, William Johnston, had a background in metaphysics and as a rural public school teacher, but he had no practical farm experience. Johnston presided over a staff divided over the purpose of the school (as described above). One teacher defined agricultural knowledge as the cultivation of facts, as opposed to the result of research conducted by a disciplined, or educated, mind capable of grappling with problems. Another, a professor of agriculture and the farm superintendent, claimed that the purpose of agricultural experimentation was to verify rather than discover. But this professor nevertheless did much to improve Ontario livestock and forest management, all with a view to greater profitability.

Johnston, who taught natural history and geology, grasped the value of both positions, although he was more inclined by background to agree that farmers needed to have some academic skills. He thus emphasized the teaching of English and arithmetic and the importance of the affiliation of the school with the University of Toronto, so that his students might be encouraged to become its graduates. But he also believed that manual labour, for three to five hours a day, should be part of the curriculum. He also wanted teachers' colleges, in addition to his own college, to teach agriculture so that the rural population might be better informed generally. In the end, however, despite his moderation, he proved insufficiently practical for his powerful farm manager, who provoked Johnston's resignation in 1879 and did not retire himself until 1888.

James Mills became principal of the Ontario School of Agriculture in 1879 and served as its president from 1880 to 1904, after it had been renamed the Ontario Agricultural College (OAC). The renaming of the institution signalled that Ontario now accepted that academic training complemented, and was of equal importance to, practical training. The charter of the college even provided for a museum of agriculture and horticulture to be attached to it. Mills's long tenure coincided with both the increasing mechanization of farms and a steep decline in Canada's rural population, from 70 per cent of the total population in 1881 to 57 per cent in 1901. These trends, combined with a widening interest in business efficiency, made formal education more acceptable to farmers. Mills saw more and more examples of projects involving agricultural improvement based on hard science, a science which, as at McGill in Montreal, was influenced by Darwin's radical new theories.

A serious economic depression from 1873 to 1879 coincided with efforts by a farmers' organization called "the Grange," or the Patrons of Husbandry of Ontario, to assert farmers' equality with manufacturers, merchants, and bankers. According to the Grange, science was transforming farmers into profit-making businessmen, making farming a profession comparable to that of mining and forestry. The depression forced farmers to rethink the profitability of their crops and make necessary adjustments. Hard times compelled them to consider other options, such as livestock raising, fruit growing, dairy production, and cheese making.

OAC developed new programs to train farmers to specialize in what they raised, and also to teach them business techniques for measuring their progress. In 1885, for example, it established a dairying department. However, the management of the college suffered from a lack of unity, with the president, the gardener, the farm superintendent, and the dairying professor all having to report separately to the provincial commissioner of agriculture. This weakened management structure reflected the increasing politicization and ineffectiveness of the college. Moreover, higher salaries at American schools were drawing some of the best staff and graduates to the United States. Two years later, however, in 1887, the University of Toronto agreed to confer the degree of bachelor of science in agriculture (BSA) on graduates of a three-year course at OAC. Ontario also unified the management of the college in that year and then established a full department of agriculture.

The future was now looking brighter for the college. One key change for the better had been Robertson's appointment in 1886 as professor of dairying or dairy husbandry, replacing the first professor of the department, who had left almost immediately, disgusted by the state of the creamery facilities of the college. Robertson's appointment coincided with a renewed effort by OAC to respond to the practical needs of farmers. In 1884–85 James Mills had established the Farmers' Institutes of Ontario, an extension of a movement started in Michigan to provide farmers with a forum for discussing their problems. OAC had been losing students, and to determine how to improve teaching at the college, college staff went out both to speak to and to learn from the Farmers' Institutes, a practice that became a venture in adult education for everyone involved.

For about half of his first year at OAC, Robertson travelled through villages in Ontario, as well as in Wisconsin, attending sixty meetings with farmers. In his lectures, he talked about the conditions that were favourable to the successful growth of crops. Experiments in Wisconsin had shown, for example, that seeded smooth land absorbed more heat than rolled land and that a difference of three degrees could make the difference between a good start and a slow start in growth.[3] Robertson learned from the farmers attending the lectures that they needed practical instruction in new farming techniques but could not afford to attend the college full-time. As a result, OAC established short-term courses for farmers, and the province invited every county to send a student to the college without fee. In 1893 OAC began to offer summer courses in agriculture to public school teachers and in butter making to others.

## ROBERTSON'S UNDERSTANDING AND IMPLEMENTATION OF PRACTICAL EDUCATION

During his first year at OAC, Robertson was in charge of the Ontario display of cheese and butter at the Colonial and Indian Exhibition in London, England. Still an exporter of dairy products as well as a teacher, he soon applied his preoccupation with temperature in agriculture to Canadian butter exports. Despite Ontario's 1888 Milk Act, intended to improve the quality and safety of milk delivered to cheese factories and creameries, butter continued to vary in quality and to be rancid before reaching the market. In 1891 OAC established travelling dairies to show farmers how to handle milk and butter safely.

In 1890, at the urging of the Dairymen's Association of the Dominion of Canada, Robertson had retired from OAC and entered government service, both as the first dairy commissioner for Canada and the first agriculturist of the Central (Dominion) Experimental Farm in Ottawa. He turned his attention to improving the quality of butter once it left the farm. For its export, he designed a system of cold-storage facilities, beginning by inducing railways to run refrigerator cars once a week. The creameries and ocean steamships were then encouraged to establish their own cold-storage chambers. By 1902 about 525,735 packages of butter were shipped from Montreal to England in cold storage throughout the crossing. Eight years earlier, only 32,000 packages had taken the same journey, and most had probably spoiled.

In 1892, again in his role as dairy commissioner, Robertson started a cooperative cheese factory as a government dairy station, in New Perth, Prince Edward Island. The venture was very successful from the start, exporting $3,600 worth of cheese to England in its first year. Before Robertson's arrival, there had been four cheese factories on the Island with an output of $8,448. By 1901 the Island could boast forty-seven cheese and butter factories with an output of $566,824. Robertson attributed the increase to "organization and education," with no increase in the acres farmed and little increase in the numbers of cows kept.[4] In Quebec in

1892, Robertson set up the St Hyacinthe Dairy School to give courses to people who had worked for at least a year in a cheese or butter factory. Between 1891 and 1901, at least in part as a result of this initiative, the value of the province's cheese and butter production increased by $9,343,371.[5]

At the end of 1895, Robertson assumed the new post of agricultural and dairy commissioner for Canada, and he became responsible for Canadian exports of food generally. His office, though still called the "Dairy Branch" of government, by 1901 included divisions overseeing livestock, fruit, marketing, poultry, and cold storage, with seeds to follow in 1902. Largely thanks to Robertson, Canadian dairy exports rose from $9.7 million in 1890 to $25 million in 1900 and to $31.5 million in 1906.[6] As commissioner, Robertson was a tireless publicist for agriculture as a vocation worthy of dedication. Whether his subject was butter making or ensilage, he spoke eloquently all over the country, to clubs, institutes, farmers, and others, never failing to advance the idea that agriculture was central to the economy. To represent Canada at the World's Columbian Exhibition in Chicago in 1893, he authorized the construction – at the Dominion Experimental Dairy Station in Perth – of the "Mammoth Cheese." Weighing 22,000 pounds, it was the biggest cheese ever made, and it crashed to the floor of the exhibition agricultural building when it arrived. This mishap only attracted more attention to it and established a global reputation for Canadian cheddar.

## THE EARLY ASSOCIATION OF MACDONALD AND ROBERTSON

By the time he met Macdonald in 1897, Robertson had been a bookkeeper at a leather factory, a successful owner of a cheese factory, a teacher at an agricultural college, and a civil servant. He had also gained fame as an exporter. Robertson had experienced one failure, as a cheese-broker in Montreal and London, Ontario, in business with his father in 1888. Money management generally was never his strong suit, and he lost a good deal of both his savings and his wife's in mining speculations. His daughter was to describe his "almost careless generosity" as coming from his conviction "that God in his great plan was keeping a watchful eye upon all the small plans of men and women."[7]

It is said that Macdonald first learned of Robertson by reading about Robertson's cheese factories in a Bank of Montreal annual report. Macdonald himself had no farm experience, but he had been very impressed by the facilities of the Massachusetts Agricultural College in Amherst while he was enrolling his eldest nephew, Fred, there in 1888. Around this time Macdonald's concern was not so much the need for agricultural education as the lack of educational opportunities for the then-sizable English-speaking Protestant minority of rural Quebec. This population was suffering from the fragmentation of the public education system originally envisioned by the Royal Institution for the Advancement of Learning. Early in the nineteenth century, the institution had begun as an effort to create a system of common or public schools for both French- and English-speaking students, but had almost immediately foundered because of the determination of the Roman Catholic Church to keep its members from being taught with Protestants. The efforts of the institution had shrunk, in effect, from trying to cover all of Quebec to covering McGill University, which, as we have seen, was Protestant culturally but effectively non-denominational or even secular in tendency. The Normal School at McGill was still supplying the Protestant schools of Montreal with teachers, but outside the city Protestant public education was dying.

Macdonald and Robertson probably first met at the experimental farm in Ottawa in June 1899. Sir Sandford Fleming was giving Macdonald a tour of the grounds with a Professor Saunders, and Robertson was also present. Macdonald spent two hours with Robertson and was duly impressed. Robertson, he felt, had "done more for the Agricultural interests in the past ten years than any other man in the Dominion."[8] At this first meeting, Macdonald expressed his concerns about education, defining his goal as being to "[b]uild up the country in its boys and girls."[9] He asked Robertson whether they could set up an institution to take in boys at the age of seven and to keep them until they were twenty-one, then to send them out as educational leaders in rural areas. This was, Macdonald admitted, the model for Roman Catholic schools, which was dominant across the province. Robertson replied that mothers might spare their sons for fourteen years to serve the church, but never to become farmers.[10]

This exchange demonstrates how little thought Macdonald had given to creating a workable plan for educational reform. It also suggests what it was that he needed from Robertson if they were to cooperate successfully. For all his experience, however, Robertson himself was not an expert in educational theory, but he was about to tour schools, apparently at Macdonald's expense, in the United States and Europe as well as in Canada. He would scrutinize and absorb their innovations with the same attention that he devoted to new agricultural practices. The knowledge he gained would form the intellectual basis of the Macdonald-Robertson movement.

It was in 1899, two years after their first meeting, that the active partnership of Macdonald, aged sixty-eight, and Robertson, aged forty-three, began. Earlier in that year Robertson had decided to set aside $100 of his own money "to encourage boys and girls on their fathers' farms to pick the best heads out of the standing crops of wheat and oats."[11] The children were to send these heads to Ottawa, and those who had submitted the best one hundred – in terms of size, number of kernels, and weight of grain – were to share the $100. This competition was a great success, with heads of grain deluging the dairy and agricultural commissioner. Although Robertson had come up with the idea of a competition, OAC alumni – now farmers – had already begun to experiment with and exchange information about seeds around 1875, keeping track of new crop varieties under actual farm conditions; in 1879 they formed the Ontario Agricultural and Experimental Union. Robertson's initiative was valuable, however, in that it stimulated children to take an active interest in seeds and crops.

Macdonald believed that holding another competition for children, with much larger prizes, would benefit Canadian farms generally. In the new competition, beginning in 1900, Macdonald offered $100 as the first prize in each province, to be given to the child with the best results in wheat after three years, and in 1902 he offered a similar prize for the best results in oats. In the intervening year, in order to keep up interest in the contest, he added another first prize, of $75, for wheat seeds cultivated in 1900–01 alone, and also a second prize. The Dominion Department of Agriculture, which was about to set up a special seed branch with a budget of $50,000 a year, administered the competition.

The contest attracted 1,500 competitors, of whom 450 would participate for all three years. Each competitor was required to pick by hand the largest heads of the most vigorous and productive plants and obtain enough seed from them to sow over a quarter of an acre. This quarter acre was to be the plot for stock seed grain. Before this plot was harvested, the competitor was to handpick the heads of the most vigorous plants on it, to produce seed to scatter on the same plot for a further harvest. As in Robertson's initial competition, each competitor submitted a hundred of the largest heads each year to Robertson and his staff, and they kept a record of both the number and the weight of grains per hundred heads. By 1903, the final year of the competition, the yield of the originally selected seeds of spring wheat, sown in 1900, was 28 per cent heavier than that of unselected seed in grains per hundred heads, and 18 per cent greater in the number of its grains. In oats, the corresponding figures were 27 per cent and 19 per cent.

The Macdonald-Robertson seed competition had proved unequivocally that crops could be improved by the systematic selection of seed. This success led to the formation in 1903 of the Macdonald-Robertson Seed Growers' Association, renamed the Canadian Seed Growers' Association in 1904, of which Robertson was president for twenty years. By 1906 it was estimated that the value of the crops that had been improved by the competition in 1900–03 alone had increased in value by $500,000. Robertson described this sum as a return of 5,000 per cent on Macdonald's investment of $10,000, which was then the price of two farms. The most famous of these improved crops was Red Fife wheat. In 1900 it had covered 360 acres on experimental farms, and by 1907 it was covering 34,000 acres and taking over the Canadian West.

## THE NATURE OF MACDONALD AND ROBERTSON'S
### GROWING PARTNERSHIP

Macdonald, as we have seen, looked to Dawson, Harrington, Bovey, and others for suggestions on what at McGill needed his financial assistance. Although it is probable that few of the McGill projects that he so generously funded were initiated by him alone, he was relentless in seeking to ensure that any buildings named after him met the highest standards. His relationship with Robertson was much the same, with Macdonald financing, but holding to high standards, the implementation of Robertson's ideas. Macdonald may have remained in the background, but he was far from passive.

The motivations of the two men in entering into their partnership remain something of a mystery. It has been speculated that together they sought to revive or preserve rural life in an industrializing society, but the evidence does not support this, at least as Macdonald's sole or even primary intention.[12] After leaving Prince Edward Island at the age of seventeen, Macdonald never again lived on a farm and likely never worked on one. Indeed, he had no special interest in rural life and seldom even ventured into the Canadian countryside. Nevertheless, agriculture was inevitably a part of his life. His tobacco business had made him acutely aware of farming issues in the southern United States. The accidental discovery of the very lucrative bright tobacco, for example, would have made him sympathetic to Robertson's interest in the crucial factors for plant growth. The rotation of crops, which tobacco farmers had adopted early, inclined him likewise. Macdonald's friendship with Principal William Dawson would also have inclined him to support Robertson, as Dawson had been doing research into agricultural improvement at least as early as 1855.[13]

Until the early 1880s Macdonald was still a landlord on Prince Edward Island, and he was well aware of his family's troubled relations, over three generation, with their tenants. Also, he remembered how limited his educational opportunities had been when he was a child. More than a deep interest in agriculture, this, together with his acquaintance with the poverty of the Island, quite probably led to his desire, expressed to Robertson, to create educational opportunities for rural children, whom he felt to be much less advantaged than city children. As most of Macdonald's life was spent in Montreal, he was also acutely aware of the decline in educational opportunities for the rural Protestants of Quebec. The Catholic Church would not permit them to be educated in common schools with Catholics, and in many places they were so few in number that they could not support a local school.

By 1897, when Macdonald first approached Robertson, the standard of schooling in Protestant rural Quebec was abysmal. The McGill Normal School, established forty years before, required all Protestant teachers in the province to obtain its certification, beginning in that year. Though well intentioned, this was a deadly blow to Protestant country schools, as farmers did not want to send their daughters to the city to learn to be teachers. By 1903, with about two hundred rural vacancies, the Normal School was certifying only fifty-three teachers and most of these found employment in the city. In 1905 three Protestant schools in Huntingdon County had no teachers, and sixty-six of the Protestant schools of the province were closed.[14]

Considered together, Macdonald's limited personal experience of rural life and his concern with the lack of opportunity for rural children suggest that the preservation of rural life was not his primary motivation in cooperating with Robertson. Macdonald, like Robertson, must have been aware of the growing exodus from the countryside to the cities that had been underway in Canada, largely as the result of industrialization, over the last quarter century, a process with no obvious end in sight. Instead of harbouring a deep nostalgia for rural life or a burning interest in agriculture, Macdonald was preoccupied with protecting rural children from the devastation that could be wrought by this demographic trend. His motivation for working with Robertson was subtle but important, for it laid the ground for the differences that would arise between them.

In contrast to Macdonald but like Dawson, Robertson was part of a group of professionals and experts, and was as much an organizer as a thinker. It was through his peculiar set of strengths that Robertson was able to convince Macdonald to support innovations in educational theory – an area that had not been one of Macdonald's original concerns. The seed competition was the such first example. In place of mere book learning, Robertson's innovations embodied the notion of learning through doing. Macdonald had probably never heard of this concept before meeting Robertson, but their goals turned out to be complementary. In Macdonald's own expression, he provided the yeast to Robertson's dough, which Robertson kneaded and made into bread.

## THE CONCEPT OF MANUAL TRAINING, 1899–1909

The idea of "manual training" had originated over a century before Macdonald met Robertson, and it gained adherents in Europe and the United States throughout the nineteenth century. It was both theoretical and practical, but was only partially utilitarian, as it was rooted in a philosophy of child development that had originated in the Enlightenment. The work and ideas of three men – Jean-Jacques Rousseau (1712–1778), Heinrich Pestalozzi (1746–1827), and Friedrich Froebel (1782–1852) – had provided a theoretical basis for manual training, stretching from Rousseau's belief in the goodness of human nature to Froebel's establishment of a kindergarten, or children's garden, a century later. They had all urged that children must work with things and learn both through their senses and through physical activity in order to reach their full potential.

This full potential would later be harnessed in practical employment. Thus, through manual training, the theoretical was expected to merge with the practical in the course of a lifetime. The pressing question for Robertson was how this shift could apply to rural education. In 1888 only 1,489 students out of a total of 487,496 in Ontario public schools, or about 3 per cent, were studying agriculture. That was one in every 327 students, even though two-thirds of Canadians were still employed on the land. Farming and even factory work in urban areas were still far from being mechanized, and so what nearly all children needed to prepare them for adulthood was manual training, or education in how to use their hands in conjunction with their eyes and their minds.

Robertson cited a wide range of authorities to show that manual training was useful to children in both rural areas and towns. The School Committee of Boston for 1892 had praised the results of manual training in that city, and the 1896 Royal Commission on National Education in Ireland had roundly endorsed it for what was still a largely rural country. It was the Irish commission that perhaps had the most influence on Robertson. Also influential was the endorsement given in 1899 by the Ontario minister of education, who observed that the acquisition of manual dexterity led to accuracy of form, dimension, colour, and proportion. More concretely, in 1900 Ontario accepted domestic science, a preeminently practical subject, as part of the curriculum of its public schools.[15] On a visit to England in 1899, Robertson was impressed by the 150 manual-training centres in London alone, attended by about 50,000 boys between the ages of nine and fourteen.

Manual training was a reaction against merely scholastic or book learning, and its promoters emphasized the development of mental power, as distinct from simple manual techniques, as the value of working with the hands. The goal of manual training was to keep the senses of children keen and alert so that they could report on whatever was presented to them accurately and fully. It was intended to prepare them for what Robertson called "the joy of clear apprehension."[16] Robertson contrasted the mere memorization that passed for education among the "decadent" Chinese with the practical training for life offered by the Germans, which included manual training. This latter was not so much the exercise of technical training as it was the guided experimentation by the child, of which the Swedish word *sloyd*, meaning dexterity, was the ultimate goal. In Sweden, the training was called "educational sloyd," but because Robertson first encountered it in England, he called his Canadian version "English sloyd."

To reach the desired dexterity through sloyd, children were given exercises that involved making objects wholly by themselves, first from models, then from drawings of models, and finally from their own drawings of models. It was the making of objects that was crucial, not the objects themselves. Beyond manual dexterity, sloyd implied accuracy, carefulness in little things, neatness, self-reliance, patience, concentration, and love for honest and well-finished work. The goal of sloyd was to inculcate the habits of industry, the ability to reason on the basis of observed facts, and hand-and-eye skills to complement memorization. The manual-training room thus only superficially resembled a carpentry workshop. Its purpose was not to produce articles of commercial value, but to offer children manual training without regard to the intrinsic value of their work or to the time they spent on a particular object.

In the year before their seed competition, Macdonald and Robertson had decided to set up a program in manual training for boys and girls in selected urban schools. Initially, the project was to extend over three years at a cost of about $40,000. Eight representatives of eight Canadian provinces visited Britain and Sweden to observe manual training in action. Trained teachers then came from England, and benches, tools, and working materials were provided to the participating schools. The breadth of the program expanded in 1901 when Macdonald deposited a further $60,000 into the Macdonald Sloyd School Fund.

Macdonald was delighted with the program, telling Robertson: "I rejoice to know that you have found so much pleasure in this patriotic work, undertaken by you with so much heartiness, and such cheerful spirit."[17] By 1903, when responsibility for the program was passed on to local authorities, forty-five schools were offering manual training to about 6,350 students, from Truro in Nova Scotia, to Brockville in Ontario, to Victoria in British Columbia. The cost to Macdonald had mounted to $180,000. By 1909 about 20,000 Canadian children were receiving manual training.

### MACDONALD CONSOLIDATED SCHOOLS, 1902–1909

In 1902 Robertson visited "consolidated schools" in rural Iowa and Ohio. These schools had been formed through the amalgamation of five or more one-room schoolhouses into a central graded school of several rooms, with a garden and a manual-training room attached to it. In Gustavus Township in Ohio, Robertson found that the consolidated school was actually cheaper to run than the nine schoolhouses that it had replaced. Instead of nine teachers working in isolation, for example, there was now one principal and four assistant teachers in a single location. Before this consolidation, the average daily attendance in the township had been 125, but on the day of his visit it was 142, out of an enrolment of 162. The cost of the nine vans to transport the children to the central school had increased the school budget of the township by $256, but the average cost of the education of each pupil had decreased by $1.59 after taking into account the increased cost of the vans. By 1902 seventeen U.S. states had adopted consolidated schools.[18]

On returning to Canada, Robertson promoted the idea of consolidated schools, and Macdonald, probably recalling his own one-room schoolhouse in Prince Edward Island and being concerned about rural schools in Quebec generally, agreed to finance them. Each of the provinces then in Canada was to receive at least one Macdonald Consolidated School, as they were called, and Macdonald made the commitment not only to have them built but also to provide the vans necessary for transporting the pupils and to cover the additional expenses incurred by school boards above the costs of the original smaller schools. In addition to a consolidated school, each province was to have Macdonald "demonstration areas." These were to make use of the former one-room schoolhouses, their properties transformed into gardens. They were to be visited weekly by travelling instructors, each of whom would divide his or her time among a group of ten or fewer schools. The students would each have their own garden plot, and there were illustration plots for comparison. Macdonald also committed himself to establishing training centres for the teachers who were to visit these schools to teach their pupils "nature study" (to be explained presently).

With a view to who would head the consolidated schools, Robertson sent eleven promising students, all men, to the University of Chicago and Cornell University to study "nature," in particular insects, horticulture, and agriculture. After those studies and a further spell at the Teachers' College at Columbia University in New York, they attended the Ontario Agricultural College in Guelph, where they cultivated their own plots before having to teach students how to do likewise. Robertson insisted on men as the heads of these schools, as he felt only men could keep discipline among the older boys. He also insisted that the school buildings be beautiful and that they be set within beautiful gardens. They also had to have adequate light and ventilation and be clean, well ordered, and decorated with pictures. Robertson wanted an atmosphere that would encourage a love of flowers, pictures, and good books.

The curriculum of the consolidated schools did not emphasize the three R's – reading, 'riting, and 'rithmetic. Instead Robertson wanted the emphasis to be put on the training of the three H's – the head, the hands, and the heart – first proposed a century before by Heinrich Pestalozzi in Switzerland. The three subjects to transform these three H's into intelligence, ability, and unselfish service were manual training, domestic economy, and nature study.

Manual training has already been described, and domestic economy is largely self-explanatory, although Robertson envisioned it as encompassing dairying, beekeeping, poultry farming, and the growing of fruit, vegetables, and flowers, in addition to household management. Nature study, however, was to be the central subject, and it was peculiar to the Macdonald-Robertson movement and distinct from the elementary science taught elsewhere. Like manual training, it was not about information but about learning, in this case from planting, drawing

Opening of Middleton Consolidated School (MSF)

plants, writing descriptions of plants, and following the seasons through school walks. It dealt with only those elementary facts and principles that Robertson believed should be the basis of an education in agriculture.[19]

After a vigorous campaign mounted by Robertson, the provinces comprising Canada passed the necessary legislation for consolidated schools in 1903. The first to open was at Middleton, in the county of Annapolis in Nova Scotia, in the same year, with four hundred students from grade 4 to grade 10. In the area around Truro, Nova Scotia, five unconsolidated schools were chosen as sites for "illustration areas" (another term for demonstration areas), to be visited by a travelling instructor for half a day each week, for three years. The Nova Scotia government, at the urging of Robertson, also set up an agricultural school in conjunction with the Normal School in Truro, in 1903.[20] By 1907 fifty-three Nova Scotia schools had been consolidated into twenty-two, inspired but not financed, except for the first at Middleton, by Macdonald.

New Brunswick followed shortly with the opening of its Macdonald Consolidated School, also in 1903, in Kingston, Kings County, where daily attendance

School wagon for Middleton Consolidated School, about 1906 (MSF)

The students of Middleton Consolidated School (MSF)

shot up by 140 per cent. Others in the county were quick to set up their own con-solidated schools, in Riverside and Florenceville. This story of much-improved school attendance was repeated in Ontario once Macdonald and Robertson had set up a model consolidated school in that province. In 1906 in Carlton County near Ottawa, unconsolidated schools saw a pass rate of only 49 per cent, while the consolidated schools – all of which had gardens – had a pass rate of 71 per cent. The beneficial effect of the movement on students also showed itself in the results of high school entrance examinations all over Canada.

### THE CONSOLIDATED SCHOOL AND THE MACDONALD INSTITUTE IN GUELPH, ONTARIO, 1901–1909

Plans were made for a Macdonald Consolidated School at Guelph early in 1902, and the school opened in 1905. Its total attendance was on average 50 per cent higher than that of the schools it was replacing, but its particular importance lay in its proximity to the Ontario Agricultural College and to the new Macdonald Institute, exclusively for women, with which it was effectively to form a com-plex.[21]

At McGill, Lord Strathcona (Sir Donald Smith) had taken the lead in the higher education of women with his establishment of Royal Victoria College in 1899–1900. Macdonald had implicitly provided for the education of both girls and boys through his Rural Schools Fund for consolidated schools (the fund would exceed $260,000 by 1909), but it took an appeal from Adelaide Hunter Hoodless of Hamilton, through Robertson, to convince him to build an institute just for women. Born on a farm, Hoodless had married a rich furniture maker and given birth to four children. A tireless advocate of domestic science instruc-tion, she had already been involved in teaching household work with the Young Women's Christian Association, was active in the National Council of Women, had set up a school of domestic science in Hamilton in 1894, and was a pioneer of the Women's Institutes, the women's equivalent of the Farmers' Institutes set up by James Mills.

As early as 1896, Hoodless had lectured in Guelph on the need for domestic science programs in rural society, and in 1900 Mills asked her to establish such a program at OAC. This she did, and as an able fundraiser, she won support from Strathcona to set up scholarships for the students of the program. Through Rob-ertson, OAC president Mills asked Macdonald to provide buildings not only for domestic science but also for training women teachers for rural schools. After meeting Hoodless, Macdonald agreed to set up in Guelph what became the Macdonald Institute (later the Family and Consumer Studies Building of the University of Guelph), just for women studying domestic science.

Macdonald Institute, Guelph (MSF)

By the autumn of 1901, Macdonald had pledged $125,000 (later raising the amount to $175,000 and ultimately to $182,500) to the Macdonald Institute, and he had agreed to build Macdonald Hall, a residence for the students at the institute, in addition to the classrooms for the institute building. The first students began their studies in 1903, although their buildings were not opened until the following year.

The Macdonald Institute was loosely conceived according to the preferences of several individuals, though Macdonald was not one of them. Beyond Macdonald's pledge of money for the buildings, Mills asked him for up to $350,000 more for scholarships in domestic science and nature study, for a small hospital, and for the operation of the institute, but Macdonald refused. Then Richard Harcourt, the Ontario minister of education, informed Robertson that Ontario premier G.W. Ross was expecting to use Macdonald's funds for a summer school for nature study and scientific agriculture. The premier wrote to Macdonald himself to thank him for his donation of $125,000 "for the training of teachers in the elements of architecture and of young women in domestic science." Macdonald responded sharply, insisting that his money should be spent specifically on the buildings of the institute rather than on rural education generally.[22] Mills and Macdonald, however, at least agreed that the buildings should be used for more than the short-term courses that Harcourt had suggested for the summer school, and their view prevailed. The content of their long-term courses remained an open question.

Early in its life, the Macdonald Institute developed along lines not foreseen by Hoodless, Mills, Robertson, and Macdonald. Originally, it was to serve in part as a Normal School, training female teachers in both nature study and manual training, but these subjects were soon dropped, essentially leaving only domestic science for aspiring teachers, with shorter courses for others. While domestic science was considered to be the equivalent in the "women's sphere" of what engineering was in the men's,[23] it turned out to be very different from the manual training for women that Hoodless had described.

Domestic science, as it had developed in the United States, never embraced the purely cognitive goals of manual training. Neither was it merely practical, as it was intended to involve much more than lessons in cooking and housekeeping. Far from being designed to enslave women in kitchens, domestic science was designed to enhance women's role by strengthening their natural abilities as homemakers, unchallenged by men. It was scientific by definition, and its purpose was to reinforce the home and the family as centres of social stability.

In the Macdonald Institute's first few years, its curriculum emphasized pedagogy, chemistry, food and cooking (including bacteriology), economics, hygiene and health (including biology), and laundry. Physics was added later. Extensive as the curriculum was, the institute was not alone in making strides in the teaching of domestic science. Several such schools had been set up almost simultaneously, including Hoodless's own Hamilton Normal School of Domestic Science and Art, which, on the verge of bankruptcy, she arranged to be absorbed into the institute, and the Truro School of Domestic Science. The University of Toronto and Acadia University also had domestic science programs. The Lillian Massey Treble Building at the University of Toronto, standing opposite the new Royal Ontario Museum, was monumental in its solidity and its ambitions.

What distinguished the Macdonald Institute from the others was its emphasis on improving rural life. Towards this goal, it provided teachers of domestic science to rural schools or Women's Institutes, and its staff and students designed simple portable equipment, such as kerosene stoves, to help farm families who lacked such essentials of modern hygiene as running water, electricity, and appliances. The institute generally awarded the Macdonald Housekeeping Certificate to more mature women who had studied for two years to become institutional managers, such as matrons of hospitals and of residential institutions. Even these women studied dairy work and horticulture in addition to sanitation, sewing, food chemistry, and other subjects. Farm girls generally took shorter courses that trained them to be homemakers.

Meanwhile, manual training at Guelph was conceived from the start as primarily a program for children at the Macdonald Consolidated School, although originally it was to be taught to the girls at the institute as well. As early as 1906 the program was moved to a newly built "machinery hall," and it switched

Nature study at the Macdonald Institute, Guelph, about 1906 (MSF)

from being described as having sloyd as its goal to being described as comprising "farm mechanics." Manual training was now almost indistinguishable from "shop" work, which included very practical woodworking, drafting, metalworking, forging, machine shop practice, and farm machinery maintenance. This sort of shop work was precisely what Robertson would have thought sloyd was not. Curiously, this early deviation from the original concept of sloyd formed the basis for the eventual faculty of engineering that was to be part of the University of Guelph decades later. In this sense, the failure of Robertson's sloyd ideal resulted in the triumph of the sort of engineering that Macdonald had done so much to foster at McGill.

Although manual training failed to catch on at the Macdonald Institute, in this early period and under pressure from Macdonald and Robertson, the institute could nevertheless emphasize methodology through the location in one place of so many different efforts. Near it stood the new Macdonald Consolidated School (now the Macdonald-Stewart Arts Centre), in which students of the institute could supplement their lessons in pedagogy with the close observation of children, both in classrooms and in the extensive gardens of the school. The gardens were designed as outdoor classrooms, with their plots a notional blackboard. The women of the institute could themselves also milk cows and plant crops.

Outsiders, too, were interested in the nature study course offered at the institute. In 1904 Macdonald specified that at least fifteen teachers from outside Ontario must be assisted in attending the summer courses that the institute offered in this subject. In 1905–06, fifty-one teachers came from the eastern provinces, all but ten on Macdonald scholarships, and altogether 202 women took the course. But when the initial Macdonald three-year subsidy came to an end in 1907, the number of teachers in nature study fell to seven and the teachers' summer program ended.

Other modifications to the Macdonald-Robertson schemes at Guelph followed. In 1913 the province stopped granting specialist teachers' certificates to students of the institute. The First World War had a devastating effect on the remainder of Robertson's projects at Guelph. Some teaching in nature study continued at the institute until 1915–17, but was then overwhelmed by the growing fashion for technical education and standardized testing. The manual training at the consolidated school ended altogether in 1921.

## THE HILLSBOROUGH (HILLSBORO') CONSOLIDATED SCHOOL, PRINCE EDWARD ISLAND, 1905–1912

Macdonald and Robertson chose Summerside and Charlottetown on Prince Edward Island for a three-year pilot project in manual training and gardening in existing schools. They also set up a consolidated school at Mount Herbert, five miles east of Charlottetown, which taught academic as well as practical subjects. Called Hillsborough and consolidating six districts, this school opened in 1905. Macdonald committed himself to funding its first three years, covering salaries and operating costs in addition to the $20,000 that he had given towards its construction.

One hundred and sixty-one children were enrolled at Hillsborough, with an average daily attendance of 119. The school was dogged at the start by overspending, especially by its principal, Walter Jones, later a premier of the province. Robertson paid for the initial deficit out of his own pocket. Exceptional local poverty also blighted the effort. In 1907 Mrs Robertson set up five scholarships to enable teachers to stay at the school for one year. The premier and the chief superintendent of education of the province urged the taxpayers to take over the consolidated school after Macdonald's funding had ceased, and Robertson promised to give two dollars out of his own pocket for every dollar raised from school fees.[24]

Nevertheless, in 1908, at the conclusion of the experimental period of three years, only three of the original six school districts consolidated at Hillsborough chose to remain in the scheme. Macdonald extended his payment of Hillsbor-

ough salaries and operating costs for a further three years, from 1908 to 1911, at
$1,200 a year, although the consolidated district also received support from taxes
and its own students. By 1910 it was clear that the Hillsborough experiment had
failed, largely owing to the ratepayers' fears about having to take over from Macdonald in the following year. The school closed definitively in 1912. Its closure
must have been a bitter disappointment to Macdonald, who had favoured his
home province with special grants only to find his generosity and imaginative
concept rejected and to see Prince Edward Island apparently reverting to the
insularity that had driven him out of it almost sixty years before.[25]

### THE MACDONALD CONSOLIDATED SCHOOL IN QUEBEC
### AND THE FOUNDING OF MACDONALD COLLEGE IN
### STE ANNE DE BELLEVUE, QUEBEC, 1903–1909[26]

The Macdonald Consolidated School in Quebec – called the Protestant Day
School of Ste Anne de Bellevue – was, like that in Guelph, funded by Macdon-
ald and the adjunct to a much more important institution. This institution was
Macdonald College, undoubtedly the best known of Macdonald's benefactions.
Twenty miles west of Montreal, the college resembled OAC and the Macdonald
Institute in Guelph, but was on a much grander scale.

The first land for Macdonald College was bought in 1903–04. Through 1906,
Macdonald bought up half a dozen farms and town lots, the largest farm belonging to his friend Robert Reford, a shipping agent. Although rural in setting, the
college was near Ste Anne de Bellevue (then a town, later a Montreal suburb),
only a short train or bus ride from the city of Montreal. Macdonald gave an
initial endowment of $2.2 million, and the college was formally approved by the
Corporation of McGill University on 12 December 1906. Over time, Macdonald
would lavish upon the college attention and gifts that no other creation of the
Macdonald-Robertson movement would receive. For its grounds, buildings, and
equipment, he would give $3,172,355.88, and he would also provide for an endow-
ment of $3,023,896.70, stipulating its increase by a further $1,000,000 after his
death.[27] Details of his gifts to the college are discussed further in chapter 8.

Macdonald College has always been associated with McGill University, but
this affiliation has been an odd and sometimes problematical one, as the college was not originally integrated into the university in the way that, say, the
Faculty of Applied Science (also funded by Macdonald) was on the main campus of McGill. Nevertheless, Macdonald College avoided many of the problems encountered at Guelph. Unlike the counterpart institutions there (with the
exception of the School for Teachers), its own School for Teachers was not dependent on provincial funding or subject to provincial politics. Instead it enjoyed

Macdonald College, main building, 1908 (MSF)

the ongoing support of Macdonald himself and had access to funding from the university. McGill was responsible for Macdonald College, whereas the University of Toronto, despite granting degrees to OAC graduates, was not responsible for OAC. McGill offered Macdonald College graduates the BSA degree from the outset, and thus the college was always watched closely by the McGill Board of Governors and for its first decade by Macdonald himself.

Robertson himself was the head of Macdonald College for its first few years – initially as acting principal in 1906 and then as principal from 19 April 1907 until 10 January 1910. Until late 1905 he worked as an unpaid colleague of Macdonald's while holding the post of Dominion commissioner for dairying and agriculture, his indulgent minister, Sydney Fisher, permitting him to devote half his time to the affairs of the movement. But the new college promised to absorb him almost totally, and so he resigned as commissioner before taking up the post of principal.

When the college opened in 1907, its property covered 561 acres and was divided into three sections: the actual campus, with demonstration and research plots for grains, grasses, and flowers (74 acres); a small-cultures farm devoted to horticulture and poultry keeping (100 acres); and a farm for livestock and grain (387 acres). And next to the college was the consolidated school.

The college consisted of three distinct schools – domestic (or household) science, agriculture, and teaching – in fireproof buildings with red tile roofs. Macdonald, with his vivid memories of fires at Glenaladale and at his factory in

Students in household science, Macdonald College (MUA PR001045)

Montreal, personally supervised the construction along with Robertson. It is said that Macdonald was so dissatisfied with the construction of the Macdonald Institute in Guelph that he refused to set foot in it, but he constantly visited his college in Ste Anne de Bellevue and from time to time would insist on improvements.

In its first year, Macdonald College registered 215 students. In 1908–09, its schools of domestic science, agriculture, and teaching had 76, 65, and 127 students respectively, 79 per cent of whom were from Quebec. Meanwhile, by 1910 the consolidated school had attracted 110 pupils, who were taught by four teachers. Improving rural life was the goal of all three schools of the college, and Macdonald constructed residences for men and women from the countryside to enable them to pursue their studies at the college. Tuition was free in agriculture and teaching for residents of Canada, and $50 each session for others. In household science, the fee was $50 a session for all.

The Macdonald School of Household Science was exclusively for women, and its housekeeping course included millinery, dressmaking, an understanding of fuels and ventilation, home nursing, and home decoration. Like its counterpart at Guelph, it did not attract much of Macdonald's direct attention. Neither did the School of Agriculture, although this was Robertson's chief interest.

At the School of Agriculture at Macdonald College, students were instructed in both theory and practice on what was in effect a vast experimental farm, built to the highest modern standards. The school inculcated Robertson's "tripod" of agricultural principles (Robertson generously called them the "Macdonald tripod"), namely, use selected seed (already discussed); protect plants against insects and funguses; and rotate crops. It was thanks to an instance of the second principle, which had entailed spraying a fertilizer on the potato plants in the twenty-nine school gardens set up under the Macdonald Rural Schools Fund, that Robertson had already seen great increases of yield.[28]

The principle of crop rotation derived from Robertson's long study of the composition of soil, including the conditions of the various constituents of plant food within it, and of the function of bacteria in the soil. He saw that humus, made of decaying plants, improved all soils. He also learned that clover could be used as a substitute for humus, as it removed four times as much nitrogen from the soil as barley did and it broke down plant foods for absorption by the plant. A new barley crop planted where clover had been planted the year before yielded 77 per cent more than a barley crop planted where nothing but barley had grown before. On a wider scale, rotation distributed the mechanical operations of the farm over the season; it gave an opportunity for the land to be refreshed; and it produced a variety of foods for livestock or for sale.[29] Macdonald College was the ideal place to test the Macdonald tripod to the full.

The part of Macdonald College to which Macdonald himself paid the closest attention was the School for Teachers. In 1902, long concerned with education in rural Quebec, he had paid $2,000 for a survey of Protestant education in Quebec. John Adams (later knighted) of the University of London conducted the survey with the assistance of Henry Marshall Tory, an instructor in mathematics at McGill. In concluding his report, Adams endorsed all the elements of the Macdonald-Robertson movement as a basis for improving standards of teaching.

Then, early in 1905, the Protestant Committee of the Council of Public Instruction refused to readjust the provincial grant for Protestant schools so as to give less to the richer Montreal institutions and more to the poorer rural ones. W.A. Weir, a provincial minister without portfolio (later minister of public works and labour), led an attack on the committee for this refusal, and Sydney Fisher, Robertson's long-time ally as minister of agriculture in Ottawa, brokered a truce between rural and urban Protestants, proposing the transfer of the Normal School from downtown Montreal to Ste Anne de Bellevue, where Macdonald was starting to build his college.[30] This proposal was followed up at a meeting in March 1905 of the Protestant Committee. The committee secretary, George Parmalee, announced that not only had Robertson become a member of the committee, but Macdonald had provided fourteen scholarships in nature

Model school at Macdonald College, 1910 (MSF)

Model gardens at Macdonald College, about 1906 (MSF)

study for rural Quebec teachers and was intending to establish a teachers' college at Ste Anne de Bellevue. This college could take over the training of all Protestant teachers in Quebec, as it was not intended just to supplement their existing training in Montreal through short courses.

The McGill Normal School, which Dawson had begun in 1855 and which had opened in 1857, had in 1888 become formally associated with the superintendent of public instruction, under the regulations of the Protestant Committee. As a consequence, the Normal School was recognized as the institution that would train all of the Protestant teachers of Quebec. Aspiring Protestant teachers thus had to take up residence in Montreal, and because many found living in the city very expensive, there was a chronic teacher shortage, especially in rural areas.

In 1906, just before the opening of the School for Teachers at Macdonald College, there were 900 Protestant elementary schools in Quebec, of which about half had an average daily attendance of 12 pupils; only 170 were open for the full academic year, and 47 were open for only four months a year.[31] Thus, the prospect of new and subsidized residences for teachers in training at Ste Anne's was an attractive one, but there arose the question of whether McGill would exercise more control over the new school than it had been exercising over the Normal School. After considerable discussion between March and October 1905, McGill explicitly disclaimed control over the Ste Anne's school, leaving the administration of the successor to the Normal School to the Council for Public Instruction.

Macdonald stipulated that the running expenses of the School for Teachers must continue to be met by the province, and that the money Quebec was saving through his gift of these new facilities should go to the improvement of Protestant education more generally. In 1907 this money amounted to $18,657, and it was directed towards rural Protestant elementary schools for bursaries and other purposes. Macdonald's grant was thus aimed at raising the standards of existing schools as well as at producing new teachers. The new school taught a broad range of subjects, from kindergarten teaching to theories of education, and like the teachers' college in Guelph, it added nature study and manual training to the curriculum. The School for Teachers was indeed one of Macdonald's most generous and imaginative achievements; within a very short period, it solved the long-standing problems of inadequate space, limited facilities, and costliness that had plagued the Normal School.

Nevertheless, it was difficult to find adequate leadership for the School for Teachers. George Locke came from the University of Chicago to head it in 1907, but he left after eighteen months, apparently because of difficulties with Robertson. Sinclair Laird came from Queen's University in Kingston in 1913 and stayed for thirty-six years, but it was J.A. Dale, who specialized in physical education and social service, who became the first Macdonald Professor of Education in

Students and staff at Macdonald College, with Principal J.W. Robertson in the front row at the extreme left, about 1909 (MSF)

1908. Macdonald endowed his chair with $60,000 and gave its occupant $1,250 to travel for research. From 1913 onwards, there were also problems in obtaining provincial funding for the School for Teachers.[32]

The years 1906–10 at Macdonald College were ones of building and consolidation. Macdonald was closely involved at every stage, but Robertson did not hesitate to take initiatives of his own. Friction developed, and Robertson's sudden resignation as principal early in 1910 came after a period of increasing tension between the two men. The financial records of the college suggest that the finances of the school may have been the issue, as apparently they were out of control. Both men were in most ways frugal Scots, but they were also perfectionists, as well as very ambitious Canadians, and they sought perfectionism in different ways. If Macdonald thought of himself as the paymaster (as seen in the citation at the head of this chapter) and believed that by paying Robertson, Robertson would operate within his budget, he was miscalculating. Robertson had never felt himself totally constrained by budgets and regulations. When appointed commissioner of agriculture, he had without authority replaced his government-issued desk with his own. He had paid for the initial seed com-

petition out of his own pocket and for some of the deficits of the Hillsborough
Consolidated School also out of his own pocket. Now he repeatedly refused to
be bound by the budget decided by the governors of McGill, and in Macdonald's
view, this was probably tantamount to gross mismanagement.

By June 1909, Robertson had incurred a deficit of $10,000, which he offered to
pay out of his own pocket. The governors of McGill were aghast. They accepted
his gift, but with an "expression of regret that the financial condition of the
College should have rendered such a contribution necessary." They went on to
note: "Through their Treasurer and Secretary they have given notice on several
occasions during the last eighteen months that they are unable to approve of
any expenditure that goes beyond the actual resources of the Institution, and in
accepting his gift they again ask Dr. Robertson to effect such retrenchment as
shall bring about an equilibrium in the financial conditions of a college funded
with such unparalleled generosity and whose interests they have so much at
heart."[33] It is clear that they saw his extravagance as disrespectful of Macdonald,
who had only three years before endowed the college with $2.2 million. In the
following October, Robertson used his own money to give bonuses of $100 to
each of three teachers at the college. The governors noted that he had also spent
$6,500 over his budget for the training of teachers at the college. In November,
the governors appointed a committee consisting of Charles Fleet, Edward Greenshields, and James Crathern to investigate the financial affairs of the college.[34]

On 1 November 1909, Macdonald wrote to Walter Vaughan and the board
referring to a letter of 11 June 1908 on Robertson's estimates of the cost of work
necessary at the college, especially $171,000 for sixteen staff residences. Only
five, Macdonald noted, had been completed, and there was no sign of the other
eleven residences after seventeen months and the payment of the deposit for their
construction.[35] Robertson was forced to resign on 10 January 1910. A few weeks
later, Macdonald noted to Vaughan that there was a shortage of $100,000 in the
amount donated by Macdonald for the staff residences. As he put it, "[O]wing to
Dr. Robertson having diverted the funds to purposes other than those for which
they were especially provided," $100,000 must be transferred from the Macdon-
ald Auxiliary Fund for the college to cover the shortfall.[36]

In view of his $1-million bequest for the college in his will, there is no ques-
tion that Macdonald could have afforded to donate far more than he did, and it
is equally clear that no one, including Robertson, would have been ungrateful
for his generosity. Still, Macdonald was seventy-nine in 1910 and likely worried
about how he would be remembered. Although remarkably vigorous until 1914,
he was a demanding and impatient man, probably more so than he had ever
been. It seems that he feared that Robertson's failure to operate within budget

was casting into public doubt the judgment of both of them, as well as Macdonald's own ability to pay for what he and the other governors deemed either necessary or sufficient.

In a struggle of wills between two such strong men, only one could prevail. Macdonald as founder had the last word. He effectively asked the McGill governors to remove Robertson, which they did with much, but hardly total, reluctance. The result for the college was at least fifteen years of uncertainty, beginning with F.C. Harrison's interim role as principal. The college continued to grow, but not as it would have done under Robertson's continued leadership. Robertson had been adored by many of his students and staff, he had involved himself in every aspect of the college, and he had also drawn international praise as an educator.

Robertson visited the college from time to time over the years, to what its official history calls Macdonald's "distaste." Macdonald himself took charge of the school's accounts and correspondence, but he lacked Robertson's energy and flair for administration. The two men probably never spoke after Robertson's resignation, and thus their quarrel marked the end of their movement. There were no further projects for what had come to be called simply the "Macdonald movement." Macdonald could never have instituted such a movement on his own, without someone such as Robertson to advise him and indeed run it. It is doubtful that he felt acute loss with its end, especially as McGill now had, in Macdonald College, a massive new undertaking for him to watch over.

## SUMMING UP THE MACDONALD-ROBERTSON MOVEMENT

The magnificent buildings Macdonald had erected for his schools – at the Macdonald Institute, Macdonald College, and McGill – were to endure for at least a century. The buildings themselves – not their specific purposes – were what he, with his fascination with architectural detail and modern construction, took a personal interest in. He built them instead of a house for himself, although he could well have afforded to erect an enormous mock castle like Casa Loma of Sir Henry Pellatt in Toronto, begun in 1911. Pellatt occupied his castle for only a few years before going bankrupt, while Macdonald's educational offspring occupy his buildings to this day. We should not be surprised, then, to learn that towards the end of their partnership Macdonald and Robertson quarrelled over the ostentatious principal's residence that Robertson had decided to build at the college, complete with a lavish suite for the founder. Robertson chose to name it Glenaladale, presumably to flatter Macdonald. This was exactly what Macdonald did not want. Robertson had no real sense of Macdonald's character, no comprehension of how someone so generous to others could be so frugal in his personal life. The residence was later used by the Macdonald College Faculty Club, and today it awaits renovation for still other purposes.

It would be misleading to suggest that the Macdonald-Robertson movement ended in failure after the two men had severed their alliance. While certain aspects of the movement faded away, others took root and flourished. The experiments in manual training, nature study, and consolidated schools had been intended to last only a few years at most. By 1908, a year before the split, these ventures were already either modified, self-sufficient, or verging on abandonment; moreover, Macdonald was no longer personally supporting them, except for the consolidated schools in Quebec and Prince Edward Island. Although it was to take years, Macdonald College would emerge stronger than it had ever been under Robertson, if only because it matured. Its graduates and teachers found positions all over the world, one being Leonard Klinck, the first president of the University of British Columbia, of which, as we shall see, Macdonald was also a founder. The facilities of Macdonald College, like those Macdonald built in Guelph, attracted wide admiration for their quality and innovation, especially as they provided a place for research of a very high order. Thus, from its early years Macdonald College was able to attract staff from outside Canada, as well as send its own graduates across Canada and beyond.

The split between Macdonald and Robertson shows not so much their personal failings as some of the limitations inherent in their movement from its start. First of all, because the scheme was probably so ambitious and rushed, it was almost fated to yield variable results. Robertson, as we have seen, held several demanding positions between 1899 and 1905, apart from his work with Macdonald. His onerous duties in provisioning Imperial troops during the Boer War led to his nervous breakdown in 1903, and he retired to the Isle of Wight to recuperate, just as the consolidated schools were opening.

Secondly, the movement undertook the daunting task of marrying nature study, manual training, and domestic science with the training of teachers in both urban and rural areas across Canada. Although conceptually arguable, this marriage was to prove stressful for all involved. Life in Canada was changing, disrupting expectations everywhere. Ste Anne de Bellevue, for example, soon became suburban rather than rural, whereas Guelph remained firmly rural in a province that was experiencing rapid industrialization and urbanization.

Thirdly, the movement was limited by its dependence on Robertson's personality and administrative ability and on Macdonald's money and interest. It needed both men and it generated no successors. Although there is no doubt that Macdonald was genuinely interested in rural education, as he told Robertson from the start, there is also no doubt that the movement was the product of Robertson's vision and planning, and without these it could only collapse.

The movement's final limitation involved certain flaws in Robertson's vision. Robertson's ideal seemed eminently practical, modern, and comprehensive. It encompassed everything conceivable from modern farming as a business to child development beyond rote learning. But it also encompassed too much, and not all of its elements cohered or survived long. Although the idea of consolidated schools in rural areas eventually became the norm, manual training and nature study were widely and swiftly abandoned. They proved to be what Robertson explicitly denied they were: fads. He insisted that manual training and nature study were meant to supplement book learning, but they also took time and energy away from book learning. Despite their appeal, even to this day, these ideals were essentially irrelevant to the transition underway in Canada at that time, from a rural society to a largely urban, industrial, and professional society, one that Robertson foresaw and to some extent promoted but nevertheless underestimated. Manual dexterity seemed perfectly appropriate when it came to helping manual workers adapt to new manual techniques on farms or in factories, but it seemed increasingly irrelevant in an increasingly mechanized society.

It is true that the Macdonald-Robertson emphasis on the practical gave rural education a good reputation even among those who had thought that farmers did not need a formal education. But this was the movement's effect rather than its intention. The two men had from the start diverged fundamentally in their emphases. Macdonald was most concerned with improving the poor educational facilities available to rural children. Robertson was more concerned with retaining a sense of craftsmanship and fostering living links to nature in rural education. Their views remained complementary for the purposes and the duration of their movement, but not longer, and they were not logically connected. And in an era that was to turn most family farms into agribusinesses, Macdonald's emphasis on bricks and mortar would prove more useful and more enduring than the bucolic, almost romantic vision – reminiscent of Ruskin – that Robertson held of rural life.

It is hard not to attribute Robertson's essential hostility to what he called scholasticism to his own failure to obtain a university degree, despite his efforts in 1888 to obtain a bachelor of arts degree from the University of Toronto. He took great pride in his honorary degrees, always calling himself "Dr" after receiving one. Yet when Professor James Cappon of Queen's University criticized Robertson for underestimating the value of classical languages, he replied, "Some knowledge of the needs of rural population and of the art of agriculture has taught me more useful and congenial employment for the 'literary faculty and instinct' than the mental exercise which that sort of thing affords."[37] He was prickly in the face of tradition, as many autodidacts are, but he did not notice that the real challenge to his theories of practical education, at least for adults, was no longer classical learning but systematic study and research. This was not a mistake that Macdonald, who was supporting the physicist Ernest Rutherford at the same time as he was supporting Robertson, could make.

Macdonald, with a considerably more meagre educational background than Robertson's, never received an honorary degree and probably never wanted one. He was not so much hostile to a traditional education based on the classics as inspired by the promise of such new disciplines as engineering, and he most likely never subscribed to Robertson's notion that manual training was an important basis for engineering. Robertson preached tirelessly and often about a host of subjects, from morality to the ruin of France after the Battle of Sedan. Macdonald seems never to have given a public speech, and yet – for all his reputation for unsociability and frugality – he seems to have retained a much more amused and tolerant – and indeed relaxed – view of human nature, or at least one more sceptical and less salvationist than Robertson's. There was not, for obvious reasons, a trace of the Presbyterian in him.

To say that there were flaws in Robertson's vision is not seriously to disparage him, for he was indisputably an effective organizer. After leaving Macdonald he was, at the invitation of Mackenzie King, the Dominion minister of labour, to chair the Royal Commission on Industrial Training. His report, published in 1913, was a masterly survey that dispelled any notion that he might be a Luddite. In 1919 he joined Sir Robert Borden on the Canadian delegation to the Paris Peace Conference. In the previous year, in recognition of his tireless years of work for Canada and the empire, he had been offered first the honour of a knight bachelor and then a knighthood in the new Order of the British Empire. He had declined both, although he had previously become a commander of the Order of St Michael and St George.

As Robertson's daughter admitted in her memoir of her father, Robertson and Macdonald could rarely have been called close friends, despite their partnership. Indeed, as we have seen, Macdonald saw himself as Robertson's paymaster. Theirs was the most formal of relationships, but one of mutual benefit. Macdonald was skilled in spotting talent, but it is doubtful that he could ever have found a more able lieutenant than Robertson; in any case, after their rupture in 1910 he never did. He remained solitary to the end, the financier of the ideas of others. As we are about to see, Macdonald did not need close friends, or even a lieutenant, in order to continue to shape higher education in new directions.

William C. Macdonald, 1890 (Notman II-92891)

*Chapter Eight*

MACDONALD COLLEGE AND McGILL UNIVERSITY:
EDUCATION AND RESEARCH FOR A NEW CENTURY,
1893–1914

In-as-much as the U.S. persists in carrying off the most valuable crop this country raises, (viz. our men) without giving us any adequate return, I propose to adopt a beneficent mode of punishment, and continuing raising and educating a superior class of men, who will go on and improve the standard of the inhabitants of that country, until the standard is sufficiently high to admit of its being annexed to Canada. Then we shall have the whole of our capital handed back, with the unearned increment besides. There Doctor, in a paragraph, is a great work laid out for a great people.

*Macdonald to Dr William Osler, 1893*[1]

Husband not life's taper at the close,
And keep the flame from wasting by repose.

*Macdonald to Lord Strathcona, 1899*[2]

At least until he was stricken with illness in 1914, the years from 1893 onwards were Macdonald's most productive and most enjoyable. He was relatively free of business cares and a rich man, and able to pursue his two chief interests – the education of young people, particularly those from rural areas, and the expansion of McGill University in the applied sciences. Through his gifts, he exercised a decisive influence on the direction of education and research in Canada.

### SHARING THE LEADERSHIP OF McGILL[3]

Despite his deep interest in the university, Macdonald was wearying of his duties as governor, and he tried to retire from the board in 1893. His fellow governors seem to have prevailed on him to stay, however, as he faithfully attended most meetings of the board until 1907, and a few even after that. It was the tradition for the meetings to be chaired by a senior businessman, especially in the absence of the chancellor. Sir Donald Smith was chancellor in 1893, having assumed this position in 1889. Macdonald's friend John H.R. Molson acted as chairman whenever Strathcona was away, and after Molson's death in 1897, Macdonald assumed this responsibility until 1907.[4] On Strathcona's death in January 1914, the governors immediately elected Macdonald chancellor. They worked for two months to encourage him to accept the position but found him "diffident." Finally, at the end of March, he gave in but only in the "earnest hope that no harm shall ever come to the university in consequence of this election." On the same day, he gave $1,021,563.37 to Macdonald College. Stricken with illness during the summer of that year, however, he was able to do little more for the remainder of his life.

When Sir William Dawson retired as principal of McGill in 1893, Macdonald, having been a governor for ten years and a major benefactor of the university for twelve, was naturally involved in the search for a successor. As irreplaceable as Dawson had seemed, the new principal turned out to be similarly impressive. William Peterson, born in Edinburgh in 1856, would head McGill from 1895 to 1919.[5] The son of a Presbyterian merchant, he had attended the Royal High School in Edinburgh, graduated in classics from the University of Edinburgh, and furthered his studies at the University of Göttingen and at Corpus Christi College, Oxford. In 1882, after teaching at Harrow and the University of Edinburgh, he had become principal and professor of classics and ancient history at the new University College of Dundee.

Like Dawson, Peterson was an able teacher and interested in all aspects of education. Where he built on Dawson's legacy most obviously was in his establishment of postgraduate studies at McGill, more along American and German lines than British. Although firmly an imperialist at the height of the British Empire and not always popular in Montreal on this account, he was open to innovation and to bringing to McGill both teachers and researchers from abroad, from countries both within and outside the empire. His connections with young academics were even better than Dawson's had been, and it was in Britain that he found most of the early Macdonald professors, whom Macdonald accepted even before meeting them. But like Macdonald, Peterson recognized that McGill also needed to strengthen its links – both academic and financial – with the United States.

## New Sources of Funding

In 1905 Andrew Carnegie, the great industrialist turned philanthropist, appointed Peterson to the board of his new Carnegie Teachers' Pension Fund, which sup-

Sir William Peterson (MUA PR009554)

ported teachers retired from non-sectarian public schools in the United States, Canada, and Newfoundland.[6] On 1 May 1906, at a testimonial dinner at McGill in conjunction with his receipt of an honorary degree, Carnegie is reported to have slapped Macdonald on the back and reflected on their success with the remark, "Not bad for two Scots, eh?" Indeed, they had much in common. Both were essentially Scots that had made their fortunes in the New World, both were fundamentally hostile to any religious influence on education, and both were perhaps unequalled in their support of educational innovation and expansion. Macdonald himself had paid $441.76 towards the expenses of Carnegie's visit, and at the dinner, Carnegie appealed to Montrealers generally to support McGill.

In 1909, through one of his several new charitable foundations – after he had satisfied himself that McGill was thoroughly non-sectarian – Carnegie himself gave the university $100,000 for its general purposes.[7] This was the greatest single gift that McGill had received apart from those of Strathcona and Macdonald, and it must have been a source of considerable relief. McGill had been suffering constant financial problems, not least because the very success of Macdonald's projects had increased the number of students it had to serve. In 1870, for example, there had been 70 students in the applied sciences, but as early as 1893 the number had increased to 160, and this was before the opening of the Macdonald Engineering and Physics Buildings, which both attracted and accommodated more.[8]

As Carnegie was the first to establish large charitable foundations, even before the Rockefellers, who established their first in 1914, his grant to McGill signalled an expansion of its future sources of support. Macdonald himself would never establish a foundation in his lifetime,[9] but he was probably especially interested to learn that this newly expanded form of charitable trust, whether Canadian or not, was willing to share the burden of financing the expansion of McGill.[10]

The Carnegie grant of 1909 foreshadowed not merely growing assistance from foundations, but also increasing sophistication in fundraising. Even before it was made but as a direct result of Carnegie's visit, the shipping agent Robert Reford issued his own challenge to Montrealers. He announced that he would contribute $50,000 to the university if others would raise, by 1 May 1907, the balance of the $1 million that McGill estimated it now required as a new endowment. This sort of challenge grant was to be used to great effect in the Young Men's Christian Association (YMCA) fundraising campaign in 1909 and in McGill's own campaign of 1911. New men were taking up the burden latterly assumed only by Macdonald, Strathcona, Molson, and a few others. Although his financial challenge to Montrealers was not to be met, in July 1906 Reford joined the board of governors of McGill, in the company of E.A. Clouston, general manager of the Bank of Montreal, and Charles Melville Hays, president of the Grand Trunk Railway.[11]

## THE UNFOLDING OF MACDONALD'S VISION FOR McGILL

In the meantime, from 1893 onwards, Macdonald was pursuing his building program at McGill. The Peterson era was a golden age of building at the university. Molson's and Strathcona's buildings, which included Royal Victoria College, the medical buildings, and many other works, would in themselves have been considered magnificent gifts by any university.[12] But Macdonald was the greatest builder of all, and he became known as the second founder of the university,

The Macdonald buildings on the campus of McGill University, 1892–93
(Notman VIEW-3223)

after James McGill himself. Yet his generosity extended far beyond his building projects. He gave hundreds of books, as well as money for their purchase, and he endowed many Macdonald chairs in different faculties.[13] Most of his appointees to these chairs turned out to be exemplary and evidence of both his shrewdness and his acquaintance with where young talent lay.

What was Macdonald's object in adopting McGill as his special cause? What motivated him to give the bulk of his hard-earned and carefully saved fortune to education? The quotation at the head of this chapter, from a letter Macdonald wrote to the renowned Canadian physician William Osler, sums up his rationale. It was to make Canada comparable to the United States in the education that it offered to its most promising young people. In addition, after his dismal experience with his nephews and nieces, he probably wanted to help deserving and talented young people whom he could observe regularly. Although he had had little formal education himself, he was a very intelligent and well-read man, and like many self-educated people he delighted in creating superior opportunities for educating others.

Ever the bookkeeper he had trained to become in 1850–52, Macdonald was a sharp observer of detail. Little escaped his piercing eyes, so evident in photo-

Macdonald Engineering Building (MSF)

graphs of him, and yet he retained a faith in the future, necessary for any investor. He financed the visions of people whose ideas aligned with his own goals, and because he could see beyond the visions, he was able to take shrewd and informed risks in realizing them. Most of his investments continue to bear fruit today, long after the eclipse of those visions and long after the passing of their originators.

It is probable that in his later years Macdonald found inspiration for his McGill venture on visits to Boston. Apart from the Massachusetts Institute of Technology, he may have admired the new Boston Public Library, a palatial temple to learning erected in 1887–95 by McKim, Mead and White, the architects of the head office of the Bank of Montreal, of which Macdonald was a director, and of the future Mount Royal Club, of which he was a founding member. The increasing grandeur of Boston's institutions, together with the support given them by their local community, reinforced in Macdonald his vision of how a modern society might develop through a mixture of private and public capital. This was the vision he had first glimpsed in the same city in 1849–52, one that he wanted to encourage for all of Canada, led by Montreal, half a century later. At the opening of the Macdonald Engineering Building in 1893, one of his guests, Ernest Barker, a physicist from the University of Pennsylvania, declared that

Macdonald experimental thermal laboratory, about 1901 (Notman MP-000.25.282)

McGill now possessed "the finest and best equipped engineering school on the continent," while warning that the Americans still intended "to overtake and surpass Montreal."[14]

Because Sir William Osler (as he became in 1911) had left his teaching post at the McGill school of medicine for the University of Pennsylvania in 1884, where he found greater opportunities, he was probably all the more appreciative of Macdonald's projects in Montreal. Although he never returned to work in Canada, one of Osler's last acts was to arrange for a grant of almost $1 million to be given to McGill by the new Rockefeller Foundation in 1918. This grant, coming just after Macdonald's death and four years after that of Strathcona, the greatest benefactor to the Faculty of Medicine, would ensure the flourishing of medicine at McGill for years to come. It was because of this grant, in tandem with Macdonald's endowments primarily for the sciences, that at least throughout the twentieth century medicine and science were the areas of study and research for which the McGill was best known. Osler bequeathed his famous

Macdonald dynamo room, about 1893 (Notman VIEW-2664)

library of medical works to McGill rather than to Johns Hopkins and Oxford, with which he had been more recently associated. In this bequest, as well as his role in winning the Rockefeller grant, he seems to have endorsed the vision articulated to him by Macdonald.

## THE MACDONALD CHAIRS IN
### ENGINEERING AND PHYSICS, 1892–1893

The opening of the Macdonald Engineering and Physics Buildings in February 1893 was just a beginning, and indeed the buildings were not actually completed until December of the same year. He had already given $248,662.57 in 1890 for the Physics Building and its equipment, to which he was to add for its maintenance $40,000 in 1892 and $110,000 in 1896.[15] Also in 1890 he had given $460,396.89 to erect the Engineering Building, in addition to $20,000 for the Workman workshops in it and $1,500 for surveying and geodetic apparatus (with $900 more for

Macdonald Physics Building, about 1893 (Notman VIEW-2630)

the building in 1894 and $1,185 still more in 1895). In 1892 his endowment for the maintenance of the Engineering Building had cost $45,000 (to be followed by a further $40,000 in 1896) and of the Physics Building $40,000 (to be followed by $110,000 in 1896). It had cost him $329.50 just for the opening ceremonies of the Engineering and Physics Buildings in 1893. But now, after the opening, their laboratories had to be continually stocked and updated, and although several professors and lecturers in the sciences were already at McGill, more teachers had to be found.

In 1893 the roles of the various faculty members reflected the earlier evolution of the sciences out of the arts and of engineering out of the engineering profession. Alexander Johnson was Peter Redpath Professor of Pure Mathematics (originally endowed as the chair in natural philosophy by Peter Redpath in 1854 but renamed in 1893), as well as dean of the Faculty of Arts. B.J. Harrington, Dawson's son-in-law, was appointed the David Greenshields Professor of Chemistry and Mineralogy in 1883 but retired from this position in 1891 to become a lecturer in mining and metallurgy. Henry Bovey was a professor of civil engineering and mechanics in 1877 and was appointed dean of the Department (not Faculty) of Engineering, within the Faculty of Arts, in the following year. Within Bovey's department were C.H. McLeod, secretary of the Canadian Society of Civil Engineers and a lecturer; C.A. Carus-Wilson, the Macdonald Professor of Electrical Engineering; and J.F. Nicholson, the first Thomas Workman Professor of Mechanical Engineering. To his original $40,000 endowment of Carus-Wilson's chair, Macdonald added $10,000 in both 1898 and 1903.

None of these scientists and engineers had been appointed as a result of the opening of Macdonald's new buildings, but they occupied them once they were open. The idea of a physics department, with its own endowment, however, was Macdonald's alone, and it was his responsibility to nominate the first teachers of physics. From his 1890 tour of American institutions with Bovey and Taylor, Macdonald had learned that physics was an integral part of the education of engineers.[16] It was not an applied science in the same sense as engineering, but research in physics led to practical applications. The research conducted by the physicists Pierre and Marie Curie had led to the use of X-rays in medical diagnosis, and there was widespread optimism that a new era of invention was dawning, that physics, a "pure" science, might lead to other practical applications scarcely conceivable, as indeed it was about to do.

In 1893, to replace the chair in experimental physics that he had endowed in 1890, Macdonald set up not one but two new chairs for physics. He added $50,000 to his endowment of 1890 to make the total endowment of the two new chairs $100,000, with a further $20,000 in 1901. John Cox became the first Macdonald Professor of Physics and Hugh Callendar the second. The two were appointed to both the Faculty of Arts and the new Faculty of Applied Science.[17] Cox was one of the most brilliant scientists of his generation to come out of Cambridge. He loved to teach, and Callendar, who was equally brilliant, was hired to supervise the researchers in physics.[18] Having two chairs in physics simultaneously made McGill perhaps uniquely endowed in the world at this time.

In Cox, Macdonald had hired a man more than worthy to set up the department. But Cox had not even been his first choice. Macdonald had favoured Oliver Lodge of Victoria University College in Liverpool, considered to be among the pre-eminent British physicists of the time along with J.J. Thomson, who had been Cox's teacher, Callendar, and Ernest Rutherford, all at the Cavendish Laboratories in Cambridge. Macdonald had heard Lodge lecture on dust at a meeting of the British Association for the Advancement of Science in 1884 in Montreal. Nine years later Macdonald would write to Lodge, "[Y]ou made an impression on my mind which I have never forgotten," adding that his decision to erect a physics building in 1890 was "coupled with the strong hope of having you as the first Professor."[19] But Lodge refused to leave England, and so Cox was appointed. Macdonald's correspondence with Lodge suggests that at the very

Macdonald science library, about 1895 (Notman N-0000.25.266)

least he had been thinking of a physics department early as six years before his trip to the United States.

Unlike the engineers, the physicists at McGill did not seek professional status. They were pure scientists, and while they had students to teach, their main concern was with having an adequate laboratory and up-to-date equipment for their study of energy. In providing them with the most advanced equipment anywhere for research, Macdonald demonstrated his enormous faith in their future. At the opening of the Macdonald Physics Building in February 1893, Cox himself complained that "the very *carte blanche* which he gave me, his very instructions to get the best that could be got, involving, as it did, difficulty of choice, became almost a source of grievance." Lord Stanley, the governor general, remarked that this was "a grievance which a great many people in this old world would be glad to be distressed with."[20]

Macdonald's largesse was not unlimited, however. Only a year after Cox's remarks, he chided the physics professor for spending $70,000 beyond the

One-hundred-ton testing machine, in one of Macdonald's science buildings, about 1895
(Notman N-0000.25.261)

$68,014.27 that he had already provided for equipment: "When you compare these figures with the original $20,000 estimate which you gave me, of the probable cost of the equipment, you will be scarcely surprised at my informing you that I am not prepared to authorize the purchase, at my cost, of the additional items in the lists handed to me, by yourself and Prof. Callendar, at my home some time ago."[21]

Nevertheless, at the end of 1897, it is estimated that he permitted Cox and Callendar to exceed their budgets for equipment by four times. His contributions to physics and to the applied sciences more generally up to this date had included, for 1894, $7,500 for accumulators of electricity and compressed air, $10,000 for deficiencies (deficits in operating expenses), and $3,200 for the salaries of demonstrators in electrical engineering and physics (this last amount was his total profit from his tobacco business in that year);[22] for 1895, $10,000 for deficiencies in the applied sciences budget; and, for 1896, $150,000 for a maintenance fund for the Macdonald Engineering and Physics Buildings. For 1895, they had included

Hydraulics laboratory, in one of Macdonald's science buildings, about 1895
(Notman MP-0000.25.263)

$10,000 for deficiencies in the applied sciences budget; and for 1896, $150,000 for a maintenance fund for the Macdonald Engineering and Physics Buildings.[23] In 1894–96 he had supplemented certain salaries in the physics department with $2,627.54, and in 1894–97 he had supplemented salaries in the engineering department with $1,920. Between 1890 and 1904, he gave a total of $74,466.29 to cover the deficits of the Faculty of Applied Science as a whole. These contributions represented Macdonald's commitment to ensuring that his buildings remained productive, but he was simultaneously supporting efforts to fulfil still greater ambitions, such as in the teaching of architecture.

## THE ARCHITECTURAL CHARACTER OF MACDONALD'S BUILDINGS AND HIS CHAIR IN ARCHITECTURE, 1896

As we have seen, Macdonald built his Engineering Building largely to meet the challenge posed by the achievements of MIT and similar institutions. But the excellence of MIT rested on much more than engineering. It could also be proud of its arts programs, no less than before now that the arts were increasingly distinct from the sciences, both pure and applied. Architecture was a subject in which MIT and similar, primarily technical institutions could excel, even over such universities as Harvard. MIT had begun teaching architecture in 1868, but Harvard would not do so until 1895. Looking to MIT as his model, Macdonald established the first chair in architecture in Canada only a year after Harvard had begun teaching the subject, giving McGill $50,000 for this purpose.

Architecture could arguably be considered a branch of engineering. Surveying is common to both, as it is to mining and geology, and yet Macdonald created a separate chair in architecture, even though it was housed in his Engineering Building. This was a subject that he was personally interested in, from an aesthetic as well as a technical point of view. In the 1870s, for example, when he had to replace the Water Street tobacco works that had been destroyed by fire, he erected new works that were not only serviceable and designed to withstand fire, but also adorned with a huge and essentially decorative tower.

Now, at McGill, Montreal architects and their suppliers, such as the ironmaster John McDougall, who had coalmines and steel mills in Cape Breton but sales offices in Montreal, would benefit from the research carried out at the university. They would benefit from Macdonald's building projects as well. Macdonald used McDougall and the architects Andrew Hutchison and Andrew Taylor, among others, more than once in the construction of his many buildings.

Hutchison (1838–1922), the son of an immigrant from Ayrshire, had been born in Montreal and followed his father as a stonecutter. He supervised the stonecutting for Christ Church Cathedral in Montreal and the Parliament Buildings in Ottawa in 1858–62 and then taught drawing at the Mechanics' Institute and the Board of Arts and Manufactures in Montreal, where he became the architect of Macdonald's new tobacco works in 1874 and of the Redpath Museum in 1880. He also built the house of Lord Strathcona and various office buildings and churches. Perhaps his largest commission was to build Macdonald College in 1905–09.[24]

Taylor (1851–1937) was the son of an Edinburgh publisher. His mother was the sister of Senator George Drummond, originally from Edinburgh, whose house on Sherbrooke Street, opposite the entrance to McGill, Taylor designed in 1889. After practising architecture in Edinburgh and London, Taylor arrived in Canada in 1883 and here he obtained commissions from the Bank of Montreal, the Church of England, and the Montreal General Hospital. He became a lecturer in drawing at McGill, with the engineer C.H. McLeod, and professor of ecclesiastical architecture at the Presbyterian College. He built the Redpath Library and the Macdonald Engineering and Physics Buildings in 1890–93,

Department of Architecture, Macdonald Engineering Building, about 1901
(Notman MP-0000.25.283)

the Strathcona Medical Building in 1894, and the Macdonald Chemistry and Mining Building in 1896.[25]

The buildings given by Macdonald to McGill incorporated laboratories and workshops reminiscent of his tobacco works. With their fine craftsmanship and machine-made precision, they taught their own lesson. They were embodiments in stone of the ideals of nature study and manual training described in chapter 7.

In 1893, three years after Macdonald, Bovey, and Taylor had toured the United States to study the architecture of existing technical schools, Cox, at the opening of the Macdonald Engineering and Physics Buildings, praised Taylor's creations for their distinctive mix of beauty and practicality. Taylor, he said, had come to his work "with an open mind": "He was not hampered by tradition. He had combined utility with beauty. There was a stability, and there was the beauty of the Romanesque type ... the stony hard details of the equipment, which was the very best, and strong touches here and there dealing with the value of research and investigation such as would be carried out in this new building, and the setting forth of the distinction between the character of the work in the engineering building and the more delicate processes demanded in the work of physics."[26]

All of Macdonald's surviving buildings at McGill and elsewhere strike visitors to this day as unusually grand and solid, even monumental and yet somehow almost domestic in inspiration. There is no doubt that they reflect his preferences. He would often supervise with real delight not only their construction but also their maintenance and improvement, and would become quite upset if his orders were not followed to the letter. On an inspection of his institute in Guelph, for example, he found some deficiency in the execution of his instructions. Furious, he left immediately for the railway station, never to return. For Macdonald, nothing but the finest materials and workmanship would do, and once the buildings were opened, only the finest equipment and the finest professors he could find would satisfy him. This applied to the appointees to his chair of architecture as to his other chairs.

The first three holders of the Macdonald Chair in Architecture were Scotsmen, the first by adoption and the two others by birth. Stewart Henbest Cappen, born in 1859 of English parents, was educated at the Royal High School in Edinburgh and at the Universities of Edinburgh and Heidelberg and the École des Beaux-Arts in Paris.[27] He spent four years attached to the household of the British minister to Lisbon and Madrid and was fluent in Spanish, Portuguese, French, and German as well as in Latin, Greek, and English. He was a noted conservationist and proponent of the Arts and Crafts style. Peterson appointed him to the architecture chair in 1896 on the recommendation of a friend at the University of Edinburgh. In his inaugural lecture at McGill, Cappen insisted that architecture was "closely combined" with engineering and was the science and art of building well, representing common sense touched by poetry. Cappen left McGill in 1903, however, joining Owens College at Victoria University in Manchester.

Percy Nobbs, born in Haddington in Scotland in 1874, succeeded Cappen.[28] He had lived and studied in St Petersburg and Edinburgh and had worked in both Edinburgh and London. Unlike Cappen, he would stay in Montreal for the rest of his life, marrying a daughter of Dr F.J. Shepherd, dean of medicine at McGill, and practising his profession with George T. Hyde from 1910 until 1944. Like Cappen, Nobbs appealed to Macdonald's love of the practical in combination with the soberly decorative. In 1904–06 Macdonald had him design the McGill Student Union at Sherbrooke and Victoria Streets, and for this project Nobbs drew upon Sir Charles Barry's clubs in the palazzo style in London. There was in Nobbs a romantic streak, in the Ruskinian tradition, evident not only in his buildings but also in his deep interest in fencing and heraldry and similar to the bravado of J.W. Robertson. His many buildings in Montreal, not least his

Percy Nobbs, 1906 (Notman II-159967)

new Macdonald Engineering Building for McGill, erected in 1907–09, embodied the simplicity and solidity of character, combined with grace, that both he and Macdonald saw as part of the best of Canada. In 1921 Nobbs designed an extension to the Redpath Library, thus concluding the legacy to McGill of a tight-knit group of benefactors and architects begun with the Redpath Museum over forty years before.

Nobbs was aware that not all architects were talented engineers, and thus he had McGill offer two distinct architecture degrees. One was called a "bachelor of science in architectural engineering degree" while the other was known simply as a "bachelor of architecture degree." Holders of the latter were spared the more demanding courses of the Faculty of Applied Science.

Despite Nobbs's obvious talents, Principal Peterson objected to the time he spent in his private architectural practice, and in 1913 Nobbs's colleague Ramsay

Traquair (1874–1952) replaced him, becoming the third Macdonald Professor of Architecture. Traquair's father had been a geologist and palaeontologist at the Royal Museum of Science and Art in Edinburgh, and his mother had been the first woman fellow of the Royal Scottish Academy. Traquair, once an apprentice under Cappen, was an authority on Byzantine, medieval, and Quebec vernacular architecture in his own right.

As in the case of his other endowments, Macdonald considered his gift of a chair in architecture as marking only the beginning of his commitment to this field. In 1897 he gave the new department casts worth $950, photographs and slides worth $400, and books worth $1,700. In the following year, he gave it $10,000 for supplies and $500 for its maintenance.[29] No detail was too small for him, and in 1899 he spent $94.83 on a bookcase for the department.

### THE MACDONALD CHEMISTRY AND MINING BUILDING, 1896, AND THE CHAIR IN CHEMISTRY, 1897[30]

Chemistry was part of the curriculum at McGill from the earliest days of Dawson's tenure. It was taught to students of both medicine and natural philosophy, and had been recognized as a branch of science even when science was taught in the Faculty of Arts. Its evolution into a distinct discipline with a separate department and a chair in chemistry (endowed by Macdonald) was similar to that of architecture and engineering, though it included a brief phase when chemical engineering constituted a department.

In September 1896 Macdonald offered McGill a total of $475,000 to erect a building that would house laboratories and lecture rooms for chemistry and mining and metallurgy ($170,000); to buy equipment ($120,000); to endow chairs in (a) mining and metallurgy and (b) architecture ($50,000 each); and to add to a maintenance fund ($85,000). His only condition was that all free tuition in certain faculties be abolished. The free tuition he was mainly concerned with was that for aspiring clergymen, although the free tuition that was provided to students nominated by specific benefactors and others had long been a burden on university finances. Never, Macdonald noted, had there ever been free tuition for students of applied science.[31]

In 1896 Macdonald is recorded as contributing $279,321.84 for the Chemistry and Mining Building and its equipment. He gave an additional $135,000 for its maintenance in that year, followed by a further $90,000 in 1897 for the same purpose. B.J. Harrington became the first Macdonald Professor of Chemistry, someone named Porter became the first Macdonald Professor of Mining and Metallurgy, and James Wallace Walker took the second chair of chemistry. Macdonald also endowed a special University Chair in Chemistry with $50,000.

Chemistry wing of the Macdonald Chemistry and Mining Building, 1913
(Notman VIEW-12882)

Lord Minto, the governor general, opened the new building on 20 December
1898, and Harrington became its director. Macdonald gave $1,222.40 to pay for
the opening ceremonies.

## MACDONALD'S FURTHER GENEROSITY TO APPLIED SCIENCES, THE ARTS, AND THE STUDENT UNION, 1897–1905

At the end of 1897, Macdonald announced further funding for McGill. He gave
$50,000 as a new endowment for the Faculty of Law and provided $225,000 for
a Macdonald Auxiliary Fund, to be used in cases of emergency. Between 1897
and 1908, he was to give a total of $395,350 to this fund. He also provided addi-
tional sums for maintenance ($150,000 for the Physics Building, $135,000 for the
Chemistry and Mining Building, $85,000 for the Engineering Building, and
$200,000 for the law department in the east wing of the Arts Building); he fur-
ther endowed his two chairs in physics, his chair in architecture, his first chair

Mining wing of the Macdonald Chemistry and Mining Building, 1913
(Notman VIEW-12876)

in chemistry, and his chair in mining with the fresh sum of $50,000 each; and he funded four Macdonald scholarships in law for $25,000. In one day, therefore, he gave the university $1,110,500.[32] Finally, in 1897, he spent $900 for surveying equipment and $12,000 for a new power station, in addition to $340 for furniture and printing for the Faculty of Law, $450 for unspecified advertising, and $1,273.35 for miscellaneous items, such as a portrait of Mr and Mrs Peter Redpath, botanical apparatus, receptions, and the Denton collection of butterflies. He was to add $60,000 to his first chair of chemistry in 1901 and $10,000 to his chair of mining in 1903.

Scarcely seven months later, in 1898, he added an endowment of $10,000 to his engineering chair, $2,500 to his auxiliary fund, $4,000 for a library and telephonic equipment for his Chemistry and Mining Building, and $1,500 for grading and macadamizing roadways and for constructing drains and waterways around the Physics Building and the Chemistry and Mining Building.[33] His passion for detail seemed bottomless. In October 1898 he gave $30,560 for modifications to

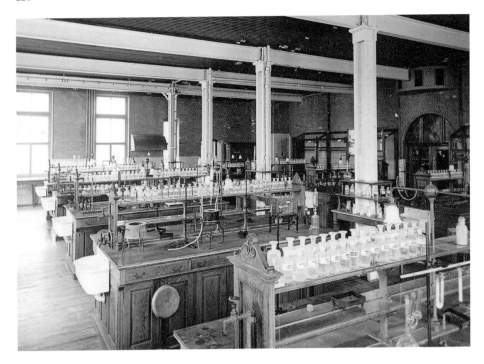

Laboratory in the Macdonald Chemistry and Mining Building, about 1901
(Notman MP-0000.25.271)

and equipment for the Department of Electrical Engineering and $2,000 for
the improvement of the walls, hardwood floors, and attic of the Chemistry and
Mining Building and for the installation of a steam pipe connection between it
and the Engineering Building.[34]

Before the end of 1898 he gave a further $50,000 to cover deficits, $50,000 to
endow a Kingsford Chair in History (named after the author of a twelve-volume
history of Canada whom he had never met), and $12,500 for his auxiliary fund;
he also provided an annuity for Mrs Kingsford of $125 a year.[35] Within the fol-
lowing six weeks, he gave a further $181,250 for the maintenance of the Chem-
istry and Mining Building.[36] For work done by students in mining engineering
during the summer, he paid $825. For the academic years 1898–1900, he gave
$1,000 to pay for assistants in the chemistry department.

In 1899 Macdonald gave the university $6,000 for equipment for the mining
department and then $50,000 for a chair in geology in honour of Sir William
Dawson, who had just died, with an additional $12,000 for the auxiliary fund
of the mining department. Out of the interest earned by the fund, $2,500 per
year was to go towards the support of Lady Dawson.[37] He also set up a special

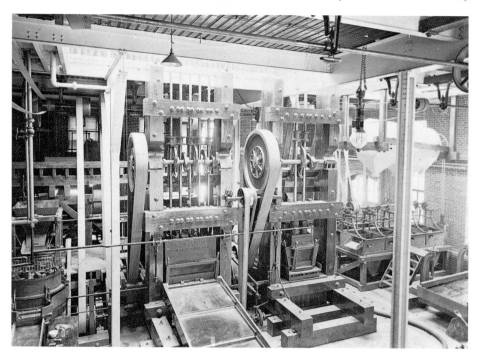

Milling room, Macdonald Chemistry and Mining Building, about 1901
(Notman MP-0000.25.273)

Macdonald Fund for Mining and Metallurgy and endowed it with $55,000. Then he asked B.J. Harrington to draw up a list of the requirements of the chemistry department, and in 1900 he gave $135,000 to endow positions for lecturers, demonstrators, and assistants in it. He topped up the auxiliary fund with $33,750, added $15,000 for necessary repairs to his Engineering, Physics, and Chemistry and Mining Buildings, and gave McGill $12,500 towards the purchase of the Ferrier collection of minerals for the Redpath Museum.[38]

He had already given eighty mounted specimens of birds to the Redpath Museum in 1893 and the Beaulieu collection of coleoptera in 1898, and in 1905 he was to promise to provide cases for the Ferrier collection and to endow it with $5,000. In 1907 he contributed $1,075 towards the purchase of B.J. Harrington's mineral collection for the museum. As late as 1911, he gave the museum a set of seven tables and six window cases for its mineral collection, valued at $1,550.69.

Macdonald's support for McGill continued into the new century. Between 1900 and his bequest of 1917, he gave a total of $42,650 for travelling scholarships in law alone, to enable law students to improve their French in France. He gave, in 1900, $30,000 for additions to the electrical engineering laboratories and

Electrical laboratory in the Macdonald Engineering Building, about 1898
(Notman MP-0000.25.267.1)

for the renewal of storage batteries, $2,000 to cover a special tax on the phys-
ics department, $300 for the maintenance of the botany laboratory, $5,000 for
apparatus for the mechanical department, and $604.91 for induction coils for the
physics laboratory.[39] All this was in addition to his endowment of the chemistry
department with $135,000 and of the Macdonald Buildings Repair Fund with
$15,000. In 1901 Macdonald gave $60,000 in increased endowment to his chair
in chemistry, $10,000 for his second chair in physics, and $50,000 for a chair in
botany, with contributions to an auxiliary fund for each of these chairs amounting respectively to $15,000, $2,500, and $12,500.[40]

Macdonald even addressed the problem of Montreal's largely unpaved streets,
in 1902–03 paying $2,800 for granolithic sidewalks to be laid all the way from
Prince of Wales Terrace through the campus to the Arts Building. His preoccupation with detail led to such simultaneous payments as $300 for insulated
wire to connect the university with an anemometer on Mount Royal, $250 for
the publication of the investigations of professors of physics, and $500 for the
construction of an animal facility for the Faculty of Medicine.[41]

Carpentry in the Macdonald Engineering Building, about 1893 (Notman VIEW-2641)

In 1903, after sitting on a committee to consider the future of the Faculty of Arts, Macdonald endowed a Macdonald Chair in Moral Philosophy with $50,000, adding $12,500 for an auxiliary fund for it. On the same day, he added $12,500 to the endowment of his mining chair, $7,500 to reduce deficits in the Faculty of Applied Science, $1,200 for a fire escape for his Physics Building, $1,800 for travelling scholarships in law, and $500 for an assistant to the professor of zoology, all followed in November by $2,000 for physics experiments.[42]

By 1904 Macdonald had become almost as interested in the arts and social sciences as he was in the pure and applied sciences. The Conservatorium of Music opened in this year, and he would eagerly attend concerts there, often with Mrs Peterson. He was to give $1,500 to the Musical Students' Fund in 1906, $3,500 in 1907, and $3,500 in 1908. In May 1904 he gave $1,050 for philosophy books and periodicals, $50 for new works in philosophy, $2,500 for the "North Western manuscripts," $250 for experiments in psychology, and $3,000 for four more travelling scholarships in law.[43] In June he gave an endowment of $6,000 to provide $250 a year for further experiments in psychology and $50 a year for the purchase of philosophical literature; $500 for an auxiliary fund for this endowment; $500

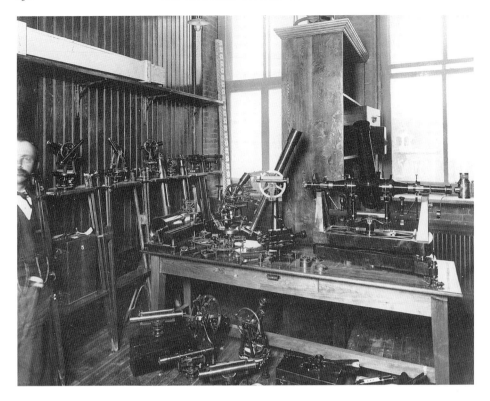

Geodetic instruments in the Macdonald Engineering Building, about 1893
(Notman VIEW-2659)

for a French-language summer school; $700 for lockers in the Physics Building; $1,000 for a mezzanine in the Mining Building; and $219,119 for a new student union.[44]

He made this last donation to protest the arrival on campus of the McGill YMCA and its occupation of Strathcona Hall at the corner of Sherbrooke Street and McGill College Avenue. Like his fellow governor C.J. Fleet and the dean of arts, Charles Moyse, he saw the YMCA's assumption of "McGill" in its name as a threat to the non-religious character of the university, and in any case, he wanted to provide a recreational centre for students whether they were Christian or not. The McGill Student Union was increasingly expensive to build, even as support for it was growing. In October 1904 Macdonald added $25,000 to his original endowment for the project, in January 1905 a further $10,000, and in May yet a further $50,000, for a total of $185,000. Macdonald, not wanting the Student Union to be financially dependent on him alone, mobilized support from the university at large for his non-sectarian project. He had already extracted a promise from McGill graduates that they would provide their own endowment of $75,000 for the union, but now, with his further contributions in 1905, he told them that they had a moral obligation to raise their endowment to $160,000.[45]

## ERNEST RUTHERFORD, MACDONALD PROFESSOR OF PHYSICS, AND HIS ATOMIC RESEARCH AT McGILL, 1898–1907

If Macdonald had given nothing else to education, he would still be remembered for funding some of the most important research of the twentieth century.[46] Although Ernest Rutherford (1871–1937) had been born in New Zealand and was to spend most of his life in England, the work that he did as a Macdonald Professor of Physics in the Macdonald Physics Laboratory in Montreal was what won him a Nobel Prize in 1908. Without Rutherford and without Macdonald's support of the physicist over seven years, nuclear physics would probably have evolved along very different lines.

Rutherford, who has been compared favourably to Einstein as the foremost scientist of the twentieth century, was one of Macdonald's favourite causes and probably his most successful investment. He was the third to occupy a Macdonald Chair in Physics, succeeding Callendar while Cox remained in the other chair. Macdonald had been unusually interested in Rutherford's appointment, and he met him "several times" just after his arrival. Later, Macdonald often visited the laboratories to see how his newest equipment was performing. Rutherford himself apparently found Macdonald pleasant, if eccentric, and yet indispensable in his moral as well as in his financial support.

Macdonald placed special monetary value on Rutherford from the start. According to the physicist himself, when he first came to McGill in 1898, Macdonald paid him £500 (or $2,000) a year, twice the amount Macdonald himself was living on, or so Rutherford was led to believe. It is doubtful that Macdonald actually lived on only $1,000 – especially since he charged Principal Peterson an annual rent of $800 (plus taxes) for the house next door – but perhaps the $1,000 referred only to what he spent on day-to-day expenses as opposed to his income. In 1901, in addition to increasing the endowment for Rutherford's chair by $10,000 and increasing Rutherford's salary by $500, Macdonald built the new laboratory that Rutherford wanted and bought whatever equipment the physicist requested, including a new liquid air machine and a microscope, each costing $1,250. In 1902 he gave him $500 towards the purchase of radium, and in 1903 he gave an additional $2,000 for physics experiments. Macdonald also paid for Rutherford's assistants, one of whom, Frederick Soddy, was to win a Nobel Prize of his own in 1921 for his work on radioactivity and isotopes.[47]

For the physics department, Macdonald had already built the finest laboratories in the world, and as already noted, he had filled them with whatever equipment his scientists requested. The department was the Los Alamos of its time,

Ernest Rutherford in his Macdonald laboratory, about 1907 (MUA PN00126)

and especially through Rutherford's work, Macdonald found himself financing the most crucial beginnings of the atomic age. Macdonald here demonstrated the vision and the confidence of a seasoned investor. Though exceedingly frugal in his personal expenses, he gave a fortune to research whose outcome was unpredictable. As we have seen in his resentment over the expenses of Cox and Callendar, he examined every detail with the closest attention, but he still took calculated risks. Physics was being taught elsewhere, of course, from Adelaide in South Australia to Edinburgh and Boston, but the Macdonald Physics Laboratory was the finest in the world and had attracted probably the finest physicist alive.

As Percy Nobbs was to recall of Rutherford's work, Macdonald in reality "did not follow the famous experiments, any more than we of other Departments were able to do," but "he was as strongly affected as any of us by this pushing back of the curtain of mystery."[48] Macdonald may even have seen Rutherford as a new Benjamin Franklin, a man he had admired since working in Boston in 1850–53. In any case, Rutherford's work offered startling glimpses of the literally earth-shattering potential of the new discipline. The work of physicists was almost intangible in comparison to, say, that of geologists and palaeontologists, and it was utterly beyond preoccupations with species and evolution. It dealt with forces invisible to the naked eye, forces far more powerful and yet removed from all the shells and the mineralogical specimens and the biblical controversies that had ensnared such men as Dawson. The subject was incomprehensible to most people, as it remains to this day.

It is possible that Macdonald hoped that speculative research such as Rutherford's might at last help free humankind from what he saw as religious superstition. Rutherford's work on subatomic particles ventured beyond what Macdonald appears to have seen as sterile questions about the origins of species. It could not come under the sway of either Christian dogma or even the Scottish School of Common Sense, the sort of apologetics then prevalent in the training of Canadian undergraduates.

At any rate, Rutherford's great discoveries at McGill, notably his theory of radioactive disintegration – with its notion of continuous change in the nature of the atom – commanded Macdonald's unequivocal support. There was no chiding of Rutherford as there had been of Cox and Callendar, and he never failed to celebrate the success of his protégé.[49] One famous occasion was the dinner for 120 that Macdonald gave Rutherford at the Windsor Hotel, in honour of his receipt of the Rumford Medal from the Royal Society of London in 1904. Macdonald himself was not present, but Nobbs was to recall it as by far the most successful social function at the university "in the last twenty years, perhaps in all her history."[50]

Rutherford left McGill in 1907 to take up a post at Victoria University (Owens College) in Manchester – also renowned for its atomic research and its teaching of physics, chemistry, and mathematics. A year later he won his Nobel Prize for his work at McGill. As late as 1935, a student of Rutherford's at Manchester, James Chadwick, won yet another Nobel Prize, for his discovery of the neutron. The achievements of Rutherford, Soddy, and Chadwick, among others, literally atomized or more precisely sub-atomized the human understanding of nature. The awards that they won, paid out of the estate of the inventor of dynamite, Alfred Nobel, epitomized what the union of a fortune from industry, scientific research, and careful investment might yield, much as Macdonald's laboratories at McGill did.

## THE ENDOWMENT OF MACDONALD COLLEGE, 1906–1917

The origins of Macdonald College in the context of Macdonald's work with J.W. Robertson were discussed in the last chapter. A description of his actual endowment for the college will put his other work described here into perspective.

Macdonald was involved in the financing for the college almost from the start. He announced in June 1906 that, along with an initial endowment of $2.2 million, he would transfer to McGill the land he had bought in Ste Anne de Belle-vue, as well as the several buildings he was erecting on it, for the use of the college.[51] This gift doubled the endowment for the university as a whole, which without it was only $2,002,333, yielding interest of $80,593.33 a year.[52] Macdonald would top up this inadequate income with $10,000 in January 1909.[53]

With additional endowments of Macdonald College in 1914 and 1917, Macdonald actually gave it a total endowment $4,023,896.70. This was in addition to the $2,684,926 that he had paid for the grounds, buildings, and equipment by 1906 and new construction at the college over the following ten years, all amounting to $3,198,355.88. If we add the total endowment to the purchase price and construction up to 1917, we find that he had given at least $7,222,252.50 to Macdonald College by then. In other words, by 1917 through his gifts to Macdonald College alone, he had increased the endowment of McGill University as a whole by almost three times. If we include his gifts to McGill University outside Macdonald College, his increase of its general endowment must be greater still.

In 1907 Macdonald gave the college a further endowment specifically for the McGill School for Teachers at Macdonald College. In 1908 he donated $326,218 to be spent on sixteen new residences, the repair of eight old residences, and the construction of stables, barns, silos, and other structures. In its entirety, the college was comparable in ambition to the complex of Macdonald buildings on the main campus in Montreal. He provided a further $76,250 of which $60,000 was to be allocated to a Macdonald Chair in Education, with $15,000 for the auxiliary fund for the chair and $1,250 to enable its first occupant to travel in preparation for assuming the position.[54] As principal, Robertson received a salary of $5,000 a year, matching that received by Rutherford, at the height of his career at McGill in 1906.[55]

Like the Macdonald buildings in Montreal, those at Macdonald College required ongoing maintenance. Macdonald gave $10,000 towards the operation of the college in 1908–09, in addition to the roughly $80,000 it was receiving each year from his main endowment.[56] In 1913 he gave the college $35,391.01 for cottages and barns, as well as 238 further arpents of land and another lot for its use at its main entrance.[57]

### MACDONALD'S LAST EFFORT IN PRINCE EDWARD ISLAND: THE EXPANSION AND MODERNIZATION OF PRINCE OF WALES COLLEGE, 1906–1907

Religion dominated the politics of Prince Edward Island in the nineteenth century. The province (as it became in 1873), with its population of less than 100,000, had both Protestant and Roman Catholic versions of the Liberal and Conservative parties. Loyalties were tested, but religious belief usually prevailed over party affiliation. In 1876, for example, an all-Protestant Liberal-Conservative coalition dominated the Legislature and faced an all-Catholic Liberal-Conservative opposition. And Bishop Peter McIntyre of Charlottetown held office from 1860 to 1891, outlasting fifteen governments and ten premiers.[58]

With the death of his brother John Archibald in 1903, Macdonald cut off all support to his remaining family on the Island. He was not about to cut off his native province, however. His consolidated school at Hillsborough was in operation, and in about 1906 he offered the province funds to expand Prince of Wales College, formerly the Central Academy, in Charlottetown, which he had attended in 1844.[59] He began by building a new wing for the college. The wing, which covered 7,000 square feet and occupied two storeys, included new classrooms for the Normal School, athletic facilities, and an examinations hall. This expansion cost $55,000, and Macdonald College principal J.W. Robertson himself oversaw the construction with Macdonald's agent H.J. Cundall.

Macdonald also made Prince of Wales College the offer of an institutional affiliation with McGill. This would be much like the affiliation of colleges in Vancouver and Ste Anne de Bellevue with the same university and the affiliation of his Guelph institute with the University of Toronto. Prince of Wales College initially agreed to this offer, which was to go into effect on 1 July 1907. Premier Arthur Peters had drafted a bill dealing with this arrangement and sent it to McGill for approval on 18 March 1907. On 17 April, however, he noted that the Farmers' Institutes were complaining that agricultural education should be given priority over university education for funding. Even though Macdonald most certainly included agricultural education in his plan, the objection of the institutes prevailed and Peters asked that a decision on Macdonald's offer be put off for a year. In the end, the province would never accept the offer. Prince of Wales College remained unfunded and it never joined McGill.

According to one historian, Roman Catholic lobbyists had been able to organize the farmers successfully because of opposition to Macdonald's offer mounted by St Dunstan's College, a seminary in Charlottetown that had not been invited to participate in Macdonald's affiliation plan.[60] The Roman Catholic Bishop of Charlottetown had been merely following church policy of the time, which was to discourage Protestant or non-denominational schools and to try to keep all levels of education as much as possible under church control. The author of a history of Prince of Wales College does not accept this explanation as definitive and instead suggests that a variety of factors kept the affiliation with McGill indefinitely on hold. The later refusal of the province in 1909 to continue to fund the Macdonald Consolidated School at Hillsborough suggests the correctness of this conclusion. But what were these factors?

At about this time, Macdonald was funding the McGill-affiliated non-denominational McGill University College of British Columbia in Vancouver. Prince Edward Island politicians and ecclesiastics were doubtless convinced that behind this funding was an implicitly secular agenda. Macdonald and others, they feared, wanted to prevent the Methodist college in New Westminster from becoming the nucleus of a projected University of British Columbia. Not only were Islanders unprepared for a similar such intrusion into their educational system, but they had probably not forgotten the terrible reputation of the Macdonalds as landlords. Moreover, the church may not have forgiven the family's obstinacy over St Andrew's College and the religious apostasy of Macdonald himself.

## THE McGILL UNIVERSITY COLLEGE
## OF BRITISH COLUMBIA, 1906–1909

The story of the Vancouver venture that did accept $15,000 from Macdonald suggests why Macdonald so ardently promoted the affiliation of various colleges with McGill.[61] The encouragement of non-denominational education was undoubtedly part of what motivated him, but so too was his desire to see the spread of practical education.

After King's College in Halifax, McGill was the oldest surviving institution of higher education in Canada. It was unique, firstly, in possessing a charter permitting it to operate both locally and outside its natural boundaries, and secondly, in being privately funded without any significant provincial aid. As the last vestige of the Royal Institution for the Advancement of Learning and with the governor general as its chancellor, it readily saw for itself a national, if not an international, role. And within Quebec, McGill was the guardian of non-Catholic education, even for French-speakers, as seen through its support of Morrin College, which trained many French Canadians.

As early as 1858, candidates across British North America were sitting for the McGill senior matriculation examination. In 1907, 550 candidates in sixty schools made the attempt.[62] The high school in Vancouver (later expanded into Vancouver College) had been affiliated with McGill since 1899. A trustee of this school, A.H.B. Macgowan, had approached Macdonald himself in 1896, seeking this affiliation and offering to name the school Macdonald College, but Macdonald had referred him to J.W. Brakenridge, the acting secretary of McGill.[63] Up to 1906, Vancouver College did its best to replicate the first two years of the McGill bachelor of arts curriculum, which was largely devoted to the study of Latin and Greek. Students would complete these first two years at the college and then go to McGill in Montreal for their final year to complete their degree.

Principal Peterson at McGill, as a classicist himself, took a special interest in the Vancouver school. But, as we have seen, McGill was not especially reputed for its arts program. It was, largely thanks to Macdonald, much more famous for its science and engineering programs, and these were subjects of great interest to the manufacturers and industrialists of the new province of British Columbia.

The head of the McGill examination board was Henry Marshall Tory (1864–1947), a mathematician and a Methodist minister. Early in the twentieth century many of the leading men in institutions of higher education in Canada were ordained ministers, although they displayed erudition and ability in widely diverse fields outside theology. Tory, however, was not to remain a minister for long. Shocked by the prosecution of the liberal theologian George Workman at the Wesleyan Theological College in Montreal in 1901, Tory resigned his ministry, finally, in 1906, and then went to Macdonald to solicit his assistance in transforming the Vancouver College into the McGill University College of British Columbia. Despite the fact that Tory had been a demonstrator in the Macdonald Physics Building and the assistant to John Adams in 1902 in the Macdonald-financed inquiry into Protestant schools in Quebec, the old man gave him a grilling. This probably occurred in the library of Macdonald's house in Prince of Wales Terrace, where he was famously reputed to conduct "long and searching" cross-examinations.[64] He immediately questioned Tory's religious background and seemed to doubt that the seed money Tory was requesting for the project would be all that would be demanded of him. Tory pledged not to ask for a penny more, and Macdonald agreed to his request.

Tory went off to Vancouver for about six months to establish the incarnation of the school as the McGill University College of British Columbia. Heeding the needs of the local business community, he effectively made the classically oriented arts program optional and dedicated its new curriculum almost entirely to science and engineering.[65] Thus, McGill University College, until its transformation into the University of British Columbia in 1915, became a technical school. J.C. Shaw, the ordained minister and classicist who had been principal of Vancouver College, became its dean of engineering.

McGill University College was essentially funded by local businessmen and not by either McGill or Macdonald. But it seems fair to say that Macdonald was its rather remote and indeed anonymous godfather, not only because of the modest amount he gave to facilitate the transformation of Vancouver College into McGill University College but also because of the support that he had given to science and engineering at McGill. Among others trained at Dalhousie and the University of Toronto, McGill-trained teachers – notably H.K. Dulcher, professor of civil engineering – went out to Vancouver to establish courses in these subjects. Finally, if McGill University College had not largely become a technical school, it would not have attracted the generous support that it did from the business and wider communities of British Columbia.

CONCLUSION

Although justly remembered for his financial contributions to McGill, Macdonald was also tireless in his contribution of time to the university. Although their work was hardly glamorous, he sat on several committees in these later years, among them one to address the problem of N.W. Trenholme's attempt to resign as dean of law, one to appoint Maxime Ingres as instructor in French, and one to reorganize the Faculty of Arts.[66] His influence is even more evident in his 1896 appointment, along with the newly appointed Principal Peterson, to a committee of two to deal with candidates for teaching positions in the Faculty of Applied Science.[67] Among his other committees, one examined sites for a tropical botany laboratory, another appointed a new bursar, another considered how office work might be reorganized, and another considered raising fees in the Faculty of Arts.[68]

Some of Macdonald's gifts to the university have been largely forgotten; records of them have disappeared or they have been absorbed into better-known parts of McGill. In 1895, for example, he bought a large amount of property on Côte-des-Neiges, thirty-nine arpents, for $70,405.12, for use by the McGill University Observatory, and he secured a restriction on the height of buildings on adjoining properties.[69] If no object of study was too small for, say, his physics department, no object was too large for his meteorological interests. And, at a cost unknown, he renovated the east wing of the Arts Building to provide space for the Faculty of Law and the university archives, as well as offices for general business, apartments for the principal, and a boardroom for the governors.[70]

Macdonald's other gifts of land to McGill, apart from those already mentioned in this chapter, included Lot 1813 of St Antoine Ward, south of the Wesleyan Theological College on University Street, and the "Little Mountain," near the summit of Mount Royal in Westmount. The purpose of the last gift is unclear, although the land may have been for a nature reserve. In any case, it was soon sold to Charles Gordon, president of the Dominion Textile Company, and Herbert Holt, president of the Montreal Light, Heat and Power Company, both of them McGill governors as well as land developers.[71] In 1911 Macdonald bought land from the Law and Molson families for the university. It cost him $1,117,639.50. Lying between Royal Victoria College and Fletcher's Field (later Jeanne Mance Park), its original dimensions and cost unclear, it became known as Macdonald Park. On it would be built Molson Stadium and the Sir Arthur Currie Gymnasium-Armoury.[72] In 1913 he made his last supplementary endowment of the Faculty of Law, $32,500, which made his total endowment of it since 1890 $232,500. It has been calculated that his total gifts to McGill amounted to $13.4 million in 1917, or about $240 million in 2006 terms.

The very variety of Macdonald's work for McGill in the eleven years covered by this chapter makes its summing up difficult. This variety underlines the fact that in offering financial gifts Macdonald was largely responding to emerging and ongoing needs. It is true that through his gifts he was promoting his own vision of a secular, largely scientific and technical university, but the implementation of the details of this vision he generally left to his appointees. Except in the case of his dispute with Robertson at Macdonald College in 1909, he allowed his appointees, as heads of his projects, to carry on without his interference. He was always interested in the most minute details of his buildings and of much else, but he knew better than to stifle his projects at their inception by interfering with what was properly their autonomous management.

Macdonald saw himself as a facilitator, a catalyst, with little relevant personal expertise, though he might have claimed a practical role in the building of his technical complex on the main campus of McGill and in the assembling of its equipment, thanks to experience gained from his tobacco works. Graduates who have spent productive years in his many extant buildings and schools can be rightly appreciative of his generosity. But as he did not head the institutions he had created and in most cases he did not initiate his projects without much advice, it would be wrong to assume that he intended or considered any of them to be more important than the others. He was keenly interested in all of them and supported each one with great sensitivity. He knew that their best days would probably dawn long after he was gone.

There was an element in Macdonald's work that was very personal, and that was his wish to redeem the Macdonald name after the decades, even centuries, of its decline. To this extent, he saw himself as a pioneer. In these later years, he corresponded with a distant cousin, Col. John A. Macdonald of Glenfinnan, where Bonnie Prince Charlie had raised his standard in 1745. Reflecting on their common heritage, Macdonald remarked that there was room in Canada for a hundred million Highlanders, the largest space in the world and it was all ripe for "improvement." What Canada was awaiting, he wrote, was the exercise of the "vast energies" of the Highlanders, "not in war, but in the beneficent arts and industries of peace."[74] Unsaid but implicit was Macdonald's vision of himself as a foot soldier in a much nobler and stirring cause than that of the Jacobites, one never even glimpsed by any previous Macdonald.

William C. Macdonald, 1901 (Notman II-137468)

*Chapter Nine*

# TOBACCO WITH A HEART:
# MACDONALD'S PERSONALITY, SCOTTISHNESS,
# LATER YEARS, AND LEGACY

With the salary you have and all the money I have you are the best [*sic*] of the two. The reason I say this [is] that you have a nice little cottage, four fine children and a wife to go home to after your day's work is over. On the other hand, I have a four-storey mansion in which I have quarters on the top floor and four servants use the rest who only look after me for what money I pay them. The result is that I am a very lonely old man.

*Macdonald to Tom Graydon, caretaker, circa 1900*[1]

I feel sure the public wd. recognize a K.C.M.G. or a Baronetcy for Sir W. Macdonald and a C.M.G. for Dr. Peterson (Principal of McGill) – the latter is no doubt proper – as to the former I am doubtful. I sd. [said] a baronetcy is certainly not advisable. I do not at present know if he has children, but he is certainly not the sort of man to keep up any social standing – also my recollection is that he was much opposed to receiving the last honour [of knight bachelor] & only consented under great persuasion.

*Lord Minto to the Right Honourable Joseph Chamberlain,*
*Colonial Secretary, 3 August 1901*[2]

## A MAN OF PARADOX

As we saw in chapter 3, Macdonald advertised his tobacco as having a heart, a reference to the tin heart that he placed in every plug of his tobacco to distinguish his product from those of his competitors. It was as unique as any trademark and might even have been considered valuable by some, for it is said that people would sometimes put Macdonald hearts into collection plates in church. This heart appears even in the arms of the Macdonald Tobacco Company. Although famous for disdaining the use of tobacco, Macdonald was saying something about himself in so advertising the source of his fortune. He, like his product, was not always in high favour everywhere, even in his own mind. Yet he definitely possessed a big heart, and despite his shyness it was his badge of choice.

However large his heart may have been, early memoirs about Macdonald placed considerable emphasis on his personal frugality. Mrs Walter Vaughan (Susan Cameron) recalled seeing him taking streetcars using cheap, off-peak tickets, while he owned a carriage and a sleigh and employed a driver. He would not butter his bread if he was also drinking milk. There are stories about how his coat was green with age and about how he wrote letters on scrap paper and boasted of collecting string rather than old master paintings. The boast was a veiled criticism of his neighbour and, for a few years, his fellow governor of McGill, Sir William Van Horne. Van Horne, president of the Canadian Pacific Railway, was a collector of paintings of world renown, but he gave almost nothing to the university. Even Van Horne's own biographer, Macdonald's friend Walter Vaughan, took the unusual step of attacking his selfishness in print. Vaughan observed that Van Horne "grudged giving" and that "his most ardent admirers could not forgive him for stinginess which in some cases fell way short of meanness."[3] A more recent biographer of Van Horne, Valerie Knowles, observed that Van Horne's will made "no provision for bequests to friends, family retainers, non-profit organizations, or charities."[4] A greater contrast to Macdonald could hardly be found.

But Macdonald's frugality led to accusations of his selfishness as well. Surviving letters of his confirm that he could be extremely abrupt and dismissive when he was not interested in entering into a business venture or in contributing to a religious cause. Neither was he especially sympathetic to his employees, whom he kept at a distance through his competitive work-bench system. And there was much criticism of him after the fire at his tobacco works. Moreover, despite his extreme conscientiousness and generosity towards them, he found his nephews and his nieces almost incomprehensible. His early biographer J.F. Snell interviewed relations who proffered the calumny that Macdonald had cut his nephews and nieces off while they were being educated overseas. In short, he was not everywhere perceived as a saint, and he would have been the first to disclaim being identified as such. Still, Macdonald, in his last years, seems to have become reconciled even with his two Jesuit relations – his cousin John Alistair MacDonald and his uncle Allan McDonnell – and he clutched the hand of his long-estranged niece Anna.[5]

It is to this chapter that has been deliberately left a consideration of his personality, in the hope that some of it might first become apparent through descriptions of some of his activities. The anecdotes recorded of him are nearly all from people who observed him as an old man, when he had become set in his ways.

Macdonald in his later years (MSF)

Macdonald's desk (MSF)

Probably none of those who recorded their memories of him, even his friends Professors Percy Nobbs and J.F. Snell, knew as much about his family as can be gleaned from other sources. Macdonald was almost as secretive about his business success as about his family sorrows. And although some of his contemporaries doubtless knew far more about manufacturing tobacco than we can know, probably few but David and Walter Stewart were privy to some of the production figures uncovered in the tables in chapter 3. With a fresh view of his many years, the paradox of his public generosity and his private frugality can be reconsidered in the context of a coherent personality. The two criticisms most frequently made of Macdonald are that he was unsociable and miserably stingy. Especially towards the end of his life, he was in fact neither.

The private man behind the normally forbidding public face could be surprising. As the quotation at the head of this chapter suggests, Macdonald became increasingly lonely as he aged, but he was not an unsociable man. He belonged to the St James Club and the Mount Royal Club, whose members were generally businessmen. He frequently visited Macdonald College, as well as his Physics and Engineering and his Chemistry and Mining Buildings, to meet the students and their teachers and to learn about their needs. At his agricultural college, he not only came to know such professors as Snell but also familiarized himself with much that went on at the college; he would watch chicks hatching for hours, for example, finding these small new lives endlessly fascinating. He frequently visited the science laboratories that he had endowed, to observe the researchers using the apparatus that he had acquired for them. Ernest Rutherford or his assistant Arthur Eve, upon being alerted of such an impending visit, would swiftly order his assistants to put out their pipes, lest the smell of tobacco offended him.

In his last two and half decades, Macdonald had more time for friends and socializing than when he had been very fully occupied with business. Most of his friends seemed beholden to him for their academic chairs, but they nonetheless found him genial and kind and thoughtful under his crusty exterior. Percy Nobbs, the second Macdonald Professor of Architecture, was especially fond of him, and he made a charming painting of Macdonald and Peterson walking through the McGill campus. How oriented his life was around McGill is apparent in his account to his niece Anna of his engagements for the first three days of one week in June 1894 and for the following week. On Sunday he was to meet his fellow governor Hugh McLennan in the afternoon and have tea with his fellow governor Charles Fleet, and then pass the evening with Dean Henry Bovey. On Monday he was to dine with Bovey. On Tuesday dinner was to be with Sir Joseph Hickson, another fellow governor, and Lady Hickson. In the following week, he was to meet the American Society of Mechanical Engineers in the Physics Building, attend a garden party given by his fellow governor J.H.R. Molson and a reception held by the chancellor of the university, Sir Donald Smith. He even went to a Miss Cantlie's wedding reception later in the month. The Reverend Mr Barclay spoke, Sir Donald Smith praised the groom – a Dr Adams – and J.H.R. Molson introduced Macdonald to the mother and the sister of the groom.[6]

Macdonald became a member of the very social St Andrew's Society of Montreal, but only late in life, in 1895, when he was sixty-four, sixty years after its foundation to aid Scottish immigrants. By that time, he lent his name to reception committees for honoured guests, but he was probably too old to join in the Scottish country dances of the society. In any case, his life membership ended inexplicably in 1913, four years before the end of his life, which probably appealed to his sense of humour. A few years earlier, when asked whether he feared death, he had replied, "Personally, I feel no interest in tragedies, other than those in which I take part on my way to the Crematorium."[7]

His reputation for stinginess probably derives from the relatively small requests for aid from others that he refused, as there is no doubt that he responded to

Sir William Macdonald and Dr William Peterson,
portrait by Percy Nobbs (MUA PN015497)

many big requests. Although he did refuse aid to religion, and even on occasion to charities without religious affiliation, he often contributed anonymously to causes in which he could not have held the least personal interest. He insisted on anonymity because he was afraid of being besieged by similar causes. He was shy and soft-spoken, and he knew well that he was a soft touch when asked for money, as his roughly one thousand surviving letters attest. Macdonald kept a worn bench outside his office for suppliants for money (described in chapter 3) – it was not for the ease of his business colleagues, of whom, as we have seen, he had almost none. Furthermore, whether he was meeting the voracious needs of the family of John Archibald or helping the kind landlady in Connecticut who looked after Augustine for seven years without payment, he was scrupulous in paying any debts that he thought might bring disrepute on his family. His generosity went much beyond his close family, to aging and ill Brecken cousins and to the bereaved even beyond his relations, including his employees. He also gave of his time and attention, serving as a governor of the Montreal General Hospital and of the Lady Stanley Institute in Ottawa, a director of the Montreal Parks and Playgrounds Association, and a vice-president of the St John's Ambulance Association.

Macdonald was indifferent to accusations of stinginess. He knew how generous he was, and he was actually equally proud of his personal frugality and his public generosity. These attributes were for him complementary aspects of the role he had defined for himself, which was to share his good fortune with others without consideration of his own comfort. His lack of comfort, however, was completely a matter of choice, for he was never forced to economize in order to meet his extensive financial and philanthropic commitments. His house was adequately furnished for his needs, and it was clearly that of a rich man, though not one given to luxury. He dressed very formally and soberly and simply. But he still hated to be underestimated or to be thought of as stinting in his support of his causes. As we have seen, this prickliness came out in his criticism of Robertson for his poor financial management of Macdonald College; Macdonald rightly saw the college as his own to watch over from the point of view of funding.

At times he could turn against fellow rich men, including his colleagues on the board of the Bank of Montreal, to which he had been elected in 1887.[8] Many other members of the Mount Royal Club, which was on Sherbrooke Street to the west of Prince of Wales Terrace, wanted to build a hotel. Led by Sir Edward Clouston, the general manager of the Bank of Montreal, and Charles R. Hosmer, the president of Ogilvie Flour Mills, they formed a syndicate with investors from England. The site that they chose was on the other side of the Terrace from the club, essentially on the McGill campus at the corner of Sherbrooke and

Dr William Peterson, Lord Strathcona, and Sir William Macdonald
at the opening of the McGill Student Union, 1906,
photograph by Arthur A. Gleason (Notman MP 0000.76)

McTavish Streets. Whether he thought that this was too close to his house or too close to McGill, or both, Macdonald, like Principal Peterson, took strong exception to the location. Macdonald was well known for hating drunkenness and rowdiness, even among students, and this fact in itself must have fuelled his opposition to a hotel so near classrooms. He is said to have threatened to bring all of the promoters of the hotel to financial ruin if they went ahead, and so they decided to build instead a few blocks to the west on Sherbrooke Street, beyond the Mount Royal Club and even farther from the Terrace. This threat seems unlikely, as collectively the promoters were richer than he. But he had his way.

Their hotel, which finally opened in 1912, had been licensed by the great Swiss hotelier César Ritz, who had opened a luxurious hotel bearing his own name in London, England. The promoters of the hotel decided to associate this name with that of the other most famous hotel in London, the Carlton, to create their new Ritz-Carlton as the most luxurious hotel in Canada – and incidentally the first of many in the world to be so called. The house of Jesse Joseph, which remained on the site originally chosen by the promoters, came to house the McCord Museum, which would move in 1968 to the Student Union Building built by Macdonald in 1906. In 1909 he paid $142,500 to give the Joseph house to McGill.

Mention of the Student Union recalls Macdonald's objection, described in the last chapter, to the erection of Strathcona Hall at the southeast corner of Sherbrooke Street and McGill College Avenue for the use of the YMCA of McGill. His reaction showed that he did not hesitate to use his money against Christians any less than against fellow members of the Mount Royal Club. Macdonald objected to the intrusion of a religious organization into university life, as well as to the name "The Young Men's Christian Association of McGill University." He lavishly funded the construction of the Student Union building a few doors away, at Sherbrooke and University Streets, a building that was to serve "all the men of McGill." To avoid the accusation of being blatantly against religion, he cannily stipulated that the Student Union should be self-financing, supported by both undergraduates and graduates. This sort of appeal – to the widest possible base of support for his cause – was characteristic of his operations. It resulted in the widespread support of innovations that otherwise would have been considered extremely controversial. Even Lord Strathcona appeared at the opening of the building with Macdonald and Principal Peterson.

### THE PARADOX UNWRAPPED

In short, Macdonald was hardly a Scrooge, but he only gave unstintingly to what he most believed in, remaining guarded in the face of appeals for other causes – hence his habitually stern public image. This image seemed to melt at McGill, where he did much more than give great sums of money. When two houses in Prince of Wales Terrace came up for sale in 1896, twenty-eight years after he had begun renting one, Macdonald bought both, his own for $16,100 and the one adjacent for $16,000, and, as we have seen, he rented the spare one to his close collaborator, Principal Peterson, presumably to enjoy easy access to him.[9] This rental arrangement Macdonald instructed his executors to maintain for two years after his death.

Macdonald himself knew of his reputation as a character, if not an ogre and a skinflint, and he would mischievously play up to it by acting as expected or feared. People would recall the twinkle in his eye and his dry, shrewd humour, which the Scots describe as pawky. He was constantly aware of his short stature of five feet five inches, and he would even draw the attention of others to it when in the presence of taller men.

Being so genuinely modest, Macdonald took his only honour very lightly. He had been winning favourable attention from the public, especially for his work with Robertson. Lord Grey, then governor general, was to write to Robertson of Macdonald in 1906, expressing how much "I envy him the satisfaction he must experience when he thinks of all the good his heart, brains and money have accomplished, with your assistance."[10] As early as October 1898, Lord Strathcona had written to Sir Wilfrid Laurier, the prime minister, recommending Macdonald for the honour of a Knight Commander of the Order of St Michael and St George (KCMG). Lord Minto, the governor general, also wrote to Laurier in December, recommending that the announcement of Macdonald's knighthood should be made in the forthcoming New Year's Honours List. Lord Minto himself offered the knighthood to Macdonald, who declined it on 1 December. Minto's predecessor, Lord Aberdeen, had already made a similar offer, but Macdonald had told him "that it would be impossible for me to consent to receive the honour as I had never desired honours."[11]

Strathcona and perhaps others prevailed on Macdonald to change his mind and accept. This he did two days later, writing to Minto that "well-meaning but unthinking friends … [had] pushed the matter so far." Persistence in his reluctance, he admitted to the governor general, would appear "as a lack of respect to the throne."[12] But on 11 December, Laurier wrote to the Colonial Office in opposition to the award, without giving reasons. The prime minister had been no friend to Macdonald, who had opposed his protection of Canadian tobacco leaf, or more precisely of the Quebec farmers who grew it.

By this time, however, the news of Macdonald's reluctant acceptance had spread, and even Cundall and the McGill governors were congratulating him on his KCMG. It was probably Minto who convinced Laurier to relent, for the announcement was duly made in January. It contained a nasty surprise, however: Macdonald was made not a knight commander but merely a knight bachelor. A knight commander of the chivalric Order of St Michael and St George was much more distinguished than a knight bachelor, and unlike the latter, it entitled him to wear the neck badge, the riband, and a knight commander's star of the order.

Laurier's degradation of the honour for Macdonald was an insult probably unprecedented. Strathcona himself had for some time been a KCMG, before his recent advancement to a knight grand cross (GCMG), which was the rank that Laurier himself had held since 1897. Also in 1897 Laurier had arranged a KCMG for the mortal enemy of the Macdonald family, Louis Davies. Sir William Dawson, it is true, had been only a knight bachelor, but Peterson was to become a KCMG in 1915, thus outranking Macdonald, who was his own chancellor.

Warrant of knighthood (MSF)

Posthumous coat of arms of Sir William C. Macdonald (MSF)

Laurier's insult was so egregious that, in 1900 and 1901, Peterson and Strathcona continued to press for Macdonald's advancement to the originally accepted dignity. Lord Minto considered but rejected the idea of advancing Macdonald to a baronetcy, which was effectively a hereditary knighthood and superior to a KCMG. He could not recall whether Macdonald was married and had sons to inherit the honour, but he did recall that Macdonald was not very social, a fact that would have made the prestige of a baronetcy, which reflected the hereditary monarchy, somewhat pointless. Baronetcies had been granted to only a few Canadians, such as Sir George-Étienne Cartier, Sir Louis-Hippolyte Lafontaine, and Sir Charles Tupper, and apart from even rarer peerages and Victoria Crosses and similar decorations, they were the highest honour in the queen's gift.[13]

Contrary to some accounts, Macdonald never did receive his KCMG. He died a knight bachelor, and although he was very content to be such, he had probably never even expected, much less wanted, the title before being knighted. When asked about his missing KCMG, he laughingly replied that he was unworthy to command St Michael and St George. Yet once people began to call him "Sir William," he came to take a childlike delight in his transformation. This transformation even involved the spelling of his surname, which he changed, for the first time, from "McDonald" to "Macdonald" in his letter of acceptance addressed to Lord Minto. He then bought copies of guides to the titled, and he joined the Society of Knights Bachelor headed in Canada by Sir Henry Pellatt, the Toronto investor and stockbroker. It was all innocent fun for him.

He did not trouble to apply for a grant of arms, as he might well have done. He contented himself instead with using the Glenaladale arms, as depicted in chapter 1. It was not until 1974 that the Macdonald-Stewart Foundation was to obtain arms for him, granted posthumously by the Lord Lyon King of Arms. Apart from the motto, there were other differences between the two arms. While the Glenaladale's showed the Tudor rose rising from behind Castle Tioram, Sir William's depicted a hand, bearing a tobacco leaf, thrusting out from the central tower, and from the two other towers, sprigs of Prince Edward Island lady slipper.

As there had been nothing calculating or grasping in his generosity, for him there was nothing paradoxical in it. He was parsimonious in order to have more to give, and giving was its own reward. Whether the Crown wished to honour him or whether others wished to caricature his apparent eccentricities was a matter of essential indifference. No snob, he probably knew, for instance, that his reputed descent from Robert the Bruce was mere mistake, and he probably also knew that Robert the Bruce, as both an excommunicate and a guerilla fighter, was in any case the very symbol of the sturdy independence that is much more a part of the Scots character than any title. There was within him a profoundly Scottish scepticism about the very appearance of wealth, as summed up in Robert Burns's poem dating back to 1795, "A Man's a Man for A' That," the third and fourth verses of which read:

> Ye see yon birkie ca'd a lord
> Wha struts an' stares an' a' that
> Tho' hundreds worship at his word
> He's but a coof for a' that
> For a' that, an' a' that
> His ribband, star and a' that
> The man o' independent mind
> He looks an' laughs at a' that
>
> A prince can mak' a belted knight
> A marquise, duke, an' a' that
> But an honest man's aboon his might
> Gude faith, he maunna fa' that
> For a' that an' a' that
> Their dignities an' a' that
> The pith o' sense an' pride o' worth
> Are higher rank than a' that

## THE ENDURING PARADOXICAL NATURE OF MACDONALD'S ACHIEVEMENT

A ripe sense of humour derives readily from Macdonald's sort of integrity, which he had developed through exceptional business challenges. At first glance, it seems that Macdonald led the simplest of lives. He spent over sixty of his eighty-six years in one business in one city. He never married or had children, and nobody has ever suggested that he led any sort of secret life, romantic or other. Nevertheless, he involved himself with people and institutions in an extraordinary way, and led a life that was far from simple and had its share of incongruity.

Although he was very private and avoided publicity of any kind, it was not because he had anything unsavoury to hide; in fact, he seems to have been extremely honest, honourable, and principled, especially when faced with adversity, as he often was. His letters to his nephews are full of admonitions about reputation, and they recall the letters that Lord Chesterfield (1694–1773) wrote to his illegitimate son, Philip.[14] The complexity of the lives of others Macdonald accepted, and he developed a shrewd estimate of human nature. His father and his brothers had caused him much grief, and he had felt impelled to make his own way in the world and to make sense of it by himself. In an era of large families – he himself was one of seven children – he became resolutely independent intellectually as well as economically, and out of his staunch independence emerged his integrity.

Macdonald's independence led him to a keen appreciation of the innovative and a firm faith in the potential of the future. In reaction to what he saw as a suffocating family legacy, he created a new one for himself, adopting as his descendants the countless young people who would benefit from his endowments. Although he certainly worked hard to make it, his vast fortune, and the relative ease with which it accumulated, probably surprised even him. Nobody in his socially prominent family had ever done anything similar within living or even documented memory. His genius lay not merely in his ability to become rich but also in his ability to invest his riches in assets that would continue to grow well beyond his own lifetime. Here was a demonstration of his faith in the future.

Above all, it was the variety and sophistication of Macdonald's causes that introduced texture into his life. Like two of the richest men of the present day, Bill Gates and Warren Buffett, he was in many respects supremely straightforward. He developed one big idea for his business, to process American tobacco leaf for the Canadian market, and he developed one big idea for his profits, to train the young to build a stronger, more rational society. It was this single-minded transference of ideas and capital that integrated his personal simplicity into his many causes, so that no academic subject, even Rutherford's physics, was so abstruse that he could not at least consider supporting it.

When he did feel perplexed, it was about how others could lead lives even simpler than his own. He reflected on happiness to Joseph Pope, a friend from Prince Edward Island but now a resident of Ottawa and the private secretary to Prime Minister John A. Macdonald. Happiness, he concluded, "does not necessarily accompany material prosperity" but "[is] purely a matter of the constitution." He was amazed at how "lighthearted & cheerful" some were "who have no provisions laid by for the future, some of whom may actually be living beyond their incomes, having to face an annual deficit as regularly as the end of the year."[15]

In the end, what is most striking about Macdonald is his humility. As he summed up his contribution, presumably to the funding of the law faculty, to N.W. Trenholme, the dean of law at McGill, in 1893, "I esteem it a privilege to have a share, indirectly though it is, in the preparation of those who will, in all probability, fill some of the most important positions our community has to offer men of character and ability."[16]

To Dawson in retirement, Macdonald wrote in lavish tribute to his "untiring industry and zeal," his "varied and extended knowledge," and above all his "long and intimate acquaintance with the implementation of the educational institutions of the Country." As for himself, Macdonald lamented: "I have always regretted that I could do so little for the University & that in only one way, but I have hoped that my limited contribution would stimulate others to similar efforts, and that as the Country increased in population and wealth the University would receive its share of the general prosperity." In the same letter to Dawson, he referred to an apparent disagreement they had had over a meeting of the board of governors:

I hope I may always enjoy the privilege of your friendship. But I do not feel that any forgiveness from me is necessary, for opposition on your part to my wishes at any time, for I hope I am not so [illegible] or unreasonable to expect my wishes to prevail, as here it is plainly understood that the decision of the majority carries, and so far as I can remember, the Board of the University has been exceedingly harmonious & nearly unanimous and on all occasions. I should indeed be a very severe critic of any views I held, that differed greatly from those of everyone about me, so great is my mistrust of myself.[17]

In this admission to his friend Dawson, we may see a paradox within the paradox of his reputation. Here we find a man of tremendous strength, achievement, and independence who fundamentally mistrusts himself. Macdonald was not the cold and harsh man that so many suspected he was, but neither was he the clear visionary that his admirers might have seen him as. In fact, he was essentially the financier of those whose careers he admired and whose ideas he liked. His opposition to Christianity and the Ritz-Carlton apart, he seldom took a public stand against anything or anyone.

His greatest satisfaction came from aiding those – such as Dawson, Peterson, Rutherford, and for many years Robertson – whom he regarded much more highly than he regarded himself. As we saw at the beginning of chapter 7, he saw his role in the Macdonald-Robertson movement only as that of the paymaster. This was modesty carried to excess, for Macdonald had contributed much beyond money to all his projects – his shrewd judgment of people, his keen understanding of buildings and their equipment, his appreciation of the importance of education. But the paymaster was how he genuinely saw himself.

To later generations brought up in a world that promotes the cultivation of public image, such humility may seem paradoxical. But it was not paradoxical to Macdonald's generation. It was good manners and it was good for the character, and that was good enough for Macdonald. For his contemporaries generally, however, the past could weigh heavily, and perhaps one reason for his humility was that he was so reluctant to share their burden.

## MACDONALD AMIDST THE INVENTION OF SCOTTISH TRADITION

In the 1870s, while the legacy of Captain John was being finally resolved, along with the troubled lives of John Archibald and Augustine, an evolution of Scottishness, begun in the eighteenth century, was proceeding apace in North America as well as in Great Britain. Although William Macdonald probably dwelt little on his ancestry after moving to Montreal in about 1853, there were many in the city to remind him often of it, including members of collateral branches of his own clan from Prince Edward Island. English-speaking Montreal was profoundly Scottish in its origins, and the vast majority of the people he worked with, in any sphere of life, were born Scots or descended from Scots. Thus, William's life became even more broadly Scottish as he grew older, and he could never forget his heritage. As Susan Cameron (later Vaughan), who worked at Royal Victoria College at McGill, was to recall of him:

Desce[n]dant of a great Highland family, with a record of thrilling personal success, he might well have been a dweller in the past. On the contrary, his thoughts seemed to be only on the future, and [on] those who were to build it up. So familiar was this characteristic that when he did turn to past history, if only to find a precedent or illustration, one was surprised. On one occasion when he suspected me of an inclination towards revolt, he astonished me by recalling the traditions of my Clan and citing an alleged saying of one of its Chiefs, to the effect that no one is fit to command who has not learned to obey.[18]

He scarcely had any choice but to be a master of his own genealogy. Macdonalds tended consciously and conscientiously to marry other Macdonalds and Macdonells and thus to form a world that was involuted if not incestuous. This world had begun in Scotland but continued in the North American colonies.[19] The two branches of Macdonalds in descent from the fifth Glenaladale, for example, were reunited again through the marriage of William's niece Margaret Jane McDonald, a daughter of John Archibald's, to Judge Aeneas A. Macdonald.[20]

By the middle of the nineteenth century, people with ancestries very similar to Macdonald's were laying the foundations of the new Dominion of Canada, and among their numbers was Sir John A. Macdonald, its first prime minister. Sir John A.'s background was not unlike that of many of the Scots settled near Kingston, one of the chief settlements of the Macdonalds and Macdonnells. His maternal grandfather, a Jacobite from Inverness-shire, had fought at Culloden with Alexander MacDonald and Bonnie Prince Charlie, and his paternal grandfather, Hugh, was a Protestant merchant from Sutherland. This intermingling was becoming characteristic of a new Scottish experience in the New World. One of Sir John A.'s closest colleagues and rivals, John Sandfield

Macdonald, the last premier of Canada West and the first premier of Ontario, was of the Catholic Clan Ranald Macdonalds who had settled in Glengarry County in eastern Ontario. His mother was a Macdonald as well. It was under this Macdonald that the Ontario Agricultural College and the technical school now known as Ryerson University were established.

### Macdonald and the Fate of the Scottish Legacy

The dissolution of the political power of the Highland chieftaincies, largely attained shortly after Culloden, was almost complete even before the start of the nineteenth century. Clan leaders, if lucky, fell prey to the lures of industrial wealth and Anglicization, and they moved to Edinburgh or London or overseas. Some remained, however, and they became colourful caricatures, much like some First Nation chiefs of North America. Take, for example, Ranald MacDonald of Staffa, born of the MacDonalds of Boisdale, who had chased away the Catholic tenants that Captain John had brought to the Island of St John in 1772. The kilted Ranald MacDonald delighted in playacting the role of a Highland chief, ferrying visitors to his home in an eight-oared galley and welcoming them with "a guard of armed tenants, pipe music and a noisy discharge of muskets and artillery," to the extreme delight of the novelist Sir Walter Scott in 1810.[21]

For the Macdonalds of Prince Edward Island, the hospitality of the chief was less jolly. It even became unclear who the reigning Glenaladale chieftain was in Macdonald's time. In 1810 or 1811, with the death of Captain John, William's father, Donald, was, according to some accounts, denied the designation of "the ninth Glenaladale" because of the loss of his father's Scottish properties. Instead, he was known by some as "the Tracadie," while the ninth Glenaladale was the Borrodale occupant of the Glenaladale house in Scotland. Curiously, the designation of "the eleventh Glenaladale" was claimed – until his death unmarried in 1932 – by William's feckless nephew Fred, presumably because he had once occupied John Archibald's house, still called New Glenaladale. This designation presumed that Donald had indeed been the ninth, followed by John Archibald as the tenth, Glenaladale, notwithstanding the Borrodale claim to the title. The justification for this presumption may have been that one of the Borrodales, probably Angus the son of Alexander, sold off the original Glenaladale within Donald's lifetime.

Despite the degradation, presumed and real, of his family, it is remarkable that there is no depiction of William Macdonald in Highland dress. This was almost undoubtedly at least in part a reflection of his extreme sobriety of nature, his hatred of display, and his deep-seated modesty. Yet this does not explain why he supported the Victoria Rifles of Montreal and the Dominion of Canada Rifle Association in preference to the Montreal Black Watch, a famously kilted Highland regiment affiliated with the Black Watch first raised by the British in 1725. Captain John's brother Donald had been with the Fraser Highlanders, decisive in Wolfe's victory at Quebec in 1759, further linking Macdonald with the central Highland contribution to Canadian history.[22]

Many others in his Montreal certainly delighted in tartans, kilts, bagpipes, and other accoutrements almost inevitably then and still associated with ancient Scotland and the Jacobites.[23] Macdonald, however, hated anything smacking of humbug, and in darker moments that is how he might have seen Highland dress. Even Captain John may never have worn the Macdonald tartan, if only because that tartan did not exist in the Scotland he had left, and he had been only a child after Culloden, when kilts and tartans were banned from wear by civilians. During his service with the Royal Highland Emigrant Regiment, however, he may have worn a kilt with a sporran of raccoon, a broadsword, and a dirk. General Small, with whom he had founded the regiment, had been a member of the Black Watch, which wore Highland dress. The general prohibition encouraged some Highland nobles to wear kilts secretly, and only after the lifting of the ban in 1782 was it legal for civilians to sport Highland dress. This was nine years after Captain John had sailed for the Island of St John. It was, moreover, only in 1819 that distinctive clan tartans were invented, in preparation for the visit of King George IV three years later, their authenticity certified by the Highland Society of London, which had earlier campaigned, through the marquess of Graham, for the restoration of Highland dress.

The Glenaladale Macdonalds became involved in the Highland Society only with Macdonald's uncle Roderick, who became its president in Nova Scotia, and with his father, Donald, who was its president on Prince Edward Island. Donald may have worn a kilt when he was greeted by pipers when assuming the presidency of the Legislative Council in 1853, but any such precedent would itself probably have deterred his sons from following suit.

For most of Macdonald's life, Scotland must have been only an imagined homeland, not only because he never lived there and did not visit it until he was fifty-five, but also because the Scottish culture in which he had been raised was already lost in Scotland itself, recoverable only in romantic or touristic form. It had taken the unlikely figure of King George IV – corpulent, pleasure-loving, and tartan-trousered – orchestrated by Sir Walter Scott, to rehabilitate the Scottishness of Scotland with his ten-day "jaunt" through his northern kingdom in August 1822. But this was long after John had left Scotland and died abroad. Macdonald could exhibit little sympathy with the invented Highland culture that royalty, the gentry, and others thereafter embraced.

He had had his fill, in particular, of the old-fashioned Scottish tenants of his family on the Island, to whom his uncle Father John had been obliged to preach in Gaelic. When asked to endow a chair of Gaelic at McGill, he is reported to have refused with the remark "Let the old language die."[24] The Scottish past in any case was by Macdonald's time an integral part of a much greater and more thrilling British experience. Through various innovations, from the incorporation of Highland regiments into the British Army even before Culloden to the British royal family's revival of interest in its Stuart legacy, Scotland had become firmly known as North Britain.

The Macdonalds were now firmly British as well as Scottish, and they lived in British and not in Scottish North America. Even Captain John had taken up arms for the Hanoverians against the American rebels in 1776, as his brother Donald had against the French in 1759, a bare thirteen years after Culloden. Culloden was now confined to the increasingly distant past, like the Campbell massacre of the Macdonalds at Glencoe. And from her beloved Scottish castle at Balmoral, with its acres of tartan wallpaper, Queen Victoria had sent out her often-kilted son-in-law, the duke of Argyll and the chief of the Campbells, to be governor general of Canada. It was to him, as the marquess of Lorne, that W.J. Rattray, in 1880, dedicated his multi-volume history, *The Scot in British North America*.[25]

Macdonald was a manufacturer and not an antiquarian by temperament, as much as he had been imbued with family history. Like most of his contemporaries, he probably thought of Jacobitism as the very epitome of romanticism and reaction. It was a curious legacy but scarcely sufficient to inspire either him or such men as the prime minister, Sir John A. Macdonald, both of only half-Jacobite ancestry, either to action or to reaction. When he did reflect on the fate of the Jacobites, Macdonald might well have concentrated on the fatal financial weakness of Bonnie Prince Charlie, whose meagre and often-empty treasury had been in the hands of Alexander MacDonald, his great-grandfather and the fifth Glenaladale. Macdonald still maintained custody of Alexander's journals, and he was sufficiently interested in his great-grandfather to make a pilgrimage to Glenfinnan in 1886 to view Bonnie Prince Charlie's standard, raised there in 1745. It had been constructed by Alexander MacDonald of Borrodale, who had taken over the original Glenaladale estate from Captain John. The monument remains an almost-overpowering column, and it attracts pilgrims even today, more than 250 years after its erection.

Macdonald probably knew that it had been the commercial and manufacturing towns of Scotland that had played the major part in the defeat of the Jacobites, on the ground that the rebels were the despoilers of peace, prosperity, and trade.[26] He must have recognized that there was no future in invoking his Jacobite heritage as part of his commercial and manufacturing present. He was in any case emotionally much closer to his Protestant mother and sister and to many of their Protestant commercially and professionally minded relations – such as the

Breckens, the De Blois, and the Hodgsons – than to the stubbornly Catholic and generally rural Macdonalds, not to mention his two sisters enclosed for life in a nunnery.

In contrast, the renaissance of Scottish thought that had begun shortly before Culloden and continued to emerge in Scottish Protestantism played no small part in Macdonald's life. The Edinburgh influence arrived at McGill not through him but through Logan, Dawson, and so many others. But to McGill he and others contributed an admixture of the still-newer influence of Boston, so that the university became in some ways the antithesis of its Catholic, French-speaking rivals. McGill gladly accepted $100,000 from his friend and fellow Scot, Andrew Carnegie, while the Catholic hierarchy had refused to permit the building of free Carnegie libraries in Quebec on the ground that they would poison the minds of the people. Nothing probably summed up better for Macdonald how much good Scots could still do.

## MACDONALD'S LAST YEARS

Macdonald was remarkably vigorous up to his illness in 1914, when he was eighty-three. Percy Nobbs noted in what must have been the 1890s: "There was a fine style about Sir William. On the small, finely arched feet, so characteristic of a high-bred Highlander, he wore the shiniest of boots, and it was a sight to see him skip, with antelope dexterity, across the March mud of Sherbrooke Street (macadamized and rutted in those days) and arrive with unspecked footgear on the far pavement."[27] Even later, probably in the period 1906–09, F.C. Harrison, successor to Robertson as principal of Macdonald College, was astonished to find Macdonald, who was touring an unfinished building at the college, scrambling across a six-inch steel beam, with a clear drop of fifty feet, and expecting Harrison to join him.[28]

In 1892, when at the age of sixty-one he was entering into his philanthropy almost full-time, he had already outlived most men of his time by about twenty years. It was a late entry into a new career, a fact that may account for his insistence that adequate funding for his projects be in place at all times and be sufficient for the foreseeable future. Sensing that he could die at any time, he gamely made provision for various emergencies, such as the paying out of his Rural Schools Fund in the event of his death. In 1900 he pointedly reminded Robertson that such a provision would take effect in the event of his, Macdonald's, death, but not Robertson's.[29]

When out riding in 1895, he had been thrown from his horse, but he suffered no long-term effects from the mishap. While still troubled by shoulder pain, he explained with characteristic good humour to his agent Landrum: "Fortunately I had on a thick tall hat, which struck the ground first, and was crushed down over my eyes, and I believe saved my forehead from being fractured."[30]

He found the cold of Montreal increasingly harsh, as he was plagued with arthritis. In winter he would often travel to cities of the American South, including Louisville and Danville, to renew contact with his agents but also to soak in the hot springs of Virginia for weeks on end.

In January 1914, Lord Strathcona, the chancellor of McGill, died. The governors, though expressing deep gratitude for Strathcona's munificence to the university, did not delay out of respect to Strathcona's memory in choosing his successor. In fact, they elected Sir William Macdonald as the new chancellor on the day they recorded the news of their loss. Strathcona had been a dynamic and forceful chancellor. He had not merely given hundreds of thousands to McGill, chiefly for the education of women and for the Faculty of Medicine, but had also served the board diligently. Despite his years as the high commissioner for Canada in London, he had returned frequently to Montreal to preside over meetings of the board. The governors doubtless hoped that Macdonald, resident in Montreal for over sixty years, would be at least as vigorous notwithstanding his advancing age. This was not to be. Very soon after assuming office, Macdonald fell seriously ill, becoming largely disabled, and he spent most of his remaining three years in his home at Prince of Wales Terrace.

On 25 August 1914, after being stricken, Macdonald made out his will and appointed Thomas Howard Stewart, Walter Monteith Stewart, and Walter Vaughan as his executors. He bequeathed the Stewart brothers his tobacco business. To the brothers, their sisters (Helen, Agnes, and Elizabeth), and their father David, also stricken, he left life annuities of $3,000 each. The other specific bequests included $25,000 each to William Peterson and Walter Vaughan; a life annuity of $500 to his coachman, Richard Cough Vincent, and to his employee Margaret Kennedy; and $2,500 to S.W. Wells, the superintendent of his factory for forty-four years. Mr Gibb, his bookkeeper, received $6,000, and Mr Green, the assistant bookkeeper, received $4,000. Georgina Teledridge, his tablemaid, received $600, and Lettie Macilwanie, his housemaid, received $400, with the residue going to the Stewart brothers. Howard Stewart was bequeathed Macdonald's residence at Prince of Wales Terrace, and Walter Stewart the residence adjacent, then rented to Peterson, which Peterson had the option of retaining for two years after Macdonald's death.

The other bequests included $25,000 to be used "to establish a permanent travelling scholarship for the purpose of enabling the English-speaking Law Students to take a course of study in France as I deem it of great importance that the English speaking people should be proficient in the French language." To Macdonald College he left an endowment of $1 million for "agricultural demonstration"; to the Faculty of Medicine at McGill $500,000; to the Conservatorium of Music at McGill $300,000; to the Montreal General Hospital $500,000; to the Montreal Maternity Hospital $100,000; and to the Crematorium Company Limited $100,000. He made it his express wish that the capital given for charitable or educational purposes should be preserved intact and that his body should be cremated.

Cremation was Macdonald's act of ultimate defiance against the Catholic Church, given its insistence on the burial of corpses, a practice he considered wasteful and unsanitary. Catholic doctrine had deemed cremation to be subversive of the Catholics' faith in the resurrection of the body, and it was only in 1963 that Catholics were permitted cremation instead of burial. For Macdonald, cremation was therefore almost a natural cause, combining as it did his disdain for religious dogma with his love of the modern. As he explained in 1900 to Senator W.J. Macdonald, a very devout and rich Methodist drygoods merchant in Toronto, he had long since ceased to support clergy and denominational charities: "My preferences drew me to endeavour to make provision for the enlargement of the store, and for the spread of knowledge, and the greater enlightenment of the human mind, rather than waste my life providing for the propagation of superstition, unworthy of our civilization, and the age in which we live."[31]

The movement for cremation was very new, and Macdonald's joining it was also the last expression of his commitment to the modern. It was only in 1873 that a Professor Brunetti of Padua had first demonstrated the efficiency of cremation in furnaces at the Vienna Exhibition. Within a year, the movement was spreading through Italy, France, England, and the United States. The first cremation in the United States took place in 1876. Canada lagged behind, with its first proposals for a crematorium, in Montreal, coming in 1888 and 1895. As late as 1933, the Mount Royal Crematorium was to be the only crematorium in Canada.

When Macdonald's dear friend John H.R. Molson died in 1897, he left money for the Mount Royal Cemetery Company in Montreal to build a crematorium. It was exactly the sort of project that the Bostonian Unitarianism that he had married into would have approved. The fact that there was no crematorium in the city at the time of Molson's death necessitated the removal of his body to Boston for cremation. This distressed his widow, Louisa Frothingham Molson, and apparently Macdonald, too. Molson's legacy, moreover, proved insufficient to complete a crematorium for Montreal. After a talk of three hours with Ormiston Roy, the superintendent of the cemetery, Macdonald pledged to remedy the shortfall. In 1900 he pushed for rapid completion no doubt mindful that he might need it himself, and made provision for a free cremation for anyone who asked for one. Andrew Taylor, the architect for many of his buildings, designed the crematorium as well, in English neo-gothic style. A committee of cemetery trustees

Mount Royal Crematorium (ANQ, Collection Michel Bazinet 6-15.d)

Macdonald's tombstone in the Mount Royal Cemetery (MSF)

headed by Richard White, the publisher of the *Gazette*, joined Macdonald in overseeing its construction.

It required a special act of the legislature to permit cremations in the province, and then on condition that they be confined to non-Catholics. In 1902 Senator A.W. Ogilvie was the first to take advantage of this legislation. He was in fact the first in Canada to be officially recorded as cremated. In the following year, Senator George A. Drummond, James Crathern, E.S. Clouston, and Senator Robert Mackay obtained a charter for the Crematorium Company Limited, and Macdonald insisted that it should be incorporated as a non-sectarian, rather than simply a Protestant, company. The fact that such prominent citizens, most of them governors of McGill, so openly supported such an innovation suggests that Macdonald was now in the mainstream of "Protestant" Montreal, which with his help was being transformed into "non-sectarian" Montreal. His espousal of the crematorium movement echoed his attempt to keep the YMCA in check by building the McGill Student Union. Mount Royal Cemetery had always been governed by members of several Protestant denominations, and now, thanks to Macdonald's insistence, it possessed a non-sectarian, effectively non-Protestant crematorium inside its very gates.

Macdonald finally died of chronic pyelonephritis, on 9 June 1917, after his long, debilitating illness. There was no public funeral, but Sir William Peterson presided over a little gathering of Macdonald's friends at Prince of Wales Terrace. "Many of those present will share my doubt as to whether our departed friend would have cared to have anyone stand forward today and use vain words about him now that he is no more," he began. He continued:

Anything that savours of a eulogy would certainly have been distasteful to him. You know how modest and retiring he was, with a kind of shy diffidence about him that made him almost to shrink from public notice. All that was, in most of the relations of life, a true indication of genuine humility. And yet he had a sort of pride about him too. Solitude had made him self-reliant; I doubt if there ever was a man who was less dependent on others. His philosophy of life rendered him absolutely detached, independent and self-contained. But with all his aloofness and reserve, there was always coupled a certain graciousness and geniality.[32]

His body duly made its last journey to his crematorium. There were no pall-bearers, but workers from Macdonald Tobacco lined parts of the route out of respect. The saving of land through cremation does not seem to have been important to him, for in Mount Royal Cemetery an impressive gravestone is placed over his ashes.[33]

## THOUGHTS ON MACDONALD'S LEGACY,
### AS VIEWED FROM 1914–1917

The question of legacy depends much on the point from which we attempt to measure it. We may start with what Macdonald himself may have taken some pride in over the last few years of his life. As he lay partially paralysed for three years, from 1914 to 1917, lucid but not strong, Macdonald might well have been contemplating his achievements. He knew that his beloved buildings and institutions would not last for ever and that in themselves they were a frail legacy. When fire destroyed much of his Engineering Building in 1907, there was much panic at McGill, but he counselled waiting until the ashes cooled. Then, equally calmly, he simply rebuilt it, just as he had rebuilt his tobacco works on Water Street and then on Ontario Street after their fires. Nobbs replaced much of Taylor's work over the following two years, and the building reopened in 1910. It was what went on within his buildings that interested him, the research, the teaching, but more particularly the men working within them – he seldom thought of women except as homemakers, even those training at the Macdonald Institute or Macdonald College.

By 1914 it was clear that with the aid of Macdonald's endowments, generations of graduates were going to make McGill known around the world for its excellent science programs and, above all, for its school of engineering. Macdonald had made the university known across Canada and beyond, and especially in Quebec, where it was located. By 1914 the privately financed McGill was producing twice as many Quebec-born engineers as the provincially funded École Polytechnique, and not all of these McGill engineers were native English-speakers. With the Macdonald endowments, in 1911, 29 of its 669 living graduates were French Canadians. If this seems to be a small proportion, the newly provincially funded École des Hautes Études Commerciales and the Polytechnique were at this stage probably exclusively French-speaking with regard to both their teachers and their students.[34]

A comparison between McGill and Laval University graduates recalls that Macdonald also had a strong influence on the bilingual character of the McGill Faculty of Law. He was deeply concerned about the competence in French of even English Canadian graduates in law, to the extent that he was eager to send McGill law students to France every year so that they might polish their language skills. He doubtless also welcomed the presence in the law school of such promising young French Canadians as Aimé Geoffrion, about to become perhaps the foremost litigator in Montreal for decades, who presided over a testimonial dinner in Macdonald's honour to thank him for saving the faculty by creating two new chairs in law.

McGill science students, class of 1909, in front of Macdonald Engineering Building
(MUA PR008891)

As Macdonald himself did not speak French and had no sympathy for the
Catholicism that dominated French Canadian life and made it highly exclusive,
mere francophilia was not his motivation for establishing travelling scholarships
in law or welcoming French-speaking Quebeckers to his engineering and other
institutions. What is fairly clear is that he believed, as many at McGill did, that
English-speaking Quebec risked losing its powerful voice in provincial affairs
if it was not both deeply aware of the opinions of the French-speaking majority
and yet fundamentally autonomous. For much of the twentieth century, Macdonald's efforts did help McGill and English Montreal retain a central place in
the life of Quebec, as well as that of Canada more generally.

Before Macdonald's death, it had already become evident that one of his greatest legacies would be what could be called the Macdonald man, the sort active in
the planning of the industrial projects that were so to enrich Quebec and Canada
over the remainder of the century, especially in the 1920s. He might never have
met Macdonald, but like him he was steady, shrewd, pragmatic, practical, and

productive. The Macdonald man was not necessarily an engineer, but he had probably pursued his teaching career or his education in one or more of Macdonald's buildings, and he was firmly oriented to the quantitative and the testable. In his last few years, Macdonald might have looked with pride on three Macdonald men in particular, Henry Bovey, Frank Dawson Adams, and Henry Marshall Tory. They were hardly his creatures, but they were men who owed much to his benefactions and who shared much of his point of view.

### *Henry Bovey*

Bovey had spent fifteen years of his career, from 1893 to 1908, as dean of applied science in Macdonald's buildings, and he was Macdonald's companion on the very important tour of American technical institutions they undertook in 1890 in order to plan them. Perhaps the ultimate vindication of the long process of increasing specialization in the sciences at McGill actually came with Bovey's retirement as dean of the Faculty of Applied Science in 1908, after exactly thirty years. He left to return to his native England – where he had first obtained his practical training as an engineer on the Mersey docks and harbour works – to become the first rector of the new Imperial College of Science and Technology in London, part of the enormous complex of buildings – including the Natural History and the Victoria and Albert Museums in South Kensington – generated by the public interest in science raised by the Great Exhibition of 1851. The exhibition had taken place just three years before Dawson's rejection for the chair in natural philosophy in Edinburgh, at least in part because he was a relatively unknown colonial. Now Bovey, an Englishman who had made his name with Dawson in the colonies, was bringing his expertise in refining and rearranging scientific studies home, with natural philosophy now definitively supplanted.

The Imperial College, which was affiliated with the University of London, combined many of the elements of the old natural history school that Bovey and others had been struggling to reorganize at McGill. Imperial College incorporated the Royal School of Mines and three other colleges that had been teaching chemistry, biology, mechanics, mathematics, and physics. The efforts of Sir Henry de la Beche, Logan's patron and head of the Geological Survey of Great Britain since 1835, had led to the foundation of the original school of mines in 1851 for the training of geologists. And so this new appointment of Bovey seems to have been a confirmation that the development of engineering at McGill – from the same origin as that of the Imperial College and along similar lines – had been sufficiently exemplary to justify his being hired as the first head of a similar institution for the entire empire.[35]

Had Dawson been alive in 1908, he certainly would have shared what was almost certainly Macdonald's immense pleasure at the news of Bovey's appointment. It was a heady time for other associates and protégés of Macdonald's as well. Ernest Rutherford had just won his Nobel Prize and was well on his way to a peerage, the Order of Merit, and the presidency of the Royal Society, all largely because of his work as Macdonald Professor of Physics in the laboratory of the Macdonald Physics Building. The architect of that building, Andrew Taylor, joined the London County Council in the same year, was to become its vice-chairman and mayor of the borough of Hampstead, and finally was to be knighted in 1926. McGill had become, by 1908, an educational institution of imperial and even global renown. It was unfortunate that Bovey was obliged to retire within a year of his appointment to Imperial College, but the fact of his appointment was gratifying and flattering in itself at a time when British imperialism was at its zenith.

*Frank Dawson Adams*

After graduating from McGill in 1878 with first-class honours in natural science, Adams joined the Geological Survey of Canada. He went on in 1884 to obtain his master of applied science degree from the Sheffield Science School at Yale University, where Bernard Harrington had obtained his doctorate. Adams obtained his own doctorate from Heidelberg in 1897, which he followed up with further studies in Zurich. In 1889 he became a lecturer in geology at McGill.[36] Three years later, he married a daughter of Macdonald's fellow governor, Samuel Finley, and in 1893 he became Logan Professor of Geology at McGill. Thus, like Harrington, Adams never cut his ties with Montreal, despite his studies abroad. In 1908 Adams succeeded Bovey as dean of applied science, and later he became vice-principal and dean of the Faculty of Graduate Studies and Research. Even before Macdonald's death, Adams had obtained honorary doctorates in science from McGill and in law from Bishop's University, the University of Toronto, and Tufts University, to which he would add several more in years to come. In 1918 he would become deputy director of educational services for the Canadian Army, and in 1919 he would succeed Sir William Peterson as (acting) principal of McGill. He then served as vice-principal under Sir Arthur Currie until 1924. If Bovey's career exemplified that of a British immigrant who had succeeded in Canada to the degree that he could return to the mother country enriched by his Canadian experience, Adams's career exemplified that of a Canadian who found the maturation of opportunities in Canada sufficient to keep him from pursuing rich opportunities abroad. He was precisely the sort of McGill graduate that

Professor Cox's group outside the Macdonald Physics Building, 1905
(Notman 11-154929)

Macdonald had envisioned in his plans for Canada as expressed in his letter to
William Osler cited at the head of chapter 8.

### Henry Marshall Tory

Tory we encountered in the last chapter with regard to the McGill University
College of British Columbia. His career in Canadian education was even more
illustrious than those of Bovey and Adams, and either Macdonald or his endowments were involved in its early stages, despite the apparent coolness between
them. We see, for example, Macdonald's effect in Tory's appointment as a demonstrator in physics in 1894, his professorship of mathematics in 1903, and his
position as assistant to John Adams in the Macdonald-funded survey of Protestant education in Quebec, all before his appointment to Vancouver. After
reorganizing the McGill University College there in 1906, Tory proceeded to
become the first president of the University of Alberta. Later he was appointed

as the first chairman of the National Research Council of Canada and the first president of Carleton University. Tory achieved most of his accomplishments after Macdonald's death, but as early as 1907 Macdonald could see Tory's star rising. In that year the governors of McGill offered the young man a rise in salary in a vain attempt to keep him from going to Alberta.[37]

## THOUGHTS ON THE BIOGRAPHICAL NATURE
## OF MACDONALD'S LEGACY

Macdonald would not recognize much of, say, Macdonald College today, and so it would be illogical to think that the college as we know it necessarily constitutes a significant part of the legacy that he envisaged. It may well be that the School for Teachers or the School of Agriculture – or the Faculty of Engineering at McGill – is *objectively* his greatest legacy, but Macdonald is not here to tell us whether he would agree and, in the absence of serious histories of these schools, it would be premature to render such a judgment.

Macdonald's life defies facile characterization in two respects, and it is in such transcendence that we can best appreciate his individuality. First, he was not a typical Victorian, if by Victorian we mean someone preoccupied by religion or fundamentally conservative. As a rebel from the start – recall his refusal to attend Stonyhurst or any other Catholic school and his expulsion from his family home – Macdonald was no less determined than his Highland forebears and no less dislocated. Few in his time could have been more imbued with Highland traditions of feudalism, and few could have repudiated them more decisively. In speech and in manner, Macdonald was a mid-Victorian gentleman, a man who, despite his early repudiation of his family heritage, exuded high breeding to his contemporaries. But he did not hold with established and traditional ways, and he became, especially with age, increasingly determined as a modernizer.

Neither was Macdonald typically Canadian, if by Canadian we imply anything exclusive. The Dominion of Canada did not exist when he was born in 1831, and it was formed only in 1867, almost twenty years after he had left Prince Edward Island. Even then, his birthplace did not join the Dominion until 1873, when he was forty-two. Macdonald became a resident of what was called the Province of Canada, the present Ontario combined with Quebec, in about 1853, when he was twenty-two. He and his brother Augustine also spent crucially formative periods of their lives in the United States, and his influence on Canadian education is largely American in inspiration.

Macdonald's life is, however, a very Canadian story. It is a tale aching with the lingering pathos of the destruction and exile of the Highlanders of Scotland, whose emigration began over a century before the birth of William and shaped much of Canada. Macdonald's story was darkened by the degradation and dispossession of his own family, a sorry history that continued throughout his long lifetime and ended only in 1932, during the reign of King George v, with the death of his nephew Fred, the last man to claim to be the Glenaladale chief.

What made Macdonald's life unique was his struggle to redeem his heritage by adopting as a cause the education of future generations of Canadians. And the education he facilitated was at once thoroughly practical and secular and democratic, and was indeed the very antithesis of the classical and theological scholarship of his forebears, paid for out of the shrinking revenues of a decaying and unsustainable feudal order. Macdonald could not have taken up the cause he did without a profound knowledge of its opposite. And so, although early in the twentieth century Macdonald financed perhaps the most crucial preliminary research of the nuclear era, inevitably there persisted in his view of the world elements that were inextricably rooted in the eighteenth century and even the Middle Ages. Throughout his life, the antiquarian and the reactionary jostled with the technological and the evolutionary. Fairly early in life he succeeded in making his peace with it all and, moreover, considerable sense of the dichotomy. He attained his relative enlightenment not as the passive observer of transition, but as the committed financier of transformation.

For teaching and research at the university level to succeed, many sorts of individuals and resources are required. Apart from the teachers and the researchers themselves, there must be support staff, such as librarians, laboratory technicians, and demonstrators. The university venture calls for buildings to house libraries, laboratories, classrooms, and offices, as well as the books and equipment, from pencils to highly specialized machinery, to be used in them. Above all, a university needs funding. Whether the source of funding is the government, a foundation, or private individuals, the university must attract and retain the attention of at least one person who can and will make the connection between the specific needs of the university and the size of grant that must be given to meet them. Macdonald was probably uniquely qualified for this role. A self-made manufacturer, he was acquainted with all the practical aspects of finance and saw his friendship with educators as the route to the most productive use of his fortune.

Although no credo or testament seems to have survived in which Macdonald defined his aims, it is clear that he wanted to spread both practical training and the scientific spirit throughout Canada. This included funding everything from his consolidated schools, to the training of homemakers and small farmers, to nuclear engineering. Little in his life would have inclined him to be interested in the education of youth, homemaking, farming, or engineering. He had no home for most of his life and no wife or children for all of his life. He never ran a farm, although he might have worked briefly on his father's and he did follow, with increasing dismay, the mismanagement of New Glenaladale by the sons of John Archibald. He was certainly never anything close to a research scientist, and he never taught any subject to a class of students. It is therefore remarkable that such a man, notorious for his penny-pinching otherwise, should have devoted his vast fortune almost entirely to the education of others.

Surprising, too, was the fact that the areas of focus for his gifts were not generally considered established fields in higher education. They were in fact very new as subjects for academic inquiry. In the nineteenth century, household management and agriculture were hardly equal in prestige to the classics, history, philosophy, and law, the mainstays of the university since the Middle Ages. Most of the universities of Canada of that time specialized in these traditional subjects and their endowments were similarly directed.

The question of why Macdonald chose to adopt very new fields of education for funding can be answered in various ways with reference to three elements in his life. Firstly, he had financed the education of several of his nephews, two at the Ontario Agricultural College, an early venture to improve farming through systematic training and study. Secondly, the failure of these nephews and other relations led him to cut off financial aid to his relatives, so that he had to search for alternative causes to support. Thirdly, it is known that he favoured a Scottish education, the tenor of which was much more practical than, say, English higher education at the time. Finally, his break with his ancestral Roman Catholicism at the age of about fifteen led to a lifetime of unwavering scepticism and perhaps agnosticism in religious matters. This break freed him from having to worry about any limits to science that religious concerns might impose.

Macdonald probably supported scientific research at least in part because he hoped that it would undermine the domination of religion and thus free future generations to lead more productive lives than those led, for example, by his two sisters in the Ursuline convent. In this regard, Macdonald was far in advance of nearly all his contemporaries. He was not ostentatiously anti-religious, but in supporting the endeavours that he did, he demonstrated a thoroughly secular approach to education. He made it his purpose to ensure that McGill University should retain this position in the face of the fiercely ultramontane Roman Catholic approach adopted by most of the province of Quebec, including by Laval University, also in Montreal. As education in Quebec and elsewhere has since Macdonald's death in 1917 become much more secular and therefore "modern," we can see Macdonald himself as curiously modern. No doubt he would have rejoiced at the banning of religious education from all the public schools of Quebec in 2006.

Macdonald was in this respect much more modern than Dawson, a prominent geologist but an apologist for Christianity. He probably sensed that Dawson was on the defensive in the face of Darwinism and was speaking in this regard for himself alone rather than for scientists generally or even for McGill. If he funded scientific research, Macdonald could be reasonably sure that his investment would yield truths unfiltered by religious revelation and unfettered by religious dogma – however much Christian apologists might try to weave these truths into a restated theistic cosmology. Dawson was presenting arguments rather than making any effort to impose his views on the staff and the students at the university. Macdonald did not have to offer arguments to influence the triumph of the scientific spirit, as he saw it, at McGill. All he had to do was back those causes that he saw as most promising.

It is safe to assume that Macdonald lacked the background to be able to estimate the precise importance of courses in chemistry and physics at the university level, and thus it is curious that he seems to have perceived their relevance to the new century. The answer to this mystery may lie in the fact that he read a good deal and was thus almost undoubtedly an energetic autodidact, like so many businessmen. What is harder to understand is how he could have found scientific research not only accessible but also vital enough to be deserving of his virtually unstinting support. Research is by definition tentative. It does not promise any particular result, much less any result with ready application, such as would appeal to a businessman with hard experience. And research into pure science is very far from the research into seeds and milk that he was also to support. But as already suggested, burning behind the vast majority of his causes was the scientific spirit.

The notion of the scientific spirit is hard to define scientifically. Its genealogy was scarcely something that Macdonald would have dwelt upon, any more than he would have read Francis Bacon and Isaac Newton. But the principle of free inquiry is part of it, and as a notoriously curmudgeonly rebel against the conventional, Macdonald would have found this element in the scientific spirit almost compelling. His rejection of Roman Catholicism in his youth did not lead to any other form of religious belief, and although he tried to be courteous to religious people, he, like many others, saw faith in science as far more useful and potent than any religion.

Even vaguer than scientific spirit is the notion of an intellectual climate. What may constitute such a climate or *Zeitgeist* is probably as complex as what may constitute a physical climate. Macdonald was a creature of his time in his very religious doubt. His language was the same as that of those scientists, in particular, whom he was funding. He was not pressing an unpopular cause in casting doubt on the value of religion to higher education. To McGill he offered the devotion that he had once offered to his mother and his sister Helen, and McGill did not hesitate to accept it. He became as integral to his McGill family as any academic or university administrator. As its principal benefactor, he was not acting out of sentimentality or even much compassion. He exemplified the social Darwinism of his time in his support of work that was competitive and not merely open-ended. Social Darwinism can seem to some heartless, but it corresponded to Macdonald's intense belief in genuine competition in a capitalist economy. It was a belief born out of experience, and it resulted in a constant demand for proof unadulterated by mere faith.

In the nineteenth century, Macdonald's former church did try in places to make its peace with scientific inquiry. Laval University, for example, had scientists on its staff. But the Catholic Church was not officially to commit itself to tolerance of plurality of belief or of freedom of thought until the second Vatican Council, over fifty years after Macdonald's death. Until then, the church was committed to severe limits on free inquiry.[38] There was therefore for Macdonald no hope of reconciliation with his former church, which was steadily veering away from any compromise with the world shaped by science as he saw it. The church was actively laying claim to a growing realm of implausible beliefs as exempt from question and debate. Thus, Macdonald could not have seen Laval University as fundamentally committed to free scientific inquiry. McGill, which had no formal religious affiliation and which did not even teach religious subjects, was the obvious alternative more suitable to his interests.

In the library of his home, which was groaning with journals and reports, he assiduously informed himself about some of the most advanced research of his time. Those possessed of the scientific spirit were therefore inclined to be receptive to his gifts and to frame their needs in such a way that Macdonald would understand them, sanction them, and most of all lend his support to them. It was his background in manufacturing and finance that made him understand that the practical spirit of their age needed to be fuelled. Thus, in Macdonald, the brutally realistic merged with the thrillingly theoretical to produce tangible and sometimes distinguished results. It was not the sort of union that most come to experience in their lives.

In thanking the physicist Oliver Lodge (knighted in 1902) for the present of a book, *Pioneers of Science*, Macdonald wrote: "I have just cut the leaves and feel a glow of warmth run through me, as I turn to the pictures of such noble men as Newton, Galileo, Darwin, and others, who have conferred such benefits upon mankind."[39] It is perhaps with a similar glow that we can leave him. We can leave him as – in his own very modest, much less cerebral, but still eminently practical way – having firmly joined their ranks. As he doubtless expected, the theories advanced by all of these men have been challenged, and in the eyes of some refuted. In any case, much subsequent research has supplemented or even supplanted them. And even if the educational ideals supported by Macdonald and Robertson now, too, seem distinctly quaint, it is a measure of Macdonald's breadth that probably none of these changes would have troubled him. The challenge that he throws out to future generations is not to believe in dogma generally, or even in his causes in particular. Macdonald wanted them to accept nothing on faith, but to think, to prove, and to do for themselves.

# NOTES

## ABBREVIATIONS OR SHORT FORMS OF MAJOR SOURCES

| | |
|---|---|
| BOG | Minutes of the Board of Governors of McGill University in the McGill University Archives, 1829–1991, RG 4 |
| Collard, Macdonald biography | Edgar Andrew Collard, unpublished, undated, and untitled draft biography of Macdonald in the Macdonald-Stewart Foundation Archives in Montreal |
| Epstein, "Macdonald" | Maurry Epstein, "Sir William C. Macdonald: Benefactor to Education" (MA thesis, McGill University, 1969) |
| *Land Purchase Testimony* | *Report of Proceedings before the Commissioners appointed under the Provisions of "The Land Purchase Act, 1875"* (Charlottetown: Queen's Printer, 1875) |
| *Mixed Commission Testimony* | *Abstract of Testimony for the Claimant in the case of Augustine Ralph McDonald vs. The United States, Nos. 42 and 334, before the Mixed Commission on British and American Claims under the Treaty of Washington of May 8th, 1871* |
| MSF/DMS | Macdonald-Stewart Foundation Archives, David Macdonald Stewart Papers |
| MSF/WCM | Macdonald-Stewart Foundation Archives, W.C. Macdonald Fonds |
| MUA | McGill University Archives |
| Snell, "Macdonald and His Kin" | John F. Snell, "Sir William Macdonald and His Kin," *Dalhousie Review*, October 1943 |
| NAC | National Archives of Canada |

UBC        Rare Books and Special Collections of the
           University of British Columbia Library

CHAPTER ONE

1  A convenient summary of the history of the Macdonalds, giving much more detail than this account, can be found in Frank Adam, *The Clans, Septs and Regiments of the Scottish Highlands*, 8th ed. (Edinburgh and London: Johnston and Bacon, 1970), 232–41.

2  The chief sources for Sir William Macdonald's genealogy are J.F. Snell, "Sir William Macdonald and His Kin," *Dalhousie Review*, October 1943 (hereafter Snell, "Macdonald and His Kin"; an unpublished, undated, and untitled draft biography of Macdonald by Edgar Andrew Collard in the Macdonald-Stewart Foundation Archives in Montreal (hereafter Collard, Macdonald biography); and Maurry Epstein's unpublished MA thesis, "Sir William C. Macdonald: Benefactor to Education" (McGill University, 1969) (hereafter Epstein, "Macdonald"). Snell had known Macdonald personally, and Collard probably knew several of Macdonald's contemporaries; both depended to some extent on oral history.

3  Certain names persist in the Macdonald story through the centuries. Six hundred and one years after the accession of Robert II (the Steward), Macdonald was to leave the bulk of his fortune to another Walter Stewart, and to this day their legacy is administered by the Macdonald-Stewart Foundation.

4  Such distant history may be followed up in Ronald Williams, *The Lords of the Isles: The Clan Donald and the Early Kingdom of the Scots* (Isle of Colonsay: House of Lochar, 1984); and Ronald Williams, *The Heather and the Gale: Clan Donald and Clan Campbell during the Wars of Montrose* (Isle of Colonsay: House of Lochar, 1997).

5  In addition to Edgar Andrew Collard and Maurry Epstein, the sources for information on John MacDonald include a paper delivered in 1964 to the Catholic Historical Society of Prince Edward Island, "Significant Scots: Captain John MacDonald, 'Glenalladale'" (Scottish Studies Foundation at www.electricscotland.com).

6  Of the vast literature on the Jacobites, two relatively modern and sound works are Frank McLynn, *Charles Edward Stuart: A Tragedy in Many Acts* (London and New York: Routledge, 1988); and Brian Fothergill, *The Cardinal King* (London: Faber and Faber, 1958).

7  See Ada Macleod, "The Glenaladale Pioneers," *Dalhousie Review* 11, no. 9 (April 1931): 311–24. For a modern study, see J.M. Bumsted, "Captain John MacDonald and the Island," *Island Magazine*, no. 6 (Spring/Summer 1979): 15–20.

8  A detailed account by A.M. Pope of the Clan Ranald Macdonalds and the Glenaladales, in particular, was published in the *Catholic World* in 1882. See www.electric-scotland.com.

9  The clearest description of the South Uist emigration is in Lorne C. Callbeck, *My Island, My People* (Charlottetown: Prince Edward Island Heritage Foundation, 1979), chap. 1. Callbeck relates that after the emigration of 1772, the Clanranald

championed the cause of the crofters, and Boisdale (Colin MacDonald) granted religious tolerance to his remaining tenants (20). South Uist did not fall into the hands of freeholders until 2005.

10 For a masterly survey of this subject, see J.M. Bumsted, *Land, Settlement and Politics on Eighteenth-Century Prince Edward Island* (Montreal and Kingston: McGill-Queen's University Press, 1987). See also Bumsted's *The People's Clearance: Highland Emigration to British North America 1770–1815* (Winnipeg: University of Manitoba Press, 1982).

11 For perspective on John MacDonald's exodus in the context of Scottish immigration to British North America more generally, see three books (among others) by Lucille H. Campey: *"A Very Fine Class of Immigrants": Prince Edward Island's Scottish Pioneers 1770–1850; The Scottish Pioneers of Upper Canada 1784–1855: Glengarry and Beyond;* and *Les Écossais: The Pioneer Scots of Lower Canada, 1763–1855,* all published in Toronto by Natural History Books, in 2001, 2005, and 2006 respectively.

12 Collard, Macdonald biography, 49.

13 John MacDonald deserves a biography in his own right. J.M. Bumsted can be said to have begun one with "Highland Emigration to the Island of St. John and the Scottish Catholic Church, 1769–1774," *Dalhousie Review* 58, no. 4 (1978/79): 511–27; and "The Catholic Church and Prince Edward Island, 1770–1810," in *Religion and Identity: The Experience of Irish and Scottish Catholics in Atlantic Canada,* ed. Terence Murphy and Cyril J. Byrne (St John's, Nfld: Jesperson Press, 1884), 19–33. See also Bumsted's *Land, Settlement and Politics* and the introduction to *The Prince Edward Island Land Commission of 1860,* ed. Ian Ross Robertson (Fredericton, N.B.: Acadiensis Press, 1988).

14 For detailed genealogical information, see Orlo Jones and Doris Haslam, eds, *An Island Refuge: Loyalists and Disbanded Troops on the Island of Saint John* (Abegweit Branch of the United Empire Loyalist Association of Canada, 1983), 175–7. There is other information, probably less accurate, in R.B. MacDonald, "The Macdonalds of P.E.I.," a typescript dated 1934, based on recollections from 1892–94, in the Special Collections of the University of Prince Edward Island Library. MacDonald of Rhetland was a branch of the house of Morar founded by MacAllan Og.

15 The regiment had another Macdonald connection. This was the famous Flora Macdonald who, though the stepdaughter of the Clanranald who was opposed Bonnie Prince Charlie, had helped the prince flee to Skye. After imprisonment in the Tower of London, she emigrated to North Carolina, where Jacobite Macdonalds had bought 100,000 acres, in 1770. In 1775, with the approach of the American Revolution, she recruited men to join the Second Battalion of the Royal Highland Emigrant Regiment; these included her cousin, Captain John MacDonald, as well as her own husband, Allan MacDonald, her brother-in-law Alexander MacDonald, and her five sons.

16 John Small became a major-general and died in 1796 as governor of Guernsey. He seems to have been related to a principal of the North West Company and through him to John Macdonald of Garth, of the Keppoch Macdonalds. In any case, one of

Captain John MacDonald's nephews was named John Small Macdonald, the trustee of St Andrew's College and an uncle of William's.

17 Bumsted, *Land, Settlement and Politics*, 183. Chapter 10 of this book is largely devoted to MacDonald.

18 Castle Tioram (or Tirrim) was the abandoned seat of the Glenaladales near Moidart. The castle had been destroyed by the English during the first Jacobite rebellion of 1715. Amy, daughter and heiress of the Roderick Macdonald who had been a follower of Robert the Bruce, had built it and brought it with her into her marriage with John Macdonald of Islay, Lord of the Isles, before his subsequent marriage to Margaret Stewart (Mrs W.M. Brehaut, "Scottish Settlers," in *Historic Highlights of Prince Edward Island* [Charlottetown: Prince Edward Island Historical Society, circa 1955], 80–5).

19 Opponents of landowners who had failed to pay quitrent were pressing for this property to revert to the Crown (the root of all title to real property), much as an appeal might be made to a landlord to repossess land from tenants for non-payment of rent. The Crown was and remains the ultimate legal landowner in Canada, and if tenants – everybody but the Crown – fail to pay their rent, then the property should properly belong to the Crown again. This is why the federal government, in the name of the Crown, can seize land, only apparently owned in fee simple by landowners today, if the landowners fail to pay their taxes.

20 Collard, Macdonald biography, 51. This is confirmed in Bumsted, *Land, Settlement and Politics*, chap. 3.

21 See Bumsted, "Captain John MacDonald and the Island," 19.

22 Collard, Macdonald biography, 46.

23 Bumsted, *Land, Settlement and Politics*, 195.

24 Macdonald-Stewart Foundation, W.C. Macdonald Fonds (hereafter MSF/WCM), folder 001.

25 Most of the genealogical information here comes from a family tree in the possession of the Macdonald-Stewart Foundation, but it is supplemented by other sources.

26 See Helen R. Neilson, "In Search of Sir William's Birthplace," *Macdonald Journal* 52, no. 1 (1992): 31. According to Neilson, the original house of the family was on Tracadie Bay. It appears that William was born in a second house that stood on the same spot. This house was probably Arisaig Cottage, which was owned by Donald, William's father, and was near St Peter's Road, nine miles from Charlottetown. It was mysteriously burned down (probably by disgruntled tenants) on 21 July 1850. In an announcement that appeared in the *Islander*, 2 August 1850, Donald McDonald offered 200 acres as a reward for evidence leading to the conviction of those responsible for destroying his "HOUSE" and the "Barn, Stables and Cow-houses at Glenaladale." Fede Heyden and John Heyden were tried for arson before the Supreme Court of Prince Edward Island on 16 January 1852, but they were acquitted on the odd ground that they had been charged with burning a house, whereas (according to the Court) it had been a barn that was destroyed. Perhaps substantiating this find-

ing, Donald was reported as having been shot several times while standing at the "Hall Door of his residence" a week after the fire (he recovered) (*Islander*, 9 August 1850). Another account of Donald's shooting relates that "a house which once gave him shelter was burnt to the ground immediately afterwards" (Lieutenant-Colonel Burrows Willart Arthur Sleigh, *Pine Forest and Hacmatack Clearings: Travel, Life and Adventure, in the British North American Provinces* [London: Richard Bentley, 1853], 170).

The first church used by the family in William's time may have been St Andrew's, near Glenaladale. The second was probably the Church of St John the Evangelist at Tracadie Cross, Scotchfort, erected by Father James MacDonald in about 1772. The St Bonaventure's Church now standing in that location was built in 1923, and it is only twenty-five yards from a predecessor of the same name. This original St Bonaventure's had been built by Father James Brady in 1840, replacing a French chapel that had survived the expulsion of the Acadians in 1758 and had later been restored by Father James MacDonald; this chapel was the St John the Evangelist that William knew as a child. It was closer to the Macdonald house than St Andrew's. See H.M. Scott Smith, *The Historic Churches of Prince Edward Island*, 2nd ed. (Halifax: SSP Publications, 2004), 84–5.

With regard to the family graves, Neilson reported visiting in 1990 the French and Scottish cemetery called the St Louis Cemetery. It was used from 1727 to 1812 and is located at Scotchfort, overlooking the Hillsborough River. The "original stones" had all been removed, but she found a plinth commemorating John MacDonald. This plinth had originally been erected in 1922 on the presumed site of the landing in 1772, but it was removed in 1964 to the cemetery of St Louis. Thus, the precise location of the earlier Macdonald graves is in some doubt, particularly in the absence of grave markers. Neilson also visited the graveyard at Tracadie Cross, that of St Bonaventure's Church, where she found "a small heap of broken markers," one of which seemed to belong to John Archibald McDonald (1825–1903).

27 Snell, "Macdonald and His Kin," xx. On Roderick, see also Jonas Howe, "A Monument and Its Story," *Acadiensis* 2, no. 2 (1901): 63–8; and no. 3 (1901): 137–42. Roderick joined the army in 1825 and became paymaster of Her Majesty's 30th Regiment of Foot. He married Elizabeth Ranaldson, daughter of Colonel Alexander Ranaldson Macdonell, chief of the Glengarry Macdonalds, a Protestant. Their son John Alistair became a Jesuit, and their daughter Elizabeth became a nun, both being cousins of William Macdonald.

28 The most extensive treatment of Captain John and St Andrew's is in Kenneth A. MacKinnon, "Captain John MacDonald and the Glenaladale Settlers," *Abegweit Review* 8, no. 2 (Fall 1995–Spring 1996), 67–96, esp. 69–86.

29 MacKinnon, "Captain John MacDonald," 79.

30 For details on St Andrew's College, see G. Edward MacDonald, *The History of St. Dunstan's University 1855–1956* (Charlottetown: Board of Governors of St Dunstan's University and Prince Edward Island Museum and Heritage Foundation, 1989).

31  Collard, Macdonald biography, 208. The incident is confirmed in Snell's notes of his own interview with Nobbs (McGill University Archives [hereafter MUA], MG 2007, C 1).

32  Epstein, "Macdonald," 7, citing the files of W.J. MacDonald, lieutenant-governor of Prince Edward Island.

33  Montreal *Gazette*, 11 January 1917.

34  Obituary of Macdonald in *Canadian Cigar and Tobacco Journal*, July 1917.

35  Collard, Macdonald biography, 78.

36  Epstein, "Macdonald," citing a letter from William to John Archibald, dated 6 January 1852.


CHAPTER TWO

1  Cited by Margaret Bennett, *Oatmeal and the Catechism: Scottish Gaelic Settlers in Quebec*, rev. ed. (Edinburgh: John Donald Publishers; Montreal and Kingston: McGill-Queen's University Press, 2003), 8.

2  Collard, Macdonald biography, 85–7. Collard never provided footnotes, but he was very accurate in citation, as can be confirmed by original documents that he used that can still be traced. The letter cited here, though it has now disappeared, seems to have been transcribed by him directly.

3  MSF/WCM, folder 008, receipt from Gabriel De Blond and Thomas Jefferson to William McDonald, 16 August 1848.

4  Epstein, "Macdonald," 9.

5  Collard, Macdonald biography, 83.

6  MUA, RG 30, C 67, Macdonald to Tom Graydon. Graydon was an athletics coach and caretaker at McGill University and left some memories in the form of notes.

7  Epstein, "Macdonald," 20, citing a letter from William to John Archibald, 10 November 1851.

8  See Ian Ross Robertson, *The Tenant League of Prince Edward Island, 1864–1867: Leasehold Tenure in the New World* (Toronto: University of Toronto Press, 1996), 133.

9  Collard, Macdonald biography, 86; and *Islander*, 9 August 1850.

10  Isabella Lucy Bird, *The Englishwoman in America* (London: John Murray, 1856; reprint, Toronto: University of Toronto Press, 1966), 47.

11  Epstein, "Macdonald," 10–11, citing letters from William to John Archibald, 1849–52, once at Macdonald College but now lost.

12  Collard, Macdonald biography, 87.

13  Epstein, "Macdonald," 13–14, citing a now-lost letter from William to John Archibald, 30 March 1852.

14  See Arthur E. Sutherland, *The Law at Harvard: A History of Ideas and Men, 1817–1967* (Cambridge: Belknap Press of Harvard University Press, 1967), chap. 5.

15  This account of Choate is derived from Jean V. Matthews, *Rufus Choate: The Law and Civic Virtue* (Philadelphia: Temple University Press, 1980); and Edward G. Parker, *Reminiscences of Rufus Choate* (New York: Mason Brothers, 1860).

16 The modern authority on this topic is Thomas H. O'Connor, especially in his books *The Athens of America: Boston 1825–1845* (Amherst and Boston: Massachusetts University Press, 2006); *Fitzpatrick's Boston 1846–1866* (Boston: Northeastern University Press, 1984); and *Lords of the Loom: The Cotton Whigs and the Coming of the Civil War* (New York: Charles Scribner's Sons, 1968). These depict the interaction of business, ideas, and religion in the city, as does Anne-Marie Taylor, *Young Charles Sumner and the Legacy of the American Enlightenment, 1811–1851* (Amherst: University of Massachusetts Press, 2001).

17 See Cleveland Amory, *The Proper Bostonians* (New York: E.P. Dutton, 1950).

18 O'Connor, *The Athens of America*, 17. The broader description of Boston as Athens is derived from chapter 5 of this same book. The Brahmins were but a small part of a much wider and generally more vigorous culture in New England in the nineteenth century. See Vernon L. Parrington, *Main Currents in American Thought*, vol. 2 (New York: Harcourt, Brace, 1927), for a description of this context.

19 O'Connor, *Lords of the Loom*, chaps 1–3, describes the origins of the Cotton Whigs.

20 See Stanley K. Schultz, *The Culture Factory: Boston Public Schools, 1789–1860* (New York: Oxford University Press, 1973).

21 MSF/WCM, letterbook, Macdonald to Letitia Rowand, 14 August 1891.

22 Peterson's eulogy on the death of Sir William Macdonald, cited in Epstein, "Macdonald," 110.

23 See *The Athenaeum Centenary: The Influence and History of the Boston Athenaeum from 1807–1907, With a Record of Its Officers and Benefactors and A Complete List of Proprietors* (1907; reprint, Boston: Gregg Press, 1972).

24 Joel Roberts Poinsett, *Discourse, on the Objects and Importance of the National Institution for the Promotion of Science, Established at Washington, 1840* (Washington: P. Force, 1841).

25 Cited in Matthews, *Choate*, 77.

26 MSF/WCM, folder 017, item 2, receipt from the Mercantile Library Association, 24 July 1850, for "first annual assessment."

27 See Connor, *The Athens of America*.

28 Matthews, *Choate*, 114.

29 The connections between Canada and MIT in the nineteenth century deserve research. See Samuel C. Prescott, *When M.I.T. Was "Boston Tech"* (Cambridge: Technology Press, 1954); and Robert Rakes Shrock, *Geology at M.I.T.* (Cambridge and London: MIT Press, 1977), especially on T. Sterry Hunt, of the Canadian Geological Survey and McGill, who went on to teach at MIT.

30 MSF/WCM, folder 011, letter dated 31 December 1851.

31 MSF/WCM, folder 013, a receipt for William from Mrs R. Ballard, 59 Murray Street, near College Place, New York, for four weeks' board at $5 a week.

32 MSF/WCM, folder 012, copy of a letter from Macdonald to an unknown correspondent, 28 September 1852.

33 Donald Creighton, *The Empire of the St. Lawrence* (Toronto: Macmillan Company of Canada, 1956), 370, 383.

34  Montreal had begun to embrace the railways in about 1844. For background to the railway situation in 1851, see Ronald Stewart Longley, *Sir Francis Hincks: A Study of Canadian Politics, Railways and Finance in the Nineteenth Century* (Toronto: University of Toronto Press, 1943), esp. chaps 8 and 9; and Ludwik Kos-Rabcewicz-Zubkowski and William Edward Greening, *Sir Casimir Stanislaus Gzowski: A Biography* (Toronto: Burns and MacEachern, 1959), chap. 4.

35  Gerald J.J. Tulchinsky, *The River Barons: Montreal Businessmen and the Growth of Industry and Transportation 1837–53* (Toronto and Buffalo: University of Toronto Press, 1977), 111, 122.

36  Ibid., 121.

37  Ibid., 135.

38  Longley, *Hincks*, 224 n. 26. See also Michael J. Piva, "Government Finance and the Development of the Canadian State," in *Colonial Leviathan: State Formation in Mid-Nineteenth-Century Canada*, eds Allan Greer and Ian Radforth (Toronto: University of Toronto Press, 1992).

39  Tulchinsky, *The River Barons*, 20, 121.

40  *Abstract of Testimony for the Claimant in the case of Augustine Ralph McDonald vs. The United States, Nos. 42 and 334, before the Mixed Commission on British and American Claims under the Treaty of Washington of May 8th, 1871* (Boston: Alfred Mudge & Son, 1873), 2 (hereafter *Mixed Commission Testimony*). On page 14 of this abstract, Augustine reportedly testified that he "[c]ommenced to reside at Montreal about 1850."

41  Abstract of the testimony of Anna Matilda McDonald in ibid., 9–10. She is also reported as testifying that in "about 1851 or 1852 he located at Montreal in business" (16). Helen McDonald, William and Augustine's sister, is reported as testifying that Augustine began business in Montreal in 1852 after returning from Massachusetts and that she did not know whether Augustine or William had arrived first (17).

42  For a description of the technical aspects of cigar-making before 1870, see Meyer Jacobstein, *The Tobacco Industry in the United States* (New York: Columbia University Press, 1907), 83.

43  The registered declaration, document 502, said that the partnership had existed since 1 April 1853 (MSF/David Macdonald Stewart Papers [hereafter DMS], 036-10). Epstein, "Macdonald," 16, summarizes the products that they dealt in, citing as his source John Lovell's *Montreal Directory* for 1854–60.

44  Collard, Macdonald biography, 88–90.

45  See Augustus H. Gill, *A Short Hand-Book of Oil Analysis* (Philadelphia and London: J.B. Lippincott Company, 1909).

46  *Mixed Commission Testimony*, 37.

47  See T.M. Devine, *The Tobacco Lords: A Study of Tobacco Merchants of Glasgow and Their Trading Activities c. 1740–90* (Edinburgh: John Donald Publishers, 1975).

48  Joseph C. Robert, *The Story of Tobacco in America* (Chapel Hill: University of North Carolina Press, 1967), 81.

49  MSF/WCM, folder 014, ticket dated 10 February 1853.

50  Epstein, "Macdonald," 20, citing a letter from Donald to John Archibald, 13 July 1854.

51 John Ferguson Snell, *Macdonald College of McGill University* (Montreal: McGill University Press, 1963), 9.

52 Epstein, "Macdonald," 22, citing a letter from Donald to John Archibald, 13 July 1854.

53 *Mixed Commission Testimony*, 36–7.

54 MSF/DMS, file 036, no. 36, registered agreement, document no. 133, 13 February 1856.

55 Douglas McCalla, *The Upper Canada Trade 1834–1872: A Study of the Buchanans' Business* (Toronto: University of Toronto Press, 1979), 95–6.

56 MSF/DMS, file 36, no. 35, document of sale, 6 April 1858.

57 See Ben Forster, *A Conjunction of Interests: Business, Politics, and Tariffs 1825–1879* (Toronto: University of Toronto Press, 1986), 30–3.

58 For a discussion of Buchanan's motivation, see McCalla, *The Upper Canada Trade*, 103–4.

59 Piva, "Government Finance and the Canadian State," 271–2, esp. Table 9:4.

60 John Charles Dent, *The Last Forty Years: Canada Since the Union of 1841* (Toronto: George Virtue, 1881), 2:392–3; and the biographical entry on Buchanan by Douglas McCalla, in *Dictionary of Canadian Biography*, vol. 11.

61 *Mixed Commission Testimony*, 37.

62 The partnership was registered as document 1411 in the Montreal Registry Office on 21 March 1859 (MSF/DMS, file 036-9). It is unclear who Alexander Ross was. It is possible that he, with Sir Francis Hincks, the prime minister of the Province of Canada and former inspector general, had been allotted shares of the Grand Trunk for distribution to Canadians at the organization of this railway in 1853 (Longley, *Hincks*, 236).

63 This description is derived from Jacobstein, *The Tobacco Industry in the United States*, 91–3.

64 For statistics on the increased use of tobacco in the early twentieth century, see *Canadian Cigar and Tobacco Journal*, September 1907, 41–2, and August 1908, 41.

65 Jacobstein, *The Tobacco Industry in the United States*, 94–5.

66 *Mixed Commission Testimony*, 37.


CHAPTER THREE

1 Cited in Margaret Bennett, *Oatmeal and the Catechism: Scottish Gaelic Settlers in Quebec*, rev. ed. (Edinburgh: John Donald Publishers; Montreal and Kingston: McGill-Queen's University Press, 2003), 8.

2 MSF/WCM, file 036, no. 27, item 4.

3 Of the vast literature on tobacco, the following have proved to be especially helpful: www.civilwar.com/tobacco; www.college.hmco.com/rcah.html.ab; and www.slaveryinamerica.org/history.

4 *Mixed Commission Testimony*, 39.

5 F.C. Harrison, "Reminiscences of the Founder of Macdonald College," *Old McGill 1927*, 102, 341; and Collard, Macdonald biography, 100–2.

6 See Frederick F. Siegel, *The Roots of Southern Distinctiveness: Tobacco and Society in Danville, Virginia, 1780–1865* (Chapel Hill and London: University of North Carolina Press, 1987), for a depiction of this most important source of Macdonald's tobacco.

7 Joseph C. Robert, *The Story of Tobacco in America* (Chapel Hill: University of North Carolina Press, 1967), 78–81.

8 This account follows the *Mixed Commission Testimony*, 37–8.

9 Ibid., 36, 86.

10 Ibid., 48–9.

11 Ibid., 45–7. Bryan thought that Macdonald "had no interest in the tobacco and cotton in the southwest," such as Augustine had had (46).

12 Ibid., 28.

13 MSF/WCM, file 036, no. 38, power of attorney dated 2 March 1866.

14 For extensive discussions of the techniques of growing tobacco and preparing it for market, see Meyer Jacobstein, *The Tobacco Industry in the United States* (New York: Columbia University Press, 1907), esp. chap. 4; and Nannie May Tucker, *The Bright-Tobacco Industry 1860–1929*, 2 vols (Chapel Hill: University of North Carolina Press, 1948).

15 *Canadian Cigar and Tobacco Journal*, August 1906, 39.

16 MSF/WCM, file 023, letter to W.P. Howland, 30 March 1868.

17 This description follows that in Robert, *The Story of Tobacco*, 83–5.

18 Collard, Macdonald biography, 185.

19 MSF/WCM, folder 022, announcement of sole proprietorship, 17 May 1863.

20 This Macdonald revealed in his testimony to the Royal Commission on the Tobacco Trade of 1902 (*Canadian Cigar and Tobacco Journal*, January 1903, 722).

21 This description follows J. Harvey Perry, *Taxes, Tariffs, & Subsidies: A History of Canadian Fiscal Development* (Toronto: University of Toronto Press, 1955), 1:30, 59, 70, 72, 96.

22 National Archives of Canada, John A. Macdonald Fonds, c-1078, v. 338, pt. 2, pp. 54444–9, Buchanan to Macdonald, 25 June 1864.

23 MSF/WCM, folder 019.

24 MSF/DMS, folder 008, "Tobacco Excise Law" resolutions, 31 January 1868.

25 Collard, Macdonald biography, 138.

26 MSF/WCM, folder 023.

27 *Illustrated Supplement to the Montreal Gazette*, 25 December 1865, 17.

28 *Canadian Cigar and Tobacco Journal*, January 1910, 45; and Collard, Macdonald biography, 142–6.

29 Collard, Macdonald biography, 144.

30 Robert Lewis, *Manufacturing Montreal: The Making of an Industrial Landscape, 1850 to 1930* (Baltimore and London: Johns Hopkins University Press, 2000), 90–1.

31 Robert, *The Story of Tobacco*, 86–91.

32 MSF/WCM, folder 074, letter from various employees to W.C. Macdonald, 31 October 1887.

33 Canada, *Report of the Royal Commission on the Relations of Capital and Labor in Canada: Evidence – Quebec* (Ottawa: Queen's Printer and Controller of Stationery, 1889), 3:529–33.

34 By comparison, the Canada Sugar Refinery at St Gabriel's Lock, which was probably then the largest sugar refinery in the country, was employing only 450 to 500 hands directly or indirectly, as testified to by its bookkeeper, Joseph Young (ibid., 3:171).

35 Ibid., 3:123.

36 The only description of Macdonald's bench-owners is in Collard, Macdonald biography, 150–62; and in the testimony of Macdonald himself and of Sam Wells to the Royal Commission on the Relations of Capital and Labor (3:552–7).

37 Forester, Moir, and Company, of 17 Helen Street, was his importing agent for 61 cases of licorice, valued at $1,643.18, on 1 May 1865. On 22 June 1865 this agent imported on Macdonald's behalf 79 gallons of high wines valued at $71.12 and sugar worth $17.98 (MSF/WCM, folder 018).

38 See George R. Dalgleish, "Aspects of Scottish-Canadian Material Culture: Heart Brooches and Scottish Pottery," in Peter E. Rider and Heather McNabb, eds, *The Kingdom of the Mind: How the Scots Helped Make Canada* (Montreal and Kingston: McGill-Queen's University Press, 2006), 122–48.

39 MSF/WCM, folder 054.

40 Collard, Macdonald biography, 136–7.

41 Macdonald seems to have been exporting manufactured tobacco to the United States as well, in the last chaotic year of the Civil War, 1864–65. There is in his papers a landing certificate from the Port of New York for the SS *Atalanta*, dated 1 July 1865, for 15 cases and 31 boxes of unstemmed or unmanufactured tobacco. But there is also a bill of entry for the same ship, which had come to New York from London and cleared, on 16 June 1865, 246 packages of Cavendish tobacco, which had entered London from Montreal on the *Peruvian* on 4 November 1864. Presumably this Cavendish tobacco had been manufactured by Macdonald (MSF/WCM, folder 018).

42 Collard, Macdonald biography, 138.

43 In 1892 Tuckett and Billings incorporated as the George E. Tuckett and Son Company; in 1902 the Tucketts incorporated a separate cigar company; in 1912 the company became the Tuckett Tobacco Company, Ltd; and in 1913 it took over the McAlpin Tobacco Company Ltd, which had only begun the year before. See MSF/WCM, folder 108, item 7; and *Canadian Cigar and Tobacco Journal*, August 1916, 19.

44 MSF/WCM, file 108.

45 MSF/WCM, folder 029.

46 MSF/WCM, folder 031.

47 "A Brief History of Tobacco in Canada" (undated typescript held by Imperial Tobacco Ltd), 11–12.

48 MSF/WCM, letterbook, Macdonald to Landrum, 4 February 1886 and 12 July 1886.

49  Lewis, *Manufacturing Montreal*, 91–2, 172–9.

50  MSF/WCM, letterbook, Macdonald to his nephew Donald Archibald Macdonald (so spelt), 28 June 1895, and Macdonald to H.J. Cundall, 9 October, 1895. For a description of the fire, see Stanley Frost and Robert Michel, "Sir William Macdonald: An Unfinished Portrait," *Fontanus* 8 (1995): 59–81.

51  MSF/WCM, letterbook, Macdonald to Landrum, 5 February 1889.

52  Macdonald had written to the Honourable Frank Smith in Toronto that he had not employed commercial travellers since 1853 (MSF/WCM, letterbook, 1 March 1891).

53  The chief sources for this subject are Michael Bliss, *A Living Profit: Studies in the Social History of Canadian Business, 1883–1911* (Toronto: McClelland and Stewart, 1974), chap. 2; and the Montreal Wholesalers' Association (later Guild) minute-books in the École des Hautes Études Commerciales Archives, Montreal Board of Trade Fonds, P019/M1H,002 (hereafter Wholesalers' minutes) in Montreal.

54  The Montreal branch did not rename itself as a "guild" until 1906.

55  Wholesalers' minutes, and letter from W.H. Gillard, 23 June 1885.

56  Wholesalers' minutes, 13 November and 21 December 1885. The *Tobacco Memorial* was simply a document circulated by the association to all manufacturers of tobacco, including Macdonald. All of them except Macdonald responded positively.

57  Bliss, *A Living Profit*, 42.

58  *Empire*, 8 November 1890.

59  *Evening Mail*, 16 February 1892.

60  John K. Winkler, *Tobacco Tycoon: The Story of James Buchanan Duke* (New York: Random House, 1942), 93.

61  A careful study of Duke is in Nannie M. Tilley, *The R.J. Reynolds Tobacco Company* (Chapel Hill and London: University of North Carolina Press, 1985), chap. 4.

62  MSF/WCM, letterbook, 3 February 1897.

63  Wholesalers' minutes, 22 October 1901. The minutes for the years from 1888 to 1900 were lost in the fire that burned down the Board of Trade Building in 1900, and so it is unclear whether Macdonald had made any concessions to the association in those years.

64  Canada, 2–3 Edward VII, Sessional Paper No. 62, A1903.

65  *Canadian Cigar and Tobacco Journal*, January 1903, 719.

66  Ibid., December 1902, 701.

67  Ibid., January 1910, 45.

CHAPTER FOUR

1  MSF/WCM, letterbook, 17 April 1890.

2  For an account of Curtis's mission, see Ian Ross Robertson, *The Tenant League of Prince Edward Island* (Toronto: University of Toronto Press, 1996), 89–92.

3  The most complete account is in ibid., 132–6.

4  Ibid., 135–6.

5  Cited in a letter dated 15 November 1865 in ibid., 244–5.

6  For a careful analysis of this period, see Ian Ross Robertson, "Political Realignment in Pre-Confederation Prince Edward Island, 1863–70," *Acadiensis* 15, no. 1 (Autumn 1985): 35–58, esp. 44.

7  P.S. Magowan (court reporter), *Report of Proceedings before the Commissioners appointed under the Provisions of "The Land Purchase Act, 1875"* (Charlottetown: Queen's Printer, 1875), 549–63 (hereafter *Land Purchase Testimony*).

8  Archives of Prince Edward Island, MG 3, H.J. Cundall Diaries, vol. 6, 7 and 14 September 1875.

9  There is much in the *Land Purchase Testimony* about Robert P. Haythorne, acting with William Cundall, John Aldous, and Francis Kelly (the commissioner of public lands), to make a division of Margaret's property (571–7). This indicates that Macdonald's interest in this land was much more obscure than Hodgson had initially suggested.

10  MSF/WCM, letterbook, 5 October 1887.

11  Robertson, *The Tenant League*, 55.

12  Cited in ibid., 133; and *Land Purchase Testimony*, 565–6.

13  Ian Ross Robertson, ed., *The Prince Edward Island Land Commission of 1860* (Fredericton: Acadiensis Press, 1988), 148–50.

14  *Land Purchase Testimony*, 561.

15  Ibid., 566–75.

16  Ibid., 575–7.

17  Ibid., 614.

18  Ibid., 615–25, 668–9.

19  Ibid., 614.

20  MSF/WCM, folder 020, receipt for $41.80 for board from H. Hogan, St Lawrence Hall, 28 July 1868.

21  Letter from William to Anna Matilda, August 1868, cited in Epstein, "Macdonald," 24. No. 3 Prince of Wales Terrace later became known as 891 (later 995) Sherbrooke Street West. In 1971 it was torn down to make room for the Bronfman Building.

22  Jean-Claude Marsan, *Montreal in Evolution* (Montreal and Kingston: McGill-Queen's University Press, 1981), 258.

23  W.B. Howell, "William Christopher Macdonald," *McGill News* 13 (June 1932).

24  MSF/WCM, letterbook, no. 526, Macdonald to Sophie H. Rowand, 30 November 1899.

25  MUA, MG 2007, C 1, notes by J.F. Snell on F.C. Harrison's memories of Macdonald.

26  The chief source for this account is in MUA, Faculty of Agriculture Fonds, MG 2007, container 7, "The Early Career of Sir William Macdonald: Supplement Concerning Augustine Ralph Macdonald [sic]," by J.F. Snell. The other source is the *Mixed Commission Testimony*. There are discrepancies between these two sources, chiefly with respect to Snell's claim that Augustine obtained $40 million of cotton in one day.

27  *Mixed Commission Testimony* (by Alexander J.D. Thurston), 90.

28 Collard, Macdonald biography, 262–3.

29 The main source for Cundall's life, containing twelve letterbooks and his diaries, is in Prince Edward Island Archives, ACC 4158, H.J. Cundall Fonds (1857–1913). A short biography is in Edward MacDonald, "The Master of Beaconsfield: Part Two: Henry J. Cundall," *Island Magazine*, no. 34 (Fall/Winter 1993): 7–14.

30 MSF/WCM, letterbook, Macdonald to John Archibald McDonald, 28 December 1886.

CHAPTER FIVE

1 Bernard J. Harrington, *Life of Sir William E. Logan, Kt.* (Montreal: Dawson Brothers, 1883), 294–5.

2 For a brief introduction to Hutton, see Alexander Broadie, *The Scottish Enlightenment: The Historical Age of the Historical Nation* (Edinburgh: Birlinn, 2001), 209–18.

3 For a comprehensive modern account of the Scottish Enlightenment, see James Buchan, *Capital of the Mind: How Edinburgh Changed the World* (London: John Murray, 2003). The discussion of Hume and Hutton here, however, more closely follows Broadie, *The Scottish Enlightenment*.

4 Broadie, *The Scottish Enlightenment*, 126.

5 Ibid., 216.

6 See Hastings Rashdall, *The Universities of Europe in the Middle Ages,* rev. ed., 3 vols (Oxford: Oxford University Press, 1936).

7 See John Henry Cardinal Newman, *The Idea of the University Defined and Illustrated* (London: Longmans, Green and Co., 1925). This volume is a collection both of lectures given in 1852 and of undelivered material. Newman's discourses II and III, "Theology a Branch of Knowledge" and "Bearing of Theology on Other Branches of Knowledge," illustrate how Dawson's and Macdonald's McGill stood in contrast to, say, Laval University.

8 When William Dawson was at Dalhousie in 1853, he learned how to deal with those who wanted it to become more of a religious institution. See P.B. Waite, *The Lives of Dalhousie University* (Montreal and Kingston: McGill-Queen's University Press, 1994), 1:80.

9 For more discussion, see Edward Grant, *A History of Natural Philosophy: From the Ancient World to the Nineteenth Century* (New York: Cambridge University Press, 2007), chap. 2.

10 On the developments of the seventeenth century in particular, see Steven Shapin, *A Social History of Truth: Civility and Science in Seventeenth-Century England* (Chicago and London: University of Chicago Press, 1994); and Lisa Jardine, *Ingenious Pursuits: Building the Scientific Revolution* (London: Little, Brown and Company, 1999).

11 See Rhodri W. Liscombe, "The Peter Redpath Museum, an Architectural Analysis," *Fontanus* 1 (1988): 50–8. On the Redpath Library, see Peter F. McNally, "Peter and Grace Redpath: Collectors and Benefactors," *Fontanus* 11 (2003): 153–73; Peter F. McNally, "Dignified and Picturesque: Redpath Library in 1893," *Fontanus* 6 (1993): 69–84; and Susan Sheets-Pyenson, *Cathedrals of Science: The Development of Colonial*

*Natural-History Museums during the Late Nineteenth Century* (Montreal and Kingston: McGill-Queen's University Press, 1988).

12 This is only one point of view but one especially suitable for understanding how the teaching of science, both pure and applied, emerged at McGill with financing from Macdonald. For another perspective, a discussion of how the applied sciences emerged from the "exact" sciences that coexisted with natural philosophy, as opposed to natural history, see Grant, *A History of Natural Philosophy*.

13 For a survey, see Frank Dawson Adams, "The History of Geology in Canada," in *A History of Science in Canada*, ed. H.M. Tory (Toronto: Ryerson Press, 1939); and Clark Blaise, *Time Lord* (Toronto: Vintage Canada, 2001), chap. 7 (a life of Sir Sandford Fleming).

14 This account is derived from Harrington, *Logan*. An extremely useful account is Suzanne Zeller, *Inventing Canada: Early Victorian Science and the Idea of a Transcontinental Nation* (Toronto, Buffalo, London: University of Toronto Press, 1987).

15 This account derives from Dawson's autobiographical notes in William Dawson, *Fifty Years of Work in Canada, Scientific and Educational,* ed. Rankine Dawson (London and Edinburgh: Ballantyne, Hanson & Co., 1901); Susan Sheets-Pyenson, *John William Dawson: Faith, Hope and Science* (Montreal and Kingston: McGill-Queen's University Press, 1996); Charles F. O'Brien, *Sir William Dawson: A Life in Science and Religion* (Philadelphia: American Philosophical Society, 1971); and B. Anne Wood, *God, Science and Schooling: John William Dawson's Pictou Years, 1820–1855* (Truro: Nova Scotia Teachers' College, 1991). For a wider context for Dawson, see Carl Berger, *Science, God and Nature in Victorian Canada* (Toronto: University of Toronto Press, 1983). See also Robert John Taylor, "The Darwinian Revolution: The Responses of Four Canadian Scholars" (PhD dissertation, McMaster University, 1976); and John Cornell, "Sir William Dawson and the Theory of Evolution" (MA thesis, McGill University, 1977). On McGill just before the appointment of Dawson, see Reginald Edwards, "1854 Revisited: McGill Seeks a New Principal," *McGill Journal of Education* 33, no. 2 (1998): 127–76; and on the origins of the university, see Stanley Brice Frost, *James McGill of Montreal* (Montreal and Kingston: McGill-Queen's University Press, 1995); Stanley Brice Frost, *McGill University for the Advancement of Learning* (Kingston and Montreal: McGill-Queen's University Press, 1980), vol. 1; and Cyrus Macmillan, *McGill and Its Story 1821–1921* (London: John Lane, 1921).

16 Harrington, *Logan*, 292–4.

17 Ibid., 322.

18 Dawson, *Fifty Years*, 98–9.

19 Both movements demonstrated how sophisticated and complicated the resistance to the more extreme ideas of the Enlightenment could be. Newman was one of the leaders of the Oxford Movement until 1845, when he converted to Rome. The Disruption led by Thomas Chalmers is even more interesting, as he was by training a natural philosopher as well as a Presbyterian minister. See Stewart J. Brown, *Thomas Chalmers and the Godly Commonwealth of Scotland* (Oxford: Oxford University Press, 1982).

20 Epstein, "Macdonald," 36–7.

21  MSF/WCM, letterbook, Macdonald to Dawson, 19 August 1893.

22  For an account of the Natural History Society of Montreal, see Stanley Brice Frost, "Science Education in the Nineteenth Century: The Natural History Society of Montreal, 1827–1925," *McGill Journal of Education* 17, no. 1 (1982): 31–43. See also Sheets-Pyenson, *Dawson*, chap. 12.

23  The charter and various annual reports of the Mercantile Association Library of Montreal are reproduced in CIHM 21954 and 00582.

24  Dawson and McGill became aware of other models as they searched for new staff. Of relevance to the early background of H.T. Bovey, the long-time dean of applied science, for example, is George W. Roderick and Michael D. Stephens, eds, *Scientific and Technical Education in Nineteenth-Century England* (Newton Abbot: David & Charles, 1971), which emphasizes engineering, mining, and chemistry in Liverpool, as well as philosophical societies. There is little evidence that technical education elsewhere in Canada East influenced them. See Jean-Pierre Charland, *L'enseignement spécialisé au Québec, 1867 à 1982* (Quebec: Institut québécois de recherche sur la culture, 1982).

25  For information on Owens College, see Robert H. Kargon, *Science in Victorian Manchester: Enterprise and Expertise* (Baltimore and London: Johns Hopkins University Press, 1977). In marked contrast to Owens College, the University of Edinburgh, where Dawson and Logan had been educated, was much less successful, despite considerable private funding. See Jack Morrell, *Science, Culture and Politics in Britain, 1750–1870* (Aldershot: Variorum, 1997), chap. 10.

26  See Sir William Dawson, "In Memoriam: Peter Redpath," a pamphlet published in 1894 and republished in "Celebrating Peter Redpath and His Library," *Fontanus* 6 (1993): 7–13.

27  This account is largely derived from J. Rodney Millard, *The Master Spirit of the Age: Canadian Engineers and the Politics of Professionalism* (Toronto: University of Toronto Press, 1988), esp. chaps 1 and 2.

28  Much material exists for the study of the development of the Faculty of Applied Science (later Engineering) under Dawson. See MUA, RG 2, Dawson Official Papers, vol. 2 (1859–71), esp. bundles 22–38 and 42–8.

## CHAPTER SIX

1  MSF/WCM, letterbook. For an interesting portrait of two early engineers, see Richard White, *Gentleman Engineers: The Working Lives of Frank and Walter Shanly* (Toronto: University of Toronto Press, 1999). At least one of these Shanlys lectured in engineering at McGill.

2  This account of the Fraser Institute is derived from Edgar C. Moodey, *The Fraser-Hickson Library* (London: Clive Bingley, 1977).

3  Stanley Frost and Robert Michel, "Sir William Macdonald: An Unfinished Portrait," *Fontanus* 8 (1995): 59–81, at 66, citing the *McGill Daily*, 1 October 1917.

4  See Edgar Andrew Collard, *Montreal's Unitarians 1832–2000* (Montreal: Unitarian Church, 2001).

5  Much of this chapter is derived from the minutes of the Board of Governors (BOG) of McGill University in the McGill University Archives (MUA), 1829–1991, RG 4. The short form, BOG, followed by a date, will be used to refer to these minutes. For those wishing to follow up references here to the minutes, the following is the correspondence between containers or volumes and dates: C4, 1871–84; C5, 1884–91; C6, 1891–97; C7, 1897–1910; and C8, 1910–19.

6  BOG, 31 November 1871, minutes on the acceptance of the Macdonald deed of endowment by Hon. James Ferrier, Hon. Frederick Torrance, J.H.R. Molson, and R.A. Ramsay.

7  BOG, 7 December 1871.

8  BOG, 7 December 1871.

9  BOG, 26 January, 13 April, and 31 December 1878.

10  MSF/WCM, letterbook, 19 December 1892.

11  Macdonald wrote off a loan to Rankine in 1888 (MSF/WCM, letterbook, 10 May 1888 and 16 February 1891).

12  Apart from the educational benefactions that formed the bulk of his donations, Macdonald gave to many other causes, but it is hard to estimate how much. In his papers, there is an undated list of his donations for one year, probably in the late 1890s, ranging from $10 to $200, for a total of $1,460. Although in comparison with his educational interests these causes made small claims on him, they ranged widely. Here is the list: Montreal Rifle Association, Montreal Foundling and Baby Hospital, Society for the Prevention of Cruelty to Animals, Diet Dispensary, Hervey Institute, Boys' Home, Day Nursery, Victorian Order of Nurses, Charity Organization Society, Grand Trunk Rifle Association, Toronto Orthopedic Hospital, Fredericton Deaf and Dumb Institute, Labrador Hospital Fund, Montreal Maternity Hospital, Society for the Protection of Women and Children, Sailors' Institute, Convalescent Home in Murray Bay, Ladies' Benevolent Society, Protestant Orphans' Home, Protestant Infants' Home, Sheltering Home, Citizens' League, Montreal General Hospital, Protestant Hospital for the Insane, Protestant House of Industry and Refuge, Boys' Club, Brotherhood of Railway Carmen, Canadian Free Library for the Blind, Children's Memorial Hospital, and the Montreal General Hospital.

13  MSF/WCM, letterbook, 24 November 1891.

14  MSF/WCM, letterbook, Macdonald to John J. Rogerson, 11 September 1891; Macdonald to Fred, 24 November 1891; Macdonald to Willie, 26 January 1892; Macdonald to Willie, 28 March 1892; and Macdonald to Willie, 8 May 1892.

15  MSF/WCM, letterbook, Macdonald to H.J. Cundall, 3 May 1893; Macdonald to Fred Macdonald, 2 May 1893; and Macdonald to H.J. Cundall, 8 May 1893.

16  MSF/WCM, letterbook, Macdonald to Willie, 15 September 1893.

17  MSF/WCM, letterbook, 12 October 1893.

18  MSF/WCM, letterbook, Macdonald to John Archibald Macdonald, 24 September 1896; and Macdonald to J.I. Rogerson, 28 December 1896. The family of John

Archibald seems to have adopted "Macdonald" as the spelling of the family name by this time, although William did not adopt it until accepting his knighthood in 1898.

19 Oral tradition alleges that the dispute was about whether Alain was actually seeking recognition as the Lord of the Isles with the financial aid of Macdonald. The allegation seems unlikely, as the Lordship of the Isles had been borne by the Prince of Wales for centuries, as it still is. It is more likely that Macdonald objected to Alain's Catholicism and later to the wedding between Alain and Anna by a Catholic priest in Prince Edward Island. Nevertheless, if there was any element of snobbery in this match, it seems highly unlikely that he would have approved of it either.

Alain Chartier de Lotbinière Macdonald (1867–97) was the son of de Bellefeuille Macdonald and the grandson of John Macdonald of Garton or Garth, of the North West Company, who had married Amelia McGillis. Through his mother, Louise, daughter of the Honourable Robert Renwin de Lotbinière Harwood, MLC, seigneur of Vaudreuil, Alain was related to many distinguished French Canadian families, not least the Chartier de Lotbinières, into whom married Sir Henri Joly de Lotbinière (who adopted their name), premier and lieutenant-governor of Quebec and lieutenant-governor of British Columbia. Whatever claim Alain had to the Lordship of the Isles derived from his descent from Alexander of Keppoch (Alastair Carrach), fourth son of John of Islay, first Lord of the Isles, by John's second marriage, to Princess Margaret Stewart. Apart from the fact that such a claim would have repulsed Sir William on principle, Alain was of the other line from Sir William's own in descent from John of Islay. In any case, Alain died shortly after his marriage to Anna, and she became eventually Mrs W.E. Walsh. Her sister Matilda Helen (Tillie) became Mrs R. de Lotbinière Harwood. This information comes in part from a letter from C.A. de Lotbinière Harwood (8 March 1944) in John F. Snell's notes for his history of Macdonald College (MUA, MG 2007, C 1).

20 MSF/WCM, letterbook, Macdonald to Anna Macdonald, 21 August 1893.

21 MSF/WCM, letterbook, 21 September 1894.

22 MSF/WCM, letterbook, 23 January 1896.

23 MSF/WCM, letterbook, Macdonald to John Archibald Macdonald, 2 and 24 February 1898.

24 MSF/WCM, letterbook, 24 March 1899.

25 MSF/WCM, letterbook, Macdonald to Augustine McDonald and to Mrs E.J. Davison, 2 October 1899; and Macdonald to James D. Macdonald, 5 September 1900.

26 As he put it to Judge Alley, who had borrowed his family papers, "What an amount of labor my grandfather went through, and how little money came out of the property even ninety years later" (MSF/WCM, letterbook, 13 June 1893).

27 MSF/WCM, letterbook, 19 August 1902.

28 MUA, RG 43, C 183, twenty-fifth anniversary pamphlet on Macdonald College (1932), 6–7.

29 MSF/WCM, letterbook, 10 November 1890.

30 BOG, 29 March 1880.

31 BOG, 26 February, 13 July, 21 September, 8 October, and 6 November 1881.

32 Macdonald objected to opening his own scholarships and exhibitions to women, despite the general policy to do so (BOG, 18 April 1885).

33 BOG, 1 May 1886.

34 BOG, 20 March and 24 September 1887. See MUA, RG 2, C 25, for much more on the Faculty of Law, 1887–95.

35 BOG, 25 January 1888.

36 BOG, 22 February 1889. Emphasis added.

37 MUA, C.J. Fleet Fonds, MG 3017 1263B. Though undated, the report is clearly from about 1890.

38 MSF/WCM, letterbook, Macdonald to Sir Donald Smith, 5 April 1890; and BOG, 5 April 1890.

39 According to Chaput et Frères, these were Macdonald's holdings in about 1889, as cited in Jean Hamelin and Yves Roby, *Histoire économique du Québec 1851–1896* (Montreal: Fides, 1971), 340.

40 BOG, 15 June 1889.

41 BOG, 15 June and 25 October 1889.

42 BOG, 22 November 1889.

43 MSF/WCM, letterbook, Macdonald to Miss Emily Caines, 24 March 1890.

44 MSF/WCM, letterbook, 17 June 1891.

45 BOG, 21 November 1890.

46 MSF/WCM, letterbook, Macdonald to J.W. Brakenridge, 7 and 29 April 1891.

47 MSF/WCM, letterbook, Macdonald to Sir Donald Smith, 20 February 1891.

48 BOG, 13 June 1891.

49 BOG, 24 April 1891.

50 BOG, 27 June 1890.

51 MSF/WCM, letterbook, Macdonald to Walker, 1 February 1893.

CHAPTER SEVEN

1 The chief source for many of the biographical details on Robertson is Mary Ishbel Robertson Currier, *James Wilson Robertson 1857–1930: Canada's Chore Boy* (Toronto: privately published by Catherine Currier Francis, 2006). See also E.J. Pavey, "James Wilson Robertson" (MEd thesis, University of British Columbia, 1971); Kristen Jane Greene, "The Macdonald-Robertson Movement 1899–1909" (PhD dissertation, University of British Columbia, 2003); and the James Wilson Robertson Fonds in the Rare Books and Special Collections of the University of British Columbia Library (hereafter UBC), Vancouver. The most valuable single source is probably *Macdonald Funds for Education: Evidence of James W. Robertson before the Select Standing Committee on Agriculture and Colonization* (of the House of Commons), 1903. There are also summaries of the receipts and disbursements of the Macdonald Manual Training and Rural Schools Funds, prepared by Macintosh & Hyde, Montreal accountants, covering 1899–1909, now in boxes 4-2 and 4-3 of the Robertson Fonds at UBC. There is now a vast and growing literature on the Macdonald-

Robertson movement, and the present account can only summarize it insofar as it may shed light on Macdonald. Cassandra Armsworthy is preparing a PhD thesis for Carleton University on the movement in Prince Edward Island. See her "Offering Opportunity: Sir William C. Macdonald and Prince Edward Island," *Island*, no. 47 (2005): 34–40.

2 Much of this account is derived from Alexander M. Ross and Terry Crowley, *The College on the Hill: A New History of the Ontario Agricultural College, 1874–1999* (Toronto: Dundurn Press, 1999).

3 This example is from Jas. W. Robertson, *Education for the Improvement of Agriculture* (Halifax: Wm. McNab, n.d.), an address given in the Assembly Chamber of Halifax, Nova Scotia, on 4 March 1903. Its forty-seven printed pages are a summary of Robertson's basic teachings on agriculture and the source of most of this account of his principles.

4 Ibid., 15–16. See also Marian Bruce and Elizabeth Cran, *Working Together: Two Centuries of Co-operation on Prince Edward Island* (Charlottetown: Island Studies Press, 1994), 50–4.

5 Robertson, *Education for the Improvement of Agriculture*, 17.

6 George Iles, "Dr. Robertson's Work for the Training of Canadian Farmers," *American Review of Reviews*, November 1907, 578.

7 Currier, *Robertson*, xxx.

8 MSF/WCM, letterbook, Macdonald to Mrs L.G. Drummond, 20 June 1899.

9 For the story of their first meeting, see Pavey, "James Wilson Robertson," 37–8. The story was based on an article by Robertson in the *Ottawa Citizen*, 15 July 1922.

10 Currier, *Robertson*, 127.

11 Ibid., 123.

12 "Macdonald and Robertson's primary goal had always been rural improvement," in Greene, "The Macdonald-Robertson Movement 1899–1909," 194.

13 See, for example, J.W. Dawson, *Contributions toward the Improvement of Agriculture in Nova-Scotia: With Practical Hints on the Management and Improvement of Live Stock* (Halifax: R. Hughes, 1856).

14 Robert Hill, *Voice of the Vanishing Minority: Robert Sellar and the Huntingdon Gleaner 1863–1919* (Montreal and Kingston: McGill-Queen's University Press, 1998), 238.

15 Pavey, "James Wilson Robertson," 39–47. See also Jas. W. Robertson, *The Macdonald Sloyd School Fund: Manual Training in Public Schools* (Ottawa: E.J. Reynolds, 1899), for an address to the Public School Board of Ottawa in which Robertson describes the genesis of manual training.

16 Currier, *Robertson*, 129.

17 UBC, Robertson Fonds, box 4-1, 13 February 1901.

18 Robertson, *Education for the Improvement of Agriculture*, 25–8.

19 Ibid., 30–4.

20 The agricultural school had actually been founded in 1885, but it took the stimulation of the province's consolidated school for it to be transformed into the Nova Scotia Agricultural College, which was chartered in 1899. See A. Dale Ellis, *Shaped through Service: An Illustrated History of the Nova Scotia Agricultural College* (Truro: Agrarian

Development Services [ADS] Ltd, 1999), esp. 21–5; and Kenneth Cox, "A History of the Nova Scotia Agricultural College" (unpublished typescript, 1965).

21 The details are in a confidential "Memorandum of a Plan proposed for the Improvement of Education at Rural Schools; and for the Establishment of Courses of Instruction and Training in Domestic Economy or Household Science at the Ontario Agricultural College" by Robertson and dated 6 January 1902, a copy of which is in UBC, Robertson Fonds, box 4.

22 Pavey, "James Wilson Robertson," 85.

23 This discussion follows James G. Snell, *Macdonald Institute: Remembering the Past, Embracing the Future* (Toronto: Dundurn Group, 2003), chap. 1.

24 Pavey, "James Wilson Robertson," 72–6.

25 One analysis sees Hillsborough not so much as a failure as an imperfect step in the reform of Island education. See M. Colleen Lewis, "The Macdonald Consolidated School: An Interpretation using the Havelock Model" (MEd thesis, Dalhousie University, 1989). In any case, consolidation did proceed; see Shanna Leah Fraser, "One-Room Schoolhouse Teachers in Prince Edward Island: From the 1929 Teachers' Strike until Consolidation in the 1970's" (BA honours paper, Laurentian University, 2003). It may be fair to conclude from this that the Hillsborough experiment was premature rather than wrong.

26 The chief sources on Macdonald College are John Ferguson Snell, *Macdonald College of McGill University: A History from 1906–1955* (Montreal: McGill University Press, 1963); and Helen R. Neilson, *Macdonald College of McGill University 1907–1988: A Profile of the Campus* (Montreal: ECP Corona Publishers, 1989). The MUA holds the college archives, and the material on Macdonald in them is material assembled by Snell for chapters 1 through 4 and the postscript to his history. There is also much material on the college in the Robertson Fonds at UBC, boxes 4-5 through 4-10.

27 Currier, *Robertson*, 202–3.

28 Dr James W. Robertson, "Education for Agriculture" (address to the Legislature, May 1908), *Bulletin No. 1 of the Department of Agriculture of New Brunswick*, 5.

29 Ibid., 14.

30 Hill, *Voice of the Vanishing Minority*, 238–40. See also John Adams, *The Protestant School System in the Province of Quebec* (London and New York: Longmans, Green, and Co.; Montreal: E.M. Renouf, 1902); and MUA, RG 2, C 25, for more on the move of the Normal School.

31 Pavey, "James Wilson Robertson," 92–5. The documents on which Pavey based his account are in the Robertson Fonds at UBC. See also Hill, *Voice of the Vanishing Minority*, 239.

32 Stanley Brice Frost, *McGill University for the Advancement of Learning* (Kingston and Montreal: McGill-Queen's University Press, 1984), 2:68–9.

33 BOG, 11 June 1909.

34 BOG, 11 June, 4 October, and 1 November 1909.

35 BOG, 13 November 1909.

36 BOG, 2 February 1910, citing Macdonald's letter of 21 January 1910. For details on the period leading to Robertson's resignation in January 1910, see UBC, Robertson

Fonds, box 4-8, minutes of the committee of the board of governors, December 1909, and subsequent correspondence between Walter Vaughan and Robertson.

37 Pavey, "James Wilson Robertson," 92, citing Robertson, "Professor Cappon's Article in the Queen's Quarterly," *Queen's Quarterly* 12 (April 1905): 424.

CHAPTER EIGHT

1 MSF/WCM, letterbook, 20 June 1893.

2 MSF/WCM, letterbook, 6 March 1899.

3 BOG, 30 March 1914.

4 The three men had endowed a superannuation fund for McGill staff with $150,475.83 in 1894, with roughly $50,000 each.

5 There is unfortunately no biography of Peterson. These details of his early life are from Reginald Edwards, "The Education of a Principal," *McGill Journal of Education* 28, no. 3 (1993): 373–405.

6 See Joseph Frazier Wall, *Andrew Carnegie* (Pittsburgh: University of Pittsburgh Press, 1989), 872. In 1916 the Carnegie Foundation for the Advancement of Teaching approved a project for insurance and annuities for teachers, of which McGill seems to have been a part (BOG, 20 March 1916).

7 BOG, 8 May 1906 and 4 October 1909.

8 It is unclear how well Macdonald and Carnegie knew each other. As late as 1910, Carnegie was asking J.W. Robertson how Macdonald was keeping, not realizing that Robertson had been dismissed as principal of Macdonald College. Robertson himself was fairly close to Carnegie. The figures for the numbers of students in the applied sciences are in BOG, 10 June 1893, citing a report by H.T. Bovey dated 2 June.

9 The first Canadian foundation, the Massey Foundation, was established in 1918, only a year after Macdonald's death. It made only one small grant to McGill. The foundation established by J.W. McConnell in 1937, by contrast, would remain a mainstay of the university beyond McConnell's death in 1963. For more on foundations generally and on fundraising for McGill more particularly, see William Fong's forthcoming biography of J.W. McConnell.

10 Unlike an individual benefactor, a charitable foundation need never die. Its funds can accumulate, free of tax, and through its trustees it can support a charitable cause, such as a university, indefinitely. Unlike a charitable trust, its objects need not be specific, as long as they are broadly charitable. Thus, it can not only carry on its work indefinitely but also be flexible in what it supports.

11 BOG, 8 May and 6 July 1906.

12 In 1893 Strathcona (as Sir Donald Smith) gave $100,000 to the Faculty of Medicine. In the same year, John H.R. Molson gave $60,000 to buy the house of Sir William Dawson at Walbrae Place, University Street, for use by the same faculty. Macdonald gave land on Carleton Road, above the medical buildings, but the value of this

land is not recorded (BOG, 24 March 1893, 21 April 1893, and 22 December 1894). To this he added 9,000 square feet of land behind the medical building, as announced on 15 November 1901. The work of these three benefactors went well beyond medicine. In 1894 Macdonald, Smith, and Molson each gave $50,000 towards a special retirement fund for teaching staff (BOG, 23 February 1894). In 1898 Strathcona gave $50,000 to the general funds of the university, and his endowment of Royal Victoria College, including the Donalda endowment for courses for women at McGill of $120,000, reached $1 million. In conjunction with the fundraising campaign of 1909, Strathcona gave a further $400,000 for the endowment of his medical building and $50,000 for the augmentation of university salaries (BOG, 13 July 1909).

13 Macdonald's gifts of books to McGill have not been valued. He began with 575 volumes and some pamphlets for the Faculty of Applied Science in 1891, followed by several hundred books for the Faculty of Law in 1892 and 498 more science volumes in the same year. In 1893 he gave 1,300 books, apparently on physics and chemistry, to the Redpath Library, with 244 for the law library. The year 1896 saw his presentation of architectural and French books, in addition to 339 other volumes and 32 atlases. In 1898 he purchased the 4,000 volumes of the late Professor Otto Ribbeck of Leipzig and many dissertations, and he paid for the completion of sets of books and for binding and repairing others. All this was in addition to 1,000 volumes on chemistry, mining, and metallurgy and one chart. In 1900 he gave only 36 bound and 15 unbound books, but in 1904–05 he gave 1,446 volumes. After giving 500 bound and 37 unbound volumes in 1905–06, his gifts levelled off to 76 bound and 10 unbound in the following year and to 191 bound and 19 unbound in 1907–08. Then they rose to 482 bound and 20 unbound in 1908–09. The gifts went on until after his death, and as late as 1919–20 the university found that it had failed to account for 24 stray volumes (MUA, RG 4, C 504, file 6794 [Board of Governors, Donations, Endowments and Bequests], list dated 23 March 1932 of Sir William Macdonald's donations to McGill University and Macdonald College).

14 *Witness*, 23 February 1893.

15 There is no definitive source for all of the donations that Macdonald made to McGill. The figures in this book come from the minutes of the board of governors and from a list dated 23 March 1932 in MUA, RG 4, C 504, file 6794, but even these do not place a dollar value on each gift. The total reached in the list compiled in 1932 is $13,223,112, and Epstein in "Macdonald" (107–8) has a total of $13,413,425. These totals do not include gifts to institutions and causes outside McGill University and Macdonald College.

16 Further investigation into what Macdonald learned on this trip would probably better explain how he was inspired to aid other areas of science as well. See, for example, Deran Hanesian, Angelo Perna, and Joseph Joffe, "History of Chemical Engineering at the New Jersey Institute of Technology, 1881–1988," in *One Hundred Years of Chemical Engineering,* ed. Nikolaos A. Peppas (Dordrecht and Boston: Kluwer Academic Publishers, 1989), 379–87.

17 BOG, 29 September 1893.

18 Callendar resigned in 1898 to become Quain Professor of Physics at the University of London, and C.A. Carus-Wilson resigned as professor of electrical engineering. Within months, Ernest Rutherford replaced Callendar, with Cox as director of the Macdonald Physics Building; J.W. Walker became Macdonald Professor of Chemistry, with B.J. Harrington as director of the Macdonald Chemistry and Mining Building; and Robert B. Owens succeeded Carus-Wilson. These new appointments had Macdonald's imprimatur (BOG, 23 April and 28 July 1898).

19 MSF/WCM, letterbook, 4 September 1893.

20 *Witness*, 23 February 1893.

21 MSF/WCM, letterbook, 24 January 1894.

22 MSF/WCM, letterbook, Macdonald to L.P.N. Landrum, 15 February 1895.

23 MSF/WCM, letterbook, Macdonald to J.W. Brakenridge, 2 March 1896.

24 See Rhodri W. Liscombe, "The Peter Redpath Museum, an Architectural Analysis," *Fontanus* 1 (1988): 50–8.

25 See Jean-Claude Marsan, *Montreal in Evolution* (Montreal and Kingston: McGill-Queen's University Press, 1981), 221–4; and Peter F. McNally, "Dignified and Picturesque: Redpath Library in 1893," *Fontanus* 6 (1993): 69–84.

26 *Witness*, 23 February 1893.

27 See Norbert Schoenauer, *Stewart Henbest Cappen: First Macdonald Professor of Architecture* (Montreal: McGill University School of Architecture, 1998); and John Blain, "The Growth of the McGill University School of Architecture" (ca 1975, MUA Reference Files, accession no. 1082).

28 See Norbert Schoenauer, "Percy Erskine Nobbs: Teacher and Builder of Architecture," *Fontanus* 9 (1996): 47–57.

29 MSF/WCM, letterbook, Macdonald to Walter Vaughan, 26 February 1898.

30 For a survey of the development of chemistry at McGill and in Canada, see C.J.S. Warrington and R.V.V. Nicholls, *A History of Chemistry in Canada* (Toronto: Sir Isaac Pitman and Sons [Canada], 1949), esp. chap. 17.

31 MSF/WCM, letterbook, Macdonald to Evelyn Carey, 11 September 1897.

32 MSF/WCM, letterbook, Macdonald to Walter Vaughan, 31 December 1897.

33 MSF/WCM, letterbook, Macdonald to Walter Vaughan, 25 July 1898.

34 MSF/WCM, letterbook, Macdonald to Walter Vaughan, 29 October 1898.

35 MSF/WCM, letterbook, Macdonald to Walter Vaughan, 14 December 1898. In 1902 Macdonald gave $20,000 for the purchase of books for the Faculty of Arts and $2,500 for the cataloguing of library books (BOG, 21 March and 16 May 1902).

36 MSF/WCM, letterbook, Macdonald to Walter Vaughan, 28 January 1899.

37 MSF/WCM, letterbook, Macdonald to Walter Vaughan, 11 October and 22 November 1899.

38 MSF/WCM, letterbook, Macdonald to Walter Vaughan, 31 March 1900.

39 BOG, 15 and 17 March and 21 June 1901.

40 He had already erected a plant house in 1893 with John H.R. Molson and Sir Donald Smith.

41 BOG, 16 January 1903.

42  BOG, 17 April and 20 November 1903.

43  BOG, 13 May 1904.

44  BOG, 15 June 1904.

45  BOG, 15 June 1904, 21 October 1904, 5 January 1905, and 26 May 1905.

46  Of the considerable literature on Rutherford, the most authoritative on his time at McGill are A.S. Eve, *Rutherford: Being the Life and Letters of the Rt. Hon. Lord Rutherford, O.M.* (Cambridge: Cambridge University Press, 1939); Mario Bunge and William R. Shea, eds, *Rutherford and Physics at the Turn of the Century* (New York: Dawson and Science History Publications, 1979), esp. chaps by Badash, Heilbron, and Trenn; and E.N. da C. Andrade, *Rutherford and the Nature of the Atom* (Garden City: Doubleday & Co., 1964). More popular are David Wilson, *Rutherford: Simple Genius* (Cambridge, Mass.: MIT Press, 1983); and John Campbell, *Rutherford: Scientist Supreme* (Christchurch: AAS Publications, 1999). For the historical context of his work, see Crosbie Smith, *The Science of Energy: A Cultural History of Energy Physics in Victorian Britain* (Chicago: University of Chicago Press, 1998).

47  See George B. Kauffman, ed., *Frederick Soddy (1877–1956)* (Boston: D. Reidel Publishing Company, 1986).

48  MUA, MG 2007, C 1, Nobbs's memoir of Macdonald in J.F. Snell's notes.

49  BOG, 17 March 1901 and 21 March 1902.

50  MUA, MG 2007, C 1, Nobbs's memoir of Macdonald in J.F. Snell's notes.

51  BOG, 18 June 1906. The total endowments were actually as follows: 1906, $2,002,333.33; 1914, $1,021,563.37; and 1917, $1,000,000, for a total of $4,023,896.70 for Macdonald College alone.

52  BOG, 19 October 1906.

53  BOG, 4 January 1909.

54  BOG, 14 July 1908.

55  BOG, 19 April 1907.

56  BOG, 4 January 1908.

57  BOG, 23 June and 27 October 1913.

58  Frank McKinnon, *Church Politics and Education in Canada: The P.E.I. Experience* (Calgary: Detselig Enterprises, 1995), chap. 3.

59  The basic story of these schools is told in Marian Bruce, *A Century of Excellence: Prince of Wales College, 1870–1969* (Charlottetown: Island Studies Press/PWC Alumni Association, 2005).

60  St Dunstan's itself would obtain a university charter in 1917, while Prince of Wales College – as a college – would never receive one, although in 1968 it would amalgamate with St Dunstan's to form the University of Prince Edward Island, which Macdonald had essentially foreseen in 1906. McKinnon, *Church Politics and Education in Canada*, 33–7.

61  MSF/WCM, letterbook. The gift was transmitted to Walter Vaughan, bursar of McGill, on 24 April 1906.

62  Peter F. McNally, "McGill's Role in Canadian Higher Education," in Paul Axelrod, ed., *Knowledge Matters: Essays in Honour of Bernard J. Shapiro* (Montreal and Kingston: McGill-Queen's University Press, 2004), 20.

63  MSF/WCM, letterbook, 27 July 1896.

64  W.B. Howell, "William Christopher Macdonald," *McGill News* 13 (June 1932).

65  This account is derived from the McGill College of British Columbia Fonds in the University of British Columbia Archives. The enabling legislation consisted of Bills 23 and 24 of 1906. Dr William Peterson, the Honourable F. Carter-Cotton of Vancouver, A.C. Flumerfelt of Victoria, and J.W. Creighton of New Westminster were constituted as the Royal Institution for the Advancement of Learning in British Columbia to establish "the McGill University College of British Columbia." During the fundraising campaign of 1906, Carter-Cotton and Flumerfelt contributed $10,000 each and Robert Dunsmuir, a coal merchant, contributed $50,000. Carter-Cotton became the president and chancellor of the college, and Flumerfelt became the treasurer; there were nine other governors. At the first meeting of the board, on 19 March 1906, Tory announced that the college was to teach the equivalent of the first and second year of the program in applied science at McGill, but it was also declared that the college "was ready to entertain propositions from any ecclesiastical or other association looking to supply scholastic instruction for such association." A.P. McLennan, the representative of Vancouver College on the board, however, praised the "science" in the new curriculum (first minute-book of the Royal Institution for the Advancement of Learning in British Columbia, University of British Columbia Archives, McGill College of British Columbia Fonds, box 1, file 4). See also NAC, MG 30, D 115, vol. 1, H.M. Tory Fonds.

66  BOG, 23 March 1895, 4 June 1895, and 25 January 1896. On all these committees he sat with John H.R. Molson and Hugh McLennan.

67  BOG, 25 March 1896. C.J. Fleet and H.J. Bovey later joined them (BOG, 26 May 1896).

68  BOG, 23 January, 11 February, and 27 November 1897.

69  BOG, 28 September 1895.

70  BOG, 25 January 1896.

71  BOG, 3 July and 26 September 1896.

72  BOG, 4 July 1911.

73  See note 15 of this chapter. The calculator at www.westegg.com/inflation has yielded the value as of 2006.

74  MSF/WCM, letterbook, Macdonald to Col. John A. Macdonald, 20 January 1899.

CHAPTER NINE

1  MUA, RG 20, C 67.

2  Paul Stevens and John T. Saywell, eds, *Lord Minto's Canadian Papers 1898–1904* (Toronto: Champlain Society, 1983), 2:53.

3  Walter Vaughan, *The Life and Work of Sir William Van Horne* (New York: Century Co., 1920), 280. In an alternative version of this story, Percy Nobbs recalled Macdonald as saying, "Mr. Greenshields collects Dutch paintings and Sir William Van

Horne collects Japanese snuff boxes, and I collect string" (MUA, MG 2007, C 1, notes by J.F. Snell). E.B. Greenshields, another governor, however, was not reluctant to give to McGill.

4   Valerie Knowles, *Telegraph to Titan: The Life of William C. Van Horne* (Toronto: Dundurn Group, 2004), 406.

5   The first was the only son of Macdonald's uncle Roderick. The second was a son of Captain John's daughter, Flora Anna Maria, who had been educated by the Ursulines in Quebec and then married Lt. Alexander or Allan Macdonell, a nephew of the first bishop of Kingston, Ontario. They lived in Prince Edward Island on Flora's land inherited from Captain John.

6   MSF/WCM, letterbook, 29 June 1894. Miss Cantlie was probably a daughter of Col. George Cantlie, and Dr Adams (not the same person as Dr Frank Dawson Adams) probably worked in the chemistry department.

7   MSF/WCM, letterbook, Macdonald to Wilfred Campbell, 12 December 1908.

8   He was often described as the larger shareholder of the Bank of Montreal, but Alfred Baumgarten, the president of St Lawrence Sugar, was also so described at the same time.

9   Collard, Macdonald biography, 248.

10  Robertson Fonds, UBC, box 4, 16 December 1906.

11  MSF/WCM, letterbook, Macdonald to Minto, 1 December 1898.

12  Epstein, "Macdonald," 33.

13  For a summary of this episode with reference to the Minto Papers at the National Archives of Canada, see Epstein, "Macdonald," 32–4.

14  See Philip Dormer Stanhope, *Lord Chesterfield's Letters to His Son and Others* (London: Everyman's Library, 1969). On reading both Macdonald's letters to Fred and to other miscreants and Chesterfield's letters to his son, one would find it hard to believe that Macdonald had himself not read Chesterfield.

15  MSF/WCM, letterbook, 10 June 1890. Sir Joseph Pope (1854–1926), born in Charlottetown, was later the biographer of Macdonald and undersecretary of state for external affairs.

16  MSF/WCM, letterbook, 20 July 1893.

17  MSF/WCM, letterbook, 19 August 1893.

18  MUA, RG 43, C 183, 25th Anniversary Pamphlet of Macdonald College (1932), 7.

19  A hint of the vast ongoing network of his own clan that still enmeshed him may be gleaned from following merely two other lines of Clan Ranald descent, the Glengarry and the French Macdonalds. One of the brothers of Ranald Macdonald, the first Clanranald, was Donald, the first of the Glengarry Macdonalds or Macdonnells. Six generations later, Alexander MacDonald, the seventh Glenaladale and Macdonald's great-grandfather, married Margaret MacDonnell of the Scotus branch of the Glengarry Macdonnells. John, the eighth Glenaladale and Macdonald's grandfather, married as his second wife Catherine Margaret Macdonald, Macdonald's grandmother and daughter of Ranald Macdonald of Gerinish and of Flora

Macdonnell of Scotus. Of John's children, William's aunt, Flora Anna Maria, married Alexander MacDonnell of Glengarry, and William's uncle Roderick married Elizabeth MacDonnell of Glengarry.

The first Macdonnells – to use the same convention here of a generic spelling of their name while retaining variations for individuals – had arrived in the colony (later state) of New York in 1773. Their leaders were four tacksmen from the peninsula of Knoydart and North Morar, not far from where Captain John had also served as tacksman. (This account is adopted from Lucille H. Campney, *The Scottish Pioneers of Upper Canada 1784–1855: Glengarry and Beyond* [Toronto: Natural Heritage Books, 2005], chap. 2.) Named John of Leek, Allan of Collachie, Alexander of Aberchalder, and John of Scotus, they were fleeing the unfair leases of their clan chief, Duncan McDonnell. In 1775, only thirty years after Culloden, they took up arms as the Glengarry Highlanders against the American rebels, and after their defeat, they fled north with the King's Royal Regiment of New York. They settled in the counties of Glengarry and Stormont and in the Rideau Valley in Upper Canada, just west of the Ottawa River and Montreal. Not all the Loyalists were Catholic, for with the Catholic Macdonnells there settled German and English Protestants, as well as veterans of Captain John's Royal Highland Emigrant Regiment (the 84th).

New waves of Macdonnells came from Scotland itself in 1785 and 1786, the first led via Philadelphia by Father Roderick Macdonnell of Leek, and the second arriving on the ship *Macdonald*, which landed at Quebec. In 1790 more Macdonnells and Macdonalds arrived at Quebec from the Glengarry estate but also from the Clan Ranald lands on Eigg. Other Clan Ranald Macdonalds, with Father Augustine Austin (Macdonald's great-uncle), arrived on the Island of St John from Eigg, Moidart, South Morar, and South Uist. Lord Selkirk, who it is said tried to persuade Captain John to lead settlers to the Red River, also settled Macdonnells in the west of Upper Canada after settling others in Prince Edward Island. (Although he describes Selkirk's settlement on Prince Edward Island, John Morgan Gray, in *Lord Selkirk of Red River* [Toronto: Macmillan, 1963], does not mention any proposal to Captain John MacDonald.)

With respect to the Clan Ranald Macdonalds that spread to France, from the brother of the fourth Clanranald there descended a line that included Jacques-Étienne-Josef-Alexandre Macdonald (1765–1840, also known as Stephen Joseph Alexander Macdonald), appointed by Napoleon marshal of France, chancellor of the Legion of Honour, and duke of Tarentum (or Tarente). Étienne's father, Neil MacEachen (1719–88), had fought with Bonnie Prince Charlie in 1745–46 and had fled into exile in France to serve in Ogilvie's Scottish Regiment in the service of the French crown. Étienne himself spoke Gaelic and English as well as French, and he became an honorary member of the Caledonian Society of Prince Edward Island, founded by Macdonald's uncle Roderick and with the duke of Gordon as its patron. Tarentum, part of the Macdonald estates on the Island, was named after Marshal Macdonald's dukedom. Roderick arranged for the tartan of the Caledonian Society to be the mingled colours of the Gordons and the Macdonalds, and it also became the tartan of his Castle Tioram (or Tirrim) Regiment. Much of this information is derived from Mrs W.M. Brehaut, "Scottish Settlers," in *Historic Highlights of Prince Edward Island* (Charlottetown: Prince Edward Island Historical Society, circa 1955), 80–5.

20 That was on Prince Edward Island, a province that has produced three Macdonalds as lieutenant-governors, all related to Sir William, in addition to his relatives on his mother's side who have occupied this position. Andrew Archibald Macdonald, a father of Confederation and the seventeenth lieutenant-governor (1884–89), was of the Clan Ranald Macdonalds who were descendants of Angus of Borrodale, the younger brother of the sixth Glenaladale, and settled in Three Rivers. This lieutenant-governor was also a commissioner under the Land Purchase Act of 1873. Augustine Colin Macdonald, brother of Andrew Archibald Macdonald and the twenty-third lieutenant-governor (1915–19), was the son of Hugh Macdonald of Moydart and of Catherine Macdonald of Rhue, Arisaig, Inverness-shire, and he married Mary Elizabeth, daughter of John Small Macdonald (a son of Captain John's sister, Margaret, and probably named after both him and General Small, with whom Captain John had founded the Royal Highland Emigrant Regiment), an executive councillor and a trustee of St Andrew's College with Donald McDonald. More recently, a descendant of John Small Macdonald, Willibald Joseph Macdonald, the thirty-second lieutenant-governor (1963–64), became known as devoted to the Macdonald heritage on the Island.

Probably the most valuable family trees can be found in four genealogical tables provided by John Ferguson Snell in his *History of Macdonald College of McGill University* (Montreal and Kingston: McGill-Queen's University Press, 1963), between pp. 7 and 8. Here they are supplemented by an undated family tree in the possession of the Macdonald-Stewart Foundation and by other accounts, such as James K. McDonnell and Robert B. Campbell, *Lords of the North* (Burnstown, Ont.: General Store Publishing House, 1997), 53–6.

21 John Prebble, *The King's Jaunt: George IV in Scotland, 1822* (London: Collins, 1988), 10.

22 See George F.G. Stanley, "The Scottish Military Tradition," in *The Scottish Tradition in Canada*, ed. W. Stanford Reid (Toronto: McClelland and Stewart, 1976), 144–5.

23 See Eileen Stack, "'Bonnie Lassies' and a 'Coat of Many Colours': Highland-Inspired Clothing at the McCord Museum," in *A Kingdom of the Mind: How the Scots Helped Make Canada*, ed. Peter E. Rider and Heather McNabb (Montreal and Kingston: McGill-Queen's University Press, 2006), 149–63.

24 MUA, MG 2007, C 1, notes of J.F. Snell.

25 Toronto: Maclear and Company.

26 See Linda Colley, "Jacobitism and the Economics of Loyalty," in *Britons: Forging the Nation 1707–1837* (New Haven and London: Yale University Press, 1992), 71–85.

27 MUA, MG 2007, C 1, notes by J.F. Snell, memoir of Percy Nobbs.

28 MUA, MG 2007, C 1, notes by J.F. Snell, memoir of F.C. Harrison.

29 MSF/WCM, letterbook, 11 July 1900.

30 MSF/WCM, letterbook, 28 November 1895.

31 MSF/WCM, letterbook, 4 April 1900.

32 Cited in Epstein, "Macdonald," 109.

33 For the background to the crematorium, see Brian Young, *Respectable Burial: Montreal's Mount Royal Cemetery* (Montreal and Kingston: McGill-Queen's University Press, 2003), chap. 7. There is extensive material on the crematorium in the archives of Mount Royal Cemetery, which has also been consulted for this account.

34 Ibid., 104–5.

35 In 1880 Bovey had married Emily Jane Bonar, a daughter of John Redpath by his marriage to Jane Drummond, and his sons Wilfred and Quentin remained in Montreal and were associated with McGill. Another McGill professor who went to Imperial College was Hugh Callendar, the second Macdonald Professor of Physics.

36 This information is derived from the Frank Dawson Adams Papers at MUA, MG 1014, container 8.

37 On Tory, see E.A. Corbett, *Henry Marshall Tory: Beloved Canadian* (Toronto: Ryerson Press, 1954); NAC, MG 30, D 115 (H.M. Tory Fonds); and Mario Creet, "H.M. Tory and the Secularization of Canadian Universities," *Queen's Quarterly* 88, no. 4 (1981): 718–36.

38 Pope Pius IX issued his Syllabus of Errors in 1864, and the first Vatican Council promulgated its doctrine of papal infallibility in 1870. Proposition 14 of the syllabus explicitly condemned as erroneous any claim that philosophy could be treated without taking into account supernatural revelation. The doctrine of infallibility declared that the pope was free from error when promulgating a decision on faith and morals, and Pius IX even applied it retrospectively to his declaration of the doctrine of the Immaculate Conception of Mary in 1854.

   Towards the end of Macdonald's life, in 1907, Pope Pius X issued a further encyclical against modernism, largely to the same effect as his predecessor's syllabus, and as late as 1950 Pius XII was to proclaim with infallibility the doctrine of the Assumption of Mary.

39 MSF/WCM, letterbook, 4 September 1893. Macdonald took great pleasure in the pictures of eminent scientists that hung in his Engineering Building. In 1902 he gave McGill $292.98 for pictures of eminent physicists and $60.93 for pictures of eminent chemists, all to hang in his "science building," as his complex was being called popularly (BOG, 3 July 1902).

# INDEX